D0331594

Salty Dog Talk

Salty Dog Talk

The Nautical Origins of
Everyday Expressions

Bill Beavis

and

Richard G. McCloskey

SHERIDAN HOUSE

This edition first published in the United States of America
1995 by Sheridan House
Reprinted 2002
Sheridan House Inc.
145 Palisade Street
Dobbs Ferry, NY 10522
www.sheridanhouse.com

Reprinted 1998, 2000, 2002

First published in 1983 in Great Britain by Adlard Coles

Library of Congress Cataloging-in-Publication Data
Beavis, Bill.
    Salty dog talk : the nautical origins of everyday expressions/Bill
    Beavis and Richard G.McCloskey.
        p. cm.
    Originally published: London : New York : Granada, 1983.
    ISBN 0-924486-82-1
    1. English language - Terms and phrases. 2. Seamen - Language
    (New words, slang, etc.) - Dictionaries. 3. English language -
    Etymology - Dictionaries. 4. Naval art and science - Dictionaries.
    5. Figures of speech - Dictionaries. I. McCloskey, Richard. II.
    Title.
    PE3727.S3B42 1994.
    422-dc20   94-38678
                                                             CIP

Printed in Great Britain
ISBN 0-924486-82-1

A.1

From the famous classification 'A.1 at Lloyds' which described the construction of a merchant ship as being of the highest quality. Coincidentally the same understanding is given today to what was formerly the highest qualification of warship – *first rate*. A 'First Rate' ship was one with 100 guns or more spaced over three decks. Admiral Nelson's *Victory* was a first rate ship of the line. Another expression with the same meaning is *top drawer*. This came to be used because the ship's documents and important papers were always kept in the top drawer.

Above Board

Literally the wooden boards of planking which make up the deck. Any activity which went on 'above boards' would be in the open for everyone to see. Thus it has come to mean honest and fair dealing.

Adrift

At the will of the wind and tide. Sailors began to use the word to describe anything which had become undone or gone missing, which is how it acquired its shoreside meaning of somebody late, lost or wandering in their mind. From this word has also come *drifter*, a person with no aim in life.

All My Eye (and Betty Martin)

The English never try very hard to get their tongue around a difficult foreign word or phrase, much easier they find to anglicise it. Thus 'Oh Mihi Beate Martine', an expression frequently used by Portuguese sailors fighting alongside the British in the Peninsula at War, became 'All My Eye in Betty

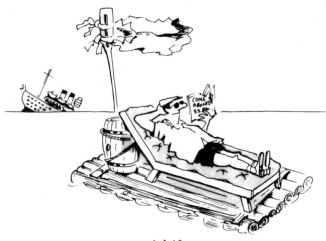

Adrift

Martin'. For the Portuguese it invoked the help of the blessed Saint Martin known for his charity; for the English it meant bullshine.

Aloof

From the old Dutch word *loef*, meaning windward. It was adopted by English sailors in the 16th and 17th centuries, and in books of old voyages it is written variously as *aluffe*, *a-luff* and *aloof*. Describes a vessel which is sailing along a lee shore with her head pointing high into the wind to prevent her being set inshore; also said of a vessel amongst a fleet of ships which sails higher into the wind so that she draws apart. Thus it has come to mean 'one who stands apart'.

Back and Fill

From the long and tedious operation of getting a large sailing ship to change tacks in light or fickle winds when the crew would have to *back* the fore and aft sails so that the wind could *fill* on their reverse side and help to blow the ship's head around. Systematic *backing* and *filling* was also used as a way of holding the ship steady in one position.

Bamboozle

The word first appears in print in the early part of the 17th century where one authority suggests it was the name of the Spanish custom of hoisting false flags to deceive or bamboozle their enemies. Certainly that was the general understanding throughout the 18th and 19th centuries, although the word also made an appearance in fairgrounds where it was the name of a betting game in which the showman placed a pea under one of three jugs and players had to guess which.

Barcarole

A song with slow tempo and sad refrain of Venetian origin. It comes from the Italian *barca*, a small boat and *barcaruoli* which was the name given to the men who sang and rowed the gondolas through the canals of Venice.

Beaker

Spelt barrico. From the Spanish *barrica*, a wooden water keg found in a ship's boat. Shoreside, it has become a 'beaker', another name for a mug or cup.

Beam Ends

A ship on her beam ends is one about to sink, i.e. laid over on her side so far that her beams, or deck supports, are in the water. It was an expressive way for the sailor to say he was broke and the expression still means impecunity. Good name for a country cottage.

Backing and filling

Bearing Up

One of several colloquialisms which describes a sailing ship's heading relative to the wind, or to another vessel. A ship is said to *bear* up when she brings her head closer into the wind; when she bears *away* it means she is steering further from the wind. To *bear* down is to steer towards an object – and frequently this meant an enemy ship, hence the suggestion of a threat; while over*bear*ing meant simply to come close.

Between the Devil and the Deep Blue Sea

The *devil* was the name given to a seam between two planks which every so often had to be 'payed' or repacked with oakum and pitch to prevent it from leaking. All seams need this routine treatment but the devil seam was the most difficult to do and so called because of it! There remains some conjecture as to which seam it actually was, devil is not a word which has survived and nobody can remember any old hands ever speaking of it. Some believe it lay next to the keel and suggest that the seaman who 'payed' it would have to hang from a rope, suspended between the devil and the deep sea. But the more likely explanation is that it was the outside seam of the deck planks next to the scuppers. This would have made it the longest seam and also the most difficult to do due to the spray coming over the side. It also gives more sense to the expression because in bad weather a man knocked over by a sea would be washed into the scuppers to find himself literally between the devil seam and the deep sea. Another expression, *the devil to pay*, supports this. Originally it ran 'The devil to pay and no hot pitch' and refers to the misfortune of either running out of pitch while paying the longest seam, or having it cool too quickly in what must have been a most exposed and draughty position. The word pay is from the French *piox* meaning pitch.

Betwixt Wind and Water

The waterline area of a sailing ship and the most vulnerable part of the ship during battle. To be hit between wind and water would be to suffer serious damage and it was always the prime target of the opponent's guns. George Bernard Shaw referred to his rumbling indigestion as 'a cave of the winds and waters,' although that is not quite the same thing.

Bilge

Rubbish talk which some wit long ago likened to the residue and cargo sweat which collected in the bilge compartment where the ship's sides curve around to the bottom.

Bitter End

The name given to the innermost end of the anchor rope, so called because it was secured to a set of 'bitts' or large pillars of oak bolted and fixed upright to the deck. In controlled circumstances an anchor rope is allowed to run out a measured amount until the anchor hits the sea bed, whereupon it is

Beam ends

checked. However, if the water is a lot deeper than expected or things go wrong, then the rope will keep running unto the bitter end. After that there is nothing left!

Black Books: to be in somebody's

Refers to the Admiralty Black Book which dates from the 14th century and is preserved in the Public Records Office near London, England. Its full title is *Rules for the Office of Lord High Admiral; Ordinances for the Admiralty in Time of War; the Laws of Oleron for the Office of Constable and Marshall; and other Rules and Precedents* – so if the librarian looks blank when you ask for the Black Book you can hit him with that lot! It is concerned with ship conduct and discipline and comes very largely from the Laws of Oleron which were the basis for sea conduct in ships throughout most of Europe. The punishments listed sound barbarous today; for repeatedly sleeping on watch the culprit was hung over the side in a basket and given a knife so he had the choice of starving to death or cutting himself into the sea; for murder the guilty one was tied to the corpse and flung overboard; for robbery the man was tarred and feathered and put ashore at the first point of land.

Blazer

In the middle of the 19th century it was the custom in the Navy for captains to buy uniforms for their boat's crew. Uniforms were not commonplace amongst the lower deck but most captains liked to show off their crews on ceremonial occasions and since the captains were paying for the uniforms out of their own money, so they were given the freedom to choose their own style and colour. The boat's crew of *HMS Harlequin*, the records state, were dressed as harlequins; the *HMS Caledonia*'s crew wore the tartan; and *HMS Tulip*'s boatmen had a green suit with a flower in their caps. But the most memorable outfits of all were the snappy blue jackets worn by the boat's crew of *HMS Blazer*. In no time the crew became known as 'the blazers' and that is how the garment got its name.

A Blind Eye

Turning a blind eye stems from the famous incident during the Battle of Copenhagen when Admiral Nelson, as second in command, complained he could not see the flag signal from his superior which

'Tween the devil and the deep blue sea

ordered him to break off the bombardment. He had deliberately placed the telescope to his blind eye, and proceeded to ignore the order, with glorious results.

Blood is Thicker than Water

These words were first spoken by Commodore Josiah Tattnall, USN to justify the intervention in the British attack in 1859 on the Peiho forts, during the China Wars. He towed boatloads of survivors from the shore with his ship *USS Toegwan*. A southern-born officer, he might well have used the words later in his career when he quit the United States Navy and joined the Confederacy.

Blood Money

Lower deck name for what was officially termed Bounty Money – monies paid to crews for sinking an enemy vessel. *Blood money* was however the more honest appellation since the amounts were reckoned not on the size or importance of the enemy ship but rather on the numbers of crew slaughtered. At one time this was as high as five guineas for every man killed.

Bottle Up

Comes from the days (before August 1970) when rum was issued daily to crews in the Royal Navy. Instead of drinking their tot at the time of issue as the rule required some men would spit their tot into a bottle and when the bottle was full drink it in one wild session.

Brace Up

Braces were the names given to the ropes which controlled the yards from which the sails were hung. Yards and sails were said to be *braced* up when they were tensioned hard against the wind. A nice comparison with someone puffing out their chest and ready for anything. Sometimes used as an order meaning get organised, stop messing about, etc.

Brought up Short; Brought up All Standing

From the practice of stopping a ship by letting go the anchor. Used only in emergencies (or by accident), it has the most dramatic effect. As the anchor bites so the ship shudders to a standstill accompanied by a cloud of chain chippings and dust, tremendous noise and the whipping and clanging of masts and rigging.

Another way to bring a vessel up short was to fire *a shot across its bows*. This was done as a warning. If the vessel failed to stop the next shot was trained upon her. This saying too has come ashore.

Blind eye

13

Buccaneers

Originally a name for the purveyors of dried meat called *boucan* which was eaten throughout the Caribbean. The word was extended to include the French settlers who hunted the meat and later to the English and Dutch who in their turn hunted the French settlers. Soon the word came to mean any lawless adventurer. It became popularised throughout the English language in 1684 after the publication of John Esquemeling's book *Bucaniers of America*. Esquemeling, a French doctor, was for a short period a buccaneer.

Burning your Boats

Although a military tactic since Roman times when it was meant to instill a backs-to-the-wall spirit, the most quoted case concerns the Spanish conquistador Herman Cortez who, having reached the shores of Mexico, and salvation so far as his men were concerned, found them in no mood to go traipsing off into the Yucatan jungle. To drive home the purpose of their mission he had the ship's boats drawn up on the beach and burnt. Then, with no alternative but to move forward, the conquest of central America could begin. Hundreds of years later during the Battle of the Falkland Islands in World War I, ships of the British squadron running short of coal used wooden boats to fire their boilers. This gave the saying a slightly different angle.

By and Large

The sailor's way of describing a passage which included bad days of headwinds when the vessel would have to be sailed *by* the wind, and good days when the *large* or square sails could be used giving more comfort and a better speed. (Sailing 'large' was to sail with the wind abaft the beam.)

Brought up all standing

By Guess and By God

From a method of navigation whereby the skipper relies on experience, intuitiveness, memory and implicit faith. Fishing boats in particular were said to find their way around by guess and by God.

By the Board

A reference to the wooden boards which made up the ship's deck; 'by the board' meant literally to throw over the side, or figuratively to let something pass. Board is a word which now occurs in a variety of meanings; we go *overboard* for something exciting, we *take aboard* or comprehend. In a literal sense, and showing how the meaning has progressed, astronauts climb *aboard* their rocket ship though there isn't so much as a splinter of wood to be seen.

Canvas

Derived from the Greek *Kannabis* which although popularly understood as a stimulating narcotic is in fact plain old-fashioned hemp. In the early days sails were woven from hemp and that is where the word canvas comes in. Even today a boat's sails are called her canvas, though the material itself might be anything from polyester to toughened paper.

Careen

From the French *caréner*. When a ship is deliberately beached and hauled over so that her bottom is accessible for scraping barnacles, repainting, or making repairs, she is careened.

Carrying Coals to Newcastle

The expression first appeared in print in 1650 when Newcastle was already well established as the centre of the North East English coal trade. Thus it means taking things to a place where they already abound.

Cash on the Nail

Immediate payment. From the English sea port of Bristol where in 1552 four brass pillars, or 'nails' were placed in front of the Council House for the convenience of merchants exchanging money. Business was discussed and money was laid down

Burning your boats

and counted on the nail. The same brass nails can still be seen today outside the Exchange in Bristol; other nails exist in the Corn Exchange in Liverpool.

Castaway

A seaman deliberately set ashore in a remote place as punishment or, and this is not generally realised, because he had gone mad! (They weren't all Robinson Crusoes.) The Irishman Paddy Watkins for example, who was castaway on the Galapagos Islands, used to come whooping and hollaring out of the trees and terrorise the boat's crews who put in for fresh water and wood for their fires. So much of a nuisance did this mad castaway become, he managed to capture and subordinate six whalermen as his personal slaves, that finally a warship was sent to arrest him.

A similar word is *outcast* – a person rejected by society. It could be connected with the high and low caste system once strong in India, although it more likely refers to the practice of *casting* a man away, either ashore or into the sea!

Cast Offs

Nowadays it particularly applies to second-hand clothing but originally it was the act of letting go, especially ropes or lashings. In an old English folk song the maiden laments:

> *Alas my love! ye do me wrong*
> *To cast me off discourteously*

She means that someone has let go her mooring.

Casting Around

When a ship is lost in a fog she will cast her sounding line into the water to find the depth which hopefully may indicate where she is. If she goes aground the first job is still to cast around and find out what the bottom is like. Whether she is on sand or a rock, an old pram, bicycle, bedstead or whatever. Hence the present meaning – to investigate or explore.

Catch a Packet

This is conjectural but the expression could relate to *packet* ships which were fast vessels that plied regularly between one port and another. The name goes back to the 16th century when State Letters and Dispatches were known as 'the packet' and their carriage entrusted to these fast ships. The term to *catch a packet* with its meaning of landing in trouble, might come from the American-owned North Atlantic packets of the mid-19th century which had a reputation amongst seamen as being particularly hard ships. In all events a trip in a packet ship must have been a miserable experience since their hulls were not 'sea kindly' and to make good time they had to be driven hard. This would have meant wet and uncomfortable conditions for the travellers.

Chance your Arm

Slang expression of World War II which means to take a risk or behave in a manner likely to prejudice rank and pay. Literally to risk losing the good conduct stripes worn on the left arm.

Channel

From the Latin 'canal', although not a defined body of water but flowing as in a stream or as water does generally. Ashore the word has been corseted, particularly by the bureaucrat who sees it not as water flowing and dancing but formalised and rigid. 'You'll have to go through the proper channels' he will say.

By guess and by God

Chew the Fat

In the days when brine was added to barrels of meat for preservative it had a hardening effect on the fat. It was still edible but it took considerable chewing, so to chew the fat has come to mean to talk endlessly.

Chock-a-Block

From the position of two pulley blocks which have been hoisted to a point where they touch and no more purchase can be gained. Block is the nautical word for pulley, and chock is to secure or render solid. Thus full to capacity. The expressions 'to be choked' or feeling 'chokker' also come from this.

Chowder

This typically New England term for a seafood soup was introduced to the American coast by the Breton fishermen who worked in the waters of the Maritime Provinces. It comes from the French *chaudière*, a cauldron. This New England version of bouillabaisse, in its different forms, has created a culinary civil war along the New England coast. In the States of Maine and Massachusetts chowder is made of milk, clams or fish and potatoes and onions. In New Hampshire and to the south it is made with water, seafood and tomatoes. These last are a pure sacrilege to the Maine and Massachusetts purists, so much so that almost every decade a semi-serious, semi-spoofing bill is introduced into the Maine Legislature making it illegal to put tomatoes into chowder within the State. The penalty? Dig a barrel of clams at high water!

Note: It is impossible to dig clams at high water for they are covered, hence the meaning of the American expression *Happy as a clam at high water* – ecstacy, the only time the clam feels safe.

Clap On

In sailing ships the order would be heard to 'clap on more sail' meaning to make the ship go faster by setting extra sails. The word clap is from the action of the crew clapping their hands around the halyards which hoisted the sail. It probably spawned that other colloquialism: *going like the clappers.*

Castaway

Clean Slate

It was the custom in the old days to record the courses and distances on a log slate and, at the end of the watch, transfer this information into the deck logbook. When this was complete, the slate was wiped clean for the next watch to take over. From this comes the notion of forgetting what has gone before and starting anew.

Clean Sweep

Term given to the effect of a monstrous sea which sweeps everything off the deck, frequently including the superstructure. The following is an extract from a letter published in *Yachting Monthly* in 1975 from someone who had survived a typhoon.

> We saw it building up astern. It grew higher and higher until we were looking up at its crest. Then it fell upon us with a terrific crash and roar. We had two lifeboats on the poop which flew into the air in a shower of planks, spars, sails and other gear. A solid wall of water rushed along the after deck carrying all before it – ventilators, hatches, tarpaulins, wire reels, hen coops, everything movable and immovable. It burst in the doors of our accommodation, knocking out all the teak panels and flattening the rails down to the deck. Then along the foredeck and up and over the foc'sle head and back into the ocean. In one minute we had been swept clean.

Clear One's Yardarm

The yardarms were the outer portions of the yard used in sailing ships for hoisting flags or, when punishment by death was current, hanging condemned men (hung from the yardarm).

The term to clear one's yardarm referred to the

job of slewing the yards or swinging them inboard so their ends would not obstruct the yards of another ship or quayside building which might have fouled them. Now, means to exonerate oneself, to prove innocence.

Clear the Decks

The preparatory order to battle which entailed lowering the ship's side rails and screens, swinging out the boats and removing all items of loose gear from the ship's upper deck. This provided a clean sweep for the guns and reduced the risk of extraneous fires breaking out.

Clew Up

A clew is a small metal ring fixed into the sail so that a rope may be attached. Clews appear in several places, the lower corner of the sails being the most significant. To 'clew up' was the order given to stow the sails which was done by furling their clews up to the yards. In time the term came to mean any job which entailed tidying up or securing. 'Clue' is merely a variant spelling but the two are usually differentiated – a clued-up person being somebody on their toes.

Close Quarters

The name given for a defensive structure used in merchant ships and erected when attacks by privateers were expected. It consisted of heavy baulks of timber placed around the after deck or quarters, to form what was virtually a small fort. Holes were cut in the timbers through which muskets could fire. They were very effective. Falconer's *Marine Dictionary* of 1771 records that the concentrated fire of an English merchant ship fitted with close quarters defeated the united efforts

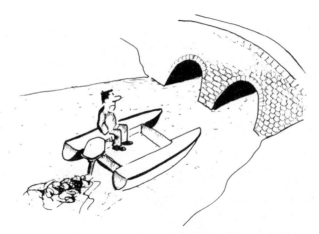

Chancing your arm

of three French privateers who attempted to board her. Incidently the holes through which the muskets were fired were called 'loopholes' from the French *louvre* or window. The word is now used to mean gaps in the law.

Coast is Clear

The phrase first appears in print in 1531 where it describes a vessel which had safely cleared the coast, then later Shakespeare used it in *Henry VI* as a reference to visibility. Neither of these references touch on its true insinuation; it is a reference to smuggling surely? Or some nefarious operation.

Cock-up

People are shy of using this in polite conversation, although quite unnecessarily so. The expression refers to the untidy custom of leaving the yards not square and neatly braced up but cock-billed or cocked-up at different angles. Considered a very unseamanlike practice, hence the allusion to something badly done.

Close quarters

Cold Enough to Freeze the Balls off a Brass Monkey

It is said that the expression dates back to the 17th century when 'ready use' cannon balls were stacked on metal trays called 'monkeys'. These had dished recesses so that each cannon ball was kept in position just touching its neighbour and in calm weather more balls could be stacked on top to form a pyramid. The monkeys were generally of iron but in some ships brass monkeys were used for ceremonial reasons. Normally, the arrangement was satisfactory, except in very cold weather when the different coefficient of expansion meant that the brass trays would contract more speedily than the iron causing the pyramid to collapse and the balls to fall off the monkey. (Although this story has been current for several years nobody has come forward to confirm or deny it. Nor has anyone complained!)

Colours

The national flag or ensign was known aboard ship as her *colours* – and a very important issue when ships engaged in battle as the survival of so many of today's expressions explain. True *colours*, false *colours*, show your *colours*, nail your *colours* to the mast, go down with *colours* flying, come off with flying *colours*, etc., etc.

Copper-bottom Investment

The term dates back to the 18th century when copper plating was first used to protect the underwater part of a ship's hull from worm and particularly the very fast nibbling toredo worm of the tropics. It was a significant step forward in shipbuilding where previously a poor defence had been to paint the ship's hull with tar. A Spanish squadron which had suffered losses in action decided to build a new ship in Equador. They completed the hull, launched it into the river at Guayaquil then sailed north to Panama to choose some suitable trees for masts and spars. When they returned, several months later, the wooden hull had all but been eaten away!

Couple of Shakes

It was the sailor's way of measuring a short period of time and alluded to the speed with which a sail would begin to shake when the helmsman's attention wandered and he allowed the ship to head too closely to the wind.

Cracking On

To 'crack on' meant to set more sail and so attain a better speed. The word almost certainly relates to the loud retorts which are heard as the straining sails and sheets are eased. The order 'crack the sheets' is to ease them, usually because the wind has freed.

Cramp One's Style

A colloquialism borrowed from boatwork where the expression was formerly to '*crab* one's style'. A smart boat's crew is the ambition of every ship in the navy where it used to be said 'a ship was known by her boats'. If an oarsman were to miss his stroke and tumble backwards, or in rowing terms 'catch a crab' it would most definitely ruin their style. Also heard 'crimp one's style'.

Cross His Bows

The founder of the Royal Navy, King Henry VIII decreed that no junior captain should *cross the bows* of his Admiral. In other words put his ship to windward in a position where it could blanket the wind of the senior vessel and stop her. It has remained a part of naval etiquette ever since (a junior ship must still request permission to cross the bows of a senior ship). In international law there exists the rule that no ship must, except under extreme circumstances, cross the bows of another.

Cut and Run

Some believe this derives from the action of cutting through the anchor rope with an axe to hurry departure, but only under extreme conditions would any captain be prepared to lose an anchor. It is more probable that the expression refers to the standard practice amongst square-rig ships anchored in an open roadstead of having their sails furled with expendable lashings. If the weather threatened or the enemy arrived, the sails could be set quickly by cutting through the lashings. The ship might then be able to *run* off before the wind. However there

Cracking on

are instances of ships trapped by an enemy, cutting through their anchor cables to effect a fast and noiseless escape. In 1782 Admiral Hood extracted his fleet from under the noses of the French in St Kitts by cutting through the hemp cables and running off before the wind.

Other nautical expressions related to this are to *cut loose*; *cut the ties* (sails held with thin lines called 'ties') and *break out*. Unfettered sails are always said to have been broken out.

Cut of His Jib

First impressions, judging a person by appearance. Sailors had a penchant for apportioning ship names to various appendages of the body, toggle, bobstay bumpkin, transom, etc. So it is quite probable that the *jib* refers to a person's nose. Some claim it has a literal meaning and does indeed refer to the shape of an approaching ship's jib sail which used to be an indication of her nationality. French and Spanish ships were supposed to have had their jibs cut very much higher than those of the British ships. On the

Cross his bows

other hand, incessant wars, prizes and privateering meant that relatively few ships ever remained under their original flag. So the practice would not have been very reliable.

Davy Jones Locker

According to mythology *Davy Jones Locker* is the final resting place for ships that sink, articles lost overboard and sailors who drown. Thus it became the sailor's phrase for death. Some believe Davy Jones was a Welshman but an older school claim the name is a corruption of Duffy Jonah – duffy being the negro word for ghost and Jonah the luckless biblical figure. In contrast, sailors who die ashore go to *Fiddlers Green* – a satellite heaven filled with chorus girls and unlimited amounts of free rum and tobacco.

Deliver a Broadside

A broadside is that crushing remark which ends all further discussion. A broadside in the sailing navy meant the simultaneous firing of every cannon which could be brought to bear on an enemy. In a three-deck ship of the line with fifty cannon aside this meant a considerable amount of ironmongery and a very fitting analogy.

Derrick

When the first cargo hoisting booms appeared in ships it was noticed that they resembled an invention by Mr Derrick, the hangman at Tynham prison. He used a single spar, topping lift and purchase to hoist condemned criminals to the gallows; up until this time only a rope had been used. Mr Derrick's name has not achieved the same ignominious fame of M. Guillotine, but it can claim a wider market.

Dogsbody

A not very popular dish aboard ship which consisted of passengers' leftovers mixed with ships biscuits and reheated. A meal without much status now applied to those who once ate it.

Doldrums; in the doldrums

State of depression or stagnation. Sailor's name for a belt of calm or variable winds which lie between the trade winds of the northern and southern hemispheres. The term signified the state of apathy as crews passed through these latitudes with no breeze to fill the sails or cool their living spaces.

Donkey Work

Apart from the obvious rural connection, the phrase was regularly used at sea and referred to heavy lifting work done by the *donkey* engine, a small steam auxiliary engine with its own boiler, fitted to sailing ships in later years.

Dressing Down

A severe scolding or reprimand. The expression dates from the late 1660s; Jane Austin wrote: 'I will give him such a dressing'. On ships the term dressing down means to *dress* or apply an oil preservative to the rigging. It was an unpleasant, sometimes dangerous job and might have been given in punishment.

Dummy Run

Originates from the torpedo training schools where practice *runs* were made with torpedoes fitted with dummy warheads.

Dutch Courage

Dates from the time of Charles II when the Anglo-Dutch Wars were at their peak and the lie was circulated that Dutch crews were so cowardly that they had to be primed with schnapps before they would come out and fight. It took some believing! At that time Dutch raids in the Thames estuary were a regular event. Van Ruyter once

Cut of his jib

managed to sink practically every British ship at anchor in Chatham. While in the English Channel Van Tromp inflicted such a devastating defeat on his enemy that he is said to have hoisted a broom to the masthead to show he had swept the English from the seas.

Embark

Barco is the Spanish word for ship, *embarcar* is to go aboard the ship. Embark is derived from this word.

Even Keel

State of normality; when the ship's keel is perfectly horizontal and her fore and aft draught are the same. (The expression is misapplied because in fact a fore and aft draught which reads the same is the last thing any sailor wants. A ship which floats on a perfectly even keel can be almost impossible to steer. It is customary to trim slightly by the stern.) The antipodean position *keeled over* with the vessel capsised and the keel sticking up in the air is the sailor's term for death.

Fagged Out

From the tendency of a rope to unlay and fray at the ends. It is the result of negligence because rope ends should be kept properly whipped. *Fag end* – tail of a rope which has been allowed to become frayed.

Fall Foul of; somebody

Foul, one of the most overworked words in the nautical vocabulary. A *foul* berth describes an obstruction; a *foul* anchorage is where one ship can swing and strike another; a *foul* area is somewhere to avoid, usually a sewer outfall; *foul* ground where

Deliver a broadside

rocks or wrecks abound. Even the anchor found in a cap badge or flag decoration is *foul* anchor because it has a rope entwined. Almost every entanglement at sea is known as a *foul* something or another . . . and that goes for human relationships.

Fathom

From the Anglo Saxon *faedm* to embrace, which loosely describes the manner by which this measure arrived. A fathom is six feet which is the span of an average man's arms. Ropes to be measured were held in each hand and stretched across the chest. Unhappily the word is dying at sea as measures and depths are now expressed in metres. However, the word still survives ashore where its figurative meaning is to get to the bottom of things to penetrate or understand.

Figurehead

Nominal leader with no real power but large in the public eye. The word is taken from the carved and ornamental figure which was carried at the stem of sailing ships. Primarily for decoration, figureheads also expressed the belief that a ship was a living thing and needed someone up front with eyes to see where it was going; ships from the Mediterranean and China had eyes painted on each bow. Symbolism too played a part and throughout the ages there have been an assortment of fierce and fast animals of which lions were probably the most common. About the time of the fast clipper ships it was felt that something more in keeping with their slender lines was required and the bare-breasted lady became fashionable. She has probably remained the number one choice ever since and not least because of a convenient superstition which has it that topless ladies calm the stormy seas.

Filibuster

The one-time name for robbers and buccaneers who seized islands off the Spanish-American coasts and used them as bases for privacy. From the Dutch *vrijbuiter* which in Spanish becomes filibustero. The word came ashore to describe the unorthodox action of one who attempts to obstruct the passage of a bill through government by endless speech making.

Floating; afloat

From the Viking *flota* meaning the sea or water. It is recorded that the Vikings had twenty-four different words for the sea and all of them derived through poetry. When the Viking was not raping, burning and pillaging, he liked nothing better than to listen to poetry about his legendary heroes, the truly great arsonists, pillagers and rapists, and their journeys across the sea. That was the problem, so often did the word *sea* crop up that the poets had to constantly find new words to avoid repetition.

Hence the invention of so many Viking words which refer to the sea and which still survive today; here are some examples; far (sea*far*er); way (under *way*; making *way*); road (*road*sted); deep; flood, float; street; water and sound.

Flogging a Dead Horse

A 'dead horse' was the seaman's term for the first month at sea – a month for which they would have been already paid and spent the money very quickly afterwards. So it seemed to them, with the money all gone, that the first month was spent working for nothing. To mark the end of the 'dead horse' month the crew would make an effigy of a horse and parade it around the decks (on passenger ships money would be collected), then with great noise and celebration the horse would be hoisted to the end of a yard, cut down and dropped in to the sea. No doubt there was the established understanding of beating a dead animal to work but to ship's officers 'flogging a dead horse' described the difficulty of getting the crew to do any extra work during this first 'unpaid' month at sea.

Fly-by-night

A large square sail used downwind or on a reach. It could be set and handed easily and quickly, which made it especially suitable for night sailing when it was expedient to take in the light sails less they prove difficult to hand in the darkness. The phrase has come to mean a shifty person, here today and gone tomorrow.

Footloose

Another case of human conduct being likened to the animations of a sail. In most sailing vessels the lower edge of the mainsail, known as the *foot*, was lashed to a boom to keep it stretched and properly

Dummy run

shaped. However, there were some exceptions, notably the London River barges. These did not have a boom and the sail was allowed to hang loose along the foot. Loose-footed sails, as they came to be called, had a mind of their own and were more difficult to control. It is from this that the meaning footloose and fancy free is believed to have come.

Freight

From the middle English *fraught* which meant earnings. Gradually the term shifted to mean the objects that provided the earnings. This was then extended when the goods were carried by ship and nowadays means any material carried by air, rail or road.

Full Flood

A phrase often used to describe oratory where the rush of words is compared to the fast moving waters

Even keel

of a flood tide. Actually the waters move much more quickly on an ebb or outgoing tide but poetry is more lasting then pedantry.

Gangway

From the Gaelic *gang* or go; ('Till all the seas *gang* dry'). Originally a gangway was the platform in the waist where the ship's boats were stowed and so called because it provided a convenient walkway from the forecastle to the poop deck. By extension the planks and ladders used for access at the ship's side became gangways and later a passageway of any kind anywhere!

Gave Us the Slip

Popular saying amongst TV cops. This could have a connection with the underworld, 'a slippery customer' for example, but then again it was not uncommon for ships to escape by slipping their ropes or anchor cables. The point of this was that it could be done secretly with no noise and no assistance from the shore.

Get Off My Back

A plea from the victimised! It is from the book about *Sinbad the Sailor* in which the 'old man of the sea' climbs onto his back and refuses to get off. Sinbad eventually dislodges the nuisance by getting him drunk. Always worth a try.

Getting into a Flap

A slang expression which arose from the excitement and confusion of preparing a warship for sea at short notice. It dates from World War I in the huge fleet anchorages such as Scapa Flow in Scotland when the order to put to sea was preceded by hurried flag signals (the 'flappings of flags'). An associated expression *there's a flap on* also derives from this. Scapa Flow was known as 'Flappa Flow'.

Glory Hole

A term which has sadly degenerated. When it first appeared in early ships it was the strong room where species and treasures were kept. It next turns up as a lazaretto or locker, then later descends to coal-burning ships where it was the name given to the stokers' accommodation. Finally, in the age of popular liner travel, the glory hole moved up into the eye of the ship to become the stewards' mess. It has remained a mess ever since.

Gone for a Burton

Popular amongst airmen of World War II to describe those missing or killed in action. It is one of several expressions which transferred from the navy when its air wing was merged into the RAF in 1918. There are two derivations, each of them plausible. The first refers to a *Spanish Burton* which was an ingenious but complicated pulley arrangement made up of three blocks. Indeed so complicated was the Spanish Burton, and so rarely used that hardly anyone could remember how to do it. Thus it became the standard answer to anyone in authority enquiring the whereabouts of a missing member of a working party 'he's gone for a burton'. The other explanation comes from the term 'a-burton' an unusual method of stowing wooden casks or barrels sideways across the ship's hold. The advantage of this was that they took up less space and were individually more accessible than when stowed in the fore-and-aft line. The disadvantage however, and the reason why it was rarely employed, was that the entire stowage could easily collapse. Hence the implication of knocking a man over.

Government

In the *Vulgate*, the Latin translation of the Bible, the word for rudder is *gubernaculum* derived from the verb *guberno* which originally meant to steer. Thus our word government comes from the Latin for one who steers.

Gripe

A vessel is said to gripe when, through bad design or sail balance, she repeatedly noses up into the wind which causes her sails to flap and her speed to fall. She will also be a pig to steer. Another of the many expressions that sailors have applied metaphorically to humans. To gripe is to complain perpetually.

Groggy

Derived from grogram, a coarse silken fabric and one particularly favoured by Admiral Vernon who had a boat cloak, and, some say, trousers made from it. It resulted in his nickname 'Old Grog'.

Vernon's great ambition was to instill a greater degree of sobriety amongst his sailors, many of whom quite regularly consumed a pint of rum per day. On his insistence, the daily ration of rum was diluted to the proportion of one part rum to three parts water and thereafter watered-down rum was always known as *grog*. Still however 50% proof and enough to make anyone feel groggy.

Groundswell

Swell is the name given to the low undulations of the sea, remnants of a faraway storm. Unlike waves, which are localised, a swell can be almost imperceptible. However, when it enters shallow water and 'feels' the ground the friction causes the swell to steepen. It then becomes a 'groundswell' and more noticeable in appearance. Figuratively the word is applied to an early change, especially in public opinion.

Figurehead

Half Mast

The world-wide custom of wearing a flag at half mast goes back to 1612 when the ship *Hearts Ease* sailed up the Thames estuary with her ensign at half staff in respect for her captain killed by eskimoes while searching the N.W. Passage. Previously ships had always worn black flags in tribute to the dead.

Half Slewed

When the yards which carry the sails are not properly braced to catch the wind they are said to be 'half slewed'. In this condition they are ineffective, they will also sway and the sail will shake. Not unnaturally the term has come to describe a drunk, or somebody well on the way.

Hammocks

From the Spanish word *hamaca*. Colombus saw natives in San Salvador sleeping in cotton nets slung

Getting into a flap

between trees and seeing the advantage for shipboard use immediately adopted the idea. Hammocks became widely used in ships in the Royal Navy and by 1660 most men shared one between two. Still popular in some backward parts of South America, the traveller brings his hammock, the hostelry provides the hooks.

Hard Up

The expression has been shortened. It was formerly 'hard up in a clinch with no knife to cut the seizing'. Hard up is the nautical description for any movement which has become checked; two pulley blocks are said to be hard up when they touch and there is no more purchase to be gained.

Harry Freemans

Gratis! but not, as popularly thought, a play on the word 'free'. The man Harry Freeman actually lived. He owned a wharehouse and quay at Tooley near London's Tower Bridge and it was his custom to give free beer to the seamen whose ships called there.

Heavy Weather

To make heavy weather or heavy going of something is to make unnecessary hard work; to meet heavy weather is to suffer unexpected difficulty. Each compares with a ship labouring in heavy seas.

Hi-Jack

The harlot's call to the sailor 'Hi-Jack!' It acquired its more sinister meaning when after their first embrace she hit him with a lead-filled handbag – or alternatively lured him into a boarding house from where he would be dragged the next morning in vest and socks to be sold to a ship in need of a crew.

This practice was prevalent along California's notorious Barbary Coast where ships, emptied of crew by the call of the goldrush, were desperate and prepared to support such intrigues. It became known as *shanghai-ing*, probably because many of the ships were employed in the China trade. Sometimes the tables were turned, seamen did occasionally drag boarding house operators off to sea, others took the girls.

Hitched

It is difficult now to know whether there was any difference implied in the two phrases; 'to get hitched' or 'to get spliced'. Both are understood to mean marriage and were the sailor's equivalent of tying the knot. Hitching however is a temporary arrangement; the whole point of making a hitch is that it can be undone again. Splicing, on the other hand, is permanent.

Horse Latitudes

An area of light winds and calms roughly between 30 and 35 degrees north but which does not have the heavy rains associated with the doldrums further south. The popular derivation suggests the name came from the unhappy job of having to destroy the horses when ships, caught in these calms, found their water supplies depleted. This however seems an unlikely explanation for while huge numbers of horses were carried by ships transporting armies, it is improbable that they would run out of water just a month or so outward bound. The name is more likely to have come from the previously mentioned custom of throwing the 'dead horse' effigy overboard. It would be about this point of the voyage that the seamen would have worked off their advance of pay.

Hot Pursuit

From the principle of naval warfare that a fight begun on the open seas can be carried into neutral waters if the enemy tries to escape; it was known then as hot chase. The most quoted example in naval history occurred in 1759 when Admiral Boscowen's fleet destroyed three French ships in Lagos Bay. The Portuguese, whose territory this was, accepted the principle and the intrusion as they were unfriendly towards the French.

Hulking

From the word *hulk* which is the hull of a derelict ship. Shakespeare describes Falstaff as a 'hulking great fellow'. Big, clumsy or unwieldy.

I'm Alright Jack

The ultimate in self-consideration. In complete form the expression is 'Blow you Jack, I'm inboard' and comes from the standard joke that the first liberty man to climb the ship's side from the boat pulls the rope ladder up behind him.

Gone for a burton

Half slewed

Jacknife

The word comes from the hinged-blade *jacknife* named after its inventor Jacques de Liege. Jack knives were carried by officers, the crews wore a sheath knife attached to a belt. Today a high diver who touches his feet before hitting the water, a man who folds in a fight, or an articulated truck which folds in a skid are all said to jacknife.

Junk

From the Latin *juncus* or *jungo* which means to join. Junk became the word for rushes which were joined together to make baskets and mats. By extension that included rope because it was also made from rushes. It came to be applied more specifically to old rope which had begun to break down and resemble its basic material. Hence its present use to describe dumped and worn out items.

Keelhaul

Used by some as an exaggerated reprimand. It comes from the very barbaric punishment of dragging the victim slowly through the water from one side of the ship to the other; literally under the keel. Another term used in the same context is *walk the plank* although there is no evidence that anyone was actually made to do this.

Know the Ropes

The rigging in a large sailing ship could comprise upwards of ten miles of cordage and all this divided into hundreds of separate parts each with its own name and function. Most of the hauling ropes were made of the same material, a great many were the same size and almost all were of the same construction, hence it was very difficult to tell one from another. Only from the precise position that ropes were secured on deck could they be identified and this was generally standardised in every ship. Nonetheless even this arrangement took time to memorise and the term 'knowing the ropes' became the distinction between the old hand and the beginner. (Interestingly only three ropes were called by name: the bolt rope, the boat rope and the manrope.)

Laid Up

Sick and unable to work. The term is taken from the description of a ship 'laid up' or out of commission. Literally with her keel 'laid' on large wooden blocks which provide a safe and level base so that her underside can be repaired or inspected. Opposite to laid up is *launched* – another sea term which has come into general use.

Landmark

A conspicuous piece of land, or prominent building on the shore, that is marked on the mariner's chart and which when identified enables the vessel to establish its position. The word has come to mean a turning point or some feature which marks a change.

Hammock

Lash Up

To lash something aboard ship is to secure it with ropes (known as *lashings*). Done either as a temporary repair or simply to stop an item breaking adrift in rough weather. Later it came to mean a hurried expediency, a badly performed job or complete disorganisation.

Lassie

In 1915 *HMS Formidable*, the first British battleship to be torpedoed by a German U-boat went down off Portland Bill. Hours later fishermen in Lyme Bay recovered a body on the beach and carried it into the Pilot Boat Inn in West Bay. While the body lay on the floor the landlord's dog pulled aside the tarpaulin which covered the victim and began licking its face. So much fuss did the dog make that it aroused the owner's attention who found that the body left for dead was in fact alive! Years later Hollywood heard the story and this inspired the dog hero movie. They named the dog after the survivor John Lassie.

Latitude

It comes from the Latin *latitudo* which means breadth. In its nautical use it is a measure and is the amount by which a vessel's position lies either north or south of the equator. Hence to allow a person *latitude* is to give them scope and freedom of action.

Lay of the Land

To study the lay of the land is to make an initial inspection, a first step. Making a landfall a sailor studies how the land 'lays' along the horizon to see whether he can recognise any prominent features which would make it familiar or if it promises landing facilities, shelter and so forth. Another expression with the same meaning is *see how the land lies*.

Leading Light

Leading lights are those which mark an entry to a port, one some distance in front of the other. There are usually two and when brought into line point a safe course between rocks and obstructions and ensure the vessel a safe entry. The phrase has come to describe a prominent person, star turn or dynamic personality.

Leeway

The distance a ship is forced sideways from her intended course by the action of wind and sea. It is correctly designated as the angle between the ship's head and the track which she will ultimately make. Colloquially *leeway* is room to operate, or falling behind with something and having to make up lost time.

Let Fly

Aboard ship the order *let fly* meant to let go quickly the sheets which held the sails whereupon they would shake uncontrollably (as a raging person can do). The order was given to stop a ship smartly. In the navy a junior ship was required to 'let fly her sheets' in salute to the flagship. Let fly has since come to mean to lose one's temper, or remonstrate angrily.

Lifeline

Its nautical origin describes a safety rope rigged along the decks which in bad weather provided the crew with a secure and convenient hand hold. It is a word which has come to mean anything upon which life depends.

Limey

The name used by Americans to describe anyone of British origin. Originally the word was limejuicers and was applied particularly to British ships, then by extension to the sailors who served in them. In effect it is a compliment by attributing to the British the wisdom of regularly issuing lime juice to the crew as a prevention against scurvy. The advantages of such a remedy were known since the Elizabethan times but it was not until 1795 when the lack of fresh food on long voyages caused so many deaths that the issue of lime juice was regularised. British ships are still required to carry lime juice.

Loggerheads

When paying the deck seams aboard ship it was necessary to heat pitch in a bucket to such consistency that it could be poured. Only the most obliging cook would permit this in his galley and so the solution was to use a *loggerhead* which was a large iron ball fixed to a handle. This was heated in the galley fire then dunked into the pitch. The expression 'to be at loggerheads' suggests it was also a popular weapon to use in an argument.

A 'loggerhead' is still used in the USA to hot-up and blend alcholic drinks – though a much smaller version of course.

Loom

To appear menacing and important, often larger than life. A ship's lookout will search for the *loom* of the land which can sometimes be projected above the horizon by a refraction of the light, thus making it visible far beyond its normal range. The word can also be used to describe the indistinct vision of something seen through a mist. At night the *loom* of shore lights is reflected in the sky.

Loose End

Rope ends which have become unravelled are called loose ends. It was a never ending job in a sailing ship putting new whippings on the ends of the running gear. If a sailor found himself idle he would

Knowing the ropes

be ordered to go around the ship looking for loose ends to tie up. Hence the idea behind the expression of being bored with nothing to do.

Low Ebb

An *ebb* tide is one which is going out. A *low ebb* or the last of the receding tide can uncover a vast expanse of mud and perhaps the expression to be at a low ebb also alludes to the emptiness which is left.

Maelstrom

The Norwegian word for a whirlpool. There are over fifty whirlpools off the Norwegian coast. The word describes any violent upheaval.

Maiden Voyage

First trip made by a ship after launching. It is a natural allusion, ships are ladies and one which is new and unused would be thought of as a maiden.

Laid up

Mainstay

Chief support. Although there are many different stays in a full rigged ship and all support the masts, and although every sailing ship has a mainmast there is no mainstay as such.

Make One's Number

To introduce oneself. Every ship has an official number which it is required to hoist as a flag signal when entering port. The authorities ashore can then read the numbers and from *Lloyd's Register* find the name of the ship long before the letters on her side become visible. It is also the custom of ships when meeting ships of the same fleet at sea to hoist their signal letters.

Making a Rod for Your Own Back

A self-imposed difficulty. Literally to fashion an instrument of punishment. The cat o' nine tails for example was always made by men awaiting flogging. They would be given a length of rope and ordered to strand it then plait it into nine ends projecting from a rope handle. If on inspection the work was found to be less than satisfactory they would be given extra lashes.

Making Headway

When a ship moves forward through the water she is said to be *making headway*. To appreciate the significance of this expression one has to imagine a large and clumsy sailing ship trying to *tack* in light airs. R. H. Dana describes the operation in which a dozen different orders were involved. Frequently the effort would come to nothing, and the drill would have to be repeated for a second or third time with the ever present risk that the ship would drift and go aground. It was with some relief that the crew watched the sails slowly fill and the cry 'She's *making headway*' was heard.

Man Friday

Factotum, handyman. The name of Robinson Crusoe's manservant in Defoe's book of that name.

Maroon

A corruption of the Spanish *cimarron* which means wild or unruly. It was the word given to runaway slaves in the Spanish colonies of the Caribbean. Later it was adopted by pirates of the area and came to describe their practice of setting unwanted men down on an inhospitable shore.

Mate

A friendly word meaning two who break bread together, or more precisely meat – two who share meat. From the old Teutonic word *gamaton* – *ga* implying a conjunction, plus *mat* for meat.

Other people think it comes from the French *matelot*, or sailor.

Mayonnaise

Believed to have been coined by the French officer Duc de Richelieu who led a successful attack on the British navy base of Port Mahon in Minorca in 1756. Finding the storehouses in flames and with no food for the victors, Richelieu improvised a meal from remnants comprising eggs, vinegar, oil, pepper, salt and mustard. The beaten ingredients so delighted the Frenchmen they named it after their victory – *Mahonnaise*.

Mess

Muddle, confusion. Derived from the ship's *mess*, the space where the men ate and slept. From the

Spanish *mesa* meaning table. Although the Anglo Saxon word *mese* means the same.

Miss the Boat

To miss the liberty boat which carried sailors returning from shore leave out to their ships. Hence to miss an opportunity.

Money for Old Rope

It was customary for ships to sell old and redundant ropes to shoreside traders and traditionally this money was shared amongst the crew. Since it was a bonus and something they did not have to work for it became the term for easy money.

Monkey Jacket

A close-fitting reefer coat of navy blue serge which reached just below the waist. It was a style popular amongst seamen in sailing ships because it left the legs free for climbing. The description *monkey* was

Lash up

Making headway

applied to anything small and included such items as wooden casks, pumps, blocks, even children. The boys who fetched and carried for the gun crews were known as powder monkies. There was also a small trading coaster in the 16th century which was known as a *monkey*.

Nausea

It is fitting that the word for this unpleasant sensation should have its origin in the sea. It comes from *naus* the Greek word for ship.

Navvy

The word came into the language when the first canals or 'navigations' were built. These constructions required huge armies of workmen or 'navvies' and the men were a familiar sight in northern England throughout the 18th and 19th centuries. When the word first appeared in print somebody obviously took a conscious decision and added the extra *v* so the corruption should not be confused with *navies*.

Nipper

In the old sailing warships anchor ropes (known as cables) were huge, as much as 8 inches in diameter and much too large to bend around the main capstan. Instead smaller endless ropes were used. These were led to the capstan and attached to the cable with *nipping* lines – so called because they nipped the ropes against the side of the cable and no awkward knots were required. Small boys were employed to do this work and inevitably they became kown as the nippers.

No Room to Swing a Cat

Most dictionaries agree that 'cat' was the short name for the cat of nine tails – nine lengths of line flayed out from a handle with which seamen were flogged. Since this required considerable arm movement there was clearly insufficient room to swing a cat below decks with clearance little more than 5½ feet. Equally important was the fact that below decks only a handful of the crew could stand witness, for flogging was very much an exemplary punishment.

The cat was also the name for a sailing collier common throughout northern Europe at one time. They were extremely handy vessels (*HMS Endeavour*, Captain Cook's ship, was formerly a Northumberland cat), but they were also very small, just 600 tons; so it is possible that the expression 'no room to swing a cat' may have referred to the minuteness of a port or anchorage, meaning not room enough for this very small vessel to swing at anchor.

Another opinion is that cat is a corruption of cot which was the sailors name for his hammock.

Now She's Talking

Pleasant and welcome sounds nowadays connected with speech but once attributed to that distinctive sound of waves dancing and rattling against the wooden hull of a sailing vessel as she moves quickly through the water. It is especially noticeable in a sailing ship where no machinery noises would mask or interfere with the sound.

Off and On

A situation in which progress is made, then lost. A ship was said to be *off and on* while sailing around waiting for daylight to enter a port. She would stand *on* towards the shore for a while then turn around and head out to sea for a safer *offing*. For those eager to get ashore at the end of a long voyage an off and on situation could be very frustrating, which is how the term came to be generally employed.

Offing: in the

Imminent, near at hand. The word 'offing' refers to the distance the ship is *off* the shore. However, it

Navvy

has become accepted to mean a safe distance from the shore clear of all rocks and danger. A ship was said to have a good *offing* when she had cleared the land but was still well in sight.

Oil on Troubled Waters

From the seamanship practice of spreading oil to calm the waves. It is frequently done in rescue or salvage work where a little vegetable oil spread from windward has a remarkable effect in modifying the seas and thus reducing the risk of accidents.

Oilskins

The name given to waterproof clothing of various manufacture although initially the sailor's word for a long linen coat made waterproof (and mighty stiff) by habitual dressings of linseed oil.

On the Beach

A seaman without ship or employment is said to be 'on the beach'. The term was associated with a stranded ship which was 'beached'. Ashore the word is slowly coming to mean the same although the more familiar derivation is 'beachcomber'. In seaman's parlance this is scrounger.

On the Make

At sea the word *make* means to increase or grow. A tide makes, a leaking ships makes water, a spur of land makes out from the coast, a vessel makes sail and a sea growing rougher is said to be *on the make*. There must be a connection with this and somebody feathering their nest but it is difficult to see what it is?

On the beach

On the Stocks

Something new or in preparation. The *stocks* refer to the keel stocks or heavy baulks of timber which support the hull, while the ship is being built. Thus the term 'on the stocks' describes a ship that has passed the planning stage and is actually under construction.

On the Wrong Tack

A vessel intent on reaching a destination upwind has to sail a zig-zag course towards it. Each of these legs, called 'tacks' represents the best heading she can make against the wind. Invariably though the destination does not lie directly upwind and one tack takes the vessel closer to her goal than the other. Without careful navigation a vessel may keep on one tack longer than necessary and pass the critical point of change. From that moment on she is said to be 'on the wrong tack'. Hence its present meaning of wrong policy or action; wrong approach to a situation.

Outfit

Collective term for gear or equipment required for a ship being made ready or *fit* for sea. The preparation period known as 'fitting out'. The word outfit has gradually come to include clothes worn for a special purpose.

> I see by your outfit that you are a cowboy,
> You see by my outfit that I'm a cowboy
> You can tell by our outfits that we are all cowboys,
> If you get an an outfit you can be a cowboy too!

Smuthers Brothers spoof on *The Streets of Lorado*.

Out of the Blue

The totally unexpected. Short for 'out of a clear blue sky' and is an analogy to a sudden change in the weather when, from a good breeze under a cloud dappled blue sky, a demon squall can appear and wreak havoc on the ship. Probably the best documented example of this was in the spring of 1878 when *HMS Eurydice* was on the last few miles of her journey home to Portsmouth from Bermuda. The day was calm the weather was sunny, all sails were set, all ports and windows were open and all men on duty were relaxing on deck. Then without warning a dark cloud appeared, a squall struck and *Eurydice* went down with 368 men. Within half an hour the weather was perfect again.

Over a Barrel

It comes from the Royal Navy practice of tying men to be flogged over a gun barrel. Secured like this they could not move. Sailors themselves referred to this punishment as being 'married to a gunner's daughter'. Thus its meaning of being placed or placing someone else in a predicament from which there is no escape.

Overhaul

Originally the word meant to feed the slack rope back through a set of pulley blocks. You hauled on a block and tackle and when the two blocks met you *over*hauled the ropes to start again. The word came into general use when the buntlines, which were long lengths of rope used for furling the sails, had to be pulled back through their blocks or else they would hang in great loops and chafe against the sails. The crew were sent aloft to *overhaul* the buntlines. Gradually the word came to include the inspection and repair of any part of the rigging and finally all the ship's gear. Since then it has come ashore.

Overreach

The word reach has several meanings; a straight stretch of river is a *reach*; to sail with the wind free is to sail on a *reach*; a vessel which overtakes another is said to *reach* past her; while a ship held steady with some sails aback will be inclined to fore*reach*. Over*reach*, which means to fail by being too clever, describes a vessel trying to reach an upwind destination but which has held one tack too long. This time it has taken her past her destination and she is said to have overreached, in other words she has to retrace her steps.

Pay Off

Literally to pay the crew their wages at the end of a voyage. Since voyages often lasted several years the amounts were comparatively large and this coupled with the release from the long engagement plus the prospect of leave gave the pay off a Christmas atmosphere. Ashore this innocence has gone, the term still has a rewarding ring, a large sum of money, a handsome return, but with curiously criminal undertones.

Pile Up

Once exclusively used in marine insurance and salvage where it described a ship which had piled on top of the rocks. Now applied to multi-vehicle accident for navigators on four wheels.

Pipe Down

In naval ships orders are given and recognised by the individual pattern of notes piped on a whistle – known as the boatswain's call. 'Pipe down' is the last pipe of the day and is the order for unwanted lights to be switched out, unnecessary noise and activity to stop, so that men preparing for night watches can sleep. The term has been adopted by sailors and is used when they want someone to stop talking or making a nuisance of themselves.

Plain Sailing

Refers to a method of navigation which assumes, over short distances, that the earth is flat. In other words the difference of longitude between the two positions is taken to be the same as the departure or actual mileage. This makes computations very much simpler. Originally *plane* sailing referred to workings on the *plane* charts of the 16th century which confidently knew the earth was flat.

Pooped

Comes from the devasting effect of a huge wave breaking over the stern or *poop* deck of the ship. Such seas could often flood even sink a ship, stoving in companionways and hatches. Yachts can be pooped while running before a big sea. It is now used as a slang term for being crushed, exhausted or satiated.

Posh

It is said that the letters P.O.S.H. were printed on the tickets of 1st class passengers travelling to and from India in the days of British rule. There is no evidence to support this although the term was current and comes from the practice of wealthy passengers booking a cabin on the port side of the ship outward bound, a starboard side cabin when coming home, which in each case was the cooler side of the ship away from the glare of the sun. The word posh stood for Port Out, Starboard Home.

Press On; Press Ahead

Press when associated with progress comes from the idea of the wind 'pressing' against the sails. Sailors spoke, and yachtsmen still do, of being under a 'full press of sail'.

Pooped

Push the Boat Out

The original nautical expression meant to pay for a round of drinks. Now more widely understood as to celebrate and not trouble about expense.

Put a New Slant on Things

A shift in emphasis, another viewpoint. *Slant* was the word sailors used to describe the position of the wind relative to their ship. A good slant was a favourable wind which could be taken advantage of to steer the intended course. A slant wind, on the other hand, was less favourable although not exactly foul. The word suggested significant change although not large in measure. A subtle analogy this.

Put Through the Hoop

When sailing ships engaged in battle it was required that every man's hammock be brought up on deck and tied to the netting along the ship's rails, where they could afford protection against musket fire and splinters and also be used as life preservers. To perform both functions properly it was necessary that they be tightly rolled and it became the drill every morning for bosun's mates to check the tightness of each man's hammock by seeing if they would pass through a regulation-sized hoop. There was trouble for the man whose hammock did not pass 'through the hoop' and the expression still suggests trouble today.

Quarantine

From the Italian *quaranta* meaning forty, which was the original period which ships with infectious disease aboard were held offshore; the practice was begun in Venice during the 14th century when a Council of Health convened to draw up the

'Quarantine Laws'. Ancient physicians ascribed many strange changes to the period of forty days. There is no medical basis for this and it seems to have more to do with the Biblical connection; forty days being the most popular period of expiation and penance. The Flood, Moses on the Mount, Jesus in the wilderness, all these lasted forty days. The most relevant though, was the forty days that Noah had to wait before opening up the doors of the Ark, perhaps that is where they got the idea.

Quarters

Strictly the area of the vessel from between 45 degrees on either side of the stern; port quarter, starboard quarter. It was the part of the ship where the officers' accommodation was situated and was known as their *quarters*. Gradually the word has come to mean lodging or billets in the military sense.

Rate of Knots

A knot is the nautical measure of speed, one nautical mile per hour. Until the mechanical log which registers the distance a ship travels came into use, speeds were calculated with a 'chip log' which was a long line with a triangular-shaped piece of wood at the end to anchor it in the water. At intervals of 24 ft 4 in. a knot was tied in the line; this represented 1/240 part of a mile. To calculate speed the line was allowed to run out from the ship, and at the same moment a sand glass was started. The glass was timed to 15 seconds which is 1/240 part of an hour. So as time and distance were of the same proportion the number of *knots* which passed through the operator's hand while the glass was running was equal to the number of miles the ship was making in the hour. To do something at a 'rate of knots' has come to mean at high speed.

Quarantine

Rats from a Sinking Ship

To walk out on a project because it seems doomed. Sailors believed that the sight of rats seen coming out of the ship's holds was a portent of disaster. There was some substance in this since the rat frequently inhabited the bilge which was the first place to flood should the vessel be foundering. However it is something else to attribute a kind of sixth sense to a rat and get alarmed just because it leaves a ship in port. Yet in 1923 at the San Francisco Navy Yard a number of seamen did become apprehensive when rats were seen leaving the *USS Young*. The following day in an unprecedented disaster the *Young* along with six more destroyers piled up on the rocks on passage to San Diego.

Real McCoy

During Prohibition in the USA (1920s and 30s), huge quantities of liquor were smuggled along a stretch of coastline between New York and Atlantic city. One of the most audacious and successful men engaged in this traffic was a boatbuilder from Nova Scotia called Bill McCoy. Over a period of four years he is credited with delivering over $70 000 000 of contraband whisky. Although later caught, and convicted for smuggling, McCoy was a man of integrity. He kept himself independent from the gangsters and was careful never to stray inside US territorial water – transfers were made at sea. He was proud of the fact that his activities brought prosperity to some poverty-stricken communities, but most importantly he never defrauded his customers and, at a time when adulteration was widespread and people were blinded or fatally poisoned from the effects of backstreet distilling, every bottle that McCoy brought in was 100% genuine and unblemished. Hence the suggestion of authenticity contained in the expression.

Reel Off

To prevent the inevitable twists and kinks which occur in ropes at the most inauspicious time, and provide greater embarrassment when handled at speed, it was found expedient to keep certain lines, such as the log and sounding line, on reels. From

Rats from a sinking ship

here the lines could be 'reeled off' without delay or hazard. The term was later applied to anyone who spoke fluently or was especially adept at quoting facts and figures.

Regatta

An Italian word, the correct spelling is *regata* and it means a boat race. In the Middle Ages it was the custom for the people of Venice to sail to the Lido to practise throwing slings. Since this was for the possible defence of the newly founded Republic the government provided boats for the trip and between them a haphazard race was begun. Subsequently it became official with the boats begun from a line. The Italian for line is *riga* and it is from this word that regatta is derived. Regattas are still very popular in Venice and take place each year.

Ride the Storm

To survive by patience and fortitude, as a vessel rides a storm. Impossible to go forward or run before it the ship lowers or shortens her sail and rides the waves until the storm abates. A vessel also 'rides' to her anchor, although this may be because the old-fashioned word for anchor was *roding*, thought to derive from roadstead, the area where craft normally anchored. The expression *let her ride* originates from here and was part of an official order to discharge the crew at the end of the voyage and 'let the vessel ride'.

Rig

The particular arrangement of masts and sails is known as the vessel's rig and it is by this she is recognised; jackass barque, hermaphrodite brig, mussel drudger, cutter, sloop and so on. Always on the lookout for words he can borrow, the sailor used the word to describe the clothes he was wearing and consequently there came the 'square rig' or the seaman's dress with bell-bottom trousers, collar, etc., and the 'fore and aft rig' which is what officers wear. The word became general in the description of dress although it does seem to have made a return to its origins with the later adoption by the oil industry.

Rostrum

The Latin name for the ram fitted to the bow on early Mediterranean ships was *rostra*. In 338 BC after a successful Battle of Actium the Romans took some of the rostra from captured vessels as souvenirs, carried them home to Rome and displayed them in front of the speaker's stage in the Forum. Gradually the entire assemblage took on the name of rostra. How the plural rostra was changed to the singular rostrum nobody knows!

Round Robin

A petition popularised by sailors who, fearful that the names at the top of the list might be held as the ringleaders, wrote their names in a circle. However, credit for the original idea must go to officers of the French government who in complaint wrote their names on the sash or ribbon worn with their tunics. Round is a corruption of the French *rond*; robin a corruption of *ruban* (ribbon).

Rummage

From the French *arrumer* which means to pack closely. The word was common in the 16th century and described the method of cargo stowage and later the cargo itself. Its later meaning, to poke about, ransack, turn over roughly or jumble, is thought to have come from the warehouses and quayside where cargo was stored awaiting shipment. Such a variation of items and materials, frequently

Regatta

intended for different destinations, would have needed some sorting out.

Running the Gauntlet

Originally a military punishment first recorded in Sweden; gauntlet being a corruption of the Swedish *gatlopp* (*gata* or gate; *lopp* running). The mode of punishment was to make the offender run between a gate or facing ranks of soldiers who would beat him with their leather belts. It entered the English language in 1661 when adopted by the Royal Navy as the punishment for stealing. Theft is a crime universally despised by sailors and there would have been no difficulty in persuading the men to partake.

Safe Passage

The word passage comes from the old French *passager* and signifies the journey a ship makes from one port to another (as opposed to voyage which is the round trip). The word *passenger* comes from here. The phrase has come to mean unharmed or unhindered. Latterly used in legislation and in government – 'the safe passage of a bill'.

Sailing too Close to the Wind

The seaman's term for conduct just within the rules and is another analogy to the sails. A helmsman who allows the ship to come too close into the wind cannot be admonished because the sails have not begun to shake. But nevertheless they will have lost their optimum pulling power and the ship will not be making her best possible speed.

Salary

It seems a long way from salary to salt but it is from this that the word is derived . . . from the Roman custom of paying soldiers and sailors a quantity of salt as a part of their wages. It was known as the *salarium* from the latin *sal* meaning salt, and also gives rise to the expression *worth his salt* meaning that a man was worth his keep.

Salt was not considered quite so precious by northern European sailors but in the early days of sail it was still a very valuable commodity where it was used principally to preserve meat, for eating (salt tablets are still issued on most ships in the tropics) and even as a crude antiseptic. It is from this that we get the expression *rub salt in the wounds*.

Scraping the Barrel

Before the days of canned foodstuffs and refrigeration, the ship's meat was supplied soaked in brine and stored in casks or barrels. The fat, which became hard, stuck to the edge of the barrel but in a hungry ship this was never allowed to waste and the cook would have to scrape the barrel, hence to use the very last, and sometimes the inferior.

Scrimshanker

From the sailors' art of scrimshaw or the making of ornamental objects from the remains of marine birds and mammals. Whale bones were the most common material. It was a popular hobby and since it involved little noise scrimshanking was frequently indulged by men on duty which was how the term came to imply malingering. Some say the word comes from the founder expert Admiral Scrimshaw, others claim there was no such person.

Scrub Round It

From the routine job of holystoning or scrubbing the decks. If an obstruction were placed on the deck the men would be told to scrub round it, hence ignoring or dismissing a problem. The 'Holystone' was a large block of sandstone which was used to scour the wooden decks. It earned its name because men kneeling down to work the stone looked as if they were praying to it.

Sculling Around

From *sculling*, the action of propelling a boat with one oar over the stern. Many of the doubtful traders and opportunists which plagued every ship at anchor would scull their boats, this could be a reference to them. Slang for an article left lying about, or a person idly employed.

Scuppered

Scuppers are the waterways or guttters at the edge of the deck which drain off the water. If a man were knocked over by a wave sweeping across the deck he would likely end up here, he was then said to be *scuppered*.

Scuttle

The act of deliberately sinking a ship of which the most dramatic example was the scuttling of the German High Seas fleet, including over fifteen battleships, after it had been interned at Scapa Flow after World War I. Rather than face the ignominy of handing them over to the British, the Germans preferred to sink their ships. Scuttle is an Anglo-Saxon word for a small hole.

Scuttlebutt

Originally a wooden cask set in a convenient part of the ship from which the men could draw their ration of water. The cask was refilled daily but to ensure that water was used sparingly it was 'scuttled' which meant it had a small hole made in its side so that only half a cask could be filled at a time. Men lining up at the scuttlebutt for their ration of water would naturally exchange gossip which is what the word in America has come to mean. But faithful to its original it remains peculiarly the gossip heard at the office water cooler or fountain.

Scuppered

Sewn up

Sailors had many sayings to express completion: *all squared up*, from the business of tidying the yards; *all clewed up* which had to do with stowing the sails; and this the final and most absolute *all sewn up*, a reference to the dead. At sea the bodies of the dead were sewn inside an old piece of sail or canvas or sometimes, their hammocks before being committed to the deep. The purpose of this was partly respectful, and partly pragmatic because it stopped the cannon balls or ballast weights slipping out. Traditionally, when sewing up, the last stitch was passed through the nose. This was done to release the soul and make sure the corpse was really dead.

Shanty

Work songs sung aboard ship which brightened up the drudgery of hand hauling and also ensured the men all *pulled* their weight together. There were different shanties for different work. Halyard shanties were brisk for the quick but comparatively easy work of hoisting sail. Capstan shanties sung when the anchor was to be hauled aboard were generally slow and sentimental. The custom goes back to the 15th century and the word shanty probably takes its name from the French *chanter*, to sing.

Shape-up

Look smart, improve oneself. Frequently used as a verb in connection with the course a vessel is to make. The navigator will draw or *shape* a course around a headland, a danger or an obstruction. A ship out of position will *shape up* a course to reach her destination.

Sheet Anchor

The sheet anchor is a name which has survived since Elizabethan times. It is a large anchor carried as a spare lest either of the main anchors should be lost or fail to hold the ship in heavy weather. Quite why the term means quintessential reliability is difficult to understand. Most sheet anchors are so covered in paint they are impossible to drag off the bulkhead.

She Won't Wear It

If the seas were too big, or the wind too strong for a square-rigged ship to be brought from one tack to the other it was the standard practice to *wear* ship, which means to put her stern through the wind rather than her bow (in yachting this is known as gybing.) Sometimes however the seas are too big to prevent this, hence the expression *she won't wear it*.

Shipshape and Bristol Fashion

For centuries Bristol was the major port on the English west coast and shipping here was the best regulated and most organised in the country, or so it was said by Bristolians. Hence its use to mean in tip top order, everything neat and tidy.

Shooting a Line

A fishing boat *shoots* its nets and lines. There is a probable link with the fact that longlines, used for catching cod, were several miles long and it took hours to bait the many hundreds of hooks. Quiet, undemanding and repetitive work would be conducive to story telling.

Show a Leg

Make a move, get started. It dates back to Napoleon times or before, when men were pressed into service and taken forcibly from the streets and their homes. Shore leave was impossible lest the men should desert, so as recompense, women were sometimes allowed to visit and it is recorded that at Spithead, the naval anchorage off Portsmouth, as many as 500 women might be entertained aboard one ship. Naturally in the mornings when work was begun there existed some confusion and the petty officers' way of sorting this out was to shout 'Show a leg!' Soft and curvy ones could stay where they were, hairy ones were kicked out of bed!

Another shout that accompanied reveille was *Rise and Shine* which again people still use today. There are more, indeed there is an entire verse but it is much too rude to publish here.

Siren

A woman with fascinating but deadly charm. A word from Greek mythology. Sirens charmed passing sailors with their singing and with such effect that the men were rooted to the spot and eventually perished from hunger. The lure of the sirens was finally ended when Odysseus, warned of

Show a leg

their danger, plugged up the ears of his crew. The women were so stricken by this reversal that they threw themselves into the sea. Cape Pelorus in Sicily, where it was reputed to have taken place, was later renamed Sirenis.

Skyscraper

Long before the word came to mean a high building it was the name given to the highest sail in the ship. Triangular shaped, made of very light cloth, it was used only in moderate weather. Sometimes a square sail was set in the same place and this was called a *moonraker*. Both skyscraper and moonraker were carried above the *skysails*. Occasionally they would run up an even higher one known as, *stargazer*. After that they ran out of names.

Sling Your Hook

One of several sayings used unkindly to urge a quick departure. This one is a reference to the sailor's hammock and the suggestion that he slings it on another hook elsewhere. From boatwork comes *shove off* which literally means to push the boat away from the ship's side or quay and is still the recognised term. Or a person may be told to *beat it*

Siren

which is to beat out of port in the first auspicious wind, or from the practice of 'beating to quarters' when ships' crews ran to battle stations to the beat of a drum.

Sloppy

Comes from the Middle English *sloppe* a loose-fitting garment. In the early days of the Royal Navy it was noticed that many of the men were in rags which not only made a poor impression but also impaired health and efficiency. In 1663, an order was passed requiring all ships to carry a supply of clothing which could be sold to the crew; a regulation which has survived to the present day. The name for the locker in which the clothes were kept was the *slop chest*, and presumably because it contained mostly *sloppes* which in those early times were the seaman's standard dress (before the introduction of the *petticoat*). The word collected its slang meaning of untidiness or a job carelessly done from the shape of the garment and the state that it must have been in after months squashed in a trunk.

Slush Fund

Slush was the unpromising name for fat scraped off the top of the barrels of meat. It was jealously guarded. The crew found it perfect for greasing masts to make sail hoisting easier and for preserving leather fittings. The cook, unhappy about this, would secrete it in his 'slush fund'. It was a perquisite so far as he was concerned. He sold it ashore, mostly to candle makers and people in the fish and chip trade.

Snub

To *snub* a ship is to cut short her progress, either by dropping the anchor onto the bottom to act as a brake, or by holding onto any ropes which might connect her to the shore. Eventually the word was applied to members of a crew, and to snub a man was to humiliate him with a curt remark, or to ignore him.

Another word with similar meaning is *jibe*. This is the sudden and dramatic movement of a sailing vessel bringing the wind across her stern and filling the sails on the other side – done carelessly it can bring the mast down. The evidence which suggests this is an authentic sea word is *jib*, the Viking word for sail.

Sold Down the River

From the perpetual threat held against slaves working in areas bordering the Northern States of America. If they misbehaved or proved lazy, they could be *sold down the river* (the Mississippi) to work in the southern sugar plantations. From this comes the notion of cheated, hoodwinked, taken for a ride.

So-long

A seaman's farewell, from the East Indian word 'salaam'. Common in shore-side use, but originally nautical.

Son of a Gun

Complimentary term for a sailor suggesting he was a natural born to the job, or more precisely born *on* the job. It comes from the time when women shared the gun deck accommodation with men aboard ships in port and sometimes at sea. Since the working spaces and gangways had to be kept clear, the only undisturbed place a woman could give birth to a child would be behind screens between the guns. The expression also meant being conceived alongside a gun, since a hammock wasn't convenient for that sort of thing.

The following is an extract from the Captain's Journal of a brig sailing off the Spanish coast in 1835:

> This day the surgeon informed me that a woman on board had been labouring in child for 12 hours and asked if I could fire a broadside to leeward. I did so and she was delivered a fine male child.

In cases where the paternity was uncertain, the child was entered in the Deck Log as *son of a gun*.

S.O.S.

The international radio signal for distress. The letters were chosen because their morse code characteristics were distinctive, easy to remember and make. The mnemonic 'save our souls' was originally 'save our ship' and the first time the signal was made at sea was in 1908 from the American ship *Azaoahe*. Years later a new international distress signal was born at sea. This time the spoken word MAYDAY from the French *m'aidez!* help me.

Sounding Out

Researchers *sound out* public opinion, which means search and enquire, in exactly the same way as the sailor does when he *sounds* the depth of water beneath his ship with an echo-sounder or sounding line. From the Anglo-Saxon *sund* – messenger.

Sou'wester

It is an abbreviation for south-westerly wind which around the shores of Northern Europe is the one which brings the rain. Hence it became the sailor's name for his oilskin cap and now more generally, a wide-brimmed waterproof hat which fastens under the chin.

Spic and Span

In pristine condition; it referred originally to a newly built ship. A *spic* was a spike or nail, a *span* a length of timber, both primary items of ship construction.

Spin a Yarn

It has the ring of a salty expression and is popularly thought to have come from wet weather days when crews would be given the job of 'spinning' or loosely twisting together yarns of old rope to be used for small tying jobs. Sheltering under the foc'sle head it would have been a great time for telling stories. However, spinning yarn was carried on ashore long before it was at sea and this is probably one of the few shore expressions adopted by seamen.

To spin a fibre, especially wool, correctly and

Spic and span

ensure it remains the right size, length and twist, the spinner has to continually stretch the material. Thus when the old-timers wanted to suggest that someone was stretching the truth they likened it to 'spinning a yarn'.

Splice the Main Brace

An extra tot of rum. There is a cynicism in this expression. The worn part of a rope would sometimes be cut out and the ends long-spliced together. It provided a reasonable repair, the rope looked as good as new although not quite so strong as before. The main brace however, was such an important rope that splicing was not often considered and at the first sign of damage or wear the rope was renewed. The expression implies that an extra tot of rum was as rare as a splicing of the main brace.

Spoil the Ship for a Ha'p'orth of Tar

This is a misquotation. Correctly it is 'spoil the *sheep* for a ha'p'orth of tar' and refers to the practice of applying bitumen or tar to a sheep's feet to prevent it contracting disease.

Square Up

From the custom of ships in harbour 'squaring' their yards horizontally to the deck and at right angles to the fore and aft line. The phrase has come to mean to repay debts; to square with somebody; the state of being normal and correct.

Stand

A ship will stand in towards the land, stand off a port, stand in with another vessel when sailing together, and stands by in case of trouble. The word has come ashore, people also stand-by, stand their ground, stand in favour, become stand-offish, or simply like to know how they stand?

Staunch

From the old French *estanche* meaning watertight. A vessel which had no leaks was described as staunch. Hence firm, reliable.

Stave Off

To stave, the operation of breaking the planks of a boat, past tense of the verb is stove. To stave off meant to thrust a boat from the stone quay or ship's side with a boathook or spar to prevent her from being damaged. Thus comes the idea of staving off a problem.

Stinkpot

An insulting term, and a form of chemical warfare used in Greek and Roman times and again by pirate ships in the 18th century. Earthernware pots filled with sulphur and a slow-burning fuse were lit and thrown onto the oponents' deck. Once ignited the mixture produced an intolerable stench and clouds of black smoke. This created a diversion as the attacker closed alongside and armed men prepared to board.

Strike

The shortened form of 'strike work'. It was a method of protest against low wages, poor conditions, etc. The crew would *strike* or lower the ship's yards to immobilise her. It was particularly done in port and not at sea which would have been mutiny.

Suck the Monkey

The phrase 'Old suck the monkey' is an insult which has attracted several variations (He doesn't give a monkey's, etc.) It comes from the practice common amongst British seamen serving in the West Indies during the American War of Independence of persuading the local women to bring coconuts aboard filled with rum which was then drunk or sucked from the small holes. There are two explanations for the word 'monkey', it was the word for the small wooden casks which were also employed for this purpose plus the obvious association that the hairy coconut looked like a monkey's face.

Sun Over the Yardarm

Time for a drink. The expression began with passengers on North Atlantic liners steeling themselves to wait for an alcoholic drink until the moment the sun had risen above the foreyard; in these latitudes that would have been around midday. There is no suitable explanation, however, for the other well known nautical toast *down the hatch*. It first appeared in print in the 1930s in a book by P. G. Wodehouse. He might even be the inventor, it sounds like him.

Sweet Fanny Adams

The most unfortunate girl in history. Not enough that she was brutally murdered and dismembered (by a deranged accountant) but her initials have become anagrammed into an ugly expletive. It was a historic coincidence that her separate parts should turn up in a trunk at the Deptford Navy Yard just at the time that the navy was switching to tinned meat. No prizes for guessing what the meat was subsequently called.

However, time has sweetened the injury and compassion, even utility has crept in. Instead of the meat it was the large square containers which were to finally immortalise her name. They were called *fannies* and were popular with sailors who used them as receptacles for collecting food from the galley. (Even today's stainless steel replacements are called 'fannies'.) The suggestion of being dispossessed, which the expression means today, comes from the idea of a completed meal and the fanny being empty. The 'sweet' followed later, with atonement.

Swinging the Lead

Before instruments were introduced, the usual method of ascertaining the depth of water was a long length of line weighted with a lump of lead. It was called the 'hand lead line', or more simply 'the lead'. A sailor would climb over the ship's rail, secure himself to the chain plates and make a continuous number of 'casts'. This entailed swinging the lead over his head several times then letting it

Swinging the lead

fly ahead. It was necessary to twirl the line and shoot it ahead so that by the time the lead had sunk to the bottom the ship's headway would have brought the line perpendicular and the correct depth could be seen. Less competent leadsmen would make a great display of twirling the lead around their heads to mask their inability to read the depth correctly. In other words they were faking it, merely pretending to work.

Another explanation is that soldiers, travelling in troopships and watching the leadsman, considered it such effortless work they borrowed the term for laziness.

Take Down a Peg

It is believed to date from the 17th century when flags began to play an important part in indicating command or rank. Admirals already had their own flag (hence the term flag officer) but from this time it became the general practice for an Admiral of the Fleet to fly a Union flag on the main, or highest mast, and lesser admirals to fly their flags from the foremast or the mizzen. Flag halyards were secured to pegs, and if a senior admiral handed over his command to a junior then the flag would have to be flown in a subordinate position, or taken down a peg. Thus the phrase has come to mean to blunt somebody's pride.

Taken Aback

A ship is said to be *taken aback* when through a dramatic shift in the wind or careless steering her sails suddenly billow out in reverse. The helmsman is then taken aback in more senses than one.

Take the Gilt off the Gingerbread

When Hans Andersen published his enormously successful *Hansel and Gretel*, the gilded scrollwork which had decorated sailing ships since mediaeval times suddenly found a name! It was called *gingerbread* after the ornate and over-embellished witch's cottage. However, the name had come too late and *gingerbread*, which had once blossomed high over the sterns and quarters of all the great warships, was in decline. Labour costs had risen so that it was now more expensive to decorate the ship then equip her with cannon. The Admiralty severely restricted its use. It spoilt the attraction, or as the saying puts it 'took the gilt off the gingerbread'.

Take the Wind Out of Your Sails

A sailing ship passing to windward of another will blanket the wind blowing on its sails thus causing her to slow or even stop. It was a tactic used in warfare, later by pirate ships and is very common in yacht racing today.

Tariff

List of duties to be paid on imports and exports, lists of prices and charges. From the Spanish sea port of Tari'fa about twenty miles from Gibraltar from where the Moors levied contributions according to a certain scale on vessels entering the Mediterranean.

Tattoo

The skin decoration produced by the injection of coloured pigments, was introduced to the western world by Captain Cook who described it in his journal after a visit to Tahiti in 1764. He also brought back Robert Stainsby, a seaman from the *Endeavour* who had allowed the natives to tattoo his body. From the Tahitian word and meaning to prick.

Tell it to the Marines

The diarist and secretary to the Royal Navy, Samuel Pepys, while relating to King Charles II in 1664 some of the stories told to him by the captain of *HMS Defyance*, mentioned the existence of flying fish. The courtiers present refused to believe this, but an officer of the Maritime Regiment of Foot, Sir William Kellegrew who was present, insisted that it was true for he had also seen them. The king is then reported to have said 'From the nature of their calling no class of our subjects can have so wide a knowledge of seas and lands as the Officers and Men of our Loyal Maritime Regiment. Henceforth ere we cast doubts upon a take that lacks likelihood we will first *Tell it to the Marines*!' The expression took on a cynical meaning when explained to the seamen of the lower deck, and ever since it has been used as a statement of disbelief.

It proved very useful to newspaperman Malcolm Muggeridge who remembered using it to fool a Kremlin censor. Obliged to report accurately the announcement that Russia was spending just 2% of her budget on defence he added the comment 'suggest you inform marines'. Incidentally, marines

Taken aback

are called *leathernecks* because of their uniform caps which once had a leather tongue to protect the back of the neck.

Three Mile Limit

The arguments between nations as to how much of the sea surrounding their coastline should belong to them was settled by a compromise suggestion from Bynkershoek in his book *De Dominio Marks* published in 1702. He proposed that a country should exercise control only over the amount of water she could defend from the shore. This was agreed to be 3 miles, the range of the smooth bore cannon.

Three Sheets in the Wind

Sails are controlled with ropes called *sheets* and the most any sail has is two – a lee side sheet and a weather sheet. The sailor's contention is that if a man who had been drinking was given as many as *three* sheets he could still not steady or control himself on a regular course. An alternative idea is

Tell it to the marines

that of a ship caught with three (jib) sheets in the wind as she goes from one tack to the other. The sails would flap and the ship would wallow and stagger in the locomotion of a drunk.

Tide Over

From the days of sail and with special reference to the English Channel where outward bound ships could make very little progress against the incoming tidal stream and the prevailing south west wind. In such conditions they would frequently *tide over* or anchor for those hours when the tide was against them. Hence to rest up and let the difficulties sort themselves out.

Tidy

The word is derived from *tide* hence the meaning of being well arranged and methodical as associated with tides. We still use the word in a seasonal connection: even*tide*, spring*tide*, etc.

Ton

In about the year 1500 many ships were built for the wine trade then carried in wooden casks or *tuns* (from the French word *tonneau*) and standardised at 2240 lb. The ships were measured and assessed according to the number of *tuns* they could carry. Hence the word ton became the measure of capacity for ships, and the measurement of weight ashore.

Touch and Go

Sailing barges trading the rivers and estuaries of the East Coast of Britain carried only two men as crew and were unable to 'sound' the depth of water. They managed by the simple expedient of running the barge to the side of the river or channel until they felt it *touch* the bottom, then promptly *go* about onto the other tack. The sudden change in direction and the force of a fifty ton barge slewing round was usually sufficient to ensure they kept going, but sometimes of course the barge would become stuck. From this comes the risk implicit in the expression 'touch and go'.

Two Six Heave

From the days when each man of a gun's crew was given a number. It was the job of Nos 2 and 6 to haul the gun back through the gun port in preparation for firing after it had been loaded.

Under the Weather

To feel ill. Originally it meant to feel seasick or to be adversely affected by bad weather. The term is correctly 'under the weather bow' which is a gloomy prospect; the weather bow is the side upon which all the rotten weather is blowing.

Under Weigh

To get started. Often spelt this way although correctly the term is *under way*. In law it means not

Touch and go

at anchor nor made fast to the shore or aground. The significance is that the vessel's rudder is effective, that she can be handled and must therefore obey the 'rule of the road'. The word *weigh* has actually nothing to do with forward movement but concerns the raising or weighing of the anchor. Another expression which means get started is *set sail*. Sails were set when the gaskets tying them to the yards were let go allowing the sails to fill with wind. It is now a figurative term and everything from hydrofoils to nuclear submarines set sail.

Under Your Own Steam

Comes from the infant days of steamships which not infrequently ran out of coal or broke down. In those uncertain times it was a matter of great satisfaction and importance for them to make port unaided. It quickly took on a metaphoric meaning – ships which sailed home under jury rig would still be said to have made it 'under their own steam'. Hence its present use – without assistance. The alternative, *taken in tow*, is another expression adopted by landsmen.

Up and a Downer

An argument or fierce row. Possibly from the continual disagreements that must have gone on between sailors and engineers drafted aboard the first steam auxiliary ships. Apart from the unaccustomed smoke and soot, sailors had the additional chore of erecting a funnel on deck and lowering the screw propeller each time the engine was used. The order 'Up funnel, down screw' prompted the ships to be known as the *up and downers*.

Under the weather

Van

The word was originally *vant*, a corruption of the French *avant*. It was the name given to the leading group of ships in a battle fleet and dates from the 17th century – in the van, up front. Previously naval ship battles had been fought at random and this was the first attempt to organise fleets into divisions.

Veer

In the nautical sense *veer* is to slack away a rope. The word takes its wider meaning from fact that when the wind moved aft, relative to the vessel, the ropes which controlled the yards and sails would have to be veered. From this developed the meteorological term, and finally it has come to describe a gradual change in direction of anything.

Wallop

After the French fleet had raised and burnt Brighton on the Sussex coast in the reign of Henry VIII Sir John Wallop was ordered by the king to carry out a reprisal raid. Sir John sailed with his fleet to Normandy where he is reported to have burnt twenty-one towns and villages and to have demolished several harbours. Ever since the name *Wallop* has been the name synonymous with a beating or good hiding.

Wash Out

A failure, disappointment – from the early days of signal flags when messages were recorded on a slate and a cancelled message was sponged or washed out.

Wasters

The word relates to the midship or centre part of a ship's deck known as her *waist*. The men who worked this part were generally older, less fit, disabled or landsmen 'pressed' into service, men who could not be trusted to work aloft. They were put to work in the ship's waist mending sails, splicing, cleaning, etc. and because they worked this part of the ship they came to be called *waisters*. Somewhere down the line the 'i' has been dropped and the term has come to describe idlers, no good layabouts.

Wedding garland

Weather Eye Open

Keep a good watch. It took an extra effort for the lookout to train his eye on the *weather* side of the ship as it would mean his having to face the wind, the spray and the rain. From the weather side however, always came the first sign of a change (in the weather).

Wedding Garland

Surprisingly the custom of the bride carrying a bouquet of flowers comes from the sea. It was traditional when a ship came home to hoist some greenery at the mast – a symbol, the men had come home safely to the good earth. Then gradually it became a signal for the women to come aboard. Later it signified nuptials and a garland of flowers was flown from the mast top whenever a crew member was about to be married. Garland comes from the Greek meaning a collection of flowers.

When My Ship Comes In

A phrase that once had legal value as shown in this extract from *Select Pleas in the Court of Admiralty 1536*; 'I promys and me bynd to pay within . . . daies after the save aryving of the said good ships into the River of Temys, the port of her right dyscharge'.

Whistling for a Wind

To hope for the impossible. It was the sailor's superstition that he could call up the desired wind by whistling, a belief still current amongst some yachtsmen. Yet whistling on ships has been either forbidden or discouraged for many years. There are a number of reasons; it can be confused with orders piped on the boatswain's call (or whistle); it was said to be the signal for the commencement of the

Mutiny of the Nore 1797; and because it is generally felt that whistling brings too much wind – a storm in fact. It is held to be unlucky for actors and stage hands to whistle backstage.

Wide Berth

From the term to give a *wide berth* which ordered the helmsman to steer well clear of a rock, a shoal, or whatever danger presented itself. Hence a generous margin.

Windbag

Originally the nickname for a sailing ship, it has somehow come to mean a talkative or boastful person.

Windfall

Some English and American landowners were prevented, by a clause in the title of their estates, to either fell or sell timber as this was reserved for building ships for the Navy. However, this did not include trees which were blown down and so a windfall came to mean a financial blessing, an unexpected gift of money.

Wreck

Figuratively somebody in poor mental or physical shape and another example of the sailor's delightful habit of likening ships to the human condition. It is interesting that quite a few of these centre around shipwreck which cannot say much for the company he was keeping. *Derelict*, for example, a ship abandoned by her crew and borrowed to describe someone who floats on a sea of misery. *Stranded*, another example, comparing the lost and helpless with a ship run aground on the strand or sandy shore. *On the rocks* describes a rather more serious

Wreck

condition: a ship will very rarely be saved once impaled by rocks. (Nothing to do with ice *in the drink* – which, incidentally, was a term coined by airmen bailing out over the sea.) Left *high and dry* is another reference to grounding, so is *touching bottom* as the economy does now and then. *Hard and fast* describes a ship hard aground and fast that she cannot be moved, a term which still means inexorable today.

Write Off

An insurance term meaning a total loss and that the item, or group of items could be 'written off' the insurance policy. Insurance is a business which began at sea as a gamble between Mediterranean bankers and merchants. The banker would suggest that a particular shipment would arrive safely and stake money to this effect. The merchant, or shipper, in effect claimed that it would not and was also prepared to put up a sum of money to back his belief. This later became the premium.

PENGUIN BOOKS

MULTITUDE

Michael Hardt teaches at Duke University, and Antonio Negri taught for years at the universities of Padua and Paris. They are the authors of *Empire*.

MULTITUDE

WAR AND DEMOCRACY
IN THE AGE OF EMPIRE

MICHAEL HARDT
ANTONIO NEGRI

PENGUIN BOOKS

PENGUIN BOOKS

Published by the Penguin Group

Penguin Group (USA) Inc., 375 Hudson Street, New York, New York 10014, U.S.A.
Penguin Group (Canada), 90 Eglinton Avenue East, Suite 700, Toronto,
Ontario, Canada M4P 2Y3 (a division of Pearson Penguin Canada Inc.)
Penguin Books Ltd, 80 Strand, London WC2R 0RL, England
Penguin Ireland, 25 St Stephen's Green, Dublin 2, Ireland (a division of Penguin Books Ltd)
Penguin Group (Australia), 250 Camberwell Road, Camberwell,
Victoria 3124, Australia (a division of Pearson Australia Group Pty Ltd)
Penguin Books India Pvt Ltd, 11 Community Centre, Panchsheel Park,
New Delhi – 110 017, India
Penguin Group (NZ), 67 Apollo Drive, Rosedale, North Shore 0632, New Zealand
(a division of Pearson New Zealand Ltd)
Penguin Books (South Africa) (Pty) Ltd, 24 Sturdee Avenue, Rosebank,
Johannesburg 2196, South Africa

Penguin Books Ltd, Registered Offices: 80 Strand, London WC2R 0RL, England

First published in the United States of America by The Penguin Press,
a member of Penguin Group (USA) Inc. 2004
Published in Penguin Books 2005

5 7 9 10 8 6

THE LIBRARY OF CONGRESS HAS CATALOGED THE HARDCOVER EDITION AS FOLLOWS:
Hardt, Michael.
Multitude : war and democracy in the Age of Empire /
Michael Hardt and Antonio Negri.
p. cm.
Sequel to: Empire.
Includes index.
ISBN 1-59420-024-6 (hc.)
ISBN 978-0-14-303559-6 (pbk.)
1. Democracy. 2. Internationalism. 3. Globalization. 4. International relations.
5. War. 6. Imperialism. I. Negri, Antonio, 1933– II. Title.
JC423.H364 2004 2004044463
321.8—dc22

Printed in the United States of America
Designed by Meighan Cavanaugh

CONTENTS

Preface: Life in Common   xi

1. WAR   *1*

1.1 Simplicissimus   *3*
Exceptions   *3*
   Golem   *10*
The Global State of War   *12*
Biopower and Security   *18*
Legitimate Violence   *25*
   Samuel Huntington, Geheimrat   *33*

1.2 Counterinsurgencies   *36*
Birth of the New War   *37*

Revolution in Military Affairs   41

   The Mercenary and the Patriot   49

Asymmetry and Full-Spectrum Dominance   51

1.3 Resistance   63

The Primacy of Resistance   64

From the People's Army to Guerrilla Warfare   69

Inventing Network Struggles   79

   Swarm Intelligence   91

From Biopower to Biopolitical Production   93

2. MULTITUDE   97

2.1 Dangerous Classes   103

The Becoming Common of Labor   103

The Twilight of the Peasant World   115

   Two Italians in India   127

The Wealth of the Poor (or, We Are the Poors!)   129

   Demonic Multitudes: Dostoyevsky
   Reads the Bible   138

      Excursus 1: Method: In Marx's Footsteps   140
      Death of the Dismal Science? 153

2.2 De Corpore   *158*

Global Apartheid   *160*

A Trip to Davos   *167*

Big Government Is Back   *176*

Life on the Market   *179*

2.3 Traces of the Multitude   *189*

The Monstrosity of the Flesh   *190*

   Invasion of the Monsters   *194*

Production of the Common   *196*

Beyond Private and Public   *202*

   Carnival and Movement   *208*

Mobilization of the Common   *211*

   Excursus 2: Organization: Multitude on the Left *219*

3. DEMOCRACY   *229*

3.1 The Long March of Democracy   *231*

Crisis of Democracy in the Era of
Armed Globalization   *231*

The Unfinished Democratic
Project of Modernity   *237*

   Debtors' Rebellion   *247*

The Unrealized Democracy of Socialism 249

Revolt, Berlin 1953 255

From Democratic Representation to Global
Public Opinion 258

White Overalls 264

3.2 Global Demands for Democracy 268

Cahiers de doléances 268

Convergence in Seattle 285

Experiments in Global Reform 289

Back to the Eighteenth Century! 306

Excursus 3: Strategy: Geopolitics and New Alliances 312

Iconoclasts 324

3.3 Democracy of the Multitude 328

Sovereignty and Democracy 328

May the Force Be with You 341

The New Science of Democracy: Madison
and Lenin 348

Notes 359

Index 407

PREFACE: LIFE IN COMMON

The possibility of democracy on a global scale is emerging today for the very first time. This book is about that possibility, about what we call the project of the multitude. The project of the multitude not only expresses the desire for a world of equality and freedom, not only demands an open and inclusive democratic global society, but also provides the means for achieving it. That is how our book will end, but it cannot begin there.

Today the possibility of democracy is obscured and threatened by the seemingly permanent state of conflict across the world. Our book must begin with this state of war. Democracy, it is true, remained an incomplete project throughout the modern era in all its national and local forms, and certainly the processes of globalization in recent decades have added new challenges, but the primary obstacle to democracy is the global state of war. In our era of armed globalization, the modern dream of democracy may seem to have been definitively lost. War has always been incompatible with democracy. Traditionally, democracy has been suspended during wartime and power entrusted temporarily to a strong central authority to confront the crisis. Because the current state of war is both global in scale and long lasting, with no end in sight, the suspension of democracy too becomes indefinite or even permanent. War takes on a generalized character, strangling all social life and posing its own political order. Democracy thus appears to be entirely irretrievable, buried deep beneath the weapons and security regimes of our constant state of conflict.

Yet never has democracy been more necessary. No other path will provide a way out of the fear, insecurity, and domination that permeates our world at war; no other path will lead us to a peaceful life in common.

This book is the sequel to our book *Empire*, which focused on the new global form of sovereignty. That book attempted to interpret the *tendency* of global political order in the course of its formation, that is, to recognize how from a variety of contemporary processes there is emerging a new form of global order that we call Empire. Our point of departure was the recognition that contemporary global order can no longer be understood adequately in terms of imperialism as it was practiced by the modern powers, based primarily on the sovereignty of the nation-state extended over foreign territory. Instead, a "network power," a new form of sovereignty, is now emerging, and it includes as its primary elements, or nodes, the dominant nation-states along with supranational institutions, major capitalist corporations, and other powers. This network power we claim is "imperial" not "imperialist." Not all the powers in Empire's network, of course, are equal—on the contrary, some nation-states have enormous power and some almost none at all, and the same is true for the various other corporations and institutions that make up the network—but despite inequalities they must cooperate to create and maintain the current global order, with all of its internal divisions and hierarchies.

Our notion of Empire thus cuts diagonally across the debates that pose unilateralism and multilateralism or pro-Americanism and anti-Americanism as the only global political alternatives. On the one hand, we argued that no nation-state, not even the most powerful one, not even the United States, can "go it alone" and maintain global order without collaborating with the other major powers in the network of Empire. On the other hand, we claimed that the contemporary global order is not characterized and cannot be sustained by an *equal* participation of all, or even by the set of elite nation-states, as in the model of multilateral control under the authority of the United Nations. Rather, severe divisions and hierarchies, along regional, national, and local lines, define our current global order. Our claim is not simply that unilateralism and multilateralism as they have been presented are not desirable but rather that they are not possible given our present conditions and that attempts to pursue them will not succeed in maintaining the current global order. When we say that Empire is a *tendency* we mean that it is the only form of power that will succeed in maintaining the current global order in a lasting way. One might thus respond to the U.S. unilateralist global projects with the ironic injunction adapted from the Marquis de Sade: *"Américains, encore un effort si vous voulez être imperials!"* ("Americans, you need to try harder if you want to be imperial!").

Empire rules over a global order that is not only fractured by internal divisions and hierarchies but also plagued by perpetual war. The state of war is inevitable in Empire, and war functions as an instrument of rule. Today's imperial peace, *Pax Imperii*, like that in the times of ancient Rome, is a false pretense of peace that really presides over a state of constant war. All of that analysis of Empire and global order, however, was part of the previous book and there is no need for us to repeat it here.

This book will focus on the multitude, the living alternative that grows within Empire. You might say, simplifying a great deal, that there are two faces to globalization. On one face, Empire spreads globally its network of hierarchies and divisions that maintain order through new mechanisms of control and constant conflict. Globalization, however, is also the creation of new circuits of cooperation and collaboration that stretch across nations and continents and allow an unlimited number of encounters. This second face of globalization is not a matter of everyone in the world becoming the same; rather it provides the possibility that, while remaining different, we discover the commonality that enables us to communicate and act together. The multitude too might thus be conceived as a network: an open and expansive network in which all differences can be expressed freely and equally, a network that provides the means of encounter so that we can work and live in common.

As a first approach we should distinguish the multitude at a conceptual level from other notions of social subjects, such as the people, the masses, and the working class. *The people* has traditionally been a unitary conception. The population, of course, is characterized by all kinds of differences, but the people reduces that diversity to a unity and makes of the population a single identity: "the people" is one. The multitude, in contrast, is many. The multitude is composed of innumerable internal differences that can never be reduced to a unity or a single identity—different cultures, races, ethnicities, genders, and sexual orientations; different forms of labor; different ways of living; different views of the world; and different desires. The multitude is a multiplicity of all these singular differences. *The masses* are also contrasted with the people because they too cannot be reduced to a unity or an identity. The masses certainly are composed of all types and sorts, but really one should not say that different social subjects make up the masses. The essence of the masses is indifference: all differences are submerged and drowned in the masses. All the colors of the population fade to gray. These masses are able to move in unison only because they form an indistinct, uniform conglomerate. In the multitude, social differences remain different. The multitude is many-colored, like Joseph's magical coat. Thus the challenge posed by the concept of multitude is for a social multiplicity to manage to communicate and act in common while remaining internally different.

Finally, we should also distinguish the multitude from the *working class*. The concept of the working class has come to be used as an exclusive concept, not only distinguishing the workers from the owners who do not need to work to support themselves, but also separating the working class from others who work. In its most narrow usage the concept is employed to refer only to industrial workers, separating them from workers in agriculture, services, and other sectors; at its most broad, working class refers to all waged workers, separating them from the poor, unpaid domestic laborers, and all others who do not receive a wage. The multitude, in contrast, is an open, inclusive concept. It tries to capture the importance of the recent shifts of the global economy: on the one hand, the industrial working class no longer plays a hegemonic role in the global economy, although its numbers have not decreased worldwide; and on the other hand, production today has to be conceived not merely in economic terms but more generally as social production—not only the production of material goods but also the production of communications, relationships, and forms of life. The multitude is thus composed potentially of all the diverse figures of social production. Once again, a distributed network such as the Internet is a good initial image or model for the multitude because, first, the various nodes remain different but are all connected in the Web, and, second, the external boundaries of the network are open such that new nodes and new relationships can always be added.

Two characteristics of the multitude make especially clear its contribution to the possibility of democracy today. The first might be called its "economic" aspect, except that the separation of economics from other social domains quickly breaks down here. Insofar as the multitude is neither an identity (like the people) nor uniform (like the masses), the internal differences of the multitude must discover *the common* that allows them to communicate and act together. The common we share, in fact, is not so much discovered as it is produced. (We are reluctant call this *the commons* because that term refers to pre-capitalist-shared spaces that were destroyed by the advent of private property. Although more awkward, "the common" highlights the philosophical content of the term and emphasizes that this is not a return to the past but a new development.) Our communication, collaboration, and cooperation are not only based on the common, but they in turn produce the common in an expanding spiral relationship. This production of the common tends today to be central to every form of social production, no matter how locally circumscribed, and it is, in fact, the primary characteristic of the new dominant forms of labor today. Labor itself, in other words, tends through the transformations of the economy to create and be embedded in cooperative and communicative networks. Anyone who works with information or knowledge—for example, from agriculturists who develop the specific properties of seeds to software programmers—relies on the common knowledge passed down from others and in turn creates new common knowledge. This is especially true for all labor that creates immaterial projects, including ideas, images, affects, and relationships. We will call this newly dominant model "biopolitical production" to highlight that it not only involves the production of material goods in a strictly economic sense but also touches on and produces all facets of social life, economic, cultural, and political. This biopolitical production and its expansion of the common is one strong pillar on which stands the possibility of global democracy today.

The second characteristic of the multitude especially important for democracy is its "political" organization (but remember that the political blends quickly into the economic, the social, and the cultural). We get a first hint of this democratic tendency when we look at the genealogy of modern resistances, revolts, and revolution, which demonstrates a tendency toward increasingly democratic organization, from centralized forms of revolutionary dictatorship and command to network organizations that displace authority in collaborative relationships. The genealogy reveals a tendency for resistance and revolutionary organizations not only to be a means to achieve a democratic society but to create internally, within the organizational structure, democratic relationships. Furthermore, democracy on a global scale is becoming an increasingly widespread demand, sometimes explicit but often implicit in the innumerable grievances and resistances expressed against the current global order. The common currency that runs throughout so many struggles and movements for liberation across the world today—at local, regional, and global levels—is the desire for democracy. Needless to say, desiring and demanding global democracy do not guarantee its realization, but we should not underestimate the power such demands can have.

Keep in mind that this is a philosophical book. We will give numerous examples of how people are working today to put an end to war and make the world more democratic, but do not expect our book to answer the question, What is to be done? or propose a concrete program of action. We believe that in light of the challenges and possibilities of our world it is necessary to rethink the most basic political concepts, such as power, resistance, multitude, and democracy. Before we embark on a practical political project to create new democratic institutions and social structures, we need to ask if we really understand what democracy means (or could mean) today. Our primary aim is to work out the conceptual bases on which a new project of democracy can stand. We have made every effort to write this in a language that everyone can understand, defining technical terms and explaining philosophical concepts. That does not mean that the reading will always be easy. You will undoubtedly at some point find the meaning of a sentence or even a paragraph not immediately clear. Please be patient. Keep reading. Sometimes these philosophical ideas take longer to work out. Think of the book as a mosaic from which the general design gradually emerges.

We conceive the movement from the one book to the other, from *Empire* to *Multitude*, as the reverse of Thomas Hobbes's development from his *De Cive* (published in 1642) to *Leviathan* (1651). The reverse progression speaks to the profound difference in the two historical moments. At the dawn of modernity, in *De Cive*, Hobbes defined the nature of the social body and the forms of citizenship that were adequate to the nascent bourgeoisie. The new class was not capable of guaranteeing social order on its own; it required a political power to stand above it, an absolute authority, a god on earth. Hobbes's *Leviathan* describes the form of sovereignty that would subsequently develop in Europe in the form of the nation-state. Today, at the dawn of postmodernity, we have first in *Empire* tried to delineate a new global form of sovereignty; and now, in this book, we try to understand the nature of the emerging global class formation, the multitude. Whereas Hobbes moved from the nascent social class to the new form of sovereignty, our course is the inverse—we work from the new form of sovereignty to the new global class. Whereas the nascent bourgeoisie needed to call on a sovereign power to guarantee its interests, the multitude emerges from within the new imperial sovereignty and points beyond it. The multitude is working through Empire to create an alternative global society. Whereas the modern bourgeois had to fall back on the new sovereignty to consolidate its order, the postmodern revolution of the multitude looks forward, beyond imperial sovereignty. The multitude, in contrast to the bourgeoisie and all other exclusive, limited class forma-tions, is capable of forming society autonomously; this, we will see, is central to its democratic possibilities.

We cannot begin our book with the project of the multitude and the possibilities of democracy. That will be the focus of chapters 2 and 3. We have to begin instead with the current state of war and global conflict, which can easily seem to be an insurmountable obstacle to democracy and liberation. This book was written under the cloud of war, primarily between September 11, 2001, and the 2003 Iraq War. We have to investigate how war has changed in our era with respect to politics and sovereignty, and we have to articulate the contradictions that run throughout our present war regime. We hope, however, that it is already clear that democracy, even when it appears distant, is necessary in our world, that it is the only answer to the vexing questions of our day, and that it is the only way out of our state of perpetual conflict and war. It is up to us in the remainder of this book to convince you that a democracy of the multitude is not only necessary but possible.

1. WAR

1.1 SIMPLICISSIMUS

> War under existing conditions compels all nations, even those professedly the most democratic, to turn authoritarian and totalitarian. —JOHN DEWEY

> The republic is lost. —CICERO

EXCEPTIONS

The world is at war again, but things are different this time. Traditionally war has been conceived as the armed conflict between sovereign political entities, that is, during the modern period, between nation-states. To the extent that the sovereign authority of nation-states, even the most dominant nation-states, is declining and there is instead emerging a new supranational form of sovereignty, a global Empire, the conditions and nature of war and political violence are necessarily changing. War is becoming a general phenomenon, global and interminable.

There are innumerable armed conflicts waged across the globe today, some brief and limited to a specific place, others long lasting and expansive.[1] These conflicts might be best conceived as instances not of war but rather *civil war*. Whereas war, as conceived traditionally by international law, is armed conflict between sovereign political entities, civil war is armed conflict between sovereign and/or nonsovereign combatants *within a single sovereign territory*. This civil war should be understood now not within the national space, since that is no longer the effective unit of sovereignty, but across the global terrain. The framework of international law regarding war has been undermined. From this perspective all of the world's current armed conflicts, hot and cold—in Colombia, Sierra Leone, and Aceh, as much as in Israel-Palestine, India-Pakistan, Afghanistan, and Iraq—should be considered imperial civil wars, even when states are involved. This does not mean that any of these conflicts mobilizes all of Empire—indeed each of these conflicts is local and specific—but rather that they exist within, are conditioned by, and in turn affect the global imperial system. Each local war should not be viewed in isolation, then, but seen as part of a grand constellation, linked in varying degrees both to other war zones and to areas not presently at war. The pretense to sovereignty of these combatants is doubtful to say the least. They are struggling rather for relative dominance within the hierarchies at the highest and lowest levels of the global system. A new framework, beyond international law, would be necessary to confront this global civil war.[2]

The attacks on the Pentagon and the World Trade Center on September 11, 2001, did not create or fundamentally change this global situation, but perhaps they did force us to recognize its generality. There is no escaping the state of war within Empire, and there is no end to it in sight. The situation was obviously already mature. Just as the "defenestration of Prague" on May 23, 1618, when two regents of the Holy Roman Empire were thrown from a window of the Hradčany castle, ignited the Thirty Years' War, the attacks on September 11 opened a new era of war. Back then Catholics and Protestants massacred each other (but soon the sides became confused), and today Christians seem to be pitted against Muslims (although the sides are already confused). This air of a war of religion only masks the profound historical transformation, the opening of a new era. In the seventeenth century it was the passage in Europe from the Middle Ages to modernity, and today the new era is the global passage from modernity to postmodernity. In this context, war has become a general condition: there may be a cessation of hostilities at times and in certain places, but lethal violence is present as a constant potentiality, ready always and everywhere to erupt. "So the nature of War," Thomas Hobbes explains, "consisteth not in actuall fighting; but in the known disposition thereto, during all the time there is no assurance to the contrary."[3] These are not isolated wars, then, but a *general global state of war* that erodes the distinction between war and peace such that we can no longer imagine or even hope for a real peace.

This world at war looks something like the one faced by Simplicissimus, the peasant protagonist of Johann Grimmelshausen's great seventeenth-century novel.[4] Simplicissimus is born in the midst of Germany's Thirty Years' War, a war in which one-third of the German population died, and true to his name Simplicissimus views this world with the simplest, most naive eyes. How else can one understand such a state of perpetual conflict, suffering, and devastation? The various armies—the French, Spanish, Swedish, and Danish, along with the different Germanic forces—pass through one after the other, each claiming more virtue and religious rectitude than the last, but to Simplicissimus they are all the same. They kill, they rape, they steal. Simplicissimus's innocent open eyes manage to register the horror without being destroyed by it; they see through all the mystifications that obscure this brutal reality. A few years earlier, across the Atlantic in Peru, an Amerindian, Huamán Poma de Ayala, wrote a similar chronicle of even more devastating destruction.[5] His text, composed in a mixture of Spanish, Quechua, and pictures, bears witness to conquest, genocide, enslavement, and the eradication of the Inca civilization. Huamán Poma could only humbly address his observations, his indictments, and his pleas for "good government" to King Philip III of Spain. Today in the face of interminable battles reminiscent of that earlier era, should we adopt something like Simplicissimus's innocent perspective or Huamán Poma's humble supplication to the ruling powers? Are those indeed our only alternatives?

The first key to understanding our brutal global state of war lies in the notion of *exception* or, specifically, in two exceptions, one Germanic and the other American in origin. We need to step back a moment and trace the development of our contemporary exceptions. It is no coincidence that our present situation should make us think of the earliest period of European modernity since European modernity was born, in certain respects, in response to generalized states of war, such as the Thirty Years' War in Germany and the civil wars in England. One central component of the political project of modern theories of sovereignty—liberal and nonliberal alike—was to put an end to civil war and destroy the constant state of war by isolating war at the margins of society and limiting it to exceptional times. Only the sovereign authority—that is, the monarch or the state— could wage war and only against another sovereign power. War, in other words, was expelled from the internal national social field and reserved only for external conflicts between states. War was thus to be the exception and peace the norm. Conflicts within the nation were to be resolved peacefully through political interaction.

The *separation of war from politics* was a fundamental goal of modern political thought and practice, even for the so-called realist theorists who focus on the central importance of war in international affairs. Carl von Clausewitz's famous claim that *war is the continuation of politics by other means,* for example, might suggest that politics and war are inseparable, but really, in the context of Clausewitz's work, this notion is based, first of all, on the idea that war and politics are in principle separate and different.[6] He wants to understand how these separate spheres can at times come into relation. Second, and more important, "politics" for him has nothing to do with political relations within a society but rather refers exclusively to political conflicts between nation-states.[7] War in Clausewitz's view is an instrument in the state's arsenal for use in the realm of international politics. It is thus completely external to the political struggles and conflicts that exist within a society. The same is true for the more general claim, also common to realist political thinkers, most notably Carl Schmitt, that all political actions and motives are based fundamentally on the friend-enemy distinction.[8] Here too it may seem at first sight that politics and war are inseparable, but again the politics in question here is not that within a society but only between sovereign entities. The only real enemy, from this perspective, is a public enemy, that is, an enemy of the state, in most cases another state. Modern sovereignty was thus meant to ban war from the internal, civil terrain. This conception was common to all the dominant veins of modern thought, among liberals and non-liberals alike: if war is isolated to the conflicts between sovereign entities, then politics within each society is, at least in normal circumstances, free from war. *War was a limited state of exception.*

This modern strategy of isolating war to interstate conflict is less and less viable today given the emergence of innumerable global civil wars, in armed conflicts from Central Africa to Latin America and from Indonesia to Iraq and Afghanistan. This strategy is also undermined in a more general way to the extent that the sovereignty of nation-states is declining and instead at a supranational level is forming a new sovereignty, a global Empire. We have to reconsider in this new light the relation between war and politics. This situation might seem to realize the modern liberal dream— from Kant's notion of perpetual peace to the practical projects that led to the League of Nations and the United Nations—that the end of war between sovereign states would be the end of the possibility of war altogether and thus the universal rule of politics. The community or society of nations would thus extend the space of domestic social peace to the entire globe, and international law would guarantee order. Today, however, instead of moving forward to peace in fulfillment of this dream we seem to have been catapulted back in time into the nightmare of a perpetual and indeterminate state of war, suspending the international rule of law, with no clear distinction between the maintenance of peace and acts of war. Because the isolated space and time of war in the limited conflict between sovereign states has declined, war seems to have seeped back and flooded the entire social field. *The state of exception has become permanent and general*; the exception has become the rule, pervading both foreign relations and the homeland.[9]

The "state of exception" is a concept in the German legal tradition that refers to the temporary suspension of the constitution and the rule of law, similar to the concept of state of siege and the notion of emergency powers in the French and English traditions.[10] A long tradition of constitutional thought reasons that in a time of serious crisis and danger, such as wartime, the constitution must be suspended temporarily and extraordinary powers given to a strong executive or even a dictator in order to protect the republic. The founding myth of this line of thinking is the legend of the noble Cincinnatus, the elderly farmer in ancient Rome who, when beseeched by his countrymen, reluctantly accepts the role of dictator to ward off a threat against the republic. After sixteen days, the story goes, the enemy has been routed and the republic saved, and Cincinnatus returns to his plow. The constitutional concept of a "state of exception" is clearly contradictory—the constitution must be suspended in order to be saved—but this contradiction is resolved or at least mitigated by understanding that the period of crisis and exception is brief. When crisis is no longer limited and specific but becomes a general omni-crisis, when the state of war and thus the state of exception become indefinite or even permanent, as they do today, then contradiction is fully expressed, and the concept takes on an entirely different character.

This legal concept alone does not give us an adequate basis for understanding our new global state of war. We need to link this "state of exception" with another exception, the exceptionalism of the United States, the only remaining superpower. The key to understanding our global war lies in the intersection between these two exceptions.

The notion of U.S. exceptionalism has a long history, and its use in contemporary political discourse is deceptively complex. Consider a statement by former secretary of state Madeleine Albright: "If we have to use force, it is because we are America. We are the indispensable nation."[11] Albright's phrase "because we are America" carries with it all the weight and ambiguity of U.S. exceptionalism. The ambiguity results from the fact that U.S. exceptionalism really has two distinct and incompatible meanings.[12] On the one hand, the United States has from its inception claimed to be *an exception from the corruption* of the European forms of sovereignty, and in this sense it has served as the beacon of republican virtue in the world. This ethical conception continues to function today, for instance, in the notion that the United States is the global leader promoting democracy, human rights, and the international rule of law. The United States is indispensable, Albright might say, because of its exemplary republican virtue. On the other hand, U.S. exceptionalism also means—and this is a relatively new meaning—*exception from the law*. The United States, for example, increasingly exempts itself from international agreements (on the environment, human rights, criminal courts, and so forth) and claims its military does not have to obey the rules to which others are subject, namely, on such matters as preemptive strikes, weapons control, and illegal detention. In this sense the American "exception" refers to the double standard enjoyed by the most powerful, that is, the notion that the one who commands need not obey. The Unites States is also indispensable in Albright's formulation simply because it is the most powerful.

Some might claim that these two meanings of U.S. exceptionalism are compatible and mutually reinforcing: since the United States is animated by republican virtue, its actions will all be good, hence it need not obey international law; the law instead must constrain only the bad nations. Such an equation, however, is at best an ideological confusion and more usually a patent mystification. The idea of republican virtue has from its beginning been aimed against the notion that the ruler, or indeed anyone, stands above the law. Such exception is the basis of tyranny and makes impossible the realization of freedom, equality, and democracy. Therefore the two notions of U.S. exceptionalism directly contradict each other.

When we say that today's global state of exception, the curtailing of legal guarantees and freedoms in a time of crisis, is supported and legitimated by U.S. exceptionalism, it should be clear that only one of the two meanings of that term applies. It is true that the rhetoric of many leaders and supporters of the United States often relies heavily on the republican virtue that makes America an exception, as if this ethical foundation made it the historical destiny of the United States to lead the world. In fact, the real basis of the state of exception today is the second meaning of U.S. exceptionalism, its exceptional power and its ability to dominate the global order. In a state of emergency, according to this logic, the sovereign must stand above the law and take control. There is nothing ethical or moral about this connection; it is purely a question of might, not right. This exceptional role of the United States in the global state of exception serves only to eclipse and erode the republican tradition that runs through the nation's history.

The intersection between the German legal notion of a state of exception and the exceptionalism of the United States provides a first glimpse of how war has changed in today's world. This is not, we should repeat, simply a matter of being for or against the United States, nor is it even a choice between unilateralist and multilateralist methods. We will return to consider the specific role of the United States in our global state of war later, but first we will have to investigate much more deeply the changing relationships among war, politics, and global order.

GOLEM

A golem is haunting us. It is trying to tell us something.

The golem has become an icon of unlimited war and indiscriminate destruction, a symbol of war's monstrosity. In the rich traditions of Jewish mysticism, however, the figure of the golem is much more complex. The golem is traditionally a man made of clay, brought to life by a ritual performed by a Rabbi. Golem *literally means unformed or amorphous matter and its animation repeats, according to the ancient mystical tradition of the kabbalah, the process of God's creation of the world recounted in Genesis. Since, according to Jewish creation myths, the name of God has the power to produce life, the golem can be brought to life by pronouncing over the clay figure the name of God in a series of permutations. Specifically, each letter of the alphabet must be combined with each letter from the tetragrammaton (YHWH), and then each of the resulting letter pairs must be pronounced with every possible vowel sound.*[13]

Creating a golem is dangerous business, as versions of the legend increasingly emphasize in the medieval and modern periods. One danger expressed particularly in medieval versions is idolatry. Like Prometheus, the one who creates a golem has in effect claimed the position of God, creator of life. Such hubris must be punished.

In its modern versions the focus of the golem legend shifts from parables of creation to fables of destruction. The two modern legends from which most of the others derive date from the sixteenth and seventeenth centuries. In one, Rabbi Elijah Baal Shem of Chem, Poland, brings a golem to life to be his servant and perform household chores. The golem grows bigger each day, so to prevent it from getting too big, once a week the Rabbi must return it to clay and start again. One time the Rabbi forgets his routine and lets the golem get too big. When he transforms it back he is engulfed in the mass of lifeless clay and suffocates. One of the morals of this tale has to do with the danger of setting oneself up as master and imposing servitude upon others.

The second and more influential modern version derives from the legend of Rabbi Judah Loew of Prague. Rabbi Loew makes a golem to defend the Jewish community of Prague and attack its persecutors. The golem's destructive violence, however, proves uncontrollable. It does attack the enemies of the Jews but also begins to kill Jews themselves indiscriminately before the rabbi can finally turn it back to clay. This tale bears certain similarities to common warnings about the dangers of instrumentalization in modern society and of technology run amok, but the golem is more than a parable of how humans are losing control of the world and machines are taking over. It is also about the inevitable blindness of war and violence. In H. Leivick's Yiddish play, The Golem, *for instance, first published in Warsaw in 1921, Rabbi Loew is so intent on revenge against the persecutors of the Jews that even when the Messiah comes with Elijah the Prophet the rabbi turns them away.[14] Now is not their time, he says, now is the time for the golem to bathe our enemies in blood. The violence of revenge and war, however, leads to indiscriminate death. The golem, the monster of war, does not know the friend-enemy distinction. War brings death to all equally. That is the monstrosity of war. "He came to save and yet he shed our blood," puzzles the rabbi. "Are we chastised because we wished to save ourselves?" If we do nothing we are destroyed by our enemies, but if we go to war against them we end up destroying ourselves the same. Rabbi Loew recognizes the horrible paradox the golem presents us. Is there no alternative to war that is nonetheless capable of freeing us from persecution and oppression?*

Perhaps we need to listen more attentively to the golem's message. The most remarkable thing about the golem in many of the modern versions is not its instrumentality or brutality but rather its emotional neediness and capacity for affection. The golem doesn't want to kill, it wants to love and be loved. Most of the versions of the legend that derive from the Rabbi Loew story emphasize how the golem's requests for comfort are constantly rebuffed by the rabbi and, moreover, how the golem's expressions of affection for the rabbi's daughter are met with horror, disgust, and panic. Rabbi Loew's golem, of course, is not the only modern monster to suffer from unrequited love. Doctor Frankenstein's monster too only wants affection, and his advances are similarly thwarted, in particular by the doctor himself, the most heartless of beings. One of the scenes of greatest pathos in Mary Shelley's novel is when the monster befriends the blind man De Lacey in his cottage in the woods but is horribly rejected once De Lacey's family sets eyes on him. The monsters in both of these tales are the ones with rich emotional lives and great capacities for human feeling, whereas the humans are emotional cripples, cold and heartless. They are just asking to be loved and no one seems to understand.

We need to find some way to heed the signs of warning and also recognize the potential in our contemporary world. Even the violent modern golems still carry all the mystery and wisdom of the kabbalah: along with the threat of destruction they also bring the promise and wonder of creation. Perhaps what monsters like the golem are trying to teach us, whispering to us secretly under the din of our global battlefield, is a lesson about the monstrosity of war and our possible redemption through love.

THE GLOBAL STATE OF WAR

Let us go back and start again from the basic elements of our global state of war. When the state of exception becomes the rule and when wartime becomes an interminable condition, then the traditional distinction between war and politics becomes increasingly blurred. The tradition of tragic drama, from Aeschylus to Shakespeare, has continually emphasized the interminable and proliferating nature of war.[15] Today, however, war tends to extend even farther, becoming a *permanent social relation*. Some contemporary authors try to express this novelty by reversing the Clausewitz formula that we cited earlier: it may be that war is a continuation of politics by other means, but politics itself is increasingly becoming war conducted by other means.[16] War, that is to say, is becoming the primary organizing principle of society, and politics merely one of its means or guises. What appears as civil peace, then, really only puts an end to one form of war and opens the way for another.

Of course, theorists of insurrection and revolutionary politics, particularly in the anarchist and communist traditions, have long made similar claims about the indistinction of war and politics: Mao Zedong, for instance, claimed that politics is simply war without bloodshed, and Antonio Gramsci in a rather different framework divided political strategies between wars of position and wars of maneuver. These theorists, however, were dealing with exceptional social periods, that is, times of insurrection and revolution. What is distinctive and new about the claim that politics is the continuation of war is that it refers to power in its normal functioning, everywhere and always, outside and within each society. Michel Foucault goes so far as to say that the socially pacifying function of political power involves constantly reinscribing this fundamental relationship of force in a sort of silent war and reinscribing it too in the social institutions, systems of economic inequality, and even the spheres of personal and sexual relations.[17] War, in other words, becomes the general matrix for all relations of power and techniques of domination, whether or not bloodshed is involved. War has become a *regime of biopower*, that is, a form of rule aimed not only at controlling the population but producing and reproducing all aspects of social life.[18] This war brings death but also, paradoxically, must produce life. This does not mean that war has been domesticated or its violence attenuated, but rather that daily life and the normal functioning of power has been permeated with the threat and violence of warfare.

Consider, as a symptom of the change in the nature of war today, how common public usage of the concept of war has changed in the late twentieth and early twenty-first centuries. The rhetoric of war has long been used, of course, to describe activities that are very different from war itself. In some cases, war metaphors are applied to forms of competition and relations of force that do not generally involve lethal violence or bloodshed, such as sports, commerce, and domestic politics. In all of these contests, one has competitors but never really enemies properly conceived. Such metaphorical usage serves to highlight the risks, competition, and conflict involved in these various activities, but it also assumes a fundamental difference from real war. In other cases, the metaphorical discourse of war is invoked as a strategic political maneuver in order to achieve the total mobilization of social forces for a united purpose that is typical of a war effort. The war on poverty, for example, launched in the United States in the mid-1960s by the Johnson administration, used the discourse of war to avoid partisan conflict and rally national forces for a domestic policy goal. Because poverty is an abstract enemy and the means to combat it are nonviolent, the war discourse in this case remains merely rhetorical.

With the war on drugs, however, which began in the 1980s, and more so with the twenty-first-century war on terrorism, the rhetoric of war begins to develop a more concrete character. As in the case of the war on poverty, here too the enemies are posed not as specific nation-states or political communities or even individuals but rather as abstract concepts or perhaps as sets of practices. Much more successfully than the war on poverty, these discourses of war serve to mobilize all social forces and suspend or limit normal political exchange. And yet these wars are not so metaphorical because like war traditionally conceived they involve armed combat and lethal force. In these wars there is increasingly little difference between outside and inside, between foreign conflicts and homeland security. We have thus proceeded from metaphorical and rhetorical invocations of war to real wars against indefinite, immaterial enemies.

One consequence of this new kind of war is that the limits of war are rendered indeterminate, both spatially and temporally. The old-fashioned war against a nation-state was clearly defined spatially, even if it could at times spread to other countries, and the end of such a war was generally marked by the surrender, victory, or truce between the conflicting states. By contrast, war against a concept or set of practices, somewhat like a war of religion, has no definite spatial or temporal boundaries. Such wars can potentially extend anywhere for any period of time. Indeed, when U.S. leaders announced the "war against terrorism" they emphasized that it would have to extend throughout the world and continue for an indefinite period, perhaps decades or even generations. A war to create and maintain social order can have no end. It must involve the continuous, uninterrupted exercise of power and violence. In other words, one cannot win such a war, or, rather, it has to be won again every day. War has thus become virtually indistinguishable from police activity.

A second consequence of this new state of war is that international relations and domestic politics become increasingly similar and intermingled. In the context of this cross between military and police activity aimed at security there is ever less difference between inside and outside the nation-state: low-intensity warfare meets high-intensity police actions. The "enemy," which has traditionally been conceived outside, and the "dangerous classes," which have traditionally been inside, are thus increasingly indistinguishable from one another and serve together as the object of the war effort. We will focus extensively on the notion of "dangerous classes" in the next chapter, but here we should emphasize that its being identified with "the enemy" tends effectively to criminalize the various forms of social contestation and resistance. In this respect, the conceptual merging of war and policing poses an obstacle to all forces of social transformation.

A third consequence is a reorientation of the conception of the sides of battle or conditions of enmity. To the extent that the enemy is abstract and unlimited, the alliance of friends too is expansive and potentially universal. All of humanity can in principle be united against an abstract concept or practice such as terrorism.[19] It should not be surprising, then, that the concept of "just war" has emerged again in the discourse of politicians, journalists, and scholars, particularly in the context of the war on terrorism and the various military operations conducted in the name of human rights. The concept of justice serves to universalize war beyond any particular interests toward the interest of humanity as a whole. Modern European political thinkers, we should keep in mind, sought to banish the concept of just war, which had been common throughout the Middle Ages, especially during the Crusades and the religious wars, because they thought it tended to generalize war beyond its proper scope and confuse it with other social realms, such as morality and religion. *Justice does not belong to the modern concept of war.*[20] When the modern realist theorists of war claimed that war is a means for political ends, for instance, they intended not only to link war to interstate politics but also separate it from other social realms, such as morality and religion. It is true that various other social realms have often throughout history been superimposed on war, especially in propaganda campaigns, such that the enemy might be presented as evil or ugly or sexually perverse, but the modern theorists insisted on this fundamental separation. War, they thought, could thus be isolated to its necessary and rational functions.

The "just" wars of the late twentieth and early-twenty-first centuries often carry explicit or implicit echoes of the old wars of religion. And the various concepts of civilizational conflict—the West versus Islam, for instance—that animate a strong vein of foreign policy and international relations theory are never far removed from the old religious paradigm of the wars of religion.[21] It seems that we are back once again in the situation defined by the seventeenth-century motto, *Cujus regio, ejus religio*, that is, the one who rules also determines religious faith—a dangerous and oppressive situation against which all the great modern movements of tolerance struggled. Along with the renewed concept of just war, then, comes also, predictably, the allied concept of evil. Posing the enemy as evil serves to make the enemy and the struggle against it absolute and thus outside of politics—evil is the enemy of all humanity. (The category of a crime against humanity, which has in effect been transformed from an element of the Geneva Convention into global penal code, is perhaps the legal concept that most clearly makes concrete this notion of evil.) Modern European philosophers tried to put to rest this problem too, the problem of evil, the great Christian debate over theodicy, that is, the justification of God with respect to the evil, the question of how God could permit evil to exist.[22] They tried to displace such problems or at least separate them from questions of politics and war. The postmodern recourse to notions of justice and evil in war may be simply irrational propaganda and moral-religious mystification, little different than old-fashioned calls to destroy the infidels or burn the witches, but since such mystifications do have very real effects, they must be confronted seriously, as was done by modern philosophers such as Voltaire. Tolerance, a central value of modern thought, is being dramatically undermined. And, more importantly for our purposes, these resurrected discourses of justice and evil are symptoms of the ways in which war has changed and lost the limitations that modernity had tried to impose on it.

We should be clear that the concept of terrorism does not (any more than the concept of evil) provide a solid conceptual or political anchor for the contemporary global state of war. Early in the twentieth century the term *terrorism* referred primarily to anarchist bombings in Russia, France, and Spain—instances of so-called propaganda of the deed. The current meaning of the term is a recent invention. Terrorism has become a political concept (a concept of war or, really, civil war) that refers to three different phenomena that are sometimes held separate and at others confused together: (1) the revolt or rebellion against a legitimate government; (2) the exercise of political violence by a government in violation of human rights (including, according to some, the rights of property); and (3) the practice of warfare in violation of the rules of engagement, including attacks on civilians. The problem with all of these definitions is that they vary according to who defines their key elements: who determines, for example, what is a legitimate government, what are human rights, and what are the rules of war. Depending on who defines these elements, of course, even the United States could be labeled a terrorist state.[23] Because of the instability of its definition, the concept of terrorism does not provide a solid foundation to understand the current global state of war.

The domestic face of just-war doctrines and the war against terrorism is a regime aimed at near complete social control, which some authors describe as a passage from the welfare state to a warfare state and others characterize as a so-called zero-tolerance society.[24] This is a society whose diminishing civil liberties and increasing rates of incarceration are in certain respects a manifestation of a constant social war. We should note that this transformation of methods of control coincides with an extremely strong social transformation, which we will describe in the next chapter in terms of biopolitical forms of production. The new forms of power and control operate increasingly in contradiction with the new social composition of the population and serve merely to block its new forms of productivity and expression. We claimed elsewhere that a similar obstruction of freedom and productive expression led to the implosion of the Soviet Union.[25] This is, in any case, a highly contradictory situation in which the actions of the ruling powers to maintain control tend to undercut their own interests and authority.

Finally, like justice, democracy does not belong to war. War always requires strict hierarchy and obedience and thus the partial or total suspension of democratic participation and exchange. "In wartime," explains the legal theorist Hans Kelsen, "the democratic principle has to yield to a strictly autocratic one: everyone must pay unconditional obedience to the leader."[26] In the modern period the wartime suspension of democratic politics was usually posed as temporary, since war was conceived as an exceptional condition.[27] If our hypothesis is correct and today the state of war has instead become our permanent global condition, then the suspension of democracy tends also to become the norm rather than the exception.

Following John Dewey's statement that serves as one of the epigraphs to this chapter, we can see that the current global state of war forces all nations, even the professedly most democratic, to become authoritarian and totalitarian. Some say that ours is a world in which real democracy has become impossible, perhaps even unthinkable.

BIOPOWER AND SECURITY

At this point we need to go back once again and try to understand this regime of biopower from another, more philosophical, perspective. Although global war, as we said, has become increasingly indistinct from global police action, it also now tends toward the *absolute*. In modernity war never had an absolute, ontological character. It is true that the moderns considered war a fundamental element of social life. When the great modern military theorists spoke of war, they considered it a destructive but inevitable element of human society. And we should not forget that war often appeared in modern philosophy and politics as a positive element that involved both the search for glory (primarily in aristocratic consciousness and literature) and the construction of social solidarity (often from the standpoint of the subaltern populations). None of this, however, made war absolute. War was an element of social life; it did not rule over life. Modern war was dialectical in that every negative moment of destruction necessarily implied a positive moment of the construction of social order.

War really became absolute only with the technological development of weapons that made possible for the first time mass and even global destruction. Weapons of global destruction break the modern dialectic of war. War has always involved the destruction of life, but in the twentieth century this destructive power reached the limits of the pure production of death, represented symbolically by Auschwitz and Hiroshima. The capacity of genocide and nuclear destruction touches directly on the very structure of life, corrupting it, perverting it. The sovereign power that controls such means of destruction is a form of *biopower* in this most negative and horrible sense of the term, a power that rules directly over death—the death not simply of an individual or group but of humanity itself and perhaps indeed of all being. When genocide and atomic weapons put life itself on center stage, then *war becomes properly ontological.*[28]

War thus seems to be heading at once in two opposite directions: it is, on one hand, reduced to police action and, on the other, raised up to an absolute, ontological level by technologies of global destruction. These two movements, however, are not contradictory: *the reduction of war to police action does not take away but actually confirms its ontological dimension.* The thinning of the war function and the thickening of the police function maintain the ontological stigmata of absolute annihilation: the war police maintain the threat of genocide and nuclear destruction as their ultimate foundation.[29]

Biopower wields not just the power of the mass destruction of life (such as that threatened by nuclear weapons) but also *individualized* violence. When individualized in its extreme form, biopower becomes torture. Such an individualized exercise of power is a central element in the society of control of George Orwell's *1984*. " 'How does one man assert his power over another, Winston?' Winston thought. 'By making him suffer,' he said. 'Exactly. By making him suffer. Obedience is not enough.' "[30] Torture is today becoming an ever more generalized technique of control, and at the same time it is becoming increasingly banalized. Methods for obtaining confessions and information through physical and psychological torments, techniques to disorient prisoners (such as sleep deprivation), and simple means of humiliation (such as strip searches) are all common weapons in the contemporary arsenal of torture. Torture is one central point of contact between police action and war; the torture techniques used in the name of police prevention take on all the characteristics of military action. This is another face of the state of exception and the tendency for political power to free itself from the rule of law. In fact, there are increasing numbers of cases in which the international conventions against torture and the domestic laws against cruel and unusual punishment have little effect.[31] Both dictatorships and liberal democracies use torture, the one by vocation and the other by so-called necessity. According to the logic of the state of exception, torture is an essential, unavoidable, and justifiable technique of power.

Sovereign political power can never really arrive at the pure production of death because it cannot afford to eliminate the life of its subjects. Weapons of mass destruction must remain a threat or be used in very limited cases, and torture cannot be taken to the point of death, at least not in a generalized way. Sovereign power lives only by preserving the life of its subjects, at the very least their capacities of production and consumption. If any sovereign power were to destroy that, it would necessarily destroy itself. More important than the negative technologies of annihilation and torture, then, is the constructive character of biopower. Global war must not only bring death but also produce and regulate life.

One index of the new, active, constituent character of war is the policy shift from "defense" to "security," which the U.S. government has promoted, particularly as an element of the war against terrorism since September 2001.[32] In the context of U.S. foreign policy, the shift from defense to security means the movement from a reactive and conservative attitude to an active and constructive one, both within and outside the national boundaries: from the preservation of the present domestic social and political order to its transformation, and similarly from a reactive war attitude, which responds to external attacks, to an active attitude that aims to preempt attack. We should keep in mind that modern democratic nations uniformly outlawed all forms of military aggression, and their constitutions gave parliaments power only to declare defensive wars. Likewise international law has always resolutely prohibited preventive or preemptive attacks on the basis of the rights of national sovereignty. The contemporary justification of preemptive strikes and preventive wars in the name of security, however, explicitly undermines national sovereignty, making national boundaries increasingly irrelevant.[33] Both within and outside the nation, then, the proponents of security require more than simply conserving the present order—if we wait to react to threats, they claim, it will be too late. Security requires rather actively and constantly *shaping the environment through military and/or police activity*. Only an actively shaped world is a secure world. This notion of security is a form of biopower, then, in the sense that it is charged with the task of producing and transforming social life at its most general and global level.

This active, constituent character of security is, in fact, already implicit in the other transformations of war we analyzed earlier. If war is no longer an exceptional condition but the normal state of affairs, if, that is, we have now entered a perpetual state of war, then it becomes necessary that war not be a threat to the existing structure of power, not a destabilizing force, but rather, on the contrary, an active mechanism that constantly creates and reinforces the present global order. Furthermore, the notion of security signals a lack of distinction between inside and outside, between the military and the police. Whereas "defense" involves a protective barrier against external threats, "security" justifies a constant martial activity equally in the homeland and abroad.

The concept of security only gestures partially and obliquely to the extensive transformative power involved in this passage. At an abstract, schematic level we can see this shift as an inversion of the traditional arrangement of power. Think of the arrangement of the elements of modern sovereign power like a Russian matrioshka doll, whose largest shell consists of disciplinary administrative power, which contains the power of political control, which in turn contains in the final instance the power to make war. The productive character of security, however, requires that the order and priority of these nested shells be reversed, such that war is now the outermost container in which is nestled the power of control and finally disciplinary power. What is specific to our era, as we claimed earlier, is that war has passed from the final element of the sequences of power— lethal force as a last resort—to the first and primary element, the foundation of politics itself. Imperial sovereignty creates order *not* by putting an end to "the war of each against all," as Hobbes would have it, but by proposing a regime of disciplinary administration and political control directly based on continuous war action. The constant and coordinated application of violence, in other words, becomes the necessary condition for the functioning of discipline and control. In order for war to occupy this fundamental social and political role, war must be able to accomplish a constituent or regulative function: war must become both a procedural activity and an ordering, regulative activity that creates and maintains social hierarchies, a form of biopower aimed at the promotion and regulation of social life.

To define war by biopower and security changes war's entire legal framework. In the modern world the old Clausewitz adage that war is a continuation of politics by other means represented a moment of enlightenment insofar as it conceived war as a form of political action and/or sanction and thus implied an international legal framework of modern warfare. It implied both a *jus ad bellum* (a right to conduct war) and a *jus in bello* (a legal framework to govern war conduct). In modernity, war was subordinated to international law and thus legalized or, rather, made a legal instrument. When we reverse the terms, however, and war comes to be considered the basis of the internal politics of the global order, the politics of Empire, then the modern model of civilization that was the basis of legalized war collapses. The modern legal framework for declaring and conducting war no longer holds. We are still nonetheless not dealing with a pure and unregulated exercise of violence. War as the foundation of politics must itself contain legal forms, indeed must construct new procedural forms of law. As cruel and bizarre as these new legal forms may be, war must nonetheless be legally regulative and ordering. Whereas war previously was *regulated* through legal structures, war has become *regulating* by constructing and imposing its own legal framework.[34]

We should note that to say imperial war is regulative and ordering, and thus contains within itself a constructive element, does not mean that it is a constituent or foundational power in the proper sense. The modern revolutionary wars were indeed instances of constituent power; they were foundational insofar as they overthrew the old order and imposed from the outside new legal codes and new forms of life. The contemporary imperial regulative state of war, in contrast, reproduces and regulates the current order; it creates law and jurisdiction from the inside. Its legal codes are strictly functional to the constant reordering of imperial territories. It is constituent in the way, for example, that the implicit powers of the U.S. Constitution are or the activities of constitutional courts can be in closed juridical systems. These are functional systems that, above all in complex societies, serve as surrogates for democratic expression—and thus function against democracy. In any case, this reordering and regulating power has little to do with constituent power in the proper, foundational sense. It is rather a means to displace and suffocate it.[35]

The political program of "nation building" in countries like Afghanistan and Iraq is one central example of the productive project of biopower and war. Nothing could be more postmodernist and antiessentialist than this notion of nation building. It reveals, on the one hand, that the nation has become something purely contingent, fortuitous, or, as philosophers would say, accidental. That is why nations can be destroyed and fabricated or invented as part of a political program. On the other hand, nations are absolutely necessary as elements of global order and security. The international divisions of labor and power, the hierarchies of the global system, and the forms of global apartheid we will discuss in the next chapter all depend on national authorities to be established and enforced. Nations must be made! Nation building thus pretends to be a constituent, even ontological, process, but it is really only a pale shadow of the revolutionary processes out of which modern nations were born. The modern revolutions and national liberations that created nations were processes that arose from within the national societies, fruit of a long history of social development. The contemporary projects of nation building are by contrast imposed by force from the outside through a process that now goes by the name "regime change." Such nation building resembles less the modern revolutionary birth of nations than it does the process of colonial powers dividing up the globe and drawing the maps of their subject territories. It resembles also, in a more benign register, the battles over redrawing electoral or administrative districts in order to gain control, cast now, of course, on a global scale. Nation building, in any case, illustrates the "productive" face of biopower and security.

For another example of the productive nature and regulative legal capacity of biopower and global war, we can turn back to the renewed conception of "just war." The current notion of just war should not be reduced to the right of the ruling power to unilateral decision-making and command that could correspond to old conceptions of raison d'etat, as it is used by some of the hawks who pursue today's imperial wars. Neither should just war be reduced to a moral principle, as various religious thinkers and utopian legal theorists seem to want (with the danger that just war is transformed into fanaticism and superstition). These are both, in fact, merely old, premodern conceptions that have recently been resurrected. It is more instructive to look at a much more recent genealogy of just war and its constituent capacity, specifically the notion of just war associated with the cold war that served as the basis for the theories of containment promoted by strategists from George Kennan to Henry Kissinger. The cold war, as we will argue later, was indeed a war, but a war that introduced novel elements, often conducted through low-intensity conflicts simultaneously on various fronts throughout the world. What is relevant for our argument here is that these cold war theorists of containment reinterpreted the traditional morality of just war. The cold war was a just war in their view not because it could destroy the Communist and Soviet threats but because it could *contain* them. Just war in this case is no longer a moral justification for temporally limited acts of violence and destruction, as it was traditionally, but rather for maintaining a permanent stasis of global order. That cold war idea of justice and containment provides a key to both the indefinite duration and the regulative and ordering functions that imperial war can have today.

The cold war, however, never arrived at an ontological concept of war. Its notion of containment was static or perhaps dialectical. Only after the end of the cold war has war begun to become truly constructive. The Bush senior foreign policy doctrine, for example, was constitutive in the sense that the 1991 Persian Gulf War, although its primary objective was to restore Kuwait's national sovereignty, was also part of a project to create a "new world order." The Clinton administration's policies of humanitarian wars, peacekeeping, and nation building had analogous aspects, aimed at constructing, for instance, a new political order in the Balkans. Both administrations promoted, at least in part, the moral criterion of just war as a constitutive element of politics in order to redraw the geopolitical map. Finally, the Bush junior administration, particularly after the attacks of September 11 and the policy shift from defense to security, has made explicit the global reach and the active, constituent function of war in global order, even though this remains an incomplete and uneven process that will advance and retreat for some time in various forms. Imperial war is charged with the task of shaping the global political environment and thus to become a form of biopower in the positive, productive sense. It may appear that we have arrived at the point of a reactionary revolution, when imperial war founds a new global order, but really this is merely a regulating process that consolidates the existing order of Empire.[36]

LEGITIMATE VIOLENCE

We need to take one more approach toward our current global state of war, this time from the standpoint of the changing ways in which legitimate violence is conceived. One of the fundamental pillars of the sovereignty of the modern nation-state is its monopoly of legitimate violence both within the national space and against other nations. Within the nation, the state not only has an overwhelming material advantage over all other social forces in its capacity for violence, it also is the only social actor whose exercise of violence is legal and legitimate. All other social violence is illegitimate a priori, or at least highly delimited and constrained as is, for example, the kind of legitimate violence involved in a labor union's right to strike, if indeed one considers the strike an act of violence at all. On the international scene, the various nation-states certainly have different military capacities, but in principle they all have equal right to use violence, that is, to conduct war. The legitimate violence wielded by the nation-state is grounded primarily in national, and later international, legal structures. (It is, in Max Weber's terms, a *legal authority* rather than a traditional or charismatic one.) The violence of the police officer, jailer, and executioner within the national territory or the general and soldier outside are legitimate not because of the characteristics of the particular individuals but on the basis of the offices they occupy. The actions of these various state functionaries who wield legitimate violence are thus accountable, at least in principle, to the national and international legal orders on which they stand. *All the theories in political science of the state of exception*—the state of siege and constitutional dictatorship just like the corresponding notions of insurrection and coup d'état—*are based explicitly on the state's monopoly of violence.*[37] The great actors and theorists of twentieth-century politics, on the right and left, agree on this point: Max Weber and Vladimir Lenin say, in almost identical words, that with regard to the use of force the state is always a dictatorship.[38]

In the second half of the twentieth century, however, the mechanisms of the legitimation of state violence began to be seriously undermined. The developments of international law and international treaties, on one hand, put limits on the legitimate use of force by one nation-state against another, and on the accumulation of weapons. The nuclear nonproliferation agreements, for example, along with various limits on the development of chemical and biological weapons, maintained during the cold war the overwhelming advantage in military capabilities and the right to conduct war in the hands of the two superpowers, and thus out of the hands of the majority of nation-states.[39] On the other hand, particularly in the final decades of the twentieth century, the legitimate use of force has also eroded within nation-states. The discourse of human rights, along with the military interventions and legal actions based on it, was part of a gradual movement to delegitimate the violence wielded by nation-states even within their own national territory.[40] By the end of the twentieth century nation-states could not necessarily legitimate the violence they exercised, neither outside nor inside their territory. Today states no longer necessarily have a legitimate right to police and punish their own populations or pursue foreign war on the basis of their own laws. We should be clear that we are not claiming that the violence wielded by states against their own citizens and against other states has declined. On the contrary! What has declined instead is the means of legitimating that state violence.

The decline of the nation-state's monopoly of legitimate violence reopens a series of troubling questions. If the violence wielded by the nation-state is no longer considered legitimate a priori, based on its own legal structures, then how is violence legitimated today? Is all violence equally legitimate? Do Bin Laden and al-Qaeda, for example, have the same legitimacy that the United States military has to exercise violence? Does the Yugoslav government have the same right to torture and murder portions of its population that the United States has to imprison and execute portions of its population? Is the violence of Palestinian groups wielded against Israeli citizens just as legitimate as the violence of the Israeli military against Palestinian citizens? Perhaps the declining ability of states to legitimate the violence they exercise can explain, at least in part, why there have appeared in recent decades increasingly strident and confused accusations of terrorism. In a world where no violence can be legitimated, all violence can potentially be called terrorism. As we noted earlier, the contemporary definitions of terrorism are all variable and depend on who defines their central elements: legitimate government, human rights, and rules of war. The difficulty of constructing a stable and coherent definition of terrorism is intimately linked to the problem of establishing an adequate notion of legitimate violence.

Many politicians, activists, and scholars invoke morality and values today as the basis of legitimate violence outside the question of legality or, rather, as the basis of a new legal structure: violence is legitimate if its basis is moral and just, but illegitimate if its basis is immoral and unjust. Bin Laden, for example, asks for legitimation by presenting himself as the moral hero of the poor and oppressed of the global South. The United States government similarly asks for legitimation of its military violence on the basis of its values, such as freedom, democracy, and prosperity. In a more general way, numerous discourses of human rights suggest that violence can be (and can only be) legitimated on moral grounds. The set of human rights, whether assumed to be universal or determined through political negotiation, stands as a moral structure above the law or as a substitute for the legal structure itself. Many traditional concepts posed human rights against all forms of violence, but in the shadow of the Holocaust and clearly after the "humanitarian intervention" in Kosovo this view shifted toward what might be called the "Annan Doctrine" after the UN secretary-general. The majority human rights position now advocates violence in the service of human rights, legitimated on its moral foundation and conducted by the blue helmets of the UN military.[41]

Such moral claims do achieve a certain kind of legitimation today, but one should keep in mind that such legitimation rests precariously on the radical plurality of moral frameworks and judgments. In 1928, as part of a disarmament campaign, Winston Churchill told a parable to illustrate the catastrophic consequences of presuming one's own use of violence to be universal.[42] Once upon a time all the animals in the zoo decided they would disarm and renounce violence. The rhinoceros proclaimed that the use of teeth was barbaric and ought to be prohibited but that the use of horns was mainly defensive and should be allowed. The stag and porcupine agreed. The tiger, however, spoke against horns and defended teeth and even claws as honorable and peaceful. Finally the bear spoke up against teeth, claws, and horns. The bear proposed instead that whenever animals disagreed all that was necessary was a good hug. Each animal, Churchill concludes, believes its own use of violence to be strictly an instrument of peace and justice. Morality can only provide a solid basis to legitimate violence, authority, and domination when it refuses to admit different perspectives and judgments. Once one accepts the validity of different values, then such a structure immediately collapses.

Legal structures have traditionally provided a more stable framework for legitimation than morality, and many scholars insist today that national and international law remain the only valid bases for legitimate violence.[43] We should keep in mind, however, that international criminal law consists of a very meager set of treaties and conventions with only minimal mechanisms of enforcement. Most efforts to apply international criminal law have been fruitless. The legal proceedings against Chile's former dictator Augusto Pinochet in British and Spanish courts, for instance, were attempts to establish the precedent that war crimes and crimes against humanity are subject to universal jurisdiction and can potentially be prosecuted under national law anywhere in the world. There are similar calls to prosecute former U.S. secretary of state Henry Kissinger for war crimes in Laos and Cambodia, but these calls have, predictably, received no legal action. New institutions are emerging to punish illegitimate violence. These institutions extend well beyond the old schema of national and international law and include such bodies as the International Criminal Tribunals for the former Yugoslavia and Rwanda, established by the UN Security Council in 1993 and 1994, and (more important), founded at the Hague in 2002, the permanent International Criminal Court (which the United States has refused to join, substantially undermining its powers). Whereas the old international law was based on the recognition of national sovereignty and the rights of peoples, the new imperial justice, for which the conception of crimes against humanity and the activities of the international courts are elements, is aimed at the destruction of the rights and sovereignty of peoples and nations through supranational jurisdictional practices. Consider, for example, the charges brought against Slobodan Milošević and the other Serbian leaders in the International Criminal Tribunal for the former Yugoslavia. The fact of whether the violence the Serbian leaders exercised violated the law of the Yugoslavian state is not at issue—in fact, it is completely irrelevant. Their violence is judged illegitimate in a framework outside of the national and even international legal context. These were crimes not against their own national laws or international laws, in other words, but against humanity. This shift signals the possible decline of international law and the rise in its stead of a global or imperial form of law.[44]

Undermining international law in this way is not, in our view, in itself a negative development. We are perfectly aware of how often international law served in the twentieth century merely to legitimate and support the violence of the strong over the weak. And yet the new imperial justice, although the axes and lines have shifted somewhat, seems similarly to create and maintain global hierarchies. One has to recognize how selective this application of justice is, how often the crimes of the least powerful are prosecuted and how seldom those of the most powerful are. Arguing that the most powerful must also abide by imperial law and sanctions seems to us a noble but increasingly utopian strategy. The institutions of imperial justice and the international courts that punish crimes against humanity, as long as they are dependent on the ruling global powers, such as the UN Security Council and the most powerful nation-states, will necessarily interpret and reproduce the political hierarchy of Empire. The refusal of the United States to allow its citizens and soldiers to be subject to the jurisdiction of the International Criminal Court illustrates the unequal application of legal norms and structures.[45] The United States will impose legal sanctions on others, either through normal domestic systems or ad hoc arrangements, such as the extraordinary imprisonment of combatants at Guantánamo Bay, but it will not allow its own to be subject to other national or supranational legal bodies. The inequality of power seems to make it impossible to establish equality before the law. In any case, the fact is that today accordance of violence with either established international law or the emerging global law does not guarantee legitimation, and violation does not mean it is considered illegitimate—far from it. We need to look beyond these legal structures for other mechanisms or frameworks that are effective today as the basis for legitimate violence.

Violence is legitimated most effectively today, it seems to us, not on any a priori framework, moral or legal, but only a posteriori, based on its results. It might seem that the violence of the strong is automatically legitimated and the violence of the weak immediately labeled terrorism, but the logic of legitimation has more to do with the effects of the violence. The reinforcement or reestablishment of the current global order is what retroactively legitimates the use of violence. In the span of just over a decade we have seen the complete shift among these forms of legitimation. The first Gulf War was legitimated on the basis of international law, since it was aimed officially at restoring the sovereignty of Kuwait. The NATO intervention in Kosovo, by contrast, sought legitimation on moral humanitarian grounds. The second Gulf War, a preemptive war, calls for legitimation primarily on the basis of its results.[46] A military and/or police power will be granted legitimacy as long and only as long as it is effective in rectifying global disorders—not necessarily bringing peace but maintaining order. By this logic a power such as the U.S. military can exercise violence that may or may not be legal or moral and as long as that violence results in the reproduction of imperial order it will be legitimated. As soon as the violence ceases to bring order, however, or as soon as it fails to preserve the security of the present global order, the legitimation will be removed. This is a most precarious and unstable form of legitimation.

The constant presence of an enemy and the threat of disorder are necessary in order to legitimate imperial violence. Perhaps it should be no surprise that when war constitutes the basis of politics, the enemy becomes the constitutive function of legitimacy. Thus this enemy is no longer concrete and localizable but has now become something fleeting and ungraspable, like a snake in the imperial paradise. The enemy is unknown and unseen and yet ever present, something like a hostile aura. The face of the enemy appears in the haze of the future and serves to prop up legitimation where legitimation has declined. This enemy is in fact not merely elusive

but completely abstract. The individuals invoked as the primary targets—
Osama Bin Laden, Saddam Hussein, Slobodan Milošević, Mu'ammar
Gadhafi, and Manuel Noriega among others—are themselves very limited
threats, but they are blown up into larger-than-life figures that serve as
stand-ins for the more general threat and give the appearance of traditional, concrete objects of war. They serve perhaps as a pedagogical tool
(or mystifying facade) by presenting this new kind of war in the old form.
The abstract objects of war—drugs, terrorism, and so forth—are not really enemies either. They are best conceived rather as symptoms of a disordered reality that poses a threat to security and the functioning of
discipline and control. There is something monstrous in this abstract, au-
ratic enemy. This monstrosity is a first indication of the fact, which we will
shortly explore at length, that the asymmetry and imbalances of power in
the world cannot be absorbed within the new legitimation of imperial
power. For now, suffice it to say that the enemy is an example or, better, an
experimentum crucis for the definition of legitimacy. The enemy must
serve as a schema of reason in the Kantian sense, but in the opposite direction: it must demonstrate not what power is but what power saves us
from. The presence of the enemy demonstrates the need for security.

We should be clear here that security in itself does not necessarily imply repression or violence. We will analyze at length in part 2 the new
forms of social labor that are based on immaterial products, such as intelligence, information, and affects. These forms of labor and the social
networks they create are organized and controlled *internally*, through cooperation. This is a real form of security. The concept of security we have
been discussing, which is based on a notion of abstract enemies and serves
to legitimate violence and restrict freedoms, is imposed *externally*. The two
notions of security, the one based on cooperation and the other grounded
in violence, are thus not only different but stand in direct conflict with one
another.[47]

There were almost two thousand sustained armed conflicts on the face
of the earth at the beginning of the new millennium, and the number is
growing. When, along with the monopoly of legitimate force, the sovereign functions of nation-states decline, conflicts begin to rise behind an

infinity of emblems, ideologies, religions, demands, and identities. And in all these cases, legitimate violence, criminality, and terrorism tend to become indistinguishable from one another. This does not mean that all wars and all armed parties have become *the same*, nor does it mean that we cannot understand the causes of wars. It means rather that the modern terms of evaluation tend to collapse: *the distinctions between legitimate and illegitimate violence, between wars of liberation and wars of oppression, tend to blur*. All violence fades to gray. War itself, regardless of the distinctions one tries to make, is oppressing us. This is Simplicissimus's cynical perspective.

Consider, for example, the barbaric, genocidal war between Hutus and Tutsis in Rwanda in the early 1990s. The causes of the conflict can certainly be understood, for example, in terms of the legacy of the Belgian colonial system that privileged the minority Tutsis as a colonized race superior to the majority Hutus.[48] Such explanations of the causes do not, of course, lead to justification, nor do they define a path to liberation. Hutu violence and Tutsi violence are both devoid of legitimacy. The same is true of Croat and Serb violence in the Balkans as well as Hindu and Muslim violence in South Asia. They all tend to become equally illegitimate and oppressive.

We can, of course, still categorize present wars according to various axes—for example, wars of the rich versus the poor, the rich versus the rich, and the poor versus the poor—but these categories tend not to matter. They matter to the participants, certainly, but not in the framework of our current global order. Only one distinction does matter, and it is superimposed over all others: violence that preserves the contemporary hierarchy of global order and violence that threatens that order. This is the perspective of the new imperial war, which we will investigate in detail in the next section. Numerous contemporary wars neither contribute to nor detract from the ruling global hierarchy, and thus Empire is indifferent to them. That does not mean they will cease, but it may help explain why they are not the object of imperial intervention.

SAMUEL HUNTINGTON, GEHEIMRAT

The great modern works of political science all provide tools for transforming or overthrowing the ruling powers and liberating us from oppression. Even Machiavelli's The Prince, *which some read as a guidebook for nefarious rulers, is in fact a democratic pamphlet that puts the understanding of violence and the cunning use of power in the service of republican intelligence. Today, however, the majority of political scientists are merely technicians working to resolve the quantitative problems of maintaining order, and the rest wander the corridors from their universities to the courts of power, attempting to get the ear of the sovereign and whisper advice. The paradigmatic figure of the political scientist has become the Geheimrat, the secret adviser of the sovereign.*

Samuel Huntington may be the best example of an imperial Geheimrat, the one who has most successfully gotten the ear of the sovereign. In 1975, together with Michel Crozier and Joji Watanuki, he published a volume for the Trilateral Commission on the "crisis of democracy."[49] Huntington's diagnosis was that "democracy" in the United States has since the 1960s been put in danger by too much participation and too many demands from organized labor and newly activated social groups, such as women and African Americans. Too much democracy, he claimed paradoxically, has made U.S. democracy sick, resulting in a "democratic distemper." Perhaps such contradictory reasoning could be seen to make sense only during the cold war, when capitalist social rule, in whatever political form it took, was necessarily considered "democratic" against the threat of Soviet totalitarianism. In fact, Huntington's text is a resolutely antirepublican, antidemocratic gospel that preaches the defense of sovereignty against the threats of all social forces and social movements. What Huntington feared most, of course, and this is the central thrust of his argument, is democracy in its proper sense, that is, as the rule of all by all. Democracy, he claimed, must be tempered with authority, and various segments of the population must be kept from participating too actively in political life or demanding too much from the state. Huntington's gospel did, in fact, serve as a guide in the subsequent years for the neoliberal destruction of the welfare state.

Twenty years later the Geheimrat Huntington is again whispering in the ear of the sovereign. The needs of power have changed and thus so too has his advice. The cold war had been a stable principle that had organized nation-states into allies and enemies, thus defining global order, but that is now gone. At the end of the twentieth century, when the cold war is over and even the sovereignty of nation-states is in decline, it is unclear how global order can be configured and how the violence necessary to maintain that order can be deployed and legitimated. Huntington's advice is that the organizing lines of global order and global conflict, the blocs that cluster nation-states in allied and enemy camps, should be defined no longer in "ideological" terms but rather as "civilizations."[50] Welcome back Oswald Spengler. The old mole of reactionary thought resurfaces again. It is very unclear what these bizarre historical identities called civilizations might be, but in Huntington's conception they are largely defined, it turns out, along racial and religious lines. The generic character of civilizations as criteria of classification makes it all the easier to subordinate "science" to political tactics and to use them to redraw the geopolitical map. The "secret adviser" of the sovereign here draws on an old reactionary hypothesis that casts political groupings as fusional communities (Gemeinschaften) and locates the reality of power (Machtrealitäten) within spiritual entities. He has conjured up the phantasm of these civilizations to find in them a grand schema that rearranges the friend-enemy division that is basic to politics. Those who belong to our civilization are our friends; other civilizations are our enemies. Gather round and hear the good news: war has become a clash of civilizations! Spinoza aptly called this conjuring up of enemies and fear superstition, and such superstition, he knew well, will always lead to the ultimate barbarity of perpetual war and destruction.

Huntington's brilliance as Geheimrat in the 1970s was to anticipate the needs of the sovereign, providing beforehand an antidemocratic how-to manual for the Reagan and Thatcher revolutions. Similarly his thesis of a "clash of civilizations" preceded September 11 and the subsequent war against terrorism, which was immediately conceived by the media and the major political powers, sometimes with prudent disclaimers but often not, as a conflict of the West against Islam. In this context, in fact, the hypothesis of a clash of civilizations seems to be not so much a description of the present state of the world but rather an explicit prescription, a call to war, a task that "the West" must realize.[51] Instead of being primordial or spiritual or even historical, in other words, these civilizations are political and strategic dictates that have to generate real political bodies in order to serve as friends and enemies in the permanent state of war.

This time Huntington has missed the mark, and the sovereign has turned his back on him. Ah, the cruel fortunes of the Geheimrat, subject to the whims of the sovereign! The U.S. government has repeated insistently since September 11 that its global security strategy has nothing to do with a clash of civilizations.[52] This is not primarily because U.S. political leaders are sensitive to the racist implications of Huntington's hypothesis/proposal, but rather because the notion of a civilization is too limited for their global vision. Huntington remains stuck in the old paradigm of world order, seeking to configure new clusters of nation-states, now in civilizations, to substitute for the cold war blocs. The vistas of Empire, however, are more vast. All of humanity must come under its rule. In this new world, Huntington's imagined civilizations and the boundaries that divide them are merely obstacles. There is something sad about an eager adviser who has been spurned by the sovereign and cast out of the court.

1.2 COUNTERINSURGENCIES

> Our challenge in this new century is a difficult one: to de-
> fend our nation against the unknown, the uncertain, the
> unseen, and the unexpected.
>
> —DONALD RUMSFELD, U.S. SECRETARY OF DEFENSE

> All of Gaul is pacified. —JULIUS CAESAR

ON THE SUICIDE OF THE REFUGEE W. B.
(for Walter Benjamin)

I'm told you raised your hand against yourself
Anticipating the butcher.
After eight years in exile, observing the rise of the enemy
Then at last, brought up against an impassable frontier
You passed, they say, a passable one.

Empires collapse. Gang leaders
Are strutting about like statesmen. The peoples
Can no longer be seen under all those armaments.

So the future lies in darkness and the forces of right
Are weak. All this was plain to you
When you destroyed a torturable body.

—BERTOLT BRECHT

In this section we will analyze the internal contradictions of the "war machine" created by the state of exception and the global civil war. The new model of warfare does have some original characteristics, but it must still respond to the conventional needs of sovereign power: to repress movements of resistance and impose order on the multitude. Even the new strategies of warfare, in other words, must be configured as *counterinsurgencies*. As we will see, two types of contradictions characterize this new model of warfare: those that derive from its departure from traditional methods of war and those that arise in relation to the new conditions of society and new forms of social labor that biopower and war must inevitably confront. These contradictions will give us a first standpoint or foothold for recognizing what forms of resistance and eventually liberation are possible in this new context, for discovering, in other words, how to get out of this global state of war.

BIRTH OF THE NEW WAR

In many respects our postmodern state of war resembles the premodern wars. The modern period in which wars were limited to temporally and spatially bounded conflicts between nation-states for political ends might merely appear now as a brief respite of a few centuries before humanity was plunged back again into an indistinct state of war continually overcoded in moral and religious terms. But really the clock of history does not turn backward. These recognitions of the reappearance of old elements are really just first, inadequate attempts to grasp the new.

One might say that the world has not really been at peace since early in the twentieth century. The First World War (1914–18), which was centered in Europe, led directly, after a tumultuous quasi-peace, to the Second (1939–45). And immediately upon completion of the Second World War we entered into the cold war, a new kind of global war, in some sense a Third World War, which in turn gave way with its collapse (1989–91) to our present state of imperial civil war. Our age might thus be conceived as the Fourth World War.[53] Such a periodization is a useful starting point insofar as it helps us recognize both the continuities with and the differences from previous global conflicts. The concept of cold war itself already established that war has become a normal state of affairs, making clear that even the cessation of lethal fire does not mean that war is over, only that it has modulated its form temporarily. In a more complete way today, perhaps, the state of war has become interminable. This periodization also makes clear how the nature of warfare has changed over the course of these different stages, as has the nature of the enemies in conflict. The First World War was a conflict among European nation-states that drew in many parts of the world primarily because of the global extension of their imperialist and colonial structures. The Second World War repeated in large part the First, centered now equally in Asia and Europe, but was resolved by the intervention of the Soviets and the United States, who subsequently determined the sides of a new global conflict. The cold war consolidated this global alternative in such a way that most nation-states were forced to line up behind one side or the other. In our present state of imperial war, however, sovereign nation-states no longer primarily define the sides of the conflict. There are new actors on the field of battle today, and identifying them more clearly is one of the central tasks in constructing such a genealogy.

It is common to date the shift in international relations to 1989 and the final collapse of the cold war, but perhaps a more suggestive date to mark the inauguration of our present state of war is May 26, 1972, the day when the United States and the Soviet Union signed the Anti-Ballistic Missile Treaty, which regulated the nuclear weapons production of the two superpowers. The specular contest of nuclear threat had reached its apotheosis. This may be the moment when war began to vacillate as a fundamental index of the power of the nation-state. The nuclear keystone of military strategy still stood for a long time resting on the heads of missiles, but in reality from that moment on the nuclear missiles began to sink in their muddy warehouses. War, at least as modernity knew it, which is to say generalized war involving unrestrained, high-intensity conflict and destruction, began to fade away. A massacre like the German bombing of London in September 1940 or the Allied bombing of Dresden in February 1945, a sustained, all-out effort aimed at killing and terrorizing an entire population, could no longer rationally be part of the art of war—

which does not mean, unfortunately, that such acts cannot be repeated. The mutual deterrence strategy of the United States and the Soviet Union may still have been perpetuated for a time, but war itself had begun to be transformed—less oriented toward defending against a coherent mega-threat and more focused on proliferating mini-threats; less intent on the general destruction of the enemy and more inclined toward the transformation or even production of the enemy. War became constrained. Rather than all-out, large-scale combat, the great superpowers began to engage in *high-intensity police actions*, such as the United States's involvement in Vietnam and Latin America and the Soviet engagement in Afghanistan. High-intensity police action, of course, is often indistinguishable from low-intensity warfare. Even when these conflicts were at times transformed into wars, they were never as extensive as the total mobilizations of the twentieth century's "great wars." On May 26, 1972, in short, war began to become an integral element of biopower, aimed at the construction and reproduction of the global social order.

The shift of the form and ends of war in the early 1970s coincided with a period of great transformation in the global economy. It is no coincidence that the ABM Treaty was signed midway between the delinking of the U.S. dollar from the gold standard in 1971 and the first oil crisis in 1973.[54] These were the years not only of monetary and economic crises but also of both the beginning of the destruction of the welfare state and the shift of the hegemony of economic production from the factory to more social and immaterial sectors. One might think of these various transformations as different facets of one common phenomenon, one grand social transformation.

This postmodern warfare of biopower is so clearly linked to the shifts in economic production because war has always been and perhaps has become increasingly tied to economic production. Many scholars emphasize that large-scale industry has played a central role in modern military affairs—in terms of technological developments, organizational models, and so forth. Modern warfare and modern industry developed hand in hand.[55] Postmodern warfare adopts and extends the technologies and form of large-scale industry and adds to them the new innovations of social and immaterial production, which we will discuss at length in chapter 2.

Today military control and organization is exercised primarily through communications and information technologies. Furthermore, particularly interesting (and dangerous) is the development for military purposes of biological technologies and industries, in addition to the development of new nuclear and chemical technologies, and when added to the communications- and information-control technologies, along with the conventional industrial technologies, these combined forces constitute a gigantic arsenal at the service of war. Postmodern warfare thus has many of the characteristics of what economists call post-Fordist production: it is based on both mobility and flexibility; it integrates intelligence, information, and immaterial labor; it raises power up by extending militarization to the limits of outer space, across the surfaces of the earth, and to the depths of the oceans. Not only have traditional, modern efforts of nonproliferation failed, but in fact the new productive technologies have provided the basis for what Laurent Murawiec calls "a proliferating proliferation"—an irresistible increase throughout the world of all kinds of weapons.[56]

When we are posing the relationship between warfare and economic production, we should be careful not to fall into the simplifications that often come under the label "military-industrial complex." This term was created to name a confluence of interests in the imperialist phase of capitalist development between the major industrial enterprises and the state military and policy apparatus: between the Krupp steel works and the German army, for instance, Lloyds insurance and British imperialist projects, Dassault aviation manufacturing and Gaullist military policies, or Boeing and the Pentagon. Beginning in the 1960s the notion of a "military-industrial complex" became a mythical emblem for the control exerted by the war industries over human destiny as a whole. It came to be considered, in other words, as the subject of history rather than the result of the complex relations among industry, warfare, and institutions in response to resistance and liberation movements.[57] The acritical reference to a "military-industrial complex" in populist terms (which sometimes smacks of anti-Semitism, recalling the old stereotypes of "Jewish bankers" as "war profiteers") has thus become a form of historical oversimplification that serves to eliminate any real considerations of class conflict, insurgency, and, today, the movements of the multitude from political and theoretical analyses of war, its causes, and its social determinations. These are movements that sovereign power must respond to and control in the entire range of their vital expressions, because, as we have seen, a war that seeks only to destroy the enemy is unable today to support a new form of command; it must not only destroy life but also create it. Perhaps rather than "military-industrial complex" we should start speaking of a "military-vital complex." It is important to recognize how intimately biopower and war are connected in reality and at every level of our analysis.

REVOLUTION IN MILITARY AFFAIRS

The close relationship between the evolving technologies of economic production and those of military destruction is not only recognized by critics of the war machine. Another perspective on this genealogy—a partial and distorted but nonetheless important one—is provided by the way the military establishments themselves, particularly the U.S. military, understand the changes of the new state of warfare. After 1989 and the end of the cold war there began what many military analysts call a "revolution in military affairs" (RMA) or, simply "defense transformation," that is, a major shift of U.S. military strategy.[58] The notion of an RMA derives from three fundamental premises: that new technologies offer the possibility of a new form of combat; that the United States now has an overwhelming dominance in military power over all other nation-states; and that with the end of the cold war the paradigm of war as predictable mass conflict has ended too. The U.S. military had been organized to engage powerful nation-states on as many as two fronts at once, but now there is no longer the need to prepare for sustained, large-scale high-intensity combat on even one front. The U.S. armed forces, which had been organized in enormous units with thousands of soldiers in a single division, need to be completely restructured. Now, battle units must be small; must combine land, air, and sea capabilities; and must be prepared for various types of missions, from search and rescue and humanitarian aid to active combat on a small or medium scale. The RMA not only restructures the combat unit but also makes maximum use of new information and communication technologies, affording the U.S. military dramatic superiority and an asymmetrical relationship with respect to all its allies and enemies. The RMA gives U.S. military operations a new standard formula, including exploitation of their almost exclusive supremacy in air power, auxiliary use of naval forces and guided missiles, integration of all possible intelligence forces, maximum use of information and communication technologies, and so forth.[59] In this context, the army and its ground troops clearly have a subordinate function with respect to the air and naval forces and especially to the intelligence and information technologies, which are able to deliver weapons efficiently to any target with low risk. The ground forces are not generally engaged in primary combat but are instead deployed in small, mobile groups to coordinate operationally and technologically the air, naval, and intelligence services. Military operations have become in this framework something like a "system of systems" of military power. These new strategies and new technologies are thought to make war practically risk free for U.S. soldiers, protecting them from the threats of any adversary.

Not all in the U.S. military establishment, however, are convinced by this notion of an RMA. Those whom we can call "traditionalists" have challenged the "technologists," who advocate the theory of an RMA, particularly on the issue of putting U.S. soldiers at risk. The traditionalists insist that the RMA has put an end to war as we knew it. For the traditionalists, the virtues of war include necessarily the conflict among bodies and thus the danger of death; for the technologists, there will be very little direct conflict among bodies. War will be conducted in an antiseptic technological manner, and the number of dead troops, at least of the U.S. armed forces, will approach zero. The precision bombing made possible by the new missile, information, and communication technologies, they argue, makes it possible to keep the majority of U.S. soldiers at a safe distance and minimize the unintended deaths of enemy populations. This is furthermore the only feasible manner to conduct war today, according to the technologists' view, because the U.S. public will not accept a war with mass U.S. casualties after Vietnam. The traditionalists, of course, are not in favor of U.S. soldiers dying, but they think that the mandate that no soldier die restricts too severely the range of military activities. The U.S. public, they think, must be convinced to accept the possibility of U.S. casualties. Some traditionalists, for example, hoped that the September 11 attacks would restore to the United States the patriotic virtues and willingness to sacrifice, which they believe are necessary for a global superpower to maintain its strength.[60]

The traditionalists are generally cast as conservatives and are often associated with the father and son Bush administrations, whereas technologists are often associated with the Clinton administration, but really the debate does not correspond neatly either to party divisions or differences between presidential administrations. During the 2003 Iraq War, for example, Secretary of Defense Donald Rumsfeld was the most ardent supporter of the technologist position, insisting that the war could be won and the occupation conducted with a minimal number of troops. The U.S. generals, in contrast, maintained the traditionalist position that large troop deployments and conventional tactics were required.

We should note that the RMA and the technologist position correspond in many ways to recent shifts in economic production. Throughout the nineteenth and twentieth centuries war was identified with a total mobilization in which the nation at war became a compact social body parallel to the body engaged in industrial production. Individual bodies may have tended to become indistinct in modern war—think of how Erich Maria Remarque describes individual bodies dissolving in the muddy trenches—but they always reemerged as a collective body, the way, for example, Ernst Jünger describes the entire army as a single steel body. Louis-Ferdinand Céline grasps this transformation of the modern body when he poses again the close relationship between the body of the infantry in war and that of the worker in the factory. The "total mobilization" of modern warfare was really the turning of the entire society into a kind of war factory in which the project of amassing bodies in the battlefields was parallel to that of amassing bodies in the factories, the anonymous body of the mass worker corresponding to that of the mass soldier, the unknown soldier.[61] Taylorist strategies of organizational efficiency, scientific planning, and technological innovations invested the battlefields just as they did the factories. The mass technology of modernity was subordinated to corporeality, and modern warfare involved the destruction of bodies by other bodies using weapons technologies.[62]

According to the ideology of the RMA, however, war no longer needs masses of soldiers who are massacred in the trenches. The humans on the battlefield, in the air, and at sea have become prostheses of the machines or, better, internal elements of the complex mechanical and electronic apparatus. (Paradoxically, postmodernist theories of the subject resurface in the notions of military theory.) The RMA depends not only on technological developments, such as computer and information systems, but also on the new forms of labor—mobile, flexible, immaterial forms of social labor. This military ideology seems to anticipate in some ways the forms of biopolitical production of the multitude we will discuss in chapter 2. According to this vision, the new soldiers must not only kill but also be able to dictate for the conquered populations the cultural, legal, political, and security norms of life. It should come as no surprise, then, that the body and brain of such a soldier, who incorporates the range of activities of biopower, must be preserved at all costs. That soldier represents an intense accumulation of social labor, a valuable commodity. What a difference between this biopolitical soldier and the industrial worker soldiers who were slaughtered in the trenches of the First and the blitzes of the Second World Wars! In these respects RMA is an anticipation and an extrapolation of the recent transformations of social labor, casting the economic figures of production into the field of battle.

There have been many indications that within the highest circles of military leadership the technologists have tended to have the upper hand in the debate with traditionalists and that the plan is going forward—from the first Gulf War to Kosovo, Afghanistan, and back to Iraq—for war gradually to be "decorporalized." Increasingly, U.S. leaders seem to believe that the vast superiority of its firepower, the sophistication of its technology, and the precision of its weapons allow the U.S. military to attack its enemies from a safe distance in a precise and definitive way, surgically removing them like so many cancerous tumors from the global social body, with minimal side effects. War thus becomes *virtual* from the technological point of view and *bodyless* from the military point of view; the bodies of U.S. soldiers are kept free of risk, the enemy combatants are killed efficiently and invisibly.[63]

There are, however, significant and growing contradictions in this technologist view of war associated with the RMA. First, at the simple level of fact, one has to question whether this ideology of war corresponds to reality. Doubts are raised, for example, by the continuing high level of "collateral damage" (when will they manage to perfect the technology?), the disproportionate number of U.S. and Allied troops lost to "friendly fire" (when will they better coordinate the information and command structures?), and the unending problems military forces face while conducting the "democratic transition" that follows after "regime change" (when will they train the army better in the social, political, and cultural tasks of nation building?). To what extent is all that even possible? Eventually, as such contradictions persist and accumulate, the ideology will become increasingly difficult to maintain.

Second, at a more abstract and symbolic level, the ideology of an RMA is also contradicted by the growing phenomenon of suicide bombings. The suicide bomber is the dark opposite, the gory doppelgänger of the safe bodyless soldier. Just when the body seemed to have disappeared from the battlefield with the no-soldiers-lost policy of the high-technology military strategy, it comes back in all its gruesome, tragic reality. Both the RMA and the suicide bomber deny the body at risk that traditionally defines combat, the one guaranteeing its life and the other its death. We in no way mean to praise the horrible practice of suicide bombing or justify it, as some do, by casting it as the ultimate weapon against a system of total control. We are suggesting rather that it might be understood as the manifestation of a contradiction in the technologist view of the new bodyless war. Suicide bombings are an extreme example of the difficulties and contradictions posed by asymmetrical conflict in general, which we will analyze in the next section, "Asymmetry and Full-Spectrum Dominance."

A third contradiction arises at the most general conceptual level in the notion of a technological war without bodies. Since the technologist dreams of automated, soldierless war machines often border on science fiction, it is perhaps appropriate that we take a lesson from Captain Kirk to illustrate this contradiction. In an episode of *Star Trek* called "A Taste of Armageddon," the starship *Enterprise* is sent on a diplomatic mission to a planet that has been at war with a neighboring planet for more than five hundred years. When Kirk and Spock beam down to the planet the local leader explains that battles in this war are conducted with computers, in a kind of virtual game, which, he emphasizes, is the most advanced way to conduct war, allowing them to preserve their civilization. Captain Kirk is horrified to learn, however, that although the computer battle is virtual, those designated as killed in battle must subsequently report to "disintegration machines" to be killed. This is not civilized, Kirk exclaims, with his characteristic indignation, it is barbaric! War must involve destruction and horror, he explains. That is what gives us incentive to avoid and put an end to war. The state of war between these two planets continues interminably, he reasons, because they have made war "rational," antiseptic, and technological. Kirk and Spock thus destroy the computers to force the planets back to actual combat, hence compelling them to begin negotiations that will eventually put an end to their protracted war. This adventure of the starship *Enterprise* illustrates a contradiction of the RMA's technological dream of a civilized, bodyless war. Without the horror of war there is less incentive to put an end to it, and war without end, as Kirk says, is the ultimate barbarity. There is an important difference between the ideology of RMA and the *Star Trek* situation, however, that further exacerbates the contradiction because, today, the two sides in battle are not equal. When U.S. leaders imagine a bodyless war or a soldier-free war they are referring, of course, only to the bodies of U.S. soldiers. Enemy bodies are certainly meant to die (and increasingly enemy casualties, civilian and military, are not reported or even calculated). This asymmetry makes the contradiction even more difficult to address, since only one side lacks an incentive to put an end to war. What incentive does a power have to put an end to war if it never suffers from it?

These contradictions arise in part because the theories of RMA completely lack a consideration of the social subject that makes war. The image of a future soldierless war seems to block consideration of the real soldiers who still conduct war today. In some cases most of the soldiers who run the most risk on the front lines are not U.S. troops but "allied forces," a varied group of soldiers from other nations—European, Canadian, and Australian soldiers, but also Pakistani, Afghan, and so forth—all ultimately under U.S. command, something like an outsourced army. The ground war in Afghanistan, for example, to the regret of the traditionalist military theorists, was largely consigned to a group of proxies. Many claim that Bin Laden and al-Qaeda leaders escaped from the mountains of Tora Bora in late 2001 because Afghan and Pakistani ground troops, not U.S. soldiers, were given the task of searching for them. The reluctance to put U.S. ground troops in danger, they claim, compromises the success of military missions.[64] Furthermore, the U.S. military makes increasing use of "private military contractors," that is, businesses, often run by former military officers, that provide recruiting, training, and a variety of support and operational functions on and off the battlefield. Such private military professionals hired on contract substitute for active soldiers but are not subject to the public accountability of military service. This practice of contracting tends to blur the line between for-hire support and for-hire soldiers, that is, mercenaries.[65] The U.S. military forces themselves, we should note, come predominantly from the poorest and least-advantaged segments of the U.S. population, with disproportionate numbers of African Americans, along with many who have only recently been granted U.S. citizenship. The representative image of the U.S. soldier is no longer that of a John Wayne, and, more important, the profiles of U.S. soldiers do not resemble the profiles of the U.S. citizenry. This is a far cry from the tradition of republican armies that reproduced and represented the social structure of the society as a whole. There is no way to conceive of the U.S. military at this point as "the people in arms." It seems rather that in postmodern warfare, as in ancient Roman times, *mercenary armies* tend to become the primary combat forces.

It is strange to have to note how backward the theories of an RMA are with respect to the classic studies of the art of war by such authors as Machiavelli and Clausewitz—something of which today's traditionalist military theorists are keenly aware. The insistence on a war without casualties, and on the technological asymmetry of the ruling armed forces with respect to all others, strips the social face from the art of war, along with the problem of bodies and their power. Machiavelli, celebrating the republican ideal in the defense of society, thought that free men in battle were more important than cannons—a counterintuitive claim, but one verified in all the modern wars and revolutions, from Valley Forge to Valmy, Stalingrad to Dien Bien Phu, Havana to Algiers. Clausewitz similarly thought that technology was completely secondary to the soldiers themselves and that every army was at base a band of armed partisans, which proved to be the decisive factor for victory. The postmodern technological strategists' dream of an army without soldiers, of war without bodies, runs counter to such classic conceptions of the subject at war.

The theory of a revolution of military affairs is a serious corruption of the art of war. Armed mercenaries are an army of corruption—corruption as the destruction of public ethics, as the unleashing of the passions of power. Can we expect revolts of the mercenaries, in line with the old classic theories? Should the attack of al-Qaeda on the Twin Towers and the Pentagon be considered a revolt of mercenaries? Should Saddam Hussein be considered a condottiere, once in the pay of the U.S. government and then rebellious against his former masters? When war constitutes the global order and when the generals become the highest magistrates, we cannot but expect such developments. It is sufficient to analyze the new role that intelligence plays at all levels, military, commercial, cultural, and so forth, to develop in infinite directions this expression of corruption. The military leaders responsible for their strategic sectors lead us like consuls, like political and military governors in wide zones of the world. All that has already happened in the age of imperialisms and colonialisms, but then the conquistadors and military leaders were still controlled to a significant degree by political leaders in their country of origin. Today the relationships between the provincial governors (and more so the political leaders of nations) and the imperial center have become as equivocal as those between Queen Elizabeth and the pirates of the Atlantic in the sixteenth century.

THE MERCENARY AND THE PATRIOT

The end of the Roman Empire and the collapse of the Italian Renaissance are two examples, among many others, of the triumph of mercenaries. When the general population no longer constitutes the armed forces, when the army is no longer the people in arms, then empires fall. Today all armies are again tending to become mercenary armies. As at the end of the Renaissance, contemporary mercenaries are led by condottieri. There are condottieri who lead national squadrons of specialists in various military technologies, other condottieri who lead battalions of guardians of order, like global Swiss Guards, and still others who lead armies of the satellite countries of the global order. Some of the most horrible massacres are conducted at the hands of mercenaries, like those at the Sabra and Shatila refugee camps in Beirut in 1982. Or rather, as Jean Genet wrote after visiting those camps, they were mercenaries of mercenaries.[66]

Today, however, war is no longer conducted as it was at the beginning of modernity. The figure of the condottiere is often filled by an engineer or, better, someone linked to a number of industries that develop new weapons, communication systems, and means of control. Today's mercenaries have to be biopolitical soldiers who must master a variety of technical, legal, cultural, and political capabilities. A mercenary can even serve as the head of state in an occupied country destined to be marginal in the global hierarchy: a Gauleiter, like the district leaders of the Nazi party, or a Karzai and a Chalabi, businessmen thrust into power, or simply a Kurtz, reigning over subordinated peoples like a god. A small group of highly skilled mercenaries with the ominous name Executive Outcomes, for example, mostly former members of the South African Defense Force, determined governmental power and controlled central industries, such as the diamond trade, for almost a decade in Uganda, Sierra Leone, and other neighboring countries of central and west Africa.[67]

The relationships that form between the imperial aristocracies and the mercenaries are at some times intimate and at others quite distant. What is most feared is that a condottieri will turn against the imperial aristocracy. Saddam Hussein did that after having served as Swiss Guard against the threats of Islamic Iran; Osama Bin Laden did that after having liberated Afghanistan from the Soviets. The mercenary taking power, according to Machiavelli, signals the

end of the republic. Mercenary command and corruption, he said, become syn-
onymous. Should we expect an uprising of mercenaries against today's global
Empire, or will the mercenaries tend simply to assimilate and serve supporting
roles in the ruling structures? Machiavelli teaches us that only good weapons
make good laws.[68] *One might infer, then, that bad weapons—and in Machi-*
avelli's language, mercenaries are bad weapons—make bad laws. The corrup-
tion of the military, in other words, implies the corruption of the entire
political order.

This road to corruption is only one possible future path. The other is the re-
birth of amor patriae, *love of one's country—a love that has nothing to do*
with nationalisms or populisms. Ernst Kantorowicz, in his wonderful essay on
the history of the notion of dying for one's country, "Pro Patria Mori," demon-
strates that the modern European concept does not really derive, as one might
expect, from the ancient Greek or Roman glorification of heroes in battle. The
concept should be traced rather to the Middle Ages and the Renaissance, when
the love of country was not really tied to any country's institutions or even na-
tional identity. When Kantorowicz scratches beneath the surface of the notion
of love of one's country, he does not find nationalism but rather republican
caritas *or sympathetic fellow-feeling, which transmutes into* amor humani-
tatis, *a love of humanity, exceeding any and all nations. Nationalism and—*
even more—the glorification of nationalist militarism is thus a distortion of
this tradition of patriotic sentiments, a distortion that finds its logical culmi-
nation in the fascist regimes of the twentieth century.[69]

We should try to make this sentiment real and concrete today and find a
way for it to oppose all the mercenaries and the mercenary appropriations of
the idea of love of country. There are numerous modern examples of this re-
newed love of country that open up to a love of humanity—the struggles of the
Sanculottes at Valmy, for example, or the Vietnamese peasants in their anti-
colonial wars—but memory is not enough here. The political times and the
mode of production have changed. We have to construct the figure of a new
David, the multitude as champion of asymmetrical combat, immaterial work-
ers who become a new kind of combatants, cosmopolitan bricoleurs* *of resis-*

---

* A bricoleur is someone who constructs by piecing things together ad hoc, something like a handyman.

tance and cooperation. These are the ones who can throw the surplus of their knowledges and skills into the construction of a common struggle against imperial power. This is the real patriotism, the patriotism of those with no nation. More than ever this patriotism takes shape in the conspiracy of the many, moving toward decisions through the common desire of the multitude. What mercenaries can stand up to that? Today the cry with which Machiavelli closes The Prince *once again has all the urgency and validity that it had almost five hundred years ago, a cry against injustice and corruption: "This barbarian domination stinks to everyone!"[70] We need to find a way to renew Machiavelli's exhortation to liberation in the vernacular of the contemporary global multitude and thus renew the real tradition of patriotism.*

ASYMMETRY AND FULL-SPECTRUM DOMINANCE

The technological advantage of the U.S. military not only raises social and political questions, but also poses practical military problems. Sometimes technological advantage turns out to be no advantage at all. Military strategists are constantly confronted by the fact that advanced technology weapons can only fulfill some very specific tasks, whereas older, conventional weapons and strategies are necessary for most applications. This is especially true in asymmetrical conflicts in which one combatant has incomparably greater means than the other or others. In a symmetrical conflict, such as that between the United States and the Soviet Union during the cold war, technological advantages can be decisive—the nuclear arms race, for instance, played a major role—but in asymmetrical conflicts the applications of advanced technologies are often undercut. In many cases the enemy simply does not have the kind of resources that can be threatened by the most advanced weapons; in other cases lethal force is inappropriate, and other forms of control are required.

The fact that a dominant military power often finds itself at a disadvantage in asymmetrical conflicts has been the key to guerrilla strategy at least since bands of Spanish peasants tormented Napoleon's army: invert the relationship of military power and transform weakness into strength. The defeat of the United States in Vietnam and the Soviets in Afghanistan to incomparably inferior forces in terms of military might and technology can serve as symbols of the potential superiority of the weak in asymmetrical conflicts. Guerrilla forces cannot survive without the support of the population and a superior knowledge of the social and physical terrain. Guerrilla attacks often rely on unpredictability: any member of the population could be a guerrilla fighter, and the attack can come from anywhere with unknown means. Guerrillas thus force the dominant military power to live in a state of perpetual paranoia. The dominant power in such an asymmetrical conflict must adopt counterinsurgency strategies that seek not only to defeat the enemy through military means but also to control it with social, political, ideological, and psychological weapons.

Today the United States, the uncontested military superpower, has an asymmetrical relationship with all potential combatants, leaving it vulnerable to guerrilla or unconventional attacks from all quarters. The counterinsurgency strategies developed to combat and control weaker enemies in Southeast Asia and Latin America in the late twentieth century must therefore now be generalized and applied everywhere by the United States. This situation is complicated by the fact that most of the current military engagements of the United States are unconventional conflicts or low-intensity conflicts that fall in the gray zone between war and peace. The tasks given the military alternate between making war and peacemaking, peacekeeping, peace enforcing, or nation building—and indeed at times it is difficult to tell the difference among these tasks. The tendency for there to be less and less difference between war and peace that we recognized earlier from a philosophical perspective reappears now as an element of military strategy. This *gray zone* is the zone in which counterinsurgency efforts must be effective, both combating and controlling the indefinite and often unknown enemy, but it is also the zone in which the dominant military power is most vulnerable to attack in an asymmetrical conflict. The U.S. occupation of Iraq, for example, illustrates all the ambiguities of this gray zone.

U.S. military analysts are very concerned about the vulnerability of the powerful in asymmetrical conflict.[71] Military might in itself, they recognize, is not sufficient. The recognition of the limitations and vulnerability of military and technological dominance leads strategists to propose an unlimited form of dominance that involves all dimensions, the full spectrum of power. What is required, they say, is a "full spectrum dominance" that combines military might with social, economic, political, psychological, and ideological control. Military theorists have thus, in effect, discovered the concept of biopower. This full-spectrum dominance follows directly from the previous developments of counterinsurgency strategies. When confronting unconventional and low-intensity conflicts, which occupy a gray zone between war and peace, these military analysts propose a "gray" strategy that mixes military and civilian components. If Vietnam remains the symbol of the failure of the United States in an asymmetrical conflict, military analysts conceive Nicaragua and El Salvador as prime examples of the success of the United States and U.S.-backed forces using a full spectrum of counterinsurgency strategies in a low-intensity conflict.

We should recognize, however, that such an unlimited strategy is still plagued by contradictions. Biopower meets resistance. According to this new counterinsurgency strategy, sovereign power—faced, on one hand, with the impossibility of establishing a stable relationship with the existing population and, on the other, given the means of such full-spectrum dominance—simply *produces* the obedient social subjects it needs. Such a notion of the production of the subject by power, the complete alienation of the citizen and the worker, and the total colonization of the lifeworld has been hypothesized since the 1960s by many authors as the defining characteristic of "late capitalism." The Frankfurt School, the Situationists, and various critics of technology and communication have focused on the fact that power in capitalist societies is becoming totalitarian through the production of docile subjects.[72] To a certain extent the nightmares of such authors correspond to the dreams of the strategists of full-spectrum dominance. Just as the capitalist yearns for a labor force of obedient worker-monkeys, military administrators imagine an army of efficient and reliable robot soldiers along with a perfectly controlled, obedient population. These nightmares and dreams, however, are not real. Dominance, no matter how multidimensional, can never be complete and is always contradicted by resistance.

Military strategy here runs up against a philosophical problem. *A sovereign power is always two-sided*: a dominating power always relies on the consent or submission of the dominated. The power of sovereignty is thus always limited, and this limit can always potentially be transformed into resistance, a point of vulnerability, a threat. The suicide bomber appears here once again as a symbol of the inevitable limitation and vulnerability of sovereign power; refusing to accept a life of submission, the suicide bomber turns life itself into a horrible weapon. *This is the ontological limit of biopower in its most tragic and revolting form.* Such destruction only grasps the passive, negative limit of sovereign power. The positive, active limit is revealed most clearly with respect to labor and social production. Even when labor is subjugated by capital it always necessarily maintains its own autonomy, and this is ever more clearly true today with respect to the new immaterial, cooperative, and collaborative forms of labor. This relationship is not isolated to the economic terrain but, as we will argue later, spills over into the biopolitical terrain of society as a whole, including military conflicts. In any case, we should recognize here that even in asymmetrical conflicts victory in terms of complete domination is not possible. All that can be achieved is a provisional and limited maintenance of control and order that must constantly be policed and preserved. Counterinsurgency is a full-time job.

It will be helpful at this point to step back and consider this problem from a different standpoint, from the perspective of *form*, because counterinsurgency, we will argue, is fundamentally a question of organizational form. One hard lesson that the leaders of the United States and its allied nation-states seemed to learn reluctantly after September 11, for example, is that the enemy they face is not a unitary sovereign nation-state but rather a *network*. The enemy, in other words, has a new form. It has in fact become a general condition in this era of asymmetrical conflicts that enemies and threats to imperial order tend to appear as distributed networks rather than centralized and sovereign subjects.[73] One essential characteristic of the distributed network form is that it has no center. Its power cannot be understood accurately as flowing from a central source or even as polycentric, but rather as distributed variably, unevenly, and indefinitely. The other essential characteristic of the distributed network form is that the network constantly undermines the stable boundaries between inside and outside. This is not to say that a network is always present everywhere; it means rather that its presence and absence tend to be indeterminate. One might say that the network tends to transform every boundary into a threshold. Networks are in this sense essentially elusive, ephemeral, perpetually in flight. Networks can thus at one moment appear to be universal and at another vanish into thin air.

These changes in form have important consequences for military strategy. For the strategies of traditional state warfare, for example, a network may be frustratingly "target poor": if it has no center and no stable boundaries, where can we strike? And, even more frighteningly, the network can appear anywhere at any time, and in any guise. The military must be prepared at all times for unexpected threats and unknown enemies. Confronting a network enemy can certainly throw an old form of power into a state of universal paranoia.

The network enemy, however, is certainly not entirely new. During the cold war, for example, communism was for the United States and the Western European nations a dual enemy. On one hand, communism was a sovereign state enemy, represented first by the Soviet Union and then China, Cuba, North Vietnam, and others, but on the other hand communism was also a network enemy. Not only insurrectionary armies and revolutionary parties but also political organizations, trade unions, and any number of other organizations could potentially be communist. The communist network was potentially ubiquitous but at the same time fleeting and ephemeral. (And this was one element that fed the paranoia of the McCarthy era in the United States.) During the cold war, the network enemy was partially hidden to the extent that it was constantly overcoded in terms of the socialist states and thus thought to be merely so many dependent agents of the primary sovereign enemy. After the end of the cold war, nation-states no longer cloud our view and network enemies have come out fully into the light. *All wars today tend to be netwars.*

In order to understand how counterinsurgency strategies can combat networks, we need to look back at how counterinsurgency developed in the course of the twentieth century, specifically in the counterinsurgency campaigns against urban and rural guerrilla movements of the national liberation struggles in Africa, Asia, and Latin America.[74] Counterinsurgency strategies evolved because guerrilla organizations were organized according to a different *form* than traditional military organizations and thus required different methods of attack and control. The traditional, sovereign military structure is organized in a pyramidal form with a vertical chain of command and communication: a small group or single leader at its top, a larger group of field commanders in the middle, and a mass of soldiers at its base. The traditional army thus forms an organic fighting body, with generals for its head, lieutenants for its midsection, and common soldier and sailors for its limbs. The traditional army generally operates from the base of its own sovereign territory across relatively clear and established lines of battle, such that the head of the military body can be kept secure away from the front lines. The traditional military structure is, then, in this sense completely knowable. Guerrilla organizations appear, at least from the standpoint of a ruling power, entirely obscure. Guerrillas generally have no sovereign territory and no secure zones; they are mobile and tend to operate exclusively in enemy territory. Even though guerrillas generally operate on obscure terrain, in jungles and in cities, that obscurity is not enough to protect them. Their organizational form itself also serves to protect them, since guerrilla organizations tend to develop polycentric forms of command and horizontal forms of communication, in which small groups or sectors can communicate independently with many other groups. The guerrilla army is therefore not a single body but something more akin to a pack of wolves, or numerous wolfpacks that counterinsurgency forces have to hunt down.

The network form is from the perspective of counterinsurgency an extension and completion of the tendency described by the evolution from traditional to guerrilla organizations. The steps in this progression appear as a movement toward increasing complex types of networks. The traditional military structure can be described as a hub, or star, network in which all lines of communication and command radiate from a central point along fixed lines. The guerrilla structure suggests a polycentric network, with numerous, relatively autonomous centered clusters, like solar systems, in which each hub commands its peripheral nodes and communicates with other hubs. The final model in the series is the distributed, or full-matrix, network in which there is no center and all nodes can communicate directly with all others. If the traditional army is like a single armed body, with organic and centralized relations among its units, and the guerrilla army is like a pack of wolves, with relatively autonomous clusters that can act independently or in coordination, then the distributed network might be imagined like a swarm of ants or bees—a seemingly amorphous multiplicity that can strike at a single point from all sides or disperse in the environment so as to become almost invisible.[75] It is very difficult to hunt down a swarm.

It is clear that the old counterinsurgency strategies will not work against a swarm. Consider, for example, the "decapitation model" of counterinsurgency, based conceptually on the organic notion that if the head is cut off the rebellion, then the body will wither and die. In practical terms "decapitation" means exiling, imprisoning, or assassinating the rebel leadership. This method was used extensively against national liberation armies and guerrilla movements, but it proves increasingly ineffective as rebel organizations adopt a more polycentric or distributed form. To the horror of the counterinsurgency strategists, each time they cut off the head another head springs up in its place like a monstrous Hydra. The guerrilla organization has many heads, and a swarm has no head at all.

A second counterinsurgency strategy is based on the "environment-deprivation" model. This strategy recognizes that its enemy is not organized like a traditional army and thus cannot simply be decapitated. It even accepts that it can never know the enemy and its organizational form adequately. Such knowledge, however, is not necessary to implement this method: the sovereign power avoids being thwarted by what it cannot know and focuses on what it can know. Success does not require attacking the enemy directly but destroying the environment, physical and social, that supports it. Take away the water and the fish will die. This strategy of destroying the support environment led, for example, to indiscriminate bombings in Vietnam, Laos, and Cambodia, to widespread killing, torture, and harassment of peasants in Central and South America, and to mass repression of activist groups in Europe and North America. Napalm could be considered metaphorically the paradigmatic weapon of the environment-deprivation strategy. This is consciously and necessarily a blunt and imprecise strategy. The many noncombatants who suffer cannot be called collateral damage because they are in fact the direct targets, even if their destruction is really a means to attack the primary enemy. The limited successes of this counterinsurgency strategy decrease as the rebellious groups develop more complex, distributed network structures. As the enemy becomes increasingly dispersed, unlocalizable, and unknowable, the support environment becomes increasingly large and indiscriminate. Faced with this tendency, the sovereign, traditional military power is tempted to throw up its hands and cry in exasperation, like Joseph Conrad's crazed antihero, "Exterminate all the brutes!"

It is clear at this point that counterinsurgency strategies can no longer rely only on negative techniques, such as the assassination of rebel leaders and mass arrests, but *must also create "positive" techniques*. Counterinsurgency, in other words, must not destroy the environment of insurgency but rather create and control the environment. The full-spectrum dominance we spoke of earlier is one conception of such a positive strategy to control network enemies, engaging the network not only militarily but also economically, politically, socially, psychologically, and ideologically. The question at this point is, what form of power can implement such a general, dispersed, and articulated counterinsurgency strategy? In fact, traditional, centralized, hierarchical military structures seem incapable of implementing such strategies and adequately combating network war machines. *It takes a network to fight a network*. Becoming a network, however, would imply a radical restructuring of the traditional military apparatuses and the forms of sovereign power they represent.

This focus on form helps us clarify the significance (and also the limitations) of the RMA and the counterinsurgency strategies of asymmetrical conflicts. Certainly, especially at a technological level, the RMA dictates that the traditional military apparatuses use networks more and more effectively—information networks, communications networks, and so forth. Distributing and blocking information and disinformation may well be an important field of battle. The mandate for transformation is much more radical than that: the military must not simply *use* networks; it must itself *become* a full matrix, distributed network. There have long been efforts by traditional militaries to mimic the practices of guerrilla warfare—with small commando units, for example—but these remain at a limited scale and on a tactical level. Some of the changes described in the current conception of an RMA focusing, for example, on the greater flexibility and mobility of combat units, do point in this direction. The more significant changes, however, would need also to involve the command structure and ultimately the form of social power in which the military apparatus is embedded. How can a command structure shift from a centralized model to a distributed network model? What transformations does it imply in the form of social and political power? This would be not merely a revolution in military affairs but a transformation of the form of power itself. In our terms, this process is part of the passage from imperialism, with its centralized and bounded form of power based in nation-states, to the network form of Empire, which would include not only the dominant state powers but also supranational administrations, business interests, and numerous other nongovernmental organizations.

Now, finally, we can come back to the questions we posed at the beginning about the "exceptional" role of U.S. power in the current global order. Our analysis of counterinsurgency strategies tells us that the U.S. military (and also U.S. power more generally) must become a network, shed its national character, and become an imperial military machine. In this context, abandoning unilateral control and adopting a network structure is not an act of benevolence on the part of the superpower but rather is dictated by the needs of counterinsurgency strategy. This military necessity recalls the debates between unilateralism and multilateralism and the conflicts between the United States and the United Nations, but it really goes beyond both of these frameworks. The network form of power is the only one today able to create and maintain order.[76]

There are some indications that, at least at an ideological level, the U.S. military has in recent decades occupied an ambivalent position, at midstream between imperialism and Empire. One could say that, at least since the early 1990s, U.S. foreign policy and military engagement have straddled imperialist and imperial logics. On one hand, each military engagement and the orientation of foreign policy in general is and has to be explained in terms of U.S. national interests, either specific interests such as access to cheap oil or more general ones such as maintaining stable markets or strategic military positions. In this regard the United States acts as a national power along the lines of the modern European imperialist states. On the other hand, each U.S. military engagement and the orientation of its foreign policy in general also carry simultaneously an imperial logic, which is cast in reference not to any limited national interests but to the interests of humanity as a whole. The logic of human rights is the most important example of such an imperial logic, which is not in the specific interest of any nation or people but rather by definition universal to humanity. We should not simply regard, in other words, the humanitarian and universalistic rhetoric of U.S. diplomacy and military action as facades designed to mask the fundamental logic of national interests. Instead we should recognize them both as equally real: two competing logics that run through one single military-political apparatus. In some conflicts, such as Kosovo, the imperial humanitarian logic may be dominant, and in others, such as Afghanistan, the national, imperialist logic appears primary, while in still others, such as Iraq, the two are mixed almost indistinguishably. Both logics, in any case, in different doses and guises, run throughout all of these conflicts.[77]

We should not get caught up here in the tired debates about globalization and nation-states as if the two were necessarily incompatible. Our argument instead is that national ideologues, functionaries, and administrators increasingly find that in order to pursue their strategic objectives they cannot act and think strictly in national terms without consideration of the rest of the globe. The administration of Empire does not require the negation of national administrators. On the contrary, today imperial administration is conducted largely by the structures and personnel of the dominant nation-states. Just as national economic ministers and central bankers can and often do act on the basis of imperial and not strictly national interests, as we will see below when we take a trip to Davos, so too can national military officers and defense ministers conduct imperial wars.[78]

The necessity of the network form of power thus makes moot the debates over unilateralism and multilateralism, since the network cannot be controlled from any single, unitary point of command. The United States cannot "go it alone," in other words, and Washington cannot exert monarchical control over the global order, without the collaboration of other dominant powers. This does not mean that what is decided in Washington is somehow secondary or unimportant but rather that it must always be set in relation to the entire network of global power. If the United States is conceived as a monarchical power on the world scene, then, to use old terminology, the monarch must constantly negotiate and work with the various global aristocracies (such as political, economic, and financial forces), and ultimately this entire power structure must constantly confront the productive global multitude, which is the real basis of the network. The necessity of the network form of global power (and consequently too the art of war) is not an ideological claim but a recognition of an ineluctable material condition. A single power may attempt—and the United States has done so several times—to circumvent this necessity of the network form and the compulsion to engage the plural relations of force, but what it throws out the door always sneaks back in the window. For a centralized power, trying to push back a network is like trying to beat back a rising flood with a stick. Consider just one example: who will pay for the unilateralist wars? Once again the United States seems in the position of the monarch who cannot finance his wars independently and must appeal to the aristocracy for funds. The aristocrats, however, respond, "No taxation without representation," that is, they will not finance the wars unless their voices and interests are represented in the decision-making process. In short, the monarch can usurp power and start wars unilaterally (and indeed create great tragedies), but soon the bill comes due. Such a unilateralist adventure is thus merely a transitory phase. Without the collaboration of the aristocracy, the monarch is ultimately powerless.[79]

In order to be able to combat and control network enemies, which is to say, in order for traditional sovereign structures themselves to become networks, imperial logics of political, military, and diplomatic activity on the part of the United States and the other dominant nation-states will have to win out over imperialist logics, and military strategy will have to be transferred from centralized structures to distributed network forms. Ideologically, national interest and national security have become too narrow a basis for explanation and action in the age of network struggle, but more important the traditional military power structure is no longer capable of defeating or containing its enemies. *The network form is imposed on all facets of power strictly from the perspective of the effectiveness of rule.* What we are heading toward, then, is a state of war in which network forces of imperial order face network enemies on all sides.

1.3 RESISTANCE

> [Pancho] Villa had to invent an entirely original method
> of warfare. . . . He knew nothing of European standards
> of strategy or discipline. . . . When Villa's army goes into
> battle he is not hampered by salutes, or rigid respect for
> officers. . . . It reminds one of the ragged Republican
> army that Napoleon led into Italy.   —JOHN REED

> Bombard the headquarters.   —MAO ZEDONG

We have seen from the perspective of counterinsurgency strategies how
the forms of rebellion, revolt, and revolution changed through the course
of the twentieth century from traditional, centralized military structures
to guerrilla organizations and finally to a more complex distributed network form. One might get the impression from such a narrative that
counterinsurgency strategies dictate the evolving forms of insurgency. Actually, as the terms themselves indicate, it is just the opposite. We need to
look now from the other side and recognize the logic that determines the
genealogy of forms of insurgency and revolt. This logic and this trajectory
will help us recognize what are today and will be in the future the most
powerful and most desirable organizational forms of rebellion and revolution. Ultimately this will help us see how to address the most important
task for resistance today, that is, resisting war.

THE PRIMACY OF RESISTANCE

Counterinsurgency came first in our exposition of war and power conflicts, even though in reality, of course, insurgency comes first and counterinsurgency must always respond to it. We began with counterinsurgency for much the same reason that Marx gives, in the preface to the first volume of *Capital,* for discussing wealth before discussing labor, its source. The method of exposition or narration of his argument (*Darstellung*), he explains, is different than the method of research (*Forschung*). His book opens with capital and, specifically, with the world of commodities: this is the logical entry point because this is how we first experience capitalist society. From here Marx develops the dynamics of capitalist production and labor, even though capital and commodities are the results of labor—both materially, since they are products of labor, and politically, since capital must constantly respond to the threats and developments of labor. Whereas Marx's exposition begins with capital, then, his research must begin with labor and constantly recognize that in reality labor is primary. The same is true of *resistance*. Even though common use of the term might suggest the opposite—that resistance is a response or reaction—*resistance is primary with respect to power*. This principle affords us a different perspective on the development of modern conflicts and the emergence of our present permanent global war. Recognizing the primacy of resistance allows us to see this history from below and illuminates the alternatives that are possible today.

The great tradition of classic German philosophy on which Marx draws has a richly developed conception of philosophical method based on the relation between the mode of exposition or representation, the *Darstellung*, and the mode of research, the *Forschung*. The Young Hegelians, philosophers who in the early nineteenth century adapted and transformed Hegel's thought for the German Left, including Ludwig Feurbach, David Friedrich Strauss, Arnold Ruge, Moses Hess, and Heinrich Heine, set out from Hegel's *Darstellung*, his account of the unfolding of Spirit in the world. Their research, however, inverts this idealist perspective on the world and sets it on its feet, developing the terms of real, material subjectivities. On the basis of this *Forschung* and its foundation in material subjectivities they can pose a *Neue Darstellung*, or new vision of reality. This new exposition not only demystifies the alienated perspective of the idealist view but also actively constructs a new reality. The subjectivities that are revealed in the research are the authors of the new reality, the real protagonists of history. This indeed is Marx's own method. His research into the nature of labor and the productivity of those exploited under capital is oriented not only toward a new vision of the world from their perspective but also a new reality created through their historical activity. We must now, in the same way, begin to understand our global state of war and its development through research into the genealogy of social and political movements of resistance. This will lead us eventually toward a new vision of our world and also an understanding of the subjectivities capable of creating a new world.

As we have already seen, military questions can never be addressed in isolation, and in the age of biopower and biopolitics they are woven together increasingly tightly with social, cultural, economic, and political issues. In order to give a first sketch of these subjectivities of resistance here we thus have to anticipate some of the results of our analysis in part 2 of both the social composition of the multitude and of its technical composition, that is, how people are integrated into the systems of economic production and reproduction, what jobs they perform, and what they produce. The contemporary scene of labor and production, we will explain, is being transformed under the hegemony of immaterial labor, that is, labor that produces immaterial products, such as information, knowledges, ideas, images, relationships, and affects. This does not mean that there is no more industrial working class whose calloused hands toil with machines or that there are no more agricultural workers who till the soil. It does not even mean that the numbers of such workers have decreased globally. In fact, workers involved primarily in immaterial production are a small minority of the global whole. What it means, rather, is that the qualities and characteristics of immaterial production are tending to transform the other forms of labor and indeed society as a whole. Some of these new characteristics are decidedly unwelcome. When our ideas and our affects, or emotions, are put to work, for instance, and when they thus become subject in a new way to the command of the boss, we often experience new and intense forms of violation or alienation. Furthermore, the contractual and material conditions of immaterial labor that tend to spread to the entire labor market are making the position of labor in general more precarious. There is one tendency, for example, in various forms of immaterial labor to blur the distinction between work time and nonwork time, extending the working day indefinitely to fill all of life, and another tendency for immaterial labor to function without stable long-term contracts and thus to adopt the precarious position of becoming flexible (to accomplish several tasks) and mobile (to move continually among locations). Some characteristics of immaterial labor, which are tending to transform other forms of labor, hold enormous potential for positive social transformation. (These positive characteristics are paradoxically the flip side of the negative developments.) First, immaterial labor tends to move out of the limited realm of the strictly economic domain and engage in the general production and reproduction of society as a whole. The production of ideas, knowledges, and affects, for example, does not merely create means by which society is formed and maintained; such immaterial labor also directly produces social relationships. Immaterial labor is *biopolitical* in that it is oriented toward the creation of forms of social life; such labor, then, tends no longer to be limited to the economic but also becomes immediately a social, cultural, and political force. Ultimately, in philosophical terms, the production involved here is the *production of subjectivity*, the creation and reproduction of new subjectivities in society. Who we are, how we view the world, how we interact with each other are all created through this social, biopolitical production. Second, immaterial labor tends to the take the social form of *networks* based on communication, collaboration, and affective relationships. Immaterial labor can only be conducted in common, and increasingly immaterial labor invents new, independent networks of cooperation through which it produces. Its ability to engage and transform all aspects of society and its collaborative network form are two enormously powerful characteristics that immaterial labor is spreading to other forms of labor. These characteristics can serve as a preliminary sketch of the social composition of the multitude that today animates the movements of resistance against the permanent, global state of war.

We also need to give a first sketch of the political orientation of this multitude, anticipating very briefly the results of our analysis in part 3. The primary forces that have guided the history of modern resistance struggles and liberation movements, along with the most productive resistance movements of today, we will argue, are driven at base not only by the struggle against misery and poverty but also by a profound desire for democracy—a real democracy of the rule of all by all based on relationships of equality and freedom. This democracy is a dream created in the great revolutions of modernity but never yet realized. Today, the new characteristics of the multitude and its biopolitical productivity give powerful new avenues for pursuing that dream. This striving for democracy permeates the entire cycle of protests and demonstrations around the issues of globalization, from the dramatic events at the WTO in Seattle in 1999 to the meetings of the World Social Forum in Porto Alegre, Brazil. This desire for democracy is also the core of the various movements and demonstrations against the 2003 war in Iraq and the permanent state of war more generally. The need for democracy coincides immediately, in the present conditions, with the need for peace. When war has become a foundational element of politics and when the state of exception has become permanent, then peace is elevated for the multitude to the highest value, the necessary condition for any liberation. It is too simple in this context, however, to identify the interests of the multitude immediately and exclusively with peace. Throughout modernity, and still today, resistance movements have had to confront war and the violence it imposes, sometimes with and sometimes without violent means. Perhaps we should say rather that the great wars of liberation are (or should be) oriented ultimately toward a "war against war," that is, an active effort to destroy the regime of violence that perpetuates our state of war and supports the systems of inequality and oppression. This is a condition necessary for realizing the democracy of the multitude.

Recognizing the characteristics of the multitude will allow us to invert our perspective on the world. After the *Darstellung,* or exposition, of our current state of war, our *Forschung,* or research, into the nature and conditions of the multitude, will allow us to reach a new standpoint where we can recognize the real, creative forces that are emerging with the potential to create a new world. The great production of subjectivity of the multitude, its biopolitical capacities, its struggle against poverty, its constant striving for democracy, all coincide here with the genealogy of these resistances stretching from the early modern era to our own.

In the following sections, therefore, we will follow the genealogy of liberation struggles, from the formation of people's armies in the great modern revolutions to guerrilla warfare and finally to contemporary forms of network struggle. When we put the genealogy in motion, in fact, the changing forms of resistance will reveal three guiding principles—principles that are really embedded in history and determine its movement. The first principle that guides the genealogy will refer to the historical occasion, that is, the form of resistance that is most effective in combating a specific form of power. The second principle will pose a correspondence between changing forms of resistance and the transformations of economic and social production: in each era, in other words, the model of resistance that proves to be most effective turns out to have the same form as the dominant models of economic and social production. The third principle that will emerge refers simply to democracy and freedom: each new form of resistance is aimed at addressing the undemocratic qualities of previous forms, creating a chain of ever more democratic movements. This genealogy of wars of liberation and resistance movements, finally, will lead us to see the most adequate form of organization for resistance and liberation struggles in the contemporary material and political situation.

We should note, before moving on, that some of the basic traditional models of political activism, class struggle, and revolutionary organization have today become outdated and useless. In some ways they have been undermined by tactical and strategic errors and in others they have been neutralized by counterinsurgency initiatives, but the more important cause of their demise is the transformation of the multitude itself. The current global recomposition of social classes, the hegemony of immaterial labor, and the forms of decision-making based on network structures all radically change the conditions of any revolutionary process. The traditional modern conception of insurrection, for example, which was defined primarily in the numerous episodes from the Paris Commune to the October Revolution, was characterized by a movement from the insurrectional activity of the masses to the creation of political vanguards, from civil war to the building of a revolutionary government, from the construction of organizations of counterpower to the conquest of state power, and from opening the constituent process to establishing the dictatorship of the proletariat. Such sequences of revolutionary activity are unimaginable today, and instead the experience of insurrection is being rediscovered, so to speak, in the flesh of the multitude. It may be that insurrectional activity is no longer divided into such stages but develops simultaneously. As we will argue in the course of this book, resistance, exodus, the emptying out of the enemy's power, and the multitude's construction of a new society are one and the same process.

FROM THE PEOPLE'S ARMY
TO GUERRILLA WARFARE

Modernity was filled with civil wars. After the great German peasant war in the early sixteenth century, peasant revolts developed throughout Europe, primarily in response to the transition to capitalism. Outside of Europe at the same time, the colonial encounter gave rise to continual conflict and rebellion. There is an enormous legacy of modern peasant wars, real civil wars, sometimes extremely cruel, that can be found from Spain to Russia and from Mexico to India.[80] The techniques of repression developed by capitalist modernization, which were extremely violent, were waged equally against rebels, bandits, and witches. The resistances and rebellions, however, were not antimodern. Modernization also served as the model of development on the other side, forming armed peasant bands into armies. People's armies were formed against the armies of kings and colonizers: Cromwell led a yeoman army in the English Revolution, and the

Sanculottes developed a modern army from a theory of class war; guerrilla fighters in the southern United States were formed into an army to defeat Cornwallis and the British troops. All the great modern revolutionary struggles against colonial powers, in North and South America as in Asia and Africa, involved the formation of armed bands, partisans, guerrillas, and rebels into a people's army. This is the fundamental passage of modern civil war: the formation of dispersed and irregular rebel forces into an army.

The various theories of civil war developed on the Left in the modern era all dwell on the transformation of the insurrection into an army, the transformation of partisan activity into an organized counterpower. Friedrich Engels, for example, analyzing the 1848 uprisings in Germany, described the necessary passage from the armed insurrection of proletarians to the formation of an army of communists. A strong relationship must be constructed, according to Engels, between insurrectional acts, specific disobedience, and sabotage on the one hand and on the other the formation of an army, that is, a united composition of military forces.[81] Leon Trotsky and the generals of the Red Army, when they engaged in civil war against the white Russian forces, posed the same problem: how to organize the mobile peasant guerrilla forces under the unity of central command. How can modern weapons and organizing structures provide the conditions for directing the peasants with modern military authority? Isaak Babel recounts how the bands of Cossacks organized by Semyon Budyenny found one solution: they transformed the work carts (*tatchankas*) that had been a staple of Cossack peasant labor into mobile machine-gun carriers, creating one of the most successful Soviet attack units.[82] The push to centralize military organization thus emerged as part of the effort to link different social classes and different levels of economic development in one common political project. The primary characteristic of the revolutionary concept of modern civil war on the Left, both socialist and communist, involves the passage from guerrilla bands to a centralized army structure.

The formation of a people's army in modern civil war thus corresponds in many cases to the transition from peasant experiences to those of industrial workers. The urban proletariat lent itself immediately to centralized military formations, whereas rebellions in the countryside tended to remain isolated and uncommunicative. The modern people's army was an industrial worker army, whereas the guerrilla forces were primarily peasant bands. The path of modernization thus seemed to many revolutionaries in peasant societies the only possible strategy. What was necessary in such instances to form a people's army was a great project of articulation and communication. Mao Zedong's long march in the mid-1930s, for example, put two relationships in play: the centripetal one brings together the dispersed bands of rebels to form something like a national army, and the centrifugal one, through the pilgrimage among the various regions of China, from the south to the north, deposits groups of revolutionaries all along the way to propagate revolution.[83] The relationship between rebellion and revolution, between insurrection and civil war, armed bands and a revolutionary people's army is thus articulated together with the notions of taking power and constructing a new society. Consider also the process of forming a ragtag people's army more than two decades earlier in the Mexican Revolution: Emiliano Zapata's peasants in the south traveled by foot and horseback; Pancho Villa's peons in the north sometimes rode on horseback and other times commandeered trains to traverse the desert plains in a moving village on rails of cannons, soldiers, and families. The grand movement of such an exodus or caravan of revolutionaries is what Diego Rivera, José Orozco, and David Siqueiros capture so beautifully in their immense murals. What was central, once again, was the perpetual movement that allowed the disparate and isolated guerrilla forces to unite in a people's army. The peasants do not become proletarians in this process of military modernization, of course, but they do manage when they become a modern army to leave behind the isolation that had previously characterized peasant guerrilla rebellion.

This same passage is an even greater preoccupation for the reactionary theories of modern civil war. Carl von Clausewitz, for example, was inspired in the early nineteenth century by the anti-Napoleonic guerrilla warfare of the Spanish peasants, but he maintained that these armed bands must never become an army, in contrast to what we find in the communist theories. Clausewitz excludes any type of revolutionary education that could lead to a partisan war of liberation. His peasant partisans will remain tied to the earth, despite or even because of the civil war. Carl Schmitt, a century and a half after Clausewitz, similarly insists that the partisan is a "telluric" figure, tied to the earth, to the existing relations of production, to folklore and tradition—and these characteristics become common to all legitimist nationalisms in Europe after 1848. This telluric conception of civil war effectively blocks the modernizing tendency of the unification of struggles in a people's army, keeping them separated in isolation and thus incompatible with republican and revolutionary projects. Schmitt's greatest fear is that the telluric partisan, the last sentinel of the earth, be transformed into a modern, "motorized" partisan.[84]

Attachments to the soil along with other kinds of divisions and internal contradictions often thwarted modern rebellions and revolutionary projects. The confused Garibaldi movement in nineteenth-century Italy, for example, which did indeed contain some profound elements of social revolution, failed every time it tried to organize itself as a people's army. This was so mainly because of such reactionary elements. The antifascist resistances in Poland, Ukraine, Russia, Italy, France, Yugoslavia, and other countries during the Second World War were predicated on a logic of articulation and unification, but many of them too contained an unstable mixture of elements: class struggle, nationalism, traditional defenses of the soil, and a variety of reactionary positions. The same kinds of mixtures and divisions were found in many of the national liberation wars that emerged in Africa and Asia in the subsequent decades.[85] It is no coincidence that counterinsurgency strategies often focus on these internal contradictions, trying to keep the different subjects separate and exacerbate their ideological differences in order to prevent a political recomposition. Often, but not always, the attempts to separate the various components of resistance follow the lines of class divisions.[86] In contrast, the path of modernization, toward a unified people's army, seemed to be the only strategy available for modern civil war.

The unified people's army, however, although it proved the most effective form in this period for resisting domination and overthrowing the structures of power, did not always lead to desirable political results. Armed resistance had to be also a constituent project for the new nation:

the victorious army had to give rise too to the new national government and administrative apparatus, but the political form of the people's army is, of course, strictly hierarchical and centralized. The people's army had either to take power itself (as was most often the case) or delegate a civilian government for the new nation, which in the postcolonial world often had to be done without the aid of any historical precedent. The centralized formation of a people's army looks like a victorious strategy up until the point when the victory is won, when the weakness of its unified and hierarchical structure become painfully clear. Democracy is far from guaranteed by the people's army.[87]

The transformation of dispersed guerrilla organizations into a united people's army thus has two distinct faces. On one hand, it coincides with the general lines of modernization. It is no accident that the theories of the transition from capitalism to socialism, or really from the precapitalist regimes to an intense phase of modernization (the two trajectories often overlap in such a way that it is difficult to tell them apart), play such an important role in the modern reflections on the art of war. Guerrilla wars and wars of liberation in their various guises act as structural motors of modernization, reformulating the relations of property and production, determining the primary forms of autonomous industrialization, redistributing populations, and educating the national population. It is not true, in fact, as many reactionaries claim, that modernization would have proceeded faster in these countries if the civil wars of liberation had not taken place. On the contrary, revolutionary civil wars were motors of modernization. On the other hand, the centralization and hierarchy involved in the formation of a people's army result in a dramatic loss of autonomy of the various local guerrilla organizations and the rebellious populations as a whole. The undemocratic character of the modern people's army may be tolerated during the phase of battle when it is deemed necessary for victory but not when it defines the nature of the postwar political structure.

The modern class wars and wars of liberation brought with them an extraordinary production of subjectivity. Imagine what happened in the Mexican countryside or in Southeast Asia or Africa when the incitement to rebellion and the formation of a people's army in a foundational, constituent war emerged from a world of misery and subjugation; imagine what profound energies this call solicited, because it is a matter of a call not simply to arms but to the construction of individual and social bodies. *What these foundational wars really produce, in the final analysis, and often subsequently cannot satisfy, is a great desire for democracy.* One example of the new production of subjectivity in the resistance and liberation movements of the twentieth century are the extraordinary anarchist experiences in the Spanish civil war, organizing political revolt through new deployments of military and social relationships. All of those who chronicled the period, even the Soviets, appreciated the importance of Buenaventura Durruti, the great Catalan anarchist leader, and the social transformation of insurrection that he accomplished.[88]

Throughout the world in the 1960s there was a rebirth of guerrilla organizations. This rebirth coincided with a *growing rejection of the centralized model of the popular army.* This rejection was based in large part on the desire for greater freedom and democracy. Certainly the military structure of the united people's army was questioned for its effectiveness and its vulnerability to counterinsurgency strategies, but that military structure also lent itself to and even required centralized, authoritarian control. The guerrilla structure seemed to provide, in comparison, a model of decentralization and relative autonomy.

The Cuban revolution was one of the primary inspirations for the resurgence of guerrilla organizations in the 1960s. The novelty of the Cuban model was seen to be its affirmation of the primacy of guerrilla military experience and its refusal to submit guerrilla forces to the control of a political party.[89] The conventional orthodoxy had been that military leaders should be subordinated to party control: General Giap to Ho Chi Minh, Zhu De to Mao Zedong during the Long March, Trotsky to Lenin during the Bolshevik revolution. By contrast, Fidel Castro and the Cuban guerrilla forces were subordinated to no political leaders and formed a party themselves only after the military victory. Che Guevara, furthermore, highlighted the primacy of guerrilla activity by example when he dramatically left the political sphere in Cuba and returned to the field of battle in the Congo and Bolivia.

This Cuban model of guerrilla struggle was seen as liberatory by many, particularly in Latin America, because it posed a means to evade the authority and control of traditional Communist and Socialist parties. The primacy of guerrilla warfare was experienced as an invitation for many groups to begin revolutionary military activity on their own. Anyone could (and should) go to the mountains like Che and form a *foco*, a small autonomous guerrilla unit. This was a do-it-yourself method for revolution. The Cuban model was also thought to be liberatory as regards the form of the guerrilla organization itself. An indefinite number of small guerrilla *focos* could act relatively independently from one another, creating a polycentric structure and a horizontal relationship among the units, in contrast to the vertical and centralized command structure of the traditional army. In both of these respects, the Cuban guerrilla model seemed to offer a less authoritarian and more democratic possibility for revolutionary organizing.

The democratic and independent nature of the Cuban guerrilla *foco* strategy, however, is extremely elusive. First of all, freedom from the control of traditional parties is merely replaced by the control of a military authority. Fidel Castro and Che Guevara both insist that the guerrilla force must ultimately come under the rule of a single authority, a single man, who will subsequently, after the victory, serve as political leader. Secondly, the horizontal and autonomous appearance of the guerrilla organization also turns out to be illusory. The guerrilla *foco* is never really an autonomous unit: the *foco* is the cell of the column, and the column is the cell of the army. The guerrilla *foco* is the vanguard party in embryonic form. In other words, *the apparently plural and polycentric structure tends to be reduced in practice to a centralized unity.*

The weakness of the democracy offered by guerrilla movements is often most apparent when they are victorious and take power—even though they are in almost all cases much more democratic than the regimes they replace. Since in the Cuban model there is no preexisting political structure separate from the guerrilla force, the postliberation government must be formed on the basis of the military structure itself. In many cases the democratic diversity and autonomy of the various guerrilla units are narrowed down as the comparatively horizontal military structure is transformed into a vertical state structure of command. In the process, various subordinated social groups that had played decisive roles in the revolutionary process are systematically excluded from positions of power. One index of the democratic nature of guerrilla military organizations is the participation of women. It was not uncommon for women to compose more than 30 percent of the combatants in Latin American guerrilla organizations in the late twentieth century, for example, with an equal percentage in leadership positions.[90] This was a much higher percentage of female participation and leadership than in other sectors of these same societies, such as political or trade union organizations, and much higher than in state military regimes elsewhere. In the Nicaraguan case, after the Sandinista victory many women combatants complained that they were not able to maintain leadership positions in the postrevolutionary power structure. An impressive number of women did hold important positions in the victorious Sandinista government, but not nearly as many as in the Sandinista guerrilla forces.[91] This is one symptom of the process of *de-democratization* of the guerrilla movements.

In addition to the Cuban model, another primary inspiration for the resurgence of guerrilla organizations in the 1960s was the Chinese Cultural Revolution. The Cultural Revolution was a complex social development whose nature and consequences historians have only begun to clarify,[92] but outside of China the image of the Cultural Revolution was greeted immediately by radical and revolutionary movements as a radical social experiment. What traveled most outside of China was not news of the actual transformations of Chinese society but rather the slogans of the Cultural Revolution, such as "Bombard the headquarters," often mixed with Mao's slogans and maxims from earlier periods about guerrilla warfare and revolution. In the Cultural Revolution, Mao himself had called upon the Chinese masses to attack the party-state apparatus and claim power for themselves. *The image of China thus served as an alternative to the Soviet model* and the various Communist parties that followed the Soviet line, but it also posed the notion of a full and free engagement of the masses with no centralized control. The external image of the Cultural Revolution was thus one of antiauthoritarianism and radical democracy.

In short, the Cultural Revolution seemed to respond to the question of the "permanent revolution," the radical and unending process of class struggle on the part of the industrial workers and peasants. How could proletarian subversion constantly produce revolutionary effects? How could this process invest and legitimate the ruling form of power, including its military organizations? At times together with the Cuban strategy and at others as an alternative to it, the Chinese model served as an example. In many respects, the decentered structures of guerrilla organizations, autonomous from state and party apparatuses, seemed already to be following the dictates of the Cultural Revolution in its most radical and expressive form.

The weakness of this Chinese model, especially outside of Asia, was primarily due to its being adopted with very little understanding of the nature of contemporary Chinese society. Information from China was minimal and analyses generally too weak to support a model of political or military organization.[93] (It is hard to imagine, for example, what the Black Panthers had in mind when they sold copies of Mao's little red book on the streets of Berkeley.) The democratic character of the Cultural Revolution is complicated and qualified, furthermore, by the position of Mao himself, since it appears from the outside at least that his calls to attack all forms of authority paradoxically reinforce his own central position and control.

The Cuban guerrilla model and the Maoist model are both fundamentally ambivalent with respect to freedom and democracy. On one hand, they answer to a certain extent the desire for more democratic forms of organization and autonomy from centralized military and political control. On the other hand, however, the plural and democratic nature of the guerrilla movements tends to be reduced to unity and centralization, both in the functioning of the military organization itself and more dramatically in the resulting political forms. Central control and hierarchy continually reappear. These models of guerrilla movements might thus be viewed best as *transitional forms* that reveal above all the continuing and unsatisfied desire for more democratic and independent forms of revolutionary organization.

When we recognize the power of these modern figures of armed popular struggle, from the people's army to guerrilla organizations, it becomes clear how mistaken are the various theories that attempt to make *the political autonomous from the social*. Consider, for example, Hannah Arendt's distinction between political revolution and social revolution, which she illustrates with reference to the American Revolution (political) and the French (social).[94] Arendt's conception tends to separate the drive for political liberation and democracy from the demands of social justice and class conflict. Even for the eighteenth-century revolutions, however, and increasingly as modernity progresses, this distinction is difficult to maintain: the pressures of economic, social, and political factors are articulated in each of the revolutionary figures, and sorting them into separate boxes only mystifies the real concrete processes of popular armed struggle and guerrilla movements. In fact, one common strategy of counterinsurgency and state repression is to pit the one against the other, the social against the political, justice against freedom. On the contrary, in the long seasons of armed resistance and liberation movements—especially in the twentieth-century antifascist resistances and the anticolonial national liberation struggles—guerrilla forces continually create tighter articulations between the political and the social, between anticolonial wars of liberation, for example, and anticapitalist class wars.[95] As we move into postmodernity this articulation between the social and the political becomes even more intense. The genealogy of resistances and struggles in postmodernity, as we will see shortly, presupposes *the political nature of social life* and adopts it as an internal key to all the movements. This presupposition is basic, in fact, to the concept of biopolitics and the biopolitical production of subjectivity. Here economic, social, and political questions are inextricably intertwined. Any theoretical effort in this context to pose the autonomy of the political, separate from the social and the economic, no longer makes any sense.

INVENTING NETWORK STRUGGLES

Looking back at the genealogy of modern revolutions and resistance movements, the idea of "the people" has played a fundamental role, in both the people's army and the guerrilla models, in establishing the authority of the organization and legitimating its use of violence. "The people" is a form of sovereignty contending to replace the ruling state authority and take power. This modern legitimation of sovereignty, even in the case of revolutionary movements, is really the product of a usurpation. *The people* often serves as a middle term between the consent given by the population and the command exerted by the sovereign power, but generally the phrase serves merely as a pretense to validate a ruling authority. The modern legitimation of power and sovereignty, even in cases of resistance and rebellion, is always grounded in a transcendent element, whether this authority be (in Max Weber's terms) traditional, rational, or charismatic. The ambiguity of the notion of the sovereign people turns out to be a kind of duplicity, since the legitimating relationship always tends to privilege authority and not the population as a whole. This ambiguous relationship between the people and sovereignty accounts for the continuing dissatisfaction we have noted with the undemocratic character of the modern forms of revolutionary organization, the recognition that the forms of domination and authority we are fighting against continually reappear in the resistance movements themselves. Furthermore, increasingly today the modern arguments for the legitimation of the violence exercised by the people suffer the same crisis that we spoke of earlier in terms of the legitimation of state violence. Here too the traditional legal and moral arguments no longer hold.

Is it possible today to imagine a new process of legitimation that does not rely on the sovereignty of the people but is based instead in the biopolitical productivity of the multitude? Can new organizational forms of resistance and revolt finally satisfy the desire for democracy implicit in the entire modern genealogy of struggles? Is there an immanent mechanism that does not appeal to any transcendent authority that is capable of legitimating the use of force in the multitude's struggle to create a new society based on democracy, equality, and freedom? Does it even make sense to talk about a war of the multitude?

One model of legitimation we find in modernity that might help us address these questions is the one that animates class struggle. We are not thinking so much of the projects of Socialist states and parties, which certainly constructed their own modern forms of sovereignty, but the daily struggles of the workers themselves, their coordinated acts of resistance, insubordination, and subversion of the relations of domination in the workplace and in society at large. The subordinate classes organized in revolt never entertained any illusions about the legitimacy of state violence, even when they adopted reformist strategies that engaged with the state, forcing it to deliver social welfare and asking it for legal sanction, such as the right to strike. They never forgot that the laws that legitimate state violence are transcendental norms that maintain the privileges of the dominant class (in particular, the rights of property owners) and the subordination of the rest of the population. They knew that whereas the violence of capital and the state rests on transcendent authority, the legitimation of their class struggle was based solely on their own interests and desires.[96] Class struggle was thus a modern model of the immanent basis of legitimation in the sense that it appealed to no sovereign authority for its justification.

We do not think, however, that the question of the legitimation of the struggles of the multitude can be resolved simply by studying the archaeology of class warfare or by trying to establish any fixed continuity with the past. Past struggles can provide some important examples, but new dimensions of power demand new dimensions of resistance. Such questions furthermore cannot be resolved merely through theoretical reflection but must also be addressed in practice. We need to take up our genealogy where we left off and see how the political struggles themselves responded.

After 1968, the year in which a long cycle of struggles culminated in both the dominant and subordinated parts of the world, the form of resistance and liberation movements began to change radically—a change that corresponded with the changes in the labor force and the forms of social production. We can recognize this shift first of all in the transformations of the nature of guerrilla warfare. The most obvious change was that guerrilla movements began to shift from the countryside to the city, from open spaces to closed ones. The techniques of guerrilla warfare began to be adapted to the new conditions of post-Fordist production, in line with information systems and network structures. Finally, as guerrilla warfare increasingly adopted the characteristics of biopolitical production and spread throughout the entire fabric of society, it more directly posed as its goal the production of subjectivity—economic and cultural subjectivity, both material and immaterial. It was not just a matter of "winning hearts and minds," in other words, but rather of creating new hearts and minds through the construction of new circuits of communication, new forms of social collaboration, and new modes of interaction. In this process we can discern a tendency toward moving beyond the modern guerrilla model toward more democratic network forms of organization.

One of the maxims of guerrilla warfare common to both the Maoist and Cuban models was the privileging of the rural over the urban. At the end of the 1960s and into the 1970s guerrilla struggles became increasingly metropolitan, particularly in the Americas and Europe.[97] The revolts of the African American U.S. ghettos of the 1960s were perhaps the prologue to the urbanization of political struggle and armed conflict in the 1970s. Many of the urban movements in this period, of course, did not adopt the polycentric organizational model typical of guerrilla movements but instead followed in large part the older centralized, hierarchical model of traditional military structures. The Black Panther Party and the Front du Libération du Québec in North America, the Uruguayan Tupamaros and the Brazilian Acçâo Libertadora Nacional in South America, and the German Red Army Faction and the Italian Red Brigades in Europe were all examples of that backward-looking, centralized military structure. In this period there also emerged decentered or polycentric urban movements whose organizations resembled the modern guerrilla model. To some extent in these cases the tactics of guerrilla warfare were simply transposed from the country to the city. The city is a jungle. The urban guerrillas know its terrain in a capillary way so that they can at any time come together and attack and then disperse and disappear into its recesses. The focus, however, was increasingly not on attacking the ruling powers but rather on transforming the city itself. In metropolitan struggles the close relationship between disobedience and resistance, between sabotage and desertion, counterpower and constituent projects became increasingly intense. The great struggles of Autonomia in Italy in the 1970s, for example, succeeded temporarily in redesigning the landscape of the major cities, liberating entire zones where new cultures and new forms of life were created.[98]

The real transformation of guerrilla movements during this period, however, has little to do with urban or rural terrain—or, rather, the apparent shift to urban spaces is a symptom of a more important transformation. *The more profound transformation takes place in the relationship between the organization of the movements and the organization of economic and social production.*[99] As we have already seen, the mass armies of regimented industrial factory workers correspond to centralized military formations of the people's army, whereas guerrilla forms of rebellion are linked to peasant production, in its relative isolation dispersed across the countryside. Beginning in the 1970s, however, the techniques and organizational forms of industrial production shifted toward smaller and more mobile labor units and more flexible structures of production, a shift often labeled as a move from Fordist to post-Fordist production. The small mobile units and flexible structures of post-Fordist production correspond to a certain degree to the polycentric guerrilla model, but the guerrilla model is immediately transformed by the technologies of post-Fordism. The networks of information, communication, and cooperation—the primary axes of post-Fordist production—begin to define the new guerrilla movements. Not only do the movements employ technologies such as the Internet as organizing tools, they also begin to adopt these technologies as models for their own organizational structures.

To a certain extent these postmodern, post-Fordist movements complete and solidify the polycentric tendency of earlier guerrilla models. According to the classic Cuban formulation of *foquismo* or *guevarismo* the guerrilla forces are polycentric, composed of numerous relatively independent *focos*, but that plurality must eventually be reduced to a unity and the guerrilla forces must become an army. Network organization, by contrast, is based on the *continuing* plurality of its elements and its networks of communication in such a way that reduction to a centralized and unified command structure is impossible. The polycentric form of the guerrilla model thus evolves into a network form in which there is no center, only an irreducible plurality of nodes in communication with each other.

One distinctive feature of the network struggle of the multitude, like post-Fordist economic production, is that it takes place on the biopolitical terrain—in other words, it directly produces new subjectivities and new forms of life. It is true that military organizations have always involved the production of subjectivity. The modern army produced the disciplined soldier who could follow orders, like the disciplined worker of the Fordist factory, and the production of the disciplined subject in the modern guerrilla forces was very similar. Network struggle, again, like post-Fordist production, does not rely on discipline in the same way: creativity, communication, and self-organized cooperation are its primary values. This new kind of force, of course, resists and attacks the enemy as military forces always have, but increasingly its focus is internal—producing new subjectivities and new expansive forms of life within the organization itself. No longer is "the people" assumed as basis and no longer is taking power of the sovereign state structure the goal. The democratic elements of the guerrilla structure are pushed further in the network form, and the organization becomes less a means and more an end in itself.

Of the numerous examples of civil war in the final decades of the twentieth century, the vast majority were still organized according to outdated models, either the old modern guerrilla model or the traditional centralized military structure, including the Khmer Rouge in Cambodia, the mujahideen in Afghanistan, Hamas in Lebanon and Palestine, the New People's Army in the Philippines, Sendero Luminoso in Peru, and the FARC and the ELN in Colombia. Many of these movements, especially when they are defeated, begin to transform and take on network characteristics. One of the rebellions that looks forward and illustrates the transition from traditional guerrilla organization toward network forms is the Palestinian Intifada, which first began in 1987 and erupted again in 2000. Reliable information about the organization of the Intifada is scarce, but it seems that two models coexist in the uprising.[100] On one hand, the revolt is organized internally by poor young men on a very local level around neighborhood leaders and popular committees. The stone throwing and direct conflict with Israeli police and authorities that initiated the first Intifada spread quickly through much of Gaza and the West Bank. On the other hand, the revolt is organized externally by the various established Palestinian political organizations, most of which were in exile at the beginning of the first Intifada and controlled by men of an older generation. Throughout its different phases, the Intifada seems to have been defined by different proportions of these two organizational forms, one internal and the other external, one horizontal, autonomous, and distributed and the other vertical and centralized. The Intifada is thus an ambivalent organization that points backward toward older centralized forms and forward to new distributed forms of organization.

That anti-Apartheid struggles in South Africa similarly illustrate this transition and the copresence of two basic organizational forms over a much longer period. The internal composition of the forces that challenged and eventually overthrew the Apartheid regime was extremely complex and changed over time, but one can clearly recognize, beginning at least in the mid-1970s with the Soweto revolt and continuing throughout the 1980s, a vast proliferation of horizontal struggles.[101] Black anger against white domination certainly was common to the various movements, but they were organized in relatively autonomous forms across different sectors of society. Student groups were important actors and labor unions, which have a long history of militancy in South Africa, played a central role. Throughout this period these horizontal struggles also had a dynamic relationship with the vertical axis of older, traditional leadership organizations, such as the African National Congress (ANC), which remained clandestine and in exile until 1990. One can pose this contrast between autonomous, horizontal organization and centralized leadership as a tension between the organized struggles (of workers, students, and others) and the ANC, but it might be more illuminating to recognize it also as a tension within the ANC, a tension that has remained and developed in some senses since the ANC's election to power in 1994.[102] Like the Intifada, then, the anti-Apartheid struggles straddled two different organizational forms, marking in our genealogy a point of transition.

The Zapatista National Liberation Army (EZLN), which first appeared in Chiapas in the 1990s, offers an even clearer example of this transformation: the Zapatistas are the hinge between the old guerrilla model and the new model of biopolitical network structures. The Zapatistas also demonstrate wonderfully how the economic transition of post-Fordism can function equally in urban and rural territories, linking local experiences with global struggles.[103] The Zapatistas, which were born and primarily remain a peasant and indigenous movement, use the Internet and communications technologies not only as a means of distributing their communiqués to the outside world but also, at least to some extent, as a structural element inside their organization, especially as it extends beyond southern Mexico to the national and global levels. Communication is central to the Zapatistas' notion of revolution, and they continually emphasize the need to create horizontal network organizations rather than vertical centralized structures.[104] One should point out, of course, that this decentered organizational model stands at odds with the traditional military nomenclature of the EZLN. The Zapatistas, after all, call themselves an army and are organized in an array of military titles and ranks. When one looks more closely, however, one can see that although the Zapatistas adopt a traditional version of the Latin American guerrilla model, including its tendencies toward centralized military hierarchy, they continually in practice undercut those hierarchies and decenter authority with the elegant inversions and irony typical of their rhetoric. (In fact, they make irony itself into a political strategy.[105]) The paradoxical Zapatista motto "command obeying," for example, is aimed at inverting the traditional relationships of hierarchy within the organization. Leadership positions are rotated, and there seems to be a vacuum of authority at the center. Marcos, the primary spokesperson and quasi-mythical icon of the Zapatistas, has the rank of subcomandante to emphasize his relative subordination. Furthermore, their goal has never been to defeat the state and claim sovereign authority but rather to change the world without taking power.[106] The Zapatistas, in other words, adopt all the elements of the traditional structure and transform them, demonstrating in the clearest possible terms the nature and direction of the postmodern transition of organizational forms.

In the final decades of the twentieth century there also emerged, particularly in the United States, numerous movements that are often grouped under the rubric of "identity politics," which were born primarily of feminist struggles, gay and lesbian struggles, and race-based struggles.[107] The most important organizational characteristic of these various movements is their insistence on autonomy and their refusal of any centralized hierarchy, leaders, or spokespeople. The party, the people's army, the modern guerrilla force all appear bankrupt from their perspective because of the tendency of these structures to impose unity, to deny their differences and subordinate them to the interests of others. If there is no democratic form of political aggregation possible that allows us to retain our autonomy and affirm our differences, they announce, then we will remain separate, on our own. This emphasis on democratic organization and independence is also borne out in the internal structures of the movements, where we can see a variety of important experiments in collaborative decision-making, coordinated affinity groups, and so forth. In this regard, the resurgence of anarchist movements, especially in North America and Europe, has been very important for their emphasis on the need for freedom and democratic organization.[108] All of these experiences of democracy and autonomy, even at the smallest levels, provide an enormous wealth for the future development of movements.[109]

Finally, the globalization movements that have extended from Seattle to Genoa and the World Social Forums in Porto Alegre and Mumbai and have animated the movements against war are the clearest example to date of distributed network organizations. One of the most surprising elements of the events in Seattle in November 1999 and in each of the major such events since then is that groups we had previously assumed to have different and even contradictory interests managed to act in common—environmentalists with trade unionists, anarchists with church groups, gays and lesbians with those protesting the prison-industrial complex. The groups are not unified under any single authority but rather relate to each other in a network structure. Social forums, affinity groups, and other forms of democratic decision-making are the basis of the movements, and they manage to act together based on what they have in common. That is why they call themselves a "movement of movements." The full expression of autonomy and difference of each here coincides with the powerful articulation of all. Democracy defines both the goal of the movements and its constant activity. These globalization protest movements are obviously limited in many regards. First of all, although their vision and desire is global in scope, they have thus far only involved significant numbers in North America and Europe. Second, so long as they remain merely protest movements, traveling from one summit meeting to the next, they will be incapable of becoming a foundational struggle and of articulating an alternative social organization. These limitations may only be temporary obstacles, and the movements may discover ways to overcome them. What is most important for our argument here, however, is the form of the movements. These movements constitute the most developed example to date of the network model of organization.

This completes our genealogy of modern forms of resistance and civil war, which moved first from disparate guerrilla revolts and rebellions toward a unified model of people's army; second, from a centralized military structure to a polycentric guerrilla army; and finally from the polycentric model toward the distributed, or full-matrix, network structure. *This is the history at our backs.* It is in many respects a tragic history, full of brutal defeats, but it is also an extraordinarily rich legacy that pushes the desire for liberation into the future and bears crucially on the means for realizing it.

From our genealogy of modern resistance have emerged the three guiding principles or criteria that we mentioned at the beginning. The first guiding principal is the simple measure of efficacy in the specific historical situation. Each form of organization must grasp the opportunity and the historical occasion offered by the current arrangement of forces in order to maximize its ability to resist, contest, and/or overthrow the ruling forms of power. The second principle is the need for the form of political and military organization to correspond to the current forms of economic and social production. The forms of movements evolve in coordination with the evolution of economic forms. Finally and most important, democracy and freedom constantly act as guiding principles in the development of organizational forms of resistance. At various points in our history these three principles have conflicted with each other, in cases when, for example, it appeared that the internal democracy and independence of movements had to be sacrificed in order to maximize their efficacy or in others when efficacy had to be sacrificed in the interest of the democracy or autonomy of the movement. Today we have arrived at a point when the three principles coincide. The distributed network structure provides the model for an absolutely democratic organization that corresponds to the dominant forms of economic and social production and is also the most powerful weapon against the ruling power structure.[110]

In this network context legality itself becomes a less effective and less important criterion for distinguishing among resistance movements. Traditionally we have conceived separately those forms of resistance that acted "inside" and "outside" the law. *Within* the established legal norms, resistance served to neutralize the repressive effects of the law: labor strikes, active civil disobedience, and various other activities that contest economic and political authority constitute a first level of insubordination. At a second level, parties, trade unions, and other movements and representative bodies that straddle the present legal order, acting simultaneously *inside and outside* the law, created counterpowers that constantly challenged the ruling authorities. At a third level, *outside* of legality, organized resistances, including various people's armies and guerrilla movements, tried to break with and subvert the present order, opening spaces for the construction of a new society. Whereas these three levels of resistance required different organizations in the past, today network movements are able to address all of them simultaneously. Furthermore, in the network context the question of legality becomes increasingly undecidable. It may be impossible to say, for instance, whether a network of protesters at a summit meeting is acting legally or illegally when there is no central authority leading the protest and when protest actions are so varied and changing. In fact, and this is our main point, the most important differences among network resistances is not simply a question of legality. The best criteria for distinguishing among network movements, in fact, are the three principles we detailed above, particularly the demand for democracy. This gives us the means to differentiate clearly, for instance, among the groups that the current counterinsurgency theorists mistakenly group together. The counterinsurgency theorists of netwar link together the Zapatistas, the Intifada, the globalization protest movements, the Colombian drug cartels, and al-Qaeda. These diverse organizations are grouped together because they appear to be similarly immune to traditional counterinsurgency tactics. When we look at such contemporary forms of organization in the context of the criteria we have established, however, we can clearly recognize important distinctions. (There are many other important differences, of course, such as their use of violence, but these are the distinctions highlighted by our analysis in this section.) The Colombian drug cartels and al-Qaeda, for example, may look like networks from the perspective of counterinsurgency, but in fact they are highly centralized, with traditional vertical chains of command. Their organizational structures are not democratic at all. The Intifada and the Zapatistas, in contrast, as we have seen, do in some respects tend toward distributed network structures with no center of command and maximum autonomy of all the participating elements. Their center rather is their resistance to domination and their protest against poverty or, in positive terms, their struggle for a democratic organization of the biopolitical commons.

Now we need to return to the question of legitimation we raised earlier. It should be clear at this point that reproposing today the problem of how the needs of the proletariat can legitimate new forms of power or, to translate the question into a slightly different idiom, asking how class struggle can be transformed into social war or, rather still, translating again, asking how the interimperialist war can become the occasion for a revolutionary war—all these questions are old, tired, and faded. We believe that the multitude poses the problem of social resistance and the question of the legitimation of its own power and violence in terms that are completely different. Even the most advanced forms of resistance and civil war in modernity do not seem to offer us adequate elements for the solution of our problem. The Intifada, for example, is a form of struggle that corresponds at least superficially with some powerful characteristics of the movement of the multitude, such as mobility, flexibility, and the capacity to adapt to and challenge changing forms of repression in a radical way. The Intifada, however, can only allude to the form we are seeking, the strategic passage that leads the proletariat to take the form of the multitude, that is, a network body. The form of organization needed must deploy the full power of today's biopolitical production and also fully realize the promise of a democratic society.

Here we find ourselves in front of a sort of abyss, a strategic unknown. Every spatial, temporal, and political parameter of revolutionary decision-making à la Lenin has been destabilized, and the corresponding strategies have become completely impractical. Even the concept of "counterpower," which was so important for the strategies of resistance and revolution in the period around 1968, loses its force. All notions that pose the power of resistance as homologous or even similar to the power that oppresses us are of no more use. Here we should take a lesson from Pierre Clastres, who, while investigating the nature of war from an anthropological perspective, argues that we should never view the wars of the oppressors as the same as the wars of the oppressed. The wars of the oppressed, he explains, represent constituent movements aimed at defending society against those in power. The history of peoples with a history is, as they say, the history of class struggle; the history of peoples without a history is, we should say with at least as much conviction, the history of their struggle against the state.[111] We need to grasp the kind of struggles that Clastres sees and recognize their adequate form in our present age.

And yet we do already know some things that can help us orient our passion for resistance. In the first place, we know that today the legitimation of the global order is based fundamentally on war. Resisting war, and thus resisting the legitimation of this global order, therefore becomes a common ethical task. In the second place, we know that capitalist production and the life (and production) of the multitude are tied together increasingly intimately and are mutually determining. Capital depends on the multitude and yet is constantly thrown into crisis by the multitude's resistance to capital's command and authority. (This will be a central theme of part 2.) In the hand-to-hand combat of the multitude and Empire on the biopolitical field that pulls them together, when Empire calls on war for its legitimation, the multitude calls on democracy as its political foundation. This democracy that opposes war is an "absolute democracy." We can also call this democratic movement a process of "exodus," insofar as it involves the multitude breaking the ties that link imperial sovereign authority to the consent of the subordinated. (Absolute democracy and exodus will be central themes of chapter 3.)

SWARM INTELLIGENCE

When a distributed network attacks, it swarms its enemy: innumerable independent forces seem to strike from all directions at a particular point and then disappear back into the environment.[112] From an external perspective, the network attack is described as a swarm because it appears formless. Since the network has no center that dictates order, those who can only think in terms of traditional models may assume it has no organization whatsoever—they see mere spontaneity and anarchy. The network attack appears as something like a swarm of birds or insects in a horror film, a multitude of mindless assailants, unknown, uncertain, unseen, and unexpected. If one looks inside a network, however, one can see that it is indeed organized, rational, and creative. It has swarm intelligence.

Recent researchers in artificial intelligence and computational methods use the term swarm intelligence *to name collective and distributed techniques of problem solving without centralized control or the provision of a global model.[113] Part of the problem with much of the previous artificial intelligence research, they claim, is that it assumes intelligence to be based in an individual mind, whereas they assert that intelligence is fundamentally social. These researchers thus derive the notion of the swarm from the collective behavior of social animals, such as ants, bees, and termites, to investigate multi-agent-distributed systems of intelligence. Common animal behavior can give an initial approximation of this idea. Consider, for example, how tropical termites build magnificent, elaborate domed structures by communicating with each other; researchers hypothesize that each termite follows the pheromone concentration left by other termites in the swarm.[114] Although none of the individual termites has a high intelligence, the swarm of termites forms an intelligent system with no central control.* The intelligence of the swarm is based fundamentally on communication. *For researchers in artificial intelligence and computational methods, understanding this swarm behavior helps in writing algorithms to optimize problem-solving computations. Computers too can be designed to process information faster using swarm architecture rather than a conventional centralized processing model.*

The swarm model suggested by animal societies and developed by these researchers assumes that each of the agents or particles in the swarm is effectively the same and on its own not very creative. The swarms that we see emerging in the new network political organizations, in contrast, are composed of a multitude of different creative agents. This adds several more layers of complexity to the model. The members of the multitude do not have to become the same or renounce their creativity in order to communicate and cooperate with each other. They remain different in terms of race, sex, sexuality, and so forth. What we need to understand, then, is the collective intelligence that can emerge from the communication and cooperation of such a varied multiplicity.

Perhaps when we grasp the enormous potential of this swarm intelligence we can finally understand why the poet Arthur Rimbaud in his beautiful hymns to the Paris Commune in 1871 continually imagined the revolutionary Communards as insects. It is not uncommon, of course, to imagine enemy troops as insects. Recounting the events of the previous year, in fact, Emile Zola in his historical novel Le débâcle *describes the "black swarms" of Prussians overrunning the French positions at Sedan like invading ants, "un si noir fourmillement de troupes allemends."*[115] *Such insect metaphors for enemy swarms emphasize the inevitable defeat while maintaining the inferiority of the enemy—they are merely mindless insects. Rimbaud, however, takes this wartime cliché and inverts it, singing the praises of the swarm. The Communards defending their revolutionary Paris against the government forces attacking from Versailles roam about the city like ants* (fourmiller) *in Rimbaud's poetry and their barricades bustle with activity like anthills (*fourmilières*). Why would Rimbaud describe the Communards whom he loves and admires as swarming ants? When we look more closely we can see that all of Rimbaud's poetry is full of insects, particularly the sounds of insects, buzzing, swarming, teeming (*bourdonner, grouiller*). "Insect-verse" is how one reader describes Rimbaud's poetry, "music of the swarm."*[116] *The reawakening and reinvention of the senses in the youthful body—the centerpiece of Rimbaud's* *poetic world—takes place in the buzzing and swarming of the flesh. This is a new kind of intelligence, a collective intelligence, a swarm intelligence, that Rimbaud and the Communards anticipated.*

FROM BIOPOWER TO BIOPOLITICAL PRODUCTION

The genealogy of resistance we just completed—from people's armies and guerrilla bands to network movements—might easily appear too mechanical and neat. We do not want to give the impression that forms of resistance evolve through some natural evolution or in some preordained linear march toward absolute democracy. On the contrary, these historical processes are not predetermined in any way nor are they drawn forward by any ideal final goal of history. History develops in contradictory and aleatory ways, constantly subject to chance and accident. The moments of struggle and resistance emerge in unforeseen and unforeseeable ways.

We should also recognize that considering the genealogy of resistances only in terms of *form* as we have done primarily up to now is not sufficient. The formal differences among centralized armies, polycentric guerrilla bands, the distributed networks do provide one criterion for evaluating and distinguishing among resistance movements but not the only or most important one. Such formal differences between, say, the globalization movements and terrorist networks or between the Zapatistas and drug rings, only capture a small fraction of what is really different between them. We have to look not only at the form but also the content of what they do. The fact that a movement is organized as a network or swarm does not guarantee that it is peaceful or democratic. Moving beyond formal questions would also allow us to grapple better with the ambiguous nature of nationalist and religious forms of resistance. Nationalist and religious resistances are indeed most often based on centralized organizations and strong notions of identity, but they should not for that reason alone be considered reactionary or backward looking. Democracy is a matter not only of formal structures and relations but also of social contents, how we relate to each other, and how we produce together.

The parallel we have drawn between the evolution of resistances and that of economic production has also been limited by the focus on form. Looking only at the formal correspondence might give the impression that technological innovation is the primary force driving social change. We need to look now at the content of what is being produced, how, and by whom. Once we look inside production and recognize the conditions of labor and the bases of exploitation we will be able to see how resistances emerge in the workplace and how they change in step with the transformations of labor and all the relations of production. This will allow us to elaborate a much more substantial connection between production and resistances.

After having talked so much about war, we need now, in part 2, to turn to production and investigate the nature and divisions of the contemporary global economy. This will not be a strictly economic investigation, however, because we will find quickly that today in many respects economic production is at the same time cultural and political. We will argue that the dominant form of contemporary production, which exerts its hegemony over the others, creates "immaterial goods" such as ideas, knowledge, forms of communication, and relationships. In such immaterial labor, production spills over beyond the bounds of the economy traditionally conceived to engage culture, society, and politics directly. What is produced in this case is not just material goods but actual social relationships and forms of life. We will call this kind of production "biopolitical" to highlight how general its products are and how directly it engages social life in its entirety.

Earlier we spoke of "biopower" to explain how the current war regime not only threatens us with death but also rules over life, producing and reproducing all aspects of society. Now we will shift from biopower to biopolitical production. Both of them engage social life in its entirety— hence the common prefix *bio*—but they do so in very different ways. Biopower stands above society, transcendent, as a sovereign authority and imposes its order. Biopolitical production, in contrast, is immanent to society and creates social relationships and forms through collaborative forms of labor. Biopolitical production will give content to our investigation of democracy, which has remained too formal up to this point. It will also make clear the social basis on which it is possible today to begin a project of the multitude.

2. MULTITUDE

Political action aimed at transformation and liberation today can only be conducted on the basis of the multitude. To understand the concept of the multitude in its most general and abstract form, let us contrast it first with that of the people.[1] The people is one. The population, of course, is composed of numerous different individuals and classes, but the people synthesizes or reduces these social differences into one identity. The multitude, by contrast, is not unified but remains plural and multiple. This is why, according to the dominant tradition of political philosophy, the people can rule as a sovereign power and the multitude cannot. The multitude is composed of a set of *singularities*—and by singularity here we mean a social subject whose difference cannot be reduced to sameness, a difference that remains different. The component parts of the people are indifferent in their unity; they become an identity by negating or setting aside their differences. The plural singularities of the multitude thus stand in contrast to the undifferentiated unity of the people.

The multitude, however, although it remains multiple, is not fragmented, anarchical, or incoherent. The concept of the multitude should thus also be contrasted to a series of other concepts that designate plural collectives, such as the crowd, the masses, and the mob. Since the different individuals or groups that make up the crowd are incoherent and recognize no common shared elements, their collection of differences remains inert and can easily appear as one indifferent aggregate. The components of the masses, the mob, and the crowd are not singularities—and this is obvious from the fact that their differences so easily collapse into the indifference of the whole. Moreover, these social subjects are fundamentally passive in the sense that they cannot act by themselves but rather must be led. The crowd or the mob or the rabble can have social effects—often horribly destructive effects—but cannot act of their own accord. That is why they are so susceptible to external manipulation. The multitude, designates an active social subject, which acts on the basis of what the singularities share in common. The multitude is an internally different, multiple social subject whose constitution and action is based not on identity or unity (or, much less, indifference) but on what it has in common.

This initial conceptual definition of the multitude poses a clear challenge to the entire tradition of sovereignty. As we will explain in part 3, one of the recurring truths of political philosophy is that only the one can rule, be it the monarch, the party, the people, or the individual; social subjects that are not unified and remain multiple cannot rule and instead must be ruled. Every sovereign power, in other words, necessarily forms a *political body* of which there is a head that commands, limbs that obey, and organs that function together to support the ruler. The concept of the multitude challenges this accepted truth of sovereignty. The multitude, although it remains multiple and internally different, is able to act in common and thus rule itself. Rather than a political body with one that commands and others that obey, the multitude is *living flesh* that rules itself. This definition of the multitude, of course, raises numerous conceptual and practical problems, which we will discuss at length in this and the next chapter, but it should be clear from the outset that the challenge of the multitude is the challenge of democracy. The multitude is the only social subject capable of realizing democracy, that is, the rule of everyone by everyone. The stakes, in other words, are extremely high.

In this chapter we will articulate the concept of the multitude primarily from a socioeconomic perspective. Multitude is also a concept of race, gender, and sexuality differences. Our focus on economic class here should be considered in part as compensation for the relative lack of attention to class in recent years with respect to these other lines of social difference and hierarchy. As we will see the contemporary forms of production, which we will call biopolitical production, are not limited to economic phenomena but rather tend to involve all aspects of social life, including communication, knowledge, and affects. It is also useful to recognize from the beginning that something like a concept of the multitude has long been part of powerful streams of feminist and antiracist politics. When we say that we do not want a world without racial or gender difference but instead a world in which race and gender do not matter, that is, a world in which they do not determine hierarchies of power, a world in which differences express themselves freely, this is a desire for the multitude. And, of course, for the singularities that compose the multitude, in order to take away the limiting, negative, destructive character of differences and make differences our strength (gender differences, racial differences, differences of sexuality, and so forth) we must radically transform the world.[2]

From the socioeconomic perspective, the multitude is the common subject of labor, that is, the real flesh of postmodern production, and at the same time the object from which collective capital tries to make the body of its global development. Capital wants to make the multitude into an organic unity, just like the state wants to make it into a people. This is where, through the struggles of labor, the real productive biopolitical figure of the multitude begins to emerge. When the flesh of the multitude is imprisoned and transformed into the body of global capital, it finds itself both within and against the processes of capitalist globalization. The biopolitical production of the multitude, however, tends to mobilize what it shares in common and what it produces in common against the imperial power of global capital. In time, developing its productive figure based on the common, the multitude can move through Empire and come out the other side, to express itself autonomously and rule itself.

We should recognize from the outset the extent of capital's domain. Capital no longer rules merely over limited sites in society. As the impersonal rule of capital extends throughout society well beyond the factory walls and geographically throughout the globe, capitalist command tends to become a "non-place" or, really, an every place. There is no longer an outside to capital, nor is there an outside to the logics of biopower we described in part 1, and that correspondence is no coincidence, since capital and biopower function intimately together. The places of exploitation, by contrast, are always determinate and concrete, and therefore we need to understand exploitation on the basis of the specific sites where it is located and specific forms in which it is organized. This will allow us to articulate both a *topology* of the different figures of exploited labor and a *topography* of their spatial distribution across the globe. Such an analysis is useful because the place of exploitation is one important site where acts of refusal and exodus, resistance and struggle arise. This analysis will thus lead to the critique of the political economy of globalization based on the resistances to the formation of the body of global capital and the liberatory potentials of the common powers shared by global laboring multitude.

2.1 DANGEROUS CLASSES

Stalin's basic error is mistrust of the peasants.

—MAO ZEDONG

We are the poors! —PROTEST SLOGAN IN SOUTH AFRICA

THE BECOMING COMMON OF LABOR

Multitude is a class concept. Theories about economic class are traditionally forced to choose between unity and plurality. The unity pole is usually associated with Marx and his claim that in capitalist society there tends to be a simplification of class categories such that all forms of labor tend to merge into a single subject, the proletariat, which confronts capital. The plurality pole is most clearly illustrated by liberal arguments that insist on the ineluctable multiplicity of social classes. Both of these perspectives, in fact, are true. It is true, in the first case, that capitalist society is characterized by the division between capital and labor, between those who own productive property and those who do not and, furthermore, that the conditions of labor and the conditions of life of the propertyless tend to take on common characteristics. It is equally true, in the second case, that there is a potentially infinite number of classes that comprise contemporary society based not only on economic differences but also on those of race, ethnicity, geography, gender, sexuality, and other factors.

That both of these seemingly contradictory positions are true should indicate that the alternative itself may be false.[3] The mandate to choose between unity and multiplicity treats class as if it were merely an empirical concept and fails to take into consideration the extent to which class itself is defined politically.

Class is determined by class struggle. There are, of course, an infinite number of ways that humans can be grouped into classes—hair color, blood type, and so forth—but the classes that matter are those defined by the lines of collective struggle. Race is just as much a political concept as economic class is in this regard. Neither ethnicity nor skin color determine race; race is determined politically by collective struggle. Some maintain that race is created by racial oppression, as Jean-Paul Sartre, for example, claims that anti-Semitism produces the Jew. This logic should be taken one step further: race arises through the collective resistance to racial oppression. Economic class is formed similarly through collective acts of resistance. An investigation of economic class, then, like an investigation of race, should not begin with a mere catalog of empirical differences but rather with the lines of collective resistance to power. Class is a political concept, in short, in that a class is and can only be a collectivity that struggles in common.

Class is also a political concept in a second respect: a theory of class not only reflects the existing lines of class struggle, it also proposes potential future lines. The task of a theory of class in this respect is to identify the existing *conditions* for potential collective struggle and express them as a political *proposition*. Class is really a constituent deployment, a project. This is clearly how one should read Marx's claim about the tendency toward a binary model of class structures in capitalist society. The empirical claim here is not that society is already characterized by a single class of labor confronted by a single class of capital. In Marx's historical writings, for example, his analysis treats separately numerous classes of labor and capital. The empirical claim of Marx's class theory is that the conditions exist that make a single class of labor possible. This claim is really part of a political proposal for the unification of the struggles of labor in the proletariat as class. This political project is what most fundamentally divides Marx's binary class conception from the liberal models of class pluralism.

At this point, in fact, the old distinction between economic and political struggles becomes merely an obstacle to understanding class relations. Class is really a biopolitical concept that is at once economic and political.[4] When we say biopolitical, furthermore, this also means that our understanding of labor cannot be limited to waged labor but must refer to human creative capacities in all their generality. The poor, as we will argue, are thus not excluded from this conception of class but central to it.

The concept of multitude, then, is meant in one respect to demonstrate that a theory of economic class need not choose between unity and plurality. A multitude is an irreducible multiplicity; the singular social differences that constitute the multitude must always be expressed and can never be flattened into sameness, unity, identity, or indifference. The multitude is not merely a fragmented and dispersed multiplicity. It is true, of course, that in our postmodern social life old identities have broken apart. We will discuss later in this chapter, for example, how the compact identities of factory workers in the dominant countries have been undermined with the rise of short-term contracts and the forced mobility of new forms of work; how migration has challenged traditional notions of national identity; how family identity has changed; and so forth. The fracturing of modern identities, however, does not prevent the singularities from acting in common. This is the definition of the multitude we started from above: singularities that act in common. The key to this definition is the fact that there is no conceptual or actual contradiction between singularity and commonality.

In a second respect the concept of multitude is meant to repropose Marx's political project of class struggle. The multitude from this perspective is based not so much on the current empirical existence of the class but rather on its conditions of possibility. The question to ask, in other words, is not "What is the multitude?" but rather "What can the multitude become?" Such a political project must clearly be grounded in an empirical analysis that demonstrates the common conditions of those who can become the multitude. Common conditions, of course, does not mean sameness or unity, but it does require that no differences of nature or kind divide the multitude. It means, in other words, that the innumerable, specific types of labor, forms of life, and geographical location, which will always necessarily remain, do not prohibit communication and collaboration in a common political project. This possible common project, in fact, bears some similarities to that of a series of nineteenth-century poet-philosophers, from Hölderlin and Leopardi to Rimbaud, who took up the ancient notion of the human struggle against nature and transformed it into an element of solidarity of all those who revolt against exploitation. (Indeed their situation facing the crisis of Enlightenment and revolutionary thought is not so different from our own.) From the struggle against the limits, scarcity, and cruelty of nature toward the surplus and abundance of human productivity: this is the material basis of a real common project that these poet-philosophers prophetically invoked.[5]

One initial approach is to conceive the multitude as all those who work under the rule of capital and thus potentially as the class of those who refuse the rule of capital. The concept of the multitude is thus very different from that of the working class, at least as that concept came to be used in the nineteenth and twentieth centuries. Working class is fundamentally a restricted concept based on exclusions. In its most limited conception, the working class refers only to industrial labor and thus excludes all other laboring classes. At its most broad, the working class refers to all waged laborers and thus excludes the various unwaged classes. The exclusions of other forms of labor from the working class are based on the notion that there are differences of kind between, for example, male industrial labor and female reproductive labor, between industrial labor and peasant labor, between the employed and the unemployed, between workers and the poor. The working class is thought to be the primary productive class and directly under the rule of capital, and thus the only subject that can act effectively against capital. The other exploited classes might also struggle against capital but only subordinated to the leadership of the working class. Whether or not this was the case in the past, the concept of multitude rests on the fact that it is not true today. The concept rests, in other words, on the claim that there is no political priority among the forms of labor: all forms of labor are today socially productive, they produce in common, and share too a common potential to resist the domination of capital. Think of it as the equal opportunity of resistance. This is not to say, we should be clear, that industrial labor or the working class are not important but rather merely that they hold no political privilege with respect to other classes of labor within the multitude. In contrast to the exclusions that characterize the concept of the working class, then, the multitude is an open and expansive concept. The multitude gives the concept of the proletariat its fullest definition as all those who labor and produce under the rule of capital. In order to verify this concept of the multitude and its political project we will have to establish that indeed the differences of kind that used to divide labor no longer apply; in other words, that the conditions exist for the various types of labor to communicate, collaborate, and become common.

Before turning to figures of labor that have traditionally been excluded from the working class we should consider briefly first the general lines along which the working class itself has changed, particularly with respect to its hegemonic position in the economy. In any economic system there are numerous different forms of labor that exist side by side, but there is always one figure of labor that exerts hegemony over the others. This hegemonic figure serves as a vortex that gradually transforms other figures to adopt its central qualities. The hegemonic figure is not dominant in quantitative terms but rather in the way it exerts a power of transformation over others. Hegemony here designates a tendency.

In the nineteenth and twentieth centuries, industrial labor was hegemonic in the global economy even though it remained a minority in quantitative terms with respect to other forms of production such as agriculture.[6] Industry was hegemonic insofar as it pulled other forms into its vortex: agriculture, mining, and even society itself were forced to industrialize. Not only the mechanical practices but also the rhythms of life of industrial labor and its working day gradually transformed all other social institutions, such as the family, the school, and the military. The transformed laboring practices, in fields such as industrialized agriculture, of course, always remained different from industry, but they also increasingly shared elements in common. That is the aspect of this process that interests us most: the multiplicity of specific concrete forms of labor remain different, but it tends to accumulate an ever greater number of common elements.

In the final decades of the twentieth century, industrial labor lost its hegemony and in its stead emerged "immaterial labor," that is, labor that creates immaterial products, such as knowledge, information, communication, a relationship, or an emotional response.[7] Conventional terms such as *service work*, *intellectual labor*, and *cognitive labor* all refer to aspects of immaterial labor, but none of them captures its generality. As an initial approach, one can conceive immaterial labor in two principle forms. The first form refers to labor that is primarily intellectual or linguistic, such as problem solving, symbolic and analytical tasks, and linguistic expressions.[8] This kind of immaterial labor produces ideas, symbols, codes, texts, linguistic figures, images, and other such products. We call the other principle form of immaterial labor "affective labor." Unlike emotions, which are mental phenomena, affects refer equally to body and mind. In fact, affects, such as joy and sadness, reveal the present state of life in the entire organism, expressing a certain state of the body along with a certain mode of thinking.[9] Affective labor, then, is labor that produces or manipulates affects such as a feeling of ease, well-being, satisfaction, excitement, or passion. One can recognize affective labor, for example, in the work of legal assistants, flight attendants, and fast food workers (service with a smile). One indication of the rising importance of affective labor, at least in the dominant countries, is the tendency for employers to highlight education, attitude, character, and "prosocial" behavior as the primary skills employees need.[10] A worker with a good attitude and social skills is another way of saying a worker adept at affective labor.

Most actual jobs involving immaterial labor combine these two forms. The creation of communication, for instance, is certainly a linguistic and intellectual operation but also inevitably has an affective component in the relationship between the communicating parties. It is common to say that journalists and the media in general not only report information but also must make the news attractive, exciting, desirable; the media must create affects and forms of life.[11] All forms of communication, in fact, combine the production of symbols, language, and information with the production of affect. In addition, immaterial labor almost always mixes with material forms of labor: health care workers, for example, perform affective, cognitive, and linguistic tasks together with material ones, such as cleaning bedpans and changing bandages.

The labor involved in all immaterial production, we should emphasize, remains material—it involves our bodies and brains as all labor does. What is immaterial is *its product*. We recognize that *immaterial labor* is a very ambiguous term in this regard. It might be better to understand the new hegemonic form as "biopolitical labor," that is, labor that creates not only material goods but also relationships and ultimately social life itself. The term *biopolitical* thus indicates that the traditional distinctions between the economic, the political, the social, and the cultural become increasingly blurred. Biopolitics, however, presents numerous additional conceptual complexities, and thus in our view the notion of immateriality, despite its ambiguities, seems easier to grasp initially and better at indicating the general tendency of economic transformation.

When we claim that immaterial labor is tending toward the hegemonic position we are not saying that most of the workers in the world today are producing primarily immaterial goods. On the contrary, agricultural labor remains, as it has for centuries, dominant in quantitative terms, and industrial labor has not declined in terms of numbers globally. Immaterial labor constitutes a minority of global labor, and it is concentrated in some of the dominant regions of the globe. Our claim, rather, is that immaterial labor has become *hegemonic in qualitative terms* and has imposed a tendency on other forms of labor and society itself. Immaterial labor, in other words, is today in the same position that industrial labor was 150 years ago, when it accounted for only a small fraction of global production and was concentrated in a small part of the world but nonetheless exerted hegemony over all other forms of production. Just as in that phase all forms of labor and society itself had to industrialize, today labor and society have to informationalize, become intelligent, become communicative, become affective.

In some respects, the classes subordinated in the period of industrial hegemony provide the key to understanding the principle characteristics of the hegemony of immaterial labor. Agriculturists, on one hand, have always used the knowledge, intelligence, and innovation typical of immaterial labor. Certainly agricultural work is extraordinarily strenuous physically—the earth is low, as anyone who has worked in the fields will tell you—but agriculture is also a science. Every agriculturist is a chemist, matching soil types with the right crops, transforming fruit and milk into wine and cheese; a genetic biologist, selecting the best seeds to improve plant varieties; and a meteorologist, watching the skies. The agriculturist must know the earth and work with it, according to its rhythms. Determining the exact best day to plant or harvest a crop is a complex calculation. This is not a spontaneous act of intuition or a rote repetition of the past but a decision based on traditional knowledges in relation to observed present conditions, constantly renovated through intelligence and experimentation. (In a similar way many agriculturists also have to be financial brokers, reading the constant fluctuation of markets for the best time to sell their products.) This kind of open science typical of agriculture that moves with the unpredictable changes of nature suggests the types of knowledge central to immaterial labor rather than the mechanistic sciences of the factory.

Another form of labor subordinated under the industrial hegemony, on the other hand, what has been traditionally called "women's work," particularly reproductive labor in the home, demonstrates not only that same kind of open science of knowledges and intelligence closely tied to nature but also the affective labor central to immaterial production. Socialist feminist scholars have described this affective labor using terms such as *kin work*, *caring labor*, and *maternal work*.[12] Certainly domestic labor does require such repetitive material tasks as cleaning and cooking, but it also involves producing affects, relationships, and forms of communication and cooperation among children, in the family, and in the community. Affective labor is biopolitical production in that it directly produces social relationships and forms of life.

The affective labor that feminists have recognized and the knowledges and intelligence typical of agricultural labor both provide important keys to understanding the characteristics of the immaterial paradigm, but this does not mean that agriculturists or women are better off under the hegemony of immaterial labor. On the one hand, agriculturists, for all their intelligence and knowledges, remain tied to the soil and, as we will see shortly, suffer ever more brutal forms of exploitation in the global economy. On the other hand, when affective labor becomes central to many productive tasks under the hegemony of immaterial labor it is still most often performed by women in subordinate positions. Indeed labor with a high affective component is generally feminized, given less authority, and paid less. Women employed as paralegals and nurses, for example, not only do the affective labor of constructing relationships with patients and clients and that of managing office dynamics, but they are also caregivers for their bosses, the lawyers and doctors, who are largely male. (The strikes and demonstrations of nurses in France in the early 1990s illustrated well the gender basis of the exploitation of affective and material labor.[13]) Furthermore, when affective production becomes part of waged labor it can be experienced as extremely alienating: I am selling my ability to make human relationships, something extremely intimate, at the command of the client and the boss.[14] Alienation was always a poor concept for understanding the exploitation of factory workers, but here in a realm that many still do not want to consider labor—affective labor, as well as knowledge production and symbolic production—alienation does provide a useful conceptual key for understanding exploitation.

The hegemony of immaterial labor, then, does not make all work pleasant or rewarding, nor does it lessen the hierarchy and command in the workplace or the polarization of the labor market. Our notion of immaterial labor should not be confused with the utopian dreams in the 1990s of a "new economy" that, largely through technological innovations, globalization, and rising stock markets, was thought by some to have made all work interesting and satisfying, democratized wealth, and banished recessions to the past.[15] The hegemony of immaterial labor does, though, tend to change the conditions of work. Consider, for example, the transformation of the working day in the immaterial paradigm, that is, the increasingly indefinite division between work time and leisure time. In the industrial paradigm workers produced almost exclusively during the hours in the factory. When production is aimed at solving a problem, however, or creating an idea or a relationship, work time tends to expand to the entire time of life. An idea or an image comes to you not only in the office but also in the shower or in your dreams. Once again, the traditional characteristics of agriculture and domestic labor can help us understand this shift. Agricultural labor, of course, traditionally has no time clocks in the fields: the working day stretches from dawn to dusk when necessary. Traditional arrangements of women's domestic labor even more clearly destroy the divisions of the working day and expand to fill all of life.

Some economists also use the terms *Fordism* and *post-Fordism* to mark the shift from an economy characterized by the stable long-term employment typical of factory workers to one marked by flexible, mobile, and precarious labor relations: *flexible* because workers have to adapt to different tasks, *mobile* because workers have to move frequently between jobs, and *precarious* because no contracts guarantee stable, long-term employment.[16] Whereas economic modernization, which developed Fordist labor relations, centered on the economies of scale and large systems of production and exchange, economic postmodernization, with its post-Fordist labor relations, develops smaller-scale, flexible systems. The basic economic ideology that runs throughout postmodernization is based on the notion that efficiency is hindered by monolithic systems of production and mass exchange and enhanced instead by production systems that respond rapidly and differentiated market schemes that target specialized strategies. An emerging post-Fordist form of agricultural production, for example, is characterized by such technological shifts. Agricultural modernization relied heavily on mechanical technologies, from the Soviet tractor to the California irrigation systems, but agricultural postmodernization develops biological and biochemical innovations, along with specialized systems of production, such as greenhouses, artificial lighting, and soilless agriculture.[17] These new techniques and technologies tend to move agricultural production away from large-scale production and allow for more specialized, small-scale operations. Furthermore, in the same way that postmodern industrial production is being informationalized, through the integration, for instance, of communication technologies into existing industrial processes, agriculture too is being informationalized, most clearly at the level of the seed. One of the most interesting struggles in agriculture, for example, which we will discuss in more detail later, is over who owns plant germplasm, that is, the genetic information encased in the seed. Seed corporations patent the new plant varieties they create, often today through genetic engineering, but farmers have long discovered, conserved, and improved plant genetic resources without any comparable legal claim to ownership. The Food and Agriculture Organization of the United Nations (FAO) has thus proposed the concept of Farmers' Rights to plant genetic resources that is meant to balance the Plant Breeders' Rights.[18] Our aim here is not to praise or condemn these practices—some scientific interventions in agriculture are beneficial and others detrimental. Our primary point is simply that the process of agricultural change and the struggle over rights are increasingly dependent on the control and production of information, specifically plant genetic information. That is one way in which agriculture is being informationalized.

In general, the hegemony of immaterial labor tends to transform the organization of production from the linear relationships of the assembly line to the innumerable and indeterminate relationships of distributed networks. Information, communication, and cooperation become the norms of production, and the network becomes its dominant form of organization. The technical systems of production therefore correspond closely to its social composition: on one side the technological networks and on the other the cooperation of social subjects put to work. This correspondence defines the new topology of labor and also characterizes the new practices and structures of exploitation. We will argue below in excursus 1 that exploitation under the hegemony of immaterial labor is no longer primarily the expropriation of value measured by individual or collective labor time but rather the capture of value that is produced by cooperative labor and that becomes increasingly common through its circulation in social networks. The central forms of productive cooperation are no longer created by the capitalist as part of the project to organize labor but rather emerge from the productive energies of labor itself. This is indeed the key characteristic of immaterial labor: to produce communication, social relations, and cooperation.

The hegemony of immaterial labor creates common relationships and common social forms in a way more pronounced than ever before. Every hegemonic form of labor, of course, creates common elements: just as economic modernization and the hegemony of industrial labor brought agriculture and all other sectors in line with the technologies, practices, and basic economic relations of industry, economic postmodernization and the hegemony of immaterial labor have similarly common transformative effects, as we have said. In part this is a matter of newly created bases of commonality and in part it is that we can recognize more clearly today bases of commonality that have long existed, such as the role of information and scientific knowledges in agriculture. The difference of immaterial labor, however, is that its products are themselves, in many respects, immediately social and common. Producing communication, affective relationships, and knowledges, in contrast to cars and typewriters, can directly expand the realm of what we share in common. This is not to say, we repeat, that the conditions of labor and production are becoming *the same* throughout the world or throughout the different sectors of the economy. The claim rather is that the many singular instances of labor processes, productive conditions, local situations, and lived experiences coexist with a "becoming common," at a different level of abstraction, of the forms of labor and the general relations of production and exchange— and that there is no contradiction between this singularity and commonality. This becoming common, which tends to reduce the qualitative divisions within labor, is the biopolitical condition of the multitude.

Reality check: what evidence do we have to substantiate our claim of a hegemony of immaterial labor? We have already said that since this claim involves a tendency it is not a question of immaterial labor being dominant today in quantitative terms. The first and most concrete evidence we have are the trends in employment. In the dominant countries, immaterial labor is central to most of what statistics show are the fastest-growing occupations, such as food servers, salespersons, computer engineers, teachers, and health workers.[19] There is a corresponding trend for many forms of material production, such as industry and agriculture, to be transferred to subordinate parts of the world. These employment trends show that the hegemony of immaterial labor is emerging in coordination with the existing global divisions of labor and power. A second type of evidence, which has to be viewed in more qualitative terms, is that other forms of labor and production are adopting the characteristics of immaterial production.

Not only have computers been integrated into all kinds of production but more generally communication mechanisms, information, knowledges, and affect are transforming traditional productive practices, the way control of information in seeds, for example, is affecting agriculture. Third, the centrality of immaterial labor is reflected in the growing importance of the immaterial forms of property that it produces. We will analyze later the complex legal issues raised with regard to patents, copyright, and various immaterial goods that have recently become eligible to be protected as private property. Finally, the most abstract and most general evidence is that the distributed network form that is typical of immaterial production is springing up throughout social life as the way to understand everything from neural functions to terrorist organizations. This is the ultimate role of a hegemonic form of production: to transform all of society in its image, a tendency that no statistics can capture. The real demonstration of this tendency, in fact, is the becoming biopolitical of production.

THE TWILIGHT OF THE PEASANT WORLD

The figure of the peasant may pose the greatest challenge for the concept of the multitude because there is such an enormous weight of economic, cultural, and political history that positions it as outside of and qualitatively different from the industrial working class and other laboring classes. It is a commonplace, in fact, to conceive of peasants and village life as unchanged for centuries and even millennia.[20] What could be more eternal and basic to humanity than the figure of the peasant in close interaction with the earth, working the soil and producing food? We should be clear that not all agriculturists are peasants; the peasant is a historical figure that designates a certain way of working the soil and producing within a specific set of social relationships. The peasantry came into being and will eventually cease to exist. This does not mean that there will no longer be agricultural production or rural life or the like. It means rather that the conditions of agricultural production change, and specifically, we will argue, that they become common to those of mining, industry, immaterial production, and other forms of labor in such a way that agriculture communicates with other forms of production and no longer poses a qualitatively different, isolated form of production and life. Agriculture, along with all other sectors, becomes increasingly biopolitical. This becoming common, as we said, is one condition that makes possible the existence of the multitude.

Peasantry is primarily an economic concept that denotes a specific position within the relations of production and exchange. Peasants can be defined in a first approximation as those who labor on the land, produce primarily for their own consumption, are partially integrated and subordinated within a larger economic system, and either own or have access to the necessary land and equipment.[21] The two central axes of the definition, then, have to do with property ownership and market relations. It is worth emphasizing to avoid confusion that peasant communities are not isolated economically as were some traditional forms of agricultural production; nor are they integrated fully into national or global markets as are capitalist farmers. They stand in a middle position of partial integration in which their production is primarily but not exclusively oriented toward their own consumption.[22]

Peasantry, however, by this commonly accepted definition, is not yet precise enough because it does not differentiate sufficiently with respect to property. Mao Zedong, for one, recognized during his early investigations of the Chinese peasantry that to make sense of the economic term politically he had to divide the peasantry according to land ownership into three categories: rich peasants, who own extensive land and equipment and hire others to help them work the land; middle peasants, who own sufficient land and equipment and rely primarily on the labor of their own family; and poor peasants, who rent land or sharecrop and often have to sell some of their labor to others.[23] The fundamental division in Mao's analysis between the peasants who own property and those who do not creates a centrifugal tendency at each end of the classification: at the top the rich peasants are very close to the landlords because they own sufficient property to employ others, and at the bottom the poor peasants are little different than agricultural workers because they own no property or insufficient property.

The so-called middle peasants stand out in this analysis as the most discrete and independent category, conceptually and socially. Perhaps for this reason middle peasants define the concept of peasantry as a whole in many common formulations, so that peasants are understood in economic terms as self-sufficient, small-holding agricultural producers. The historical tendency of the changes in class composition of the peasantry through the modern era reduces dramatically the numbers of the middle peasantry, corresponding to the centrifugal conceptual tendency in Mao's analysis. At the top end a few rich peasants manage to gain more land and become indistinguishable from landowners, and at the bottom most poor peasants tend to be excluded from their traditional forms of land tenure (such as sharecropping) and become simple agricultural laborers. Middle peasants all but vanished in the process, being forced to fall one way or the other along the general cleavage of ownership.

This centrifugal historical tendency corresponds to the processes of modernization in both its capitalist and socialist forms. When Stalin launched the program of collectivization, the Soviet regime thought the strategy would boost agricultural production through economies of scale and facilitate the use of more advanced equipment and technologies: collectivization, in short, would bring tractors to the farm.[24] The cruel process of collectivization was clearly understood from the beginning—not only by the leaders but also by the peasants themselves—as a war not simply against the rich peasants, the *kulaks*, who were accused of hoarding grain, but against all the peasants who owned property, and really against the entire peasantry as a class. In the short term the process of collectivization was certainly not a success in terms of agricultural productivity and efficiency (the fierce resistance of the peasants guaranteed that failure[25]), and it may not have succeeded in realizing the economies of scale either in the long term—that is a matter of debate that was long clouded by cold war propaganda. Our primary point here is that the socialist modernization of agriculture, which the Chinese to a large extent adopted and repeated,[26] not only brought tractors to the countryside but, more important, irreversibly transformed the agricultural relations of production and exchange, ultimately eliminating the peasantry as an economic class. It makes little sense to continue to use the term *peasant* to name the agricultural worker on a massive collective or state farm who owns no property and produces food to be distributed on a national scale. Nor does it make sense to continue to call "peasants" the populations that have left the fields to work in the factories. Furthermore, subsequent processes of decollectivization of agricultural production in the post-Soviet and post-Mao eras have in various degrees reestablished private ownership of the land but they have not reconstructed the relations of exchange that define the peasantry, that is, production primarily for the family's own consumption and partial integration into larger markets. The transformation of state and collective property toward forms of private property is not a return to the peasantry and the way things were but the creation of a new condition linked to the global capitalist relations of production and exchange.[27]

The transformation of agricultural relations of production in the capitalist countries took a different route, or really several different routes, but arrived at a similar conclusion. In the United States, for example, the capitalist market (and ultimately the banks) declared small-holding agricultural production to be unviable in the early twentieth century and provoked a massive population shift from rural to urban and semiurban areas. The radical consolidation of property in large farms and ultimately in the hands of huge agribusiness corporations was accompanied by a great leap forward in productivity through water management, mechanization, chemical treatment, and so forth. The family farm and all independent, small-scale agricultural producers quickly disappeared.[28] Like the Joad family in John Steinbeck's *Grapes of Wrath*, farmers were forced from the land and compelled to pack up and make out the best they could. In Europe the process was more varied and took place over a longer period. In England, for example, agricultural land was consolidated into large estates in the early modern period, whereas small-scale ownership long remained in France. There was also a significant difference between the continuing serfdom in eastern Europe and the relative freedom of agricultural labor in western Europe.[29] By the end of the twentieth century, however, even the small agricultural ownership that remained was so embedded in the national and global relations of exchange that it could no longer be considered peasant.[30]

The history of the peasantry and agricultural production in the subordinated capitalist countries is much more complex. One should keep in mind, first of all, that in many areas peasant relations of production and exchange are a relatively recent phenomenon created by the European colonizers. Before the colonial intrusion agricultural property was in most cases owned collectively and the communities were almost completely self-sufficient and isolated economically.[31] The colonial powers destroyed the systems of collective ownership, introduced capitalist private property, and integrated local agricultural production partially into much larger economic markets—thereby creating conditions that resembled what in Europe was known as peasant production and exchange.[32] A very small portion of the rural population in Asia, Africa, and Latin America, however, have ever fit comfortably into the ideologically central category of middle peasant—independent, small-holding farmers who produce primarily for their own consumption. Latin American agriculture, for example, has been dominated at least since the nineteenth century by an extreme polarization of land ownership, with at one end huge *latifundio* estates that employ numerous families and at the other landless workers or farmers with holdings too small and infertile to support themselves. Land reform, which was a liberal and revolutionary battle cry in Latin America throughout the twentieth century, from Zapata's ragged troops to guerilla revolutionaries in Nicaragua and El Salvador, held something like the figure of the middle peasant as its goal. Aside from a few brief exceptions, most notably in Mexico and Bolivia, the tendency in Latin America has constantly moved in the opposite direction, exacerbating the polarization of land tenure and ownership.[33]

Throughout the subordinated capitalist world small-holding agricultural producers are systematically deprived of land rights as property is gradually consolidated into large holdings, controlled either by national landowners or mammoth foreign corporations.[34] This process may appear as a haphazard and undirected movement carried out by an extended and disunited series of agents, including national governments, foreign governments, multinational and transnational agribusiness corporations, the World Bank, the International Monetary Fund (IMF), and many others. At a more abstract and fundamental level, as we will see in chapter 2.2,

"De Corpore," these various agents are united by a common ideology, which spans from capitalist modernization to neoliberalism and global economic integration. According to this economic ideology, small-holding subsistence agriculture is economically backward and inefficient, not only because of its technological and mechanical limitations but also and more importantly because of its relations of exchange. In a globally integrated market, according to this view, an economic actor in agriculture or any other sector can survive only by focusing productive energies on a single commodity it can produce better than others and distribute on a wide scale. The resulting export-oriented single-crop agriculture inevitably mandates large-scale production and the concentration of ownership. Capitalist collectivization has thus tended toward creating a virtual monopoly of the soil with huge units of agricultural production employing armies of agricultural workers that produce for the world market.[35] Outside of this is left a growing rural poor that owns either no land or insufficient land for survival.

The figure of the peasant has thus throughout the world faded into the background of the economic landscape of agriculture, which tends to be populated now by huge corporations, agricultural workers, and an increasingly desperate rural poor. The great movement of modernization in both its socialist and capitalist forms has been one of general convergence. Since the 1970s some authors have emphasized the growing similarities between agriculturists and the industrial working class, that is, the proletarianization of agricultural labor and the creation of "factories in the fields."[36] One should be careful, however, not to conceive of this as a process of the homogenization of productive practices and forms of life. Agriculturists have not become the *same* as the industrial working class. Agricultural labor is still utterly different from mining, industrial labor, service labor, and other forms of labor. Agricultural life has a unique relationship to the earth and develops a symbiotic relationship with the life of the elements—soil, water, sunshine, air. (And here we can recognize clearly the potential for agriculture to become biopolitical.) Agriculture is and will always remain a singular form of production and life, and yet— this has been our primary point—the processes of modernization have created common relations of production and exchange that agriculture and other forms of production share.

This disappearance of the figure of the peasant, which we have described in economic terms, can also be recognized from a cultural standpoint. This gives us another perspective on the same process. Much of modern European literature up to the nineteenth and twentieth centuries, for example, centered on the peasant world—not so much on the peasantry as a social class but more often on all the complementary social formations it made possible, such as the knowable community of country manor houses, the urban aristocratic circuit of salons and leisure, and the limited horizons of village life.[37] In fact the peasants themselves were not as important in European literature as was the traditional rural life in which the peasants, like the land, played the role of natural and stable backdrop. This peasant world was linked to the innocence and naturalness of traditional social arrangements—class divisions, relations of property and production, and so forth—that were really, of course, neither innocent nor natural. First in England and then throughout Europe, however, there was a growing recognition that this happy rural peasant world had disappeared or was fast in the process of disappearing. And yet long after it had disappeared in reality the peasant world remained in European literature in the form of nostalgia for times gone by, for a corresponding traditional structure of feeling, set of values, or form of life.[38] This European cultural figure of the traditional peasant world, and even the nostalgia for it, eventually came to an end. One explanation of the passage from realism to modernism, a common trope in European literary studies and art history, points to the end of the peasant world: when the proximate past of the peasant world is no longer accessible, many European authors and artists shift to the more archaic past of the primitive and the mythical. The birth of modernism, in other words, according to this conception, is the discovery of an ancient, immemorial past, a kind of eternal primitive of the psyche or myth or instinct. D. H. Lawrence, T. S. Eliot, and Michel Leiris, along with Paul Gauguin, Henri Matisse, and Pablo Picasso, to cite only some of the most obvious examples, adopt figures of primitive existence and being as elements in their aesthetic constructions. This tension between primitivism and constructedness is indeed one characteristic that defines modernism.[39]

Whereas in modern European literature and art we can trace a cultural movement from the peasant to the primitive, the history of anthropology moves in the opposite direction, from the primitive to the peasant.[40] Classical anthropology was born in the late nineteenth century on the basis of the binary division between the European self and the primitive other, but in the middle of the twentieth century this was displaced by a different binary couple, European self–peasant other, which served as the foundation of much of modern anthropology. One important aspect of the shift from primitive to peasant is a new conception of otherness: whereas the anthropological fascination with the primitive poses a relationship of extreme difference and strangeness, the peasant is a familiar and proximate figure, and with this shift the degree of otherness is reduced. Eventually, as the economic figure of the peasant, which always stood on a tenuous footing outside of Europe, loses validity in the final decades of the twentieth century, the anthropological paradigm of the peasant too goes into crisis. The field of anthropology today at the beginning of the twenty-first century is moving beyond its modern paradigm and developing a new conception of difference, which we will return to later.

Finally, in addition to its economic and cultural aspects, the peasant is also a political figure or, rather, in many conceptions, a nonpolitical figure, disqualified from politics.[41] This does not mean that peasants do not rebel against their own subordination and exploitation, because indeed modern history is punctuated by massive explosions of peasant rebellion and marked too by a continuous stream of small-scale peasant resistances. It does not mean either that the peasantry does not play an important political role. It means that the peasantry is fundamentally conservative, isolated, and capable only of reaction, not of any autonomous political action of its own. As we saw in part 1, peasant wars, according to this view, at least since the sixteenth century, have been primarily telluric, tied to the defense of the soil and aimed at preserving tradition.

Marx claimed that the political passivity of the peasantry is due to its lack of both communication and large-scale circuits of social cooperation. The French small-holding peasant communities that Marx studied in the mid-nineteenth century were dispersed in the countryside and remained separate and isolated. Their inability to communicate is why Marx believed that the peasants cannot represent themselves (and must therefore be represented).[42] In Marx's view, political subjectivity requires of a class not only self-representation but first and most fundamentally internal communication. Communication, in this sense, is the key to the political significance of the traditional division between city and country and the political prejudice for urban political actors that followed from the nineteenth century into the twentieth. Not so much idiocy but incommunicability defined rural life. The circuits of communication that gave the urban working class a great political advantage over the rural peasantry were also due to the conditions of work. The industrial labor force, working in teams around a common machine, is defined by cooperation and communication, which allows it to become active and emerge as a political subject.

There was indeed a rich debate among socialists and communists in the nineteenth and twentieth centuries on the "agrarian question" and the role of the peasants in revolutionary politics. Marx himself proposed at one point basing a communist political project on the Russian peasant communes.[43] The major lines of Marxist and socialist thought, however, conceived of the peasantry as a class that could have revolutionary potential only by following the urban industrial proletariat—an unequal partnership in which the proletariat played the active, leading agent and the peasantry the passive body.[44] When the industrial proletariat has led and spoken for the peasantry, however, it has certainly not always been in the peasants' interest. This tragic history has taught us, once again, the injustice and dire consequences of one subject speaking for a subordinated other, even when that other is unable to speak for itself.[45]

It may seem that Mao Zedong is the figure that most clearly breaks with this Marxian line, but his declarations too, from the days of his early political activity through the period of revolutionary struggle, remain faithful to the two basic tenets of Marx's thinking on the political role of the peasantry: the peasantry is fundamentally passive and must be allied with and led by the only properly political revolutionary subject, the industrial proletariat.[46] The twentieth-century Chinese peasantry is no less isolated and no more communicative than the peasants Marx studied in nineteenth-century France. Mao recognized that in the context of Chinese society, with such a small industrial proletariat and such a large peasantry, the political engagement of the peasantry had to be much more extensive than elsewhere—and indeed that the Chinese revolution would have to invent a peasant form of communist revolution. The role of the peasantry in China up to this point is really only quantitatively different from its role in previous communist revolutionary struggles. The Chinese revolution itself was really a revolution conducted *with* the peasantry, not a revolution *by* the peasantry. The qualitative difference emerged only later. During the revolutionary struggle and increasingly during the periods of the Great Leap and the Cultural Revolution, Mao's political focus turned toward the peasantry—not toward the peasants *as they were* but toward the peasants *as they could be*.[47] The essence of the Maoist project was the effort to transform the peasants politically. The peasants, through the long revolutionary process in its various phases, overcome the passivity and isolation that Marx had recognized; the peasants become communicative, cooperative, and articulate as an active collective subject. This is the primary sense in which the Maoist project is applicable throughout the world: wars and struggles of peasants should no longer be oriented toward the defense of the soil in a strictly conservative relationship. They should instead become biopolitical struggles aimed at transforming social life in its entirety. As the peasantry becomes communicative and active it ceases to exist as a separate political category, causing a decline in the political significance of the division between town and country.[48] Paradoxically, *the final victory of the peasant revolution is the end of the peasantry* (as a separate political category). In other words, the ultimate political goal of the peasantry is its own destruction as a class.[49]

The figure of the peasant that emerges from its passive and isolated state, like a butterfly emerging from its chrysalis, discovers itself to be part of the multitude, one of numerous singular figures of labor and forms of life that despite their differences share common conditions of existence. The tendency of the figure of the peasant, then, to become a less separate and distinct category today is indicative of the more general trend of the socialization of all the figures of labor. In the same way that the figure of the peasant tends to disappear, so too does the figure of the industrial worker, the service industry worker, and all other separate categories. And in turn the struggles of each sector tend to become the struggle of all. The most innovative struggles of agriculturists today, for example, such as those of the *Confédération paysanne* in France or the *Movimento sem terra* in Brazil, are not closed struggles limited to a single sector of the population. They open new perspectives for everyone on questions of ecology, poverty, sustainable economies, and indeed all aspects of life.[50] Certainly, each form of labor remains singular in its concrete existence, and every type of worker is different from every other—the autoworker from the rice farmer from the retail salesperson—but this multiplicity tends to be inscribed in a common substrate. In philosophical terms we can say that these are so many singular modes of bringing to life a common laboring substance: each mode has a singular essence and yet they all participate in a common substance.

Lessons from the field of anthropology can help clarify this relationship between singularity and commonality. As we said earlier, the decline of classical anthropology and its paradigmatic figure of otherness, the primitive, gave rise to modern anthropology and its paradigmatic figure of the peasant. Now the decline of the figure of the peasant as other and consequently of modern anthropology gives rise to a global anthropology.[51] The task of global anthropology, as many contemporary anthropologists formulate it, is to abandon the traditional structure of otherness altogether and discover instead a concept of cultural difference based on a notion of singularity. In other words, the "others" of classical and modern anthropology, the primitive and the peasant, were conceived in their difference from the modern European self. The differences from modern Europe were posed in both cases in temporal terms, such that the non-European was an anachronistic survival of the past, either the primordial past of the primitive or the historical past of the peasant. Global anthropology must overcome the fundamental Eurocentrism of these conceptions that think of difference primarily as difference from the European. Cultural difference must be conceived in itself, as singularity, without any such foundation in the other.[52] Similarly it must think all cultural singularities not as anachronistic survivals of the past but as equal participants in our common present.

Consider, as an example of this new global paradigm, how anthropologists have begun to reconceive African modernity. As long as we view European society strictly as the standard by which the modern is measured, then of course many parts of Africa, along with other subordinated regions of the world, will never match up; but as soon as we recognize the singularities and plurality within modernity we can begin to understand how Africa is equally as modern as, yet different from, Europe. Africans, moreover, in our age of globalizing relationships, are just as cosmopolitan as those in the dominant regions in the sense that their social life is constantly changing and characterized by cultural exchange and economic interaction with various distant parts of the world.[53] Some of the phenomena that pose the strongest challenge for this conception of African modernity and cosmopolitanism are the forms of ritual and magic that continue to be integral elements of contemporary life. In post-apartheid South Africa, for instance, there has been a marked increase in reports of occult phenomena and violence, such as witchcraft, Satanism, monsters, zombies, ritual murder, and the like.[54] This is not a resurgence of the primitive premodern, nor is it a local phenomenon. It is rather one common element emerging in comparable contexts all over the planet, albeit in a variety of local guises. Indonesia, Russia, and parts of Latin America, for example, have similarly experienced a resurgence of occult phenomena and violence. These are all societies in which new dreams of wealth in the global capitalist economy have for the first time been plunged into the icy realities of the imperial hierarchies. Magic and monsters are means to understand in each of these contexts this shared contradictory social situation. The local singularity and global commonality of these modes of life do not contradict but rather together determine our plural collective planetary condition.

This kind of study helps us understand the primary anthropological characteristics of the multitude. When we approach a different population we are no longer forced to choose between saying either "They are the same as us" or "They are other to us" (as was the case with the discourse on primitives and, to some extent, peasants). The contradictory conceptual couple, identity and difference, is not the adequate framework for understanding the organization of the multitude. Instead we are a multiplicity of singular forms of life and *at the same time* share a common global existence. The anthropology of the multitude is an anthropology of singularity and commonality.

TWO ITALIANS IN INDIA

Once upon a time, two Italian writers go on vacation together in India, and each writes a book about his travels. One sees in India only what is different and the other only what is the same.

The one writer, Alberto Moravia, titles his book An Idea of India *(Un'idea dell'India) and tries to explain how different India is, but he is frustrated that he can grasp it only in the most abstract, metaphysical terms and through a series of tautologies. The experience teaches him why Europeans are Europeans and Indians Indians, but that is so hard to capture in words. The difference of religion, he thinks, will help him put his finger on it. India is the land of religion par excellence, he explains. Not only are its religions different than ours but also in India religion envelops all of life. The religious idea completely permeates experience. Indians go about their daily lives living their religions in countless strange and incomprehensible rituals. But this notion of a living religious idea, he finds, does not really capture the difference either. The difference of India is much more than that. In fact, this extreme difficulty of expressing it proves to him that the difference of India is ineffable. My fellow Italians, he concludes, I cannot describe India to you. You must go there and experience its enigma yourself. All I can say is, India is India.*

The other writer, Pier Paolo Pasolini, titles his book The Scent of India *(L'odore dell'India) and tries to explain how similar India is. He walks the crowded streets at night in Bombay, and the air is filled with odors that remind him of home: the rotting vegetables left over from the day's market, the hot oil of a vendor cooking food on sidewalk, and the faint smell of sewage. The writer comes upon a family conducting an elaborate ritual on the riverbank, making offerings of fruit, rice, and flowers. This is not new to him either. The peasants back home in Friuli have similar customs, ancient pagan rituals that have survived for ages. And then, of course, there are the boys. The writer talks playfully in broken English with groups of boys who congregate on street corners. Eventually in Cochin (Kochi) he befriends Revi, a poor, laughing orphan who is continually tormented and robbed by older boys. Before leaving town the writer convinces a Catholic priest with the promise of sending money from Italy to take the boy in and protect him, just as he would have done back home. All of these boys, the writer finds, are just like the boys in every poor neighborhood of Rome or Naples. My fellow Italians, he concludes, Indians are just the same as us. In his eyes, in fact, all the differences of India melt away and all that remains is another Italy.*

It makes you wonder if the travel companions even saw the same country. In fact, although polar opposites, their two responses fit together perfectly as a fable of the two faces of Eurocentrism: "They are utterly different from us" and "They are just the same as us." The truth, you might say, lies somewhere between the two—they are somewhat like us and also a little different—but really that compromise only clouds the problem. Neither of the two Italian writers can escape the need to use European identity as a universal standard, the measure of all sameness and difference. Even Indians (and Indonesians, Peruvians, and Nigerians too) have to measure themselves to the standard of European identity. That is the power of Eurocentrism.

India, however, is not merely different from Europe. India (and every local reality within India) is singular—not different from any universal standard but different in itself. If the first Italian writer could free himself of Europe as standard he could grasp this singularity. This singularity does not mean, however, that the world is merely a collection of incommunicable localities. Once we recognize singularity, the common begins to emerge. Singularities do communicate, and they are able to do so because of the common they share. We share bodies with two eyes, ten fingers, ten toes; we share life on this earth; we share capitalist regimes of production and exploitation; we share common dreams of a better future. Our communication, collaboration, and cooperation, furthermore, not only are based on the common that exists but also in turn produce the common. We make and remake the common we share every day. If the second Italian writer could free himself of Europe as standard, he could grasp this dynamic relation of the common.

Here is a non-Eurocentric view of the global multitude: an open network of singularities that links together on the basis of the common they share and the common they produce. It is not easy for any of us to stop measuring the world against the standard of Europe, but the concept of the multitude requires it of us. It is a challenge. Embrace it.

THE WEALTH OF THE POOR
(OR, WE ARE THE POORS!)

When we say that the becoming common of labor is a central condition necessary for the construction of the multitude, this might suggest that those who are excluded from waged labor—the poor, the unemployed, the unwaged, the homeless, and so forth—are also by definition excluded from the multitude. This is not the case, however, because these classes are in fact included in social production. Despite the myriad mechanisms of hierarchy and subordination, the poor constantly express an enormous power of life and production. To understand this, an inversion of perspective is necessary. Certainly, we need to recognize and protest the ways increasing numbers of people across the world are deprived of adequate income, food, shelter, education, health care—in short, recognize that the poor are victims of the global order of Empire. More important, we need to recognize that the poor are not merely victims but also powerful agents. All of those who are "without"—without employment, without residency papers, without housing—are really excluded only in part. The closer we look at the lives and activity of the poor, the more we see how enormously creative and powerful they are and indeed, we will argue, how much they are part of the circuits of social and biopolitical production. To the extent that the poor are increasingly included in the processes of social production, they are becoming, along with all of the traditional laboring classes, participants in a common condition and are thus potentially part of the multitude. The poor's inclusion in various forms of service work, their increasingly central role in agriculture, and their mobility in vast migrations demonstrate how far this process has already developed. At the most general level, biopolitical production—including the production of knowledge, information, linguistic forms, networks of communication, and collaborative social relationships—tends to involve all of society, including the poor.

Communists and socialists have generally reasoned that since the poor are excluded from the capitalist production process they must also be excluded from any central role in political organization. The party is thus traditionally composed primarily of the vanguard workers employed in the hegemonic form of production, not the poor workers and much less the unemployed poor. The poor are thought to be dangerous, either morally dangerous because they are unproductive social parasites—thieves, prostitutes, drug addicts, and the like—or politically dangerous because they are disorganized, unpredictable, and tendentially reactionary. In fact, the term *lumpenproletariat* (or rag proletariat) has functioned at times to demonize the poor as a whole. To make complete the disdain for the poor, finally, they are often thought to be merely a residue of preindustrial social forms, a kind of historical refuse.[55]

In economic terms, the poor have often been considered by Marxists and others as an "industrial reserve army," that is, a reservoir of potential industrial workers who are temporarily unemployed but could at any time be drafted into production.[56] The industrial reserve army is a constant threat hanging over the heads of the existing working class because, first of all, its misery serves as a terrifying example to workers of what could happen to them, and, second, the excess supply of labor it represents lowers the cost of labor and undermines workers' power against employers (by serving potentially as strike breakers, for example). These old theories of the industrial reserve army reappear in globalization when corporations take advantage of the vast differences in wages and labor conditions in different countries through a kind of labor "dumping," moving jobs around the world to lower their costs. Workers in the dominant countries constantly live under the threat that their plants will be closed and their jobs exported. The poor global south thus appears in the position of an industrial reserve army, wielded by global capital against the workers not only in the global north but also in other portions of the global south. (The threat of moving jobs to China, for example, is used against workers in both

North and South America.) Just as traditionally many communist and socialist political projects sought to save the working class from the destructive pressures of the industrial reserve army within each nation, so too
today many labor unions in the dominant countries adopt strategies to
save workers from the threat of the poor workers in the subordinated
countries.

Whether this logic was valid in the past, it is mistaken today to think
of either the poor or the global south as an industrial reserve army. First,
there is no "industrial army" in the sense that industrial workers no longer
form a compact, coherent unity but rather function as one form of labor
among many in the networks defined by the immaterial paradigm. In fact,
more generally, the social division between the employed and the unemployed is becoming ever more blurred. As we said earlier, in the era of
post-Fordism the stable and guaranteed employment that many sectors of
the working class could previously count on in the dominant countries no
longer exists. What is called the flexibility of the labor market means that
no job is secure. There is no longer a clear division but rather a large gray
area in which all workers hover precariously between employment and unemployment. Second, there is no "reserve" in the sense that no labor
power is outside the processes of social production. The poor, the unemployed, and the underemployed in our societies are in fact active in social
production even when they do not have a waged position. It has never
been true, of course, that the poor and the unemployed do nothing. The
strategies of survival themselves often require extraordinary resourcefulness and creativity.[57] Today, however, to the extent that social production
is increasingly defined by immaterial labor such as cooperation or the construction of social relationships and networks of communication, the activity of all in society including the poor becomes more and more directly
productive.

In many respects the poor are actually extraordinarily wealthy and productive. From the perspective of biodiversity, for example, some of the
poorest regions of the world, generally speaking the global south, have the
greatest wealth of different plant and animal species, whereas the rich
global north is home to relatively few. In addition, poor populations, particularly indigenous populations, know how to live with these plant and

animal species, keeping them alive and profiting from their beneficial qualities. Think, for example, of the indigenous populations of the Amazon, who know how to live with the forest and whose activity is necessary for keeping the forest alive.[58] Or think, alternatively, of the indigenous knowledges of the medical uses of plants. This wealth of knowledge and this wealth of plant and animal genetic resources does not translate into economic wealth—in fact, we will see later in this chapter that some of the most interesting property debates today have to do with the ownership of indigenous knowledges and plant genetic materials. It is important to recognize nonetheless that, even though the profit goes elsewhere, this enormous wealth plays an essential role in global social production.

This common nature of creative social activity is further highlighted and deepened by the fact that today production increasingly depends on linguistic competencies and community.[59] All active elements of society are agents of linguistic creativity in the constant generation of common languages. To an ever greater extent, this linguistic community comes before profit and the construction of local and global hierarchies. Language maintains hierarchical relations in at least three respects: within each linguistic community with the maintenance of signs of social superiority and inferiority; among linguistic communities, determining the dominance of one language over others—for example, the dominance of global English; and within technical languages as a relationship between power and knowledge. We find, however, that despite these hierarchies the subordinated are often the most creative agents of a linguistic community, developing new linguistic forms and mixtures and communicating them to the community as a whole. (The creative role of African American speech within American English is one obvious example.) In fact, the contradiction between linguistic hierarchies and linguistic production and commonality is what makes language today such a powerful site of conflict and resistance. This paradox helps invert the traditional image of the poor: since the poor participate in and help generate the linguistic community by which they are then excluded or subordinated, the poor are not only active and productive but also antagonistic and potentially rebellious. The paradoxical position of the poor within the linguistic community is indicative of their position in social production more generally. And, in fact, the poor can serve in this regard as the representative or, better, the common expression of all creative social activity. To complete the inversion of the traditional image, then, we can say that *the poor embody the ontological condition not only of resistance but also of productive life itself.*

Migrants are a special category of the poor that demonstrates this wealth and productivity. Traditionally the various kinds of migrant workers, including permanent immigrants, seasonal laborers, and hobos, were excluded from the primary conception and political organization of the working class. Their cultural differences and mobility divided them from the stable, core figures of labor. In the contemporary economy, however, and with the labor relations of post-Fordism, mobility increasingly defines the labor market as a whole, and all categories of labor are tending toward the condition of mobility and cultural mixture common to the migrant. Not only are workers often forced to change jobs several times during a career, they are also required to move geographically for extended periods or even commute long distances on a daily basis. Migrants may often travel empty-handed in conditions of extreme poverty, but even then they are full of knowledges, languages, skills, and creative capacities: each migrant brings with him or her an entire world. Whereas the great European migrations of the past were generally directed toward some space "outside," toward what were conceived as empty spaces, today many great migrations move instead toward fullness, toward the most wealthy and privileged areas of the globe. The great metropolises of North America, Europe, Asia, and the Middle East are magnets for the migrants, and, in turn, these regions need the migrants to power their economies. Just like in Democritus's physics, a fullness attracts another fullness.

Part of the wealth of migrants is their desire for something more, their refusal to accept the way things are. Certainly most migrations are driven by the need to escape conditions of violence, starvation, or depravation, but together with that negative condition there is also the positive desire for wealth, peace, and freedom. This combined act of refusal and expression of desire is enormously powerful. Fleeing from a life of constant insecurity and forced mobility is good preparation for dealing with and resisting the typical forms of exploitation of immaterial labor. Ironically, the great global centers of wealth that call on migrants to fill a lack in their economies get more than they bargained for, since the immigrants invest the entire society with their subversive desires. The experience of flight is something like a training of the desire for freedom.

Migrations, furthermore, teach us about the geographical divisions and hierarchies of the global system of command. Migrants understand and illuminate the gradients of danger and security, poverty and wealth, the markets of higher and lower wages, and the situations of more and less free forms of life. And with this knowledge of the hierarchies they roll up-hill as much as possible, seeking wealth and freedom, power and joy. Migrants recognize the geographical hierarchies of the system and yet treat the globe as one common space, serving as living testimony to the irreversible fact of globalization. Migrants demonstrate (and help construct) the general commonality of the multitude by crossing and thus partially undermining every geographical barrier. This does not mean that everyone in the world is in the same situation. The vast differences in income, working conditions, and living conditions are not only the cause of great misery but also, as we argue in the next section, essential to the management of the contemporary global economy. Our point rather is that these should be conceived not as a matter of exclusion but one of differential inclusion, not as a line of division between workers and the poor nationally or globally but as hierarchies within the common condition of poverty. All of the multitude is productive and all of it is poor.

We do not mean to suggest that the poor or the migrants are better off and that we should all give up our wealth and hit the road. On the contrary, every kind of poverty brings its own special suffering. In chapter 3.2 we will present grievances against the enormous and growing forms of poverty and inequality in the global system. These should be combated in every way possible. But despite their poverty and their lack of material resources, food, housing, and so forth, the poor do have an enormous wealth in their knowledges and powers of creation.

There is no qualitative difference that divides the poor from the classes of employed workers. Instead, there is an increasingly common condition of existence and creative activity that defines the entire multitude. The creativity and inventiveness of the poor, the unemployed, the partially employed, and the migrants are essential to social production. Just as social production takes place today equally inside and outside the factory walls, so too it takes place equally inside and outside the wage relationship. No social line divides productive from unproductive workers. In fact, the old Marxist distinctions between productive and unproductive labor, as well as that between productive and reproductive labor, which were always dubious, should now be completely thrown out. Like the notion of industrial reserve army, these distinctions too have often been used to exclude women, the unemployed, and the poor from central political roles, entrusting the revolutionary project to the men (with calloused hands from the factories) who were thought to be the primary producers. Today we create as active singularities, cooperating in the networks of the multitude, that is, in the common.

The struggles of the poor against their conditions of poverty are not only powerful protests but also affirmations of biopolitical power—the revelation of a common "being" that is more powerful than their miserable "having." Throughout the twentieth century in the dominant countries, poor people's movements have overcome the fragmentation, discouragement, resignation, and even panic that poverty can create and posed grievances against national governments, demanding a redistribution of wealth.[60] Today's struggles of the poor take on a more general, biopolitical character and tend to be posed on a global level. Ashwin Desai recounts, for example, the development of a contemporary protest movement against evictions and water and electricity cutoffs that began in Chatsworth, near Durban in South Africa. One remarkable element of the movement is its common basis. Black South Africans and South Africans of Indian descent march together saying "We are not Indians, we are the poors!" "We are not Africans, we are the poors!"[61] Another remarkable aspect is the global level on which the poor pose these grievances. They certainly direct their protests against local officials and the South African government, which they claim has since the end of apartheid deepened the misery of the majority of the poor, but they also target neoliberal globalization as the source of their poverty, and they found the occasion to express this in Durban during the 2001 UN World Conference Against Racism. These

South African protesters are certainly right—"We are the poors!"—and perhaps in a way more general than they intend that slogan. We all participate in social production; this is ultimately the wealth of the poor.

Eventually protests against the common conditions of poverty will have to reveal this common productivity in constituent political projects. The demands for "guaranteed income," for example, an income due to all citizens regardless of employment, which have circulated in Europe, Brazil, and North America for several years, is such a constituent project aimed against poverty.[62] If extended beyond the national realm to become a global demand of guaranteed income for all, this could become an element of a project for the democratic management of globalization. Such a common scheme for the distribution of wealth would correspond to the common productivity of the poor.

Our claims of the wealth, productivity, and commonality of the poor have immediate implications for trade union organizing. The old form of trade union, which was born in the nineteenth century and aimed primarily at negotiating wages for a specific trade, is no longer sufficient. First of all, as we have been arguing, the old trade unions are not able to represent the unemployed, the poor, or even the mobile and flexible post-Fordist workers with short-term contracts, all of whom participate actively in social production and increase social wealth. Second, the old unions are divided according to the various products and tasks defined in the heyday of industrial production—a miners' union, a pipefitters' union, a machinists' union, and so forth. Today, insofar as the conditions and relations of labor are becoming common, these traditional divisions (or even newly defined divisions) no longer make sense and serve only as an obstacle. Finally, the old unions have become purely economic, not political, organizations. In the dominant capitalist countries, working-class organizations were granted legal, constitutional status in exchange for focusing narrowly on economic workplace and wage issues and renouncing any social or political demands. In the paradigm of immaterial labor, however, and as production becomes increasingly biopolitical, such an isolation of economic issues makes less and less sense.

What is necessary and possible today is a form of labor organizing that overcomes all the divisions of the old unions and manages to represent the becoming common of labor in all its generality—economically, politically, and socially. Whereas traditional trade unions defend the economic interests of a limited category of workers, we need to create labor organizations that can represent the entire network of singularities that collaboratively produce social wealth. One modest proposal that points in this direction, for example, involves opening up trade unions to other segments of society by merging them with the powerful social movements that have emerged in recent years in order to create a form of "social-movement unionism."[63] A more militant example is provided by the "piqueteros," the movements of unemployed workers in Argentina that have begun to function like activist, politicized unions of the unemployed. Another example of labor activism outside the traditional framework of labor unions can be recognized in the 2003 strikes conducted in France by the "intérimaires" workers—that is, part-time workers in entertainment, media, and the arts.[64] In any case, a union worthy of the name today—and worthy of the legacy of labor struggles—must be the organized expression of the multitude, capable of engaging the entire global realm of social labor. The poor have no need of poor laws—in fact, the old poor laws only kept them poor.

It is easy to see now why from the perspective of capital and the global power structure all these classes are so dangerous. If they were simply excluded from the circuits of global production, they would be no great threat. If they were merely passive victims of injustice, oppression, and exploitation, they would not be so dangerous. They are dangerous rather because not only the immaterial and the industrial workers but also the agricultural workers and even the poor and the migrants are *included* as active subjects of biopolitical production. Their mobility and their commonality is constantly a threat to destabilize the global hierarchies and divisions on which global capitalist power depends. They slide across the barriers and burrow connecting tunnels that undermine the walls. Moreover, these dangerous classes continually disrupt the ontological constitution of Empire: at each intersection of lines of creativity or lines of flight the social subjectivities become more hybrid, mixed, and misceginated, further escaping the fusional powers of control. They cease to be identities and become singularities. In the inferno of poverty and the odyssey of migration we have already begun to see emerge some of the outlines of the figure of the multitude. Languages mix and interact to form not a single unified language but rather a common power of communication and cooperation among a multitude of singularities.

DEMONIC MULTITUDES:
DOSTOYEVSKY READS THE BIBLE

The multitude has a dark side. The well-known New Testament parable of the Gerasene Demoniac, recounted with variations by Mark, Luke, and Matthew, throws some light on the demonic face of the multitude. Jesus comes across a man possessed by devils and asks him his name, since a name is required for exorcism. The demoniac responds enigmatically, "My name is Legion; for we are many." The devils ask Jesus to send them from the man into a nearby herd of pigs. The pigs, now possessed, rush off a cliff and drown in the water below in an act of mass suicide. The man, now free of the devils, sits gratefully at the feet of Jesus.

One of the curious and troubling aspects of this parable is the grammatical confusion of singular and plural subjects. The demoniac is at once both "I" and "we." There is a multitude in there. Perhaps this confusion between the singular and the plural subject is itself a demonic attribute. The threat is emphasized by the demoniac's name, Legion. The Latin word legio *was widely used in Aramaic and Greek to mean a great number but the term also referred, as it continues to today in modern languages, to the Roman military unit of about six thousand men. Why is Legion the demoniac's name? Because he has such powerful destructive force? Because the multitude inside him can act together? Perhaps the real threat of this demonic multitude is more metaphysical: since it is at once singular and plural, it destroys numerical distinction itself. Think of the great lengths to which theologians have gone to prove there are not many gods but only one. Linguists similarly have long been troubled by nouns that have indeterminate number, at once singular and plural, such as deer and sheep. The threat to political order is perhaps even more clear: politi-*

cal thought since the time of the ancients has been based on the distinctions among the one, the few, and the many. The demonic multitude violates all such numerical distinctions. It is both one and many. The indefinite number of the multitude threatens all these principles of order. Such trickery is the devil's work.

Fyodor Dostoyevsky grapples with the torment caused by these demonic multitudes in his great 1873 novel, The Devils.[65] Dostoyevsky's Russia is infested with dark, dangerous forces. The serfs have been liberated, the traditional social order is collapsing, and foreign influences are leading toward moral and social catastrophe. Good Russians are acting as if they have been possessed—but what or who possesses them? Who are Dostoyevsky's devils? The novel is set in a calm Russian village where we find the widower Stepan Verkhovensky spending his twilight years courting the affections of the widow Varvara Stavrogina, the wealthiest woman in town. Verkhovensky's son Peter, recently returned from years of traveling in the capitals of Europe, charms the young women in town. Perhaps he could fall in love with a respectable young woman in the village, and the social order could be reproduced as it has been for all eternity. As the novel develops, however, we learn that beneath the timeless rituals of Russian village life is breeding an ultrasecret pseudorevolutionary political organization, which is bent on mindless destruction and includes members of some of the village's best families, with Peter Verkhovensky himself its egotistical leader. The mysterious group's activities lead to a series of catastrophic events. Everyone in the village seems to be unknowingly manipulated or influenced by the sinister plot in some way. By the end of the novel, however, all the members of the clandestine conspiracy have either committed suicide, been killed by their own comrades, or are safely away in prison or exile. Stepan Verkhovensky reflects in the final pages of the novel on the biblical parable of the Gerasene demoniac. It is exactly like our Russia, he exclaims, which has been infected by devils for centuries! Perhaps we are the pigs who have been possessed by the devils and we will thus now rush over the cliff to drown in the water so that Russia can be saved at the feet of Jesus!

Stepan Verkhovensky (and Dostoyevsky himself) tries to soothe his fears with a naive view of the exorcism of demonic multitudes and the Christian redemption of Russia.[66] Once he casts the political conspiracy, and especially its

scheming leader, as demonic, then he can isolate it from the real, eternal, re-
deemable essence of Russia. That may be a consoling conception, but what he
refuses to see is that the real demonic force is the Russian multitude itself. The
liberation of the serfs and the great radical movements of the 1860s set in mo-
tion a wave of agitation that threatened the old order and would in the com-
ing years bring it tumbling down completely. What is so fearsome about the
multitude is its indefinite number, at the same time many and one. If there
were only one unified conspiracy against the old social order, like Dostoyevsky
imagines, then it could be known, confronted, and defeated. Or if instead
there were many separate, isolated social threats, they too could be managed.
The multitude, however, is legion; it is composed of innumerable elements that
remain different, one from the other, and yet communicate, collaborate, and
act in common. Now that is really demonic!

Excursus 1: Method: In Marx's Footsteps

Here's a riddle. The key to Marx's method of historical materialism is
that social theory must be molded to the contours of contemporary
social reality. In contrast to various idealisms that propose independent, transhistorical theoretical frameworks, adequate for all social realities—one size fits all—Marx explains in his 1857 introduction to
the *Grundrisse*, a wonderfully compact discourse on method, that our
mode of understanding must be fitted to the contemporary social
world and thus change along with history: the method and the substance, the form and the content must correspond.[67] That means,
however, that once history moves on and the social reality changes,
then the old theories are no longer adequate. We need new theories
for the new reality. To follow Marx's method, then, one must depart
from Marx's theories to the extent that the object of his critique,
capitalist production and capitalist society as a whole, has changed.
Put simply, to follow in Marx's footsteps one must really walk be-

yond Marx and develop on the basis of his method a new theoretical apparatus adequate to our own present situation. We need to write a new introduction that can update Marx's method and take account of the changes between 1857 and today. Strangely, however, as we will see, after beginning to walk ahead of Marx in this way we continually have the haunting suspicion that he was already there before us.

The primary elements of Marx's method that will guide us in developing our own are (1) the historical tendency, (2) the real abstraction, (3) antagonism, and (4) the constitution of subjectivity.[68] We already employed Marx's notion of the tendency when we claimed earlier that the contemporary economy is defined by a hegemony of immaterial production. Even though immaterial labor is not dominant in quantitative terms, our claim is that it has imposed a tendency on all other forms of labor, transforming them in accordance with its own characteristics, and in that sense it has adopted a hegemonic position. Remember that, as Marx himself notes in the opening pages of *Capital,* when he studied industrial labor and capitalist production they occupied only a portion of the English economy, a smaller portion of the German and other European economies, and only an infinitesimal fraction of the global economy. In quantitative terms agriculture was certainly still dominant, but Marx recognized in capital and industrial labor a tendency that would act as the motor of future transformations. When orthodox Marxists tell us today that the numbers of the industrial working class worldwide have not declined and that therefore industrial labor and the factory must remain the guiding core of all Marxist analysis, we have to remind them of Marx's method of the tendency. Numbers are important, but the key is to grasp the direction of the present, to read which seeds will grow and which wither. Marx's great effort in the mid-nineteenth century was to interpret the tendency and project capital, then in its infancy, as a complete social form.

Implicit in the idea of the tendency is the idea of historical periodization. Infinitesimal changes in history do occur every day, but there are also great paradigms that for extended periods define our modes of thought, structures of knowledge, what appears as normal and abnormal, what is obvious and obscure, and even what is thinkable and not, and then change dramatically to form new paradigms. The passage between periods is the shift from one tendency to another. Contemporary capitalist production is characterized by a series of passages that name different faces of the same shift: from the hegemony of industrial labor to that of immaterial labor, from Fordism to post-Fordism, and from the modern to the postmodern. Periodization frames the movement of history in terms of the passage from one relatively stable paradigm to another.[69]

Each period is characterized by one or several common forms that structure the various elements of social reality and thought. These common forms, or *isomorphisms*, of each period are, for example, what Michel Foucault describes in his studies of the spatial distributions and architectures of the various modern disciplinary institutions. It is no coincidence, he argues, that the prison resembles the factory, which resembles the school, which resembles the barracks, which resembles the hospital, and so forth. They all share a common form that Foucault links to the disciplinary paradigm.[70] Today, by contrast, we see networks everywhere we look—military organizations, social movements, business formations, migration patterns, communications systems, physiological structures, linguistic relations, neural transmitters, and even personal relationships. It is not that networks were not around before or that the structure of the brain has changed. It is that network has become a common form that tends to define our ways of understanding the world and acting in it. Most important from our perspective, networks are the form of organization of the cooperative and communicative relationships dictated by the immaterial paradigm of production. The tendency of this common form to emerge and exert its hegemony is what defines the period.

As an illustration of this notion of the tendency and its formal correspondences between thought and social reality for extended periods, let us consider what might seem to be the most powerful counterexample: Descartes's methodological foundation, "I think, therefore I am," which is aimed at the certainty of the individual mind, autonomous from the body and its physical world. Descartes can conceive that he has no body and that there is no world or place where he might be, but his very thinking convinces him with certainty of his own existence. It might seem puzzling, then, that in the very text where he formulates this notion, his *Discourse on Method*, Descartes situates his revelation in a very specific place in the world. "I was then in Germany, to which country I had been attracted by the wars which are not yet at an end."[71] Descartes arrives at his discovery of the certainty of the individual mind on a day in 1619, probably November 10, when, as a soldier in the German Thirty Years' War, he is bivouacked alone for the winter in a stove-heated room. What does the war and Descartes's own role in it have to do with an eternal truth such as "I think, therefore I am"? Why does Descartes bother to tell us the time and place? It would certainly be easy to understand how such a devastating reality, such a hopeless, senseless war, could make someone want to stop "studying the book of the world" and instead make oneself an object of study. I can imagine that horrible world does not exist and that my thinking self is the only clear and certain reality. Certainly, it would be extremely reductive to conceive of Descartes's methodological discovery as merely the reaction of a distraught soldier at war. That would pose too narrow, mechanical, and linear a relation of cause and effect. It would be equally mistaken, however, to separate Descartes's revelation from his social reality. Indeed the greatness of Descartes is to have recognized a form and mode of thought that corresponds to an entire era that was in the process of emerging. The sovereign, individual, thinking self that Descartes discovers has the same *form* as a variety of other figures that would spring up more or less contemporaneously in modern Europe, from the individual economic actor to the sovereign nation-state. Neither the Thirty Years' War nor any other historical event "causes" Descartes's theory. Rather, the entire set of relations that constitutes the reality of his situation make his theory thinkable. His discovery corresponds in form to the emerging tendency of his social reality.

For Marx, of course, everything starts with production, and we can turn to the matter of production to understand the idea of the *real abstraction*, the second element of his method that we should follow. Marx adopts from the classical political economists, such as Adam Smith and David Ricardo, the maxim that in capitalist society labor is the source of all value and wealth. The labor of the individual, however, will not help us understand capitalist production, despite the fondness that political economists have for the Robinson Crusoe myth. Capital creates a collective, socially connected form of production in which the labor of each of us produces in collaboration with innumerable others. It would be as absurd to see value in capitalist production springing from the labor of an isolated individual, Marx explains, as it would to conceive the development of language without people living together and talking to each other (*Grundrisse*, 84). To understand capital we have to start from the concept of social labor—an abstraction but, as Marx claims, a rational abstraction that is in fact more real and basic to understanding the production of capital than any concrete instances of individual labor. In capitalist production the specific labors of the mason, the welder, the shop clerk, and so forth are equivalent or commensurable because they each contain a common element, abstract labor, labor in general, labor without respect to its specific form. This abstract labor, Marx explains, is key to understanding the capitalist notion of value. If, as we said, in capitalist society labor is the source of all wealth, then abstract labor must be the source of value in general. Money is the ultimate representation of the indifference and abstraction of capitalist value.

Once we articulate Marx's concept of abstract labor and its relation to value, we quickly recognize an important difference between Marx's time and ours. Marx poses the relation between labor and value in terms of corresponding quantities: a certain quantity of time of abstract labor equals a quantity of value. According to this law of value, which defines capitalist production, value is expressed in measurable, homogeneous units of labor time. Marx eventually links this notion to his analyses of the working day and surplus value. This law, however, cannot be maintained today in the form that Smith, Ricardo, and Marx himself conceived it. The temporal unity of labor as the basic measure of value today makes no sense. Labor does remain the fundamental source of value in capitalist production, that does not change, but we have to investigate what kind of labor we are dealing with and what its temporalities are. We noted earlier that the working day and the time of production have changed profoundly under the hegemony of immaterial labor. The regular rhythms of factory production and its clear divisions of work time and nonwork time tend to decline in the realm of immaterial labor. Think how at the high end of the labor market companies like Microsoft try to make the office more like home, offering free meals and exercise programs to keep employees in the office as many of their waking hours as possible. At the low end of the labor market workers have to juggle several jobs to make ends meet. Such practices have always existed, but today, with the passage from Fordism to post-Fordism, the increased flexibility and mobility imposed on workers, and the decline of the stable, long-term employment typical of factory work, this tends to become the norm. At both the high and low ends of the labor market the new paradigm undermines the division between work time and the time of life.

This intimate relationship between labor and life, this blurring of time divisions that we see in post-Fordist production is even more clear in terms of the products of immaterial labor. Material production—the production, for example, of cars, televisions, clothing, and food—creates the *means of social life*. Modern forms of social life would not be possible without these commodities. Immaterial production, by contrast, including the production of ideas, images, knowledges, communication, cooperation, and affective relations, tends to create not the means of social life but *social life itself*. Immaterial production is biopolitical. This standpoint allows us to look back with new eyes on the entire evolution of capitalist production—somewhat in the way human anatomy contains a key to the anatomy of the ape (*Grundrisse*, 105). Capital has always been oriented toward the production, reproduction, and control of social life. Marx is gesturing toward this fact, for instance, when he says that although capital can be defined, as is commonplace, as an accumulation of social wealth in the form of commodities or money, most fundamentally capital is a social relation. The production of capital is, ever more clearly and directly today, the production of social life. Marx is also pointing in this direction with his concept of "living labor," the form-giving fire of our creative capacities. Living labor is the fundamental human faculty: the ability to engage the world actively and create social life. Living labor can be corralled by capital and pared down to the labor power that is bought and sold and that produces commodities and capital, but living labor always exceeds that. Our innovative and creative capacities are always greater than our productive labor—productive, that is, of capital. At this point we can recognize that this biopolitical production is on the one hand *immeasurable*, because it cannot be quantified in fixed units of time, and, on the other hand, always *excessive* with respect to the value that capital can extract from it because capital can never capture all of life. This is why we have to revise Marx's notion of the relation between labor and value in capitalist production.

The central aspect of the paradigm of immaterial production we have to grasp here is its intimate relation with cooperation, collaboration, and communication—in short, its foundation in the common. Marx insists that one of the great progressive elements of capital historically is to organize armies of workers in cooperative productive relationships. The capitalist calls workers to the factory, for example, directing them to collaborate and communicate in production and giving them the means to do so. In the paradigm of immaterial production, in contrast, labor itself tends to produce the means of interaction, communication, and cooperation for production directly. Affective labor always directly constructs a relationship. The production of ideas, images, and knowledges is not only conducted in common—no one really thinks alone, all thought is produced in collaboration with the past and present thought of others—but also each new idea and image invites and opens new collaborations. The production of languages, finally, both natural languages and artificial languages, such as computer languages and various kinds of code, is always collaborative and always creates new means of collaboration. In all these ways, in immaterial production the creation of cooperation has become internal to labor and thus external to capital.

Economists register the common in mystified form through the notion of "externalities." Positive externalities are benefits that accrue through no action of one's own. The common classroom example is that when my neighbor makes his house and yard more beautiful the value of *my* property also goes up. More generally and fundamentally, positive externalities refer to social wealth created outside the direct productive process, the value of which can be captured only in part by capital. The social knowledges, relationships, and forms of communication that result from immaterial production generally fit into this category. As they become common to society they form a kind of raw material that is not consumed in production but actually increases with use. An enterprise in Michigan, northeastern Italy, or southern

India benefits from the education system, the public and private infrastructure of roads, railways, phone lines, and fiber optic cable, as well as the general cultural development of the population. The intelligence, affective skills, and technical knowledges of these populations are positive externalities from the standpoint of businesses. Capital does not have to pay for these external sources of wealth, but neither can it control them entirely. Such externalities, which are common to all of us, increasingly define economic production as a whole.

A theory of the relation between labor and value today must be based on the common. The common appears at both ends of immaterial production, as presupposition and result. Our common knowledge is the foundation of all new production of knowledge; linguistic community is the basis of all linguistic innovation; our existing affective relationships ground all production of affects; and our common social image bank makes possible the creation of new images. All of these productions accrue to the common and in turn serve as foundation for new ones. The common, in fact, appears not only at the beginning and end of production but also in the middle, since the production processes themselves are common, collaborative, and communicative. Labor and value have become biopolitical in the sense that living and producing tend to be indistinguishable. Insofar as life tends to be completely invested by acts of production and reproduction, social life itself becomes a productive machine.

These new properties of value in the paradigm of immaterial and biopolitical production, such as its immeasurable character and its tendency to be common and shared, undermine all the traditional mechanisms of accounting. The standard measures of production, reproduction, circulation, consumption, and investments all have to be rethought. Such methods cannot, for example, account for positive externalities and all the other collaborative social forms of production that occur outside narrow wage relationships. In the nineteenth century, French physiocrats such as François Quesnay created a *Tableau économique* to depict the total quantities of value in an economy's annual production, circulation, and consumption. Today we need a new *Tableau économique* that goes beyond the traditional measures and is able to describe more accurately where value is created and where it goes in the national and the global economy. This would require a revolution of the methods of accounting, something akin to the way Einstein's theory of relativity transformed our understanding of the regular, metrical spaces of Euclidean geometry. Once again, however, when we move so far beyond Marx we can look down and see that he too was already walking here with a very similar notion of common production and common wealth. "In fact," he writes in his notebooks, "when the limited bourgeois form is stripped away, what is wealth other than the universality of individual needs, capacities, pleasures, productive forces, etc., created through universal exchange? . . . The absolute working-out of his creative potentialities, with no presupposition other than the previous historic development, which makes this totality of development, i.e.[,] the development of all human powers as such the end in itself, not as measured on a *predetermined* yardstick? . . . Strives not to remain something he has become, but is in the absolute movement of his becoming?" (*Grundrisse*, 488). When we take off the blinders of capitalist society that limit our vision, we can see with Marx that material wealth, including commodities, property, and money, is not an end in itself. This recognition should not send us to some ascetic abnegation. The real wealth, which is an end in itself, resides in the common; it is the sum of the pleasures, desires, capacities, and needs we all share. The common wealth is the real and proper object of production.

We do not mean to suggest that the paradigm of immaterial production is some paradise in which we produce freely in common and share equally the common social wealth. Immaterial labor is still exploited under the rule of capital as material labor is. In other words, the labor of women, men, and children is still controlled by capitalists who appropriate the wealth their labor produces. This is where *antagonism* comes into play, the third element of Marx's method that we should follow. The term *exploitation* today, as ever, gives a name to the workers' constant experience of antagonism. The theory of exploitation must reveal the daily structural violence of capital against workers that generates this antagonism and serves, in turn, as the basis for workers to organize and refuse capitalist control. Marx insists that any conception of exploitation must be based on a theory of value. Insofar as the relationship between labor and value has changed, then, so too must our understanding of exploitation change. For Marx, exploitation is defined in terms of quantities of labor time, just like the theory of value. The degree of exploitation corresponds to the quantity of surplus labor time, that is, the portion of the working day that extends beyond the time necessary for the worker to produce value equal to the wage he or she is paid. Surplus labor time and the surplus value produced during that time are the key to Marx's definition of exploitation. This temporal measure gave Marx a clear and convenient conceptual framework and also made his theory directly applicable in his era to the workers' struggle to shorten the length of the working day.

But today, in the paradigm of immaterial production, the theory of value cannot be conceived in terms of measured quantities of time, and so exploitation cannot be understood in these terms. Just as we must understand the production of value in terms of the common, so too must we try to conceive exploitation as *the expropriation of the common*. The common, in other words, has become the locus of surplus value. Exploitation is the private appropriation of part or all of the value that has been produced as common. Produced relationships and communication are by their very nature common, and yet capital manages to appropriate privately some of their wealth. Think, for example, of the profit extracted from affective labor. The same is true for the production of languages, ideas, and knowledges: what is made in common becomes private. This is true, for example, when traditional knowledges produced in indigenous communities or when the knowledge produced collaboratively in scientific communities becomes private property. In some respects, one might say that money and the financialization of the economy summarize the obscure logic by which the traditional characteristics of capitalist production fall away, and yet capital still manages to exert its control and extract wealth. Money, of course, is not only a general equivalent that facilitates exchange but also the ultimate representation of the common. Financial instruments, such as derivatives, as we will see further in part 3, cast this representation of the common into the future. Through financial markets, in other words, money tends to represent not only the present but also the future value of the common. Finance capital bets on the future and functions as a general representation of our common future productive capacities. The profits of finance capital are probably in its purest form the expropriation of the common.

The logic of exploitation, however, is not by any means the same for everyone in the world. Already when we pose the theory of the tendency, with the notion that one form of labor functions as hegemonic over the others, we should recognize that this implies divisions of labor that correspond to geographical, racial, and gender hierarchies. We will focus in the next section on the topography of exploitation that defines these hierarchies. Managing the global divisions of labor and power is one weapon at capital's disposal for maintaining command over global production and wealth.

The fourth and final element of Marx's method that we should follow here involves *the production of subjectivity*. Subjectivity is produced, according to Marx, in the material practices of production. "Production thus not only creates an object for the subject," he writes, "but also a subject for the object" (*Grundrisse*, 92). Workers' subjectivity is also created in the antagonism of the experience of exploitation. It seems to us that, in our age of the hegemony of immaterial production, *the poor* designate the paradigmatic figure of production.

This does not mean that there is a constant immiseration of workers, as Marx hypothesized, or that all workers in the world suffer conditions of extreme poverty (although, in fact, many do). "The poor" is the only figure that can designate society in all its generality as an inseparable whole, defined by its base, just like the protesters in South Africa use the term to indicate the generality of the different groups in struggle. In the paradigm of immaterial production, in production based on communication and collaboration, "the poor" is the primary figure of production in the sense that society tends to produce as a coordinated ensemble. "The poor" also highlights the contradictory relation of production to the world of value: "the poor" is excluded from wealth and yet included in its circuits of social production. "The poor" is the flesh of biopolitical production. We are the poors.

Here at the end of our journey to outline a new method that goes beyond Marx and takes account of the changes in our world, we have the strange suspicion once again that Marx was here before us. In the fragmented style typical of his notes in the *Grundrisse*, he explains that labor under capital implies a state of absolute poverty. "This living labour, existing as an *abstraction* from these moments of actual reality . . . ; this complete denudation, purely subjective existence of labour, stripped of all objectivity. Labour as *absolute poverty*: poverty not as shortage, but as total exclusion of objective wealth." (*Grundrisse*, 295–96). As soon as Marx poses this negative view of poverty as exclusion, however, he inverts the definition of poverty in a positive form. "Labor not as an object, but as activity; not as itself *value*, but as the *living source* of value. [Namely, it is] general wealth (in contrast to capital in which it exists objectively, as reality) as the *general possibility* of [wealth], which proves itself as such in action." (*Grundrisse*, 296). Living labor thus has a double character: from one side it appears as absolute poverty, since it is deprived of wealth, but from the other side Marx recognizes poverty as the ground zero of human activity, as the figure of general possibility and thus the source of all wealth.

What we humans are at base is general possibility or general productive capacity. This double character of poverty and possibility defines the subjectivity of labor increasingly clearly in the immaterial paradigm. The wealth it creates is taken away, and this is the source of its antagonism. Yet it retains its capacity to produce wealth, and this is its power. In this combination of antagonism and power lies the makings of a revolutionary subjectivity.

DEATH OF THE DISMAL SCIENCE?

Nothing annoys our economist friends more than reminding them that economics is a deeply reactionary discipline. Really ever since it was born between Scotland and France in the era that thought it had reached enlightenment, economics has evolved as a theory of the measure and the equilibrium among the parts of a whole—the economic whole of the production, reproduction, and distribution of wealth. Sure, the internal movements are dynamic, there is constant growth, the forms and foundation are always open to discussion, and thus conflict is never lacking, but the stability of the whole always overrules the movements of the parts. As in Aristotle's world, for the economists, matter and form, movement and ends are necessarily compatible and united. For this reason economics, despite the appearance of constant movement, is really completely fixed and static. It is no coincidence that French physiocrats and Scottish moralists were the first to formulate the presuppositions of the analytic that would become in the course of a century the neoclassical "general theory of equilibrium." It was inevitable that statisticians and mathematicians would take over economics because they are the only ones with the techniques to manage it. The calculations and models are every day a confirmation, beyond the academic libraries and govern-

ment dossiers, of the utopia of political reaction. Why reaction? Because the reproduction of society is analyzed with the goal of keeping it exactly as is and formulating it in terms of quantitative measures that can make the relations of exploitation inevitable and natural, an ontological necessity. Economics is more disciplinary than any other discipline, and it has been ever since its origins.

In the course of modernity, proceeding toward our times, there emerge more and more phenomena and institutions that do not square with the equilibria of the good and happy science of economics. Immeasurable quantities, imperfections and distortions of information, cruel and barbaric forms of exploitation, legislative and institutional changes, in addition to social and political revolutions—in short, all that catastrophic phenomena that can be grouped under the title of crisis—*demonstrate that the theory of equilibrium cannot serve as the general schema of economics, but rather it is a matter of ruling over disequilibria. Revolutionaries have proclaimed this fact. In the academic context, Thorstein Veblen suspected it. The doubt, which became a certainty, was that measure and equilibrium does not exist in nature at all!*

In the twentieth century, along with tragic wars and other cataclysms, came the era of reconstruction, the glory years of political economy. With the recognition of the collapse of natural measures, reconstruction involved political tactics of adjustment aimed at restoring the traditional equilibria of economics. The tactics sometimes led to a new strategy, as when after the stock market crash of 1929, for example, John Maynard Keynes tried to reconstruct scientifically the knowledge of (and rule over) the social figures of the production, reproduction, and distribution of wealth. If the natural measures of value no longer hold (or, at least, no longer function under the pressures of class struggle), then one has to construct a function of measuring that brings equilibrium to development, even in the crises, in relation to the political ideologies, the relations of producers, and productive sectors. This was a rare example in the history of economics when an effort was made to free political economy from the reactionary apparatus that supports it. To do so it was necessary to open up the system to social forces and political subjects in order to mediate between antagonistic social tensions. Political economy had to become a New Deal.

Is it possible, however, to preserve the parameters of reproduction of the capitalist order in the long term once state regulation is open to social antagonism or, better, after social antagonism has been recognized as the framework of reference (if not actually legitimation) of the political order? Is it possible to maintain capitalist order once political economy has been opened to the opportunity of ever new rules of the distribution of wealth? It is still possible when economic intervention, either through welfare (even in its crisis) or warfare (in its crude effectiveness), has invested all the contradictory forces that constitute social life? Keynesianism, putting an end to the naturalist illusion, opened an insolvable problem that political economy would have to face. By the 1970s Keynes's rethinking of economics was showing negative results. With the expansion of the cold war, Keynesianism was first scaled back by Paul Samuelson to resemble the old mainstream neoclassical doctrine, and then Milton Friedman and the Chicago School arrived to undermine it completely, proposing to establish certain measures of equilibrium by confiding every power of regulation to money, that is, to the market. We were thus taken back, one might say, to the science of economics—but what a strange science! It is now based on a kind of "monetary essentialism" in which the standards of measure no longer have any relationship with the real world of production and exchange, except according to the norms that the Central Bank or the Federal Reserve dictate. Monetary Aristotelianism has been restored, and the Central Bank has now become the fixed motor of monetary ontology. All of this is highly dubious. Common sense, in addition to daily experience, teaches us (in good Keynesian form) that money, rather than a presupposition of productive social reality, an a priori, is a result, created a posteriori by regulatory instruments.

Furthermore, even criticizing the centrality of money, we have to recognize nonetheless, without irony, that this metaphysical figure economists attribute to money (as often happens in philosophy) does resemble reality to a certain extent. The more that production is socialized and globalized, in fact, the more the monetary connections (which serve as the basis for financial instruments) are presented as indexes and expressions of general social production and the set of relations that bring together different economic actors. Only the power of money, in fact, can represent the generality of the values of production when they are expressions of the global multitudes. In order to understand this analogy, however, we have to recognize once again the crisis of economics and its various attempts to define the standards of measure, going in search of the foundation no longer of nature but of the common *recomposition of labor and the concrete cooperation of singular subjects (individuals and groups) that make up production. One can no longer hope to find any natural units of measure and even when such units appear they are merely fleeting results that arise a posteriori from the common organization of society and the continuous resolution of the antagonisms that run throughout it. Economics, then, which has exhausted its powers, has to open itself to politics; it has to yield to political practice and recognize that it cannot do otherwise. Economics, if it is to be a science, has to return to something closer to the ancient Greek meaning of the term and take* all of social life *into consideration.*

While we wait for an Imre Lakatos or a Paul Feyerabend to overturn economics, it is interesting to note how even though the discipline is lost in its dogmatic slumber some economists reach conclusions close to what we suggest here. Take Gary Becker, for example, who for a half century has been asking the same question: what can it mean to ask if humans can be content or fulfilled in purely economic terms without investing the entire field of biopolitical existence? Surely, the methodological individualism of the Chicago School cannot solve such problems, even if they add new concepts like human capital and cognitive capital. The dismal science, as Thomas Carlisle called it, however, is not doomed. It can be reborn when it takes stock of the new common anthropology and the intellectual and affective power of productive labor, and when it can in addition to capitalists and wage laborers account for the poor and the excluded who nonetheless always constitute the productive articulations of social being. For economics to function today it has to be formed around the common, the global, and social cooperation. Economics, in other words, must become a biopolitical science. *Economic engineering, as Amartya Sen says, must turn to ethics.*

2.2 DE CORPORE

The body without organs now falls back on desiring-production, attracts it, and appropriates it for its own. The organ-machines now cling to the body without organs as though it were a fencer's padded jacket, or as though these organ-machines were medals pinned onto the jersey of a wrestler who makes them jingle as he starts toward his opponent.

—GILLES DELEUZE AND FÉLIX GUATTARI

But, in general, the protective system of our day is conservative, while the free trade system is destructive. It breaks up old nationalities and pushes the antagonism of the proletariat and the bourgeoisie to the extreme point. In a word, the free trade system hastens the social revolution. It is in this revolutionary sense alone, gentlemen, that I vote in favor of free trade.

—KARL MARX

Up to this point we have addressed the question of labor and poverty primarily in economic terms, seeking to demonstrate that there exist sufficient common basis, interaction, and communication among the various singular figures of production to make possible the construction of the multitude. We have already recognized, however, that treating labor and poverty today is not merely a matter of economics. The figures that coalesce in the multitude—industrial workers, immaterial workers, agricultural workers, the unemployed, migrants, and so forth—are biopolitical figures that represent distinct forms of life in concrete places, and we have to grasp the material specificity and spatial distribution of each. We need to investigate furthermore the political and social institutions that maintain the global hierarchies and the geography of poverty and subordination. Our analysis must move now, in short, from the *topology* of exploitation to its *topography*. Whereas the topology examined the logic of exploitation in production, the topography will map the hierarchies of the system of power and its unequal relations in the north and south of the globe. These spatial relations of control and subordination are key to understanding how the contradictions of the system are transformed into antagonism and conflict.

Since we have begun to recognize (from the standpoint of the critique of political economy) how the singular figures of postmodern labor do not remain fragmented and dispersed but tend through communication and collaboration to converge toward a common social being, we must now immerse ourselves in this social being as in something that is at once both rich and miserable, full of productivity and suffering and yet devoid of form. This common social being is the powerful matrix that is central in the production and reproduction of contemporary society and has the potential to create a new, alternative society. We should regard this common social being as a new flesh, amorphous flesh that as yet forms no body. The important question at this point is what kind of body will these common singularities form? One possibility is that they will be enlisted in the global armies at the service of capital, subjugated in the global strategies of servile inclusion and violent marginalization. This new social flesh, in other words, may be formed into the productive organs of the global social body of capital. Another possibility, however, is that these common singularities organize themselves autonomously through a kind of "power of the flesh" in line with the long philosophical tradition that stretches back at least to the apostle Paul of Tarsus.[72] The power of the flesh is the power to transform ourselves through historical action and create a new world. From this abstract, metaphysical perspective, then, the political conflict is posed between two forms by which the social flesh of the multitude can be organized into a global social body.

GLOBAL APARTHEID

Early modern European treatises of political philosophy usually begin with a section entitled *De Corpore*, which analyzes both the human body and the body politic. The political body is the law incarnate as a regulated social order.[73] The analogy with the human body reinforces the naturalness of this order—we have a head to make decisions, arms to fight our battles, and various other classes or organs that each serves its natural function. And in the early modern analyses this entire order is usually confirmed and guaranteed by the authority of God. Two streams of this tradition developed in modern European political thought. According to one stream a sovereign that stands above society determines and guarantees the order of the political body: all are subject to the sovereign and united under the sovereign's will. This is a political production of subjectivity in which the entire population is formed into an identity. The resulting political body, most often a national body politic, is absolutist in the reactionary sense, that is, the various different social classes or functions are absolutely united under the command of the sovereign. A second modern stream of this tradition casts the political body in the image of the republic, that is, a *res publica*, a public object. In this case sovereignty is internal to the political body and grounded in some state of nature that is prior to both the social contract and the transfer of rights and powers to the sovereign. Here too the political body is absolute and the power of the sovereign united despite that republican thought insists on the limitations of sovereignty. The production of subjectivity in this modern republican version takes the form of constitutionalism, which regulates the hierarchical political body: like organs and limbs of an individual body, every segment of society has its own organic place and function in the political body of a constitutional republic.

Since later we will discuss this alternative with English and French examples, referring to Hobbes and Rousseau, let us pose it now in the German tradition of legal theory. The most developed example of the first stream is the German conception of *Reich*, which, whether translated as government or empire, is really a *Gemeinschaft*, that is, a community of bodies, blood, and earth that form a *Heimat*, or home. From this perspective, authority is an organic element of the social whole, but, as in the tribe and the family, it is patriarchal and expressed at the highest point above society. Martin Luther calls this wellspring of obligation to command *Obrigkeitsstaat* (the state based on authority). The other stream, the republican and constitutional stream, is illustrated by the great nineteenth-century tradition of German public law, which reached its democratic apex in the work of Rudolf von Jhering and his students. Here too, however, there is no alternative to the unity of sovereign command. No subjective right, even on the political terrain, is valid unless it is sanctioned by the ordered public body. Even in the tradition of institutionalism, from Otto von Gierke to Ernst Forsthoff, which does allow for a strong autonomy of social bodies and thus theorizes the "subsidiary nature" of various social sources of authority, the central axis of command is still absolutely united. The public constitutional body is still an organic body of power. In both of these streams, modern theories of the political body are explicit formulations of biopower, posing an absolute and total ordering of the social subjectivity and social life as a whole under a unified sovereign power.

Contemporary scholars who study the political forms of globalization generally repeat these two versions of the modern body politic.[74] On one hand, there are those authors who read global society as a regime of global security. Since nation-states and the old international order, they reason, are no longer sufficient to protect us from the threats we face in the world, other forms of sovereignty will have to be created to manage conflict and maintain global order. For most authors in this stream, the United States as sole superpower (sometimes in conjunction with other major powers or with "the West" more generally) has to exercise the sovereignty that will guarantee the order of global society as a political body. On the other hand, some contemporary "republican" authors seek a new social contract between society and the sovereign, now at a global level, in order to alleviate the excesses and reduce the conflicts of the new world order. They assume once again that sovereignty resides within the global society, based on implicit principles or values, and their goal is to extend the modern political institutions beyond national boundaries and establish a cosmopolitan governance through a global constitutional order, creating thereby a global political body. We will argue in part 3 that neither of these versions of global society allows for a full conception of democracy because, by continuing to organize all elements of society in an organic body politic, they necessarily reduce the differences and freedom of the parts and establish hierarchies among them. A democratic multitude cannot be a political body, at least not in the modern form. The multitude is something like singular flesh that refuses the organic unity of the body.

Here we should focus, first of all, on the fact that none of these theories will understand the new nature of the global political body without recognizing how it is composed of divisions and hierarchies that are equally economic and political. The organs of the political body are really primarily economic divisions, and thus a critique of political economy is necessary to understand the body's *anatomy*. We should focus second on the fact that these modern traditions of constructing the body politic cannot grasp the new forms of the global political body because they are so dependent on national models. When these theories do not continue to pose power and sovereignty strictly in terms of nation-states or clusters of nation-states, they merely expand the modern national concepts and institutions to a larger regional or even global scale. The recent processes of globalization and specifically the declining sovereignty of the nation-states have undermined the conditions that made possible the modern construction of a political body. The global political body is not merely a national body grown overlarge. It has a new *physiology*.[75]

We are in a period of transition or, better, interregnum. Historians have debated for centuries who rules in periods of interregnum and how the bases of new institutions are constructed, but one thing that is clear is that there is never a vacuum of power. Power may at times be more widely distributed or at others divided between two or several rulers, but the only thing that can never exist is a total absence of power, a void. In effect, when scholars use the term *anarchy* to characterize such periods they usually refer not to an absence of power but merely to institutional chaos, excesses or defects of the production of norms, or conflicts among powers—and all of this was certainly present in England's seventeenth-century interregnum as it is in today's era of globalization. As Joseph Schumpeter says, just when it seems that the field is clear and empty, there are really already the seeds of "a tropical growth of new legal structures."[76] Our contemporary interregnum, in which the modern national paradigm of political bodies is passing toward a new global form, is also populated by an abundance of new structures of power. The only thing that remains constantly present and never leaves the scene is power itself.

To avoid confusion we should emphasize that we are not arguing here that in this interregnum nation-states are no longer powerful but rather that their powers and functions are being transformed in a new global framework. Too often in contemporary discussions about globalization authors assume that this is an exclusive alternative: either nation-states are still important or there has been a globalization of the figures of authority. We must understand instead that both are true: nation-states remain important (some, of course, more than others), but they have nonetheless been changed radically in the global context. Saskia Sassen calls this a process of "denationalization." States continue to play a crucial role in determining and maintaining the legal and economic order, she argues, but their actions are increasingly oriented not toward national interests but rather toward the emerging global power structure.[77] There is no contradiction between the nation-state and globalization from this perspective. States continue to perform many of their traditional functions in the interregnum but are transformed by the emerging global power they tend increasingly to serve.

The critique of political economy must address this interregnum and recognize how its temporal transition corresponds to a spatial transformation of global power. Economic wealth and power continue to be distributed unevenly across the world today, but the national lines that used to define the map of power are shifting. The concepts of uneven development and unequal exchange, which were battlehorses of third worldist economists in the 1960s, were meant to highlight the radical difference of the level of exploitation between first and third world countries.[78] The concepts helped explain the stubborn persistence of global divisions and hierarchies—why rich countries stayed rich and poor countries poor. Uneven development describes how the privileged countries of the world create ever more advanced regimes of productivity and profit with the support and at the expense of the subordinated countries. Unequal exchange refers to the fact that the production in poor countries is constantly undervalued in the world market, so that in fact poor countries subsidize the rich, not vice versa. Moreover, these systems of inequality were thought to represent a contradiction within capitalist development that could, under certain political conditions, threaten to bring down the entire scaffolding of capitalist rule. Capitalist globalization, however, has managed to solve this problem in the worst possible way—not by making labor relationships equal in countries throughout the world but rather by generalizing the perverse mechanisms of unevenness and inequality everywhere. Today there is uneven development and unequal exchange between the richest and poorest neighborhoods of Los Angeles, between Moscow and Siberia, between the center and periphery of every European city, between the northern and southern rims of the Mediterranean, between the southern and northern islands of Japan—one could continue indefinitely. In both South-Central Los Angeles and Lagos, Nigeria, there are processes of biopolitical dumping through the differentiation of the price of labor power so that the labor of certain workers has more value, the labor of others less, and the labor of some has almost no economic value at all. There are still, of course, speaking in general and approximate terms, important differences among nations and between the large geographical zones of the world, between Europe and Africa, between North and South America, between the global north and the global south, but these are not homogeneous zones. The lines of hierarchy and division are much more complex. One has to be a geographer today to map the topography of exploitation.[79]

The global political body is defined not only by global divisions of labor but also by closely related global divisions of power. The classic textbooks of political economy by Adam Smith and David Ricardo present the international divisions of labor as if they were natural phenomena that intelligent capitalists, knowledgeable of the various costs and benefits, could put to use. There have always been, however, hierarchies of power that coordinate and maintain these international divisions of labor, from colonial administrations to postcolonial power relations. The divisions of labor and the hierarchies of power in the global system are so intimately related that they must be grasped together. And furthermore, these divisions tend today not to run strictly along national lines so that rather than "international" we should call these, following James Mittelman, "global divisions of labor and power."[80] The concept of global divisions of labor and power implies, on the one hand, that it is not possible to determine in a *fixed* way the degrees of development and exploitation but that one has to recognize instead the shifting status of the divisions among geographical areas and among populations. The global divisions are the results and the objects of power struggles. On the other hand, it implies that an equilibrium of stable divisions is achieved only through the imposition of rules that normalize, naturalize, and control the divisions. One complex example of the shifting lines of hierarchy and exploitation under the control of the global system is the rising and falling economic fortunes of the so-called Asian dragons and tigers. In the 1980s these economies were transformed by what some economists call "peripheral Fordism," in which industrial production exported from the dominant countries helped fuel dramatic economic development under the guidance of the global economic powers and institutions, such as the IMF. The economies of South Korea, Singapore, and other Southeast Asian countries soared up the global hierarchy, in some cases well above the pack of midlevel countries such as India and Brazil. The economic crisis in the late 1990s, however, struck these same countries particularly hard, and, still under the guidance of the global economic institutions, their star fell in the global hierarchy almost as fast as it had risen.[81] The topography of global divisions of labor, poverty, and exploitation, in short, is a shifting matrix of politically constructed hierarchies. We will consider in more detail in the next section some of the political institutions that rule over these hierarchies of the global system.

Finally we should add, as in a sinister cookbook, one final ingredient that completes the recipe of the global topography of poverty and exploitation, one final portion about demography, the social science most firmly linked to biopower. Already in nineteenth-century England, Thomas Malthus, an economist and Anglican minister, warned of the catastrophic consequences of overpopulation. It is not uncommon today to hear similar calls for population control from international aid organizations and the NGO community. What these organizations propose (in charitable and humanitarian tones) is often in fact dictated and enacted in much more sinister terms by the major international agencies and national governments. Today's Malthusianism often takes the form of withholding from some populations aid for food or sanitation infrastructure and even coercive sterilization campaigns. The strategies of national and international organizations are complemented here by the thirst for profit of the multinational corporations, who are disinclined to invest in the most impoverished parts of the world and sometimes even refuse to sell them medicines at prices they can afford. Poverty and disease become indirect tools of population control. We are certainly in favor of birth control and family-planning programs that are adopted voluntarily. Most discussions of demographic explosions and population crises, however, we should be clear, are not really oriented toward either bettering the lives of the poor or maintaining a sustainable total global population in line with the capacities of the planet but are rather concerned primarily with which social groups reproduce and which do not. The crisis, in other words, is specifically that *poor* populations are increasing both in the dominant and subordinated parts of the world. (Liberal economic theories of population control, ever since the time when Reverend Malthus tested them in his Anglican parish, have always detested the poor's disgusting proclivity to reproduce.) This is particularly clear when we link the talk of population crisis to the catastrophic announcements that white populations, especially in Europe, are declining both in absolute terms and more dramatically relative to nonwhite populations in Europe and worldwide. The fundamental crisis, in other words, is that the color of the global population is changing, becoming darker. It is difficult to separate most contemporary projects of population control from a kind of racial panic. This is primarily what leads to the political machinations and the global state of demographic alert. The reproduction of life must be adjusted to preserve the hierarchies of global space and guarantee the reproduction of the political order of capital. This is perhaps the basest form of biopower: if as they used to say numbers are power, then the reproduction of all populations must be controlled.

In the contemporary period of transition, the global interregnum, we can see emerging a new topography of exploitation and economic hierarchies the lines of which run above and below national boundaries. We are living in a system of global apartheid. We should be clear, however, that apartheid is not simply a system of *exclusion*, as if subordinated populations were simply cut off, worthless, and disposable. In the global Empire today, as it was before in South Africa, apartheid is a productive system of *hierarchical inclusion* that perpetuates the wealth of the few through the labor and poverty of the many. The global political body is in this way also an economic body defined by the global divisions of labor and power.

A TRIP TO DAVOS

Davos, Switzerland, is the place where each year, except when protests make it impractical, the financial, industrial, and political oligarchies of the world go for a few days in winter to hold the World Economic Forum and plan the destiny of capitalist globalization. Many of the proponents and detractors of the present world order conceive of globalization as if it were determined by an unregulated capitalism—with free markets and free trade—which often goes by the name of "neoliberalism." A brief trip to snow-covered Davos, however, can help dispel this notion of an unregulated capitalism because there we can see clearly the need for leaders of major corporations to negotiate and cooperate with the political leaders of the dominant nation-states and the bureaucrats of the supranational economic institutions. And there too we can see that the national and global levels of political and economic control do not, in fact, conflict with each other but actually work together hand in glove. At Davos, in short, we can see the institutional relationships that support and regulate the global political and economic system. This is a nerve center of the global body politic.

The most important lesson to learn from Davos is simply that such a meeting is necessary: the economic, political, and bureaucratic elites of the world need to work together in constant relation. In more general terms, it demonstrates the old lesson that *no economic market can exist without political order and regulation.* If by free market one means a market that is autonomous and spontaneous, free from political controls, then there is no such thing as a free market at all. It is simply a myth. With the persistence of this myth it seems that the nostalgia for the old Indian Bureau, where the great economists of the British Empire who circulated fearlessly between the Foreign Office and the Bank of England were trained, is still alive and powerful. Even the free market of British capitalism's liberal heyday in the mid-nineteenth century, however, was created and sustained by state power, an articulated legal structure, national and international divisions of labor, wealth, and power, and so forth. An economic market is always necessarily embedded in a social market and ultimately in political structures of power.[82] Those who advocate freeing markets or trade from state control are not really asking for *less* political control but merely a *different kind* of political control. It is not a question of whether the state is weak or strong or whether political forces intervene in the economy. It is only a question of *how* the state and other political forces will intervene. Later in this chapter we will investigate how political and legal intervention is necessary today to protect and expand the realm of private property. For now, it is sufficient to illustrate this point simply by referring to the fact that political control is needed to placate and defeat labor struggles against capital. Behind every labor negotiation stands political power and its threat of force. If there were no political regulation, that is, no relationship of force to solve labor conflicts, then there would be no capitalist market. This is, for example, how neoliberalism triumphed in the late twentieth century. That period of market freedom would not have existed if Prime Minister Thatcher had not defeated the miners in Wales and if President Reagan had not destroyed the union of air traffic controllers. All the proponents of free markets know deep down that only political regulation and force allow for the free market. The compatibility between political control and economic markets is clear, furthermore, when we look at the form and management of business firms themselves. Throughout the twentieth century, scholars have noted how the institutional structures of corporations and state offices develop to resemble each other ever more closely and how business firms become ever more solidly inserted into public institutions.[83] It should be no surprise that the same few individuals so often pass effortlessly from the highest government offices to corporate boardrooms and back in the course of their careers. The business, bureaucratic, and political elites are certainly no strangers when they gather at the World Economic Forum. They already know each other quite well.

Globalization therefore does not mean an end or even a lessening of political and legal controls over corporations and economic markets but indicates rather shifts in the kinds of controls. The constant interplay between global market forces and legal or political institutions can be grouped into three general categories or levels: private agreements and private forms of authority in the global market that are created and managed by corporations themselves; regulatory mechanisms established through trade agreements between nation-states that directly control specific practices of international trade and production; and general norms that operate at the international or global level and are supported by international or supranational institutions.

The first level is characterized by the many emerging forms of private authority whereby businesses govern global economic activity outside the controls of nation-states or other governmental structures.[84] One example of such private authority is the new, global form of *lex mercatoria*, or "law merchant." *Lex mercatoria* traditionally names a legal system that has allowed merchants or businesses (particularly shipping, insurance, banking, and commercial enterprises) to make contracts independently in areas outside of state controls based on shared customary legal understandings.[85] *Lex mercatoria* originally referred to the legal structures that governed trade among merchants in medieval Europe at centers outside the jurisdictions of all the sovereign powers. Today in the world market there is an extensive realm of private business contracts that might be considered a new *lex mercatoria*. One can certainly imagine many instances when businesses need a legal framework that does not depend on any one national legal system but rather functions outside and supplements the national structures in the realm of global business. Imagine, for example, that at their offices in New York a French company contracts with a German company to deliver a supply of oil from its wells in Kazakhstan. Does U.S. law govern the contract or French, German, or Kazakhstan law? The customary structures of *lex mercatoria* are intended to address such cases and provide a common framework. Indeed many of the business contracts signed in today's global economy are not validated by nation-states but simply constructed by the law firms that serve the multi- and transnational corporations.

Today's *lex mercatoria* and the markets it regulates are much more extensive than in the past. Markets have changed not only with respect to space and time—exchangeable goods no longer ride on the back of the mule of the Florentine merchant to Burgundy but travel at high speeds across the globe—and not only with respect to the nature of the goods exchanged, which now include all kinds of immaterial goods, such as services, ideas, images, and codes. The markets we speak of today have also extended their domain to all aspects of economic life, encompassing now not only circulation but also the production of both material and immaterial goods, and even the social reproduction of populations. Furthermore, the regulation that the new *lex mercatoria* exerts over these markets is more extensive. Economic theories that focus on "transaction costs," for example, that is, costs other than the money price incurred in trading goods or services, highlight the capacity of self-management of businesses in the field of international trade and detail the minimum conditions that make this possible. The elements of market cohesion that such theories identify as necessary conditions really become in this context rules of conduct or legal norms for interactions among businesses. To the extent that corporations and their law firms develop an international and even global regime of *lex mercatoria* and thereby establish the normative processes that regulate globalization, capital creates in its weakest form a kind of "global governance without government." The resulting regime of global law is no longer a captive of state structures and no longer takes the form of written codes or preestablished rules but is purely conventional and customary. Law here is not an external constraint that regulates capital but rather an internal expression of agreement among capitalists. This is really a kind of capitalist utopia.

The generality of this "law through contracts" developed in the new *lex mercatoria* and the governing capacity of corporate law firms, however, should not be exaggerated. The dream of capital's self-rule is, in fact, very limited. It is true that to a certain extent the new global *lex mercatoria* has been able to develop in the period of interregnum because the grasp of nation-states on the powers of economic regulation has been loosened and corporations are partially able to pry themselves away. One should never forget, however, that the private authority that emerges in this realm of business contracts can exist only with the backing of political authorities: behind every utopia of capitalist self-government there is a strong, supporting political authority. For such a system to function, for example, the different national markets must be stable and configured similarly to one another. Most important, the rights of capital, such as the rights to defend property and control labor, must be guaranteed similarly in the different national markets to allow productive activities to engage one another with a continuous circulation and minimum friction. Furthermore, since private law always depends on public law to guarantee obligations and sanctions, *lex mercatoria* turns out to be completely insufficient when the regulation of business interactions requires legal sanction. Nation-states stand behind international business contracts and carry constantly the threat of sanction. Some nation-states, of course, wield overwhelming authority and others almost none at all. Perhaps we should say that law in this context represents not really the opportunity of all but the privilege of the few.

At a second level we find that nation-states provide a more substantial notion of global governance, which introduces stronger elements of authority. Bilateral and multilateral trade agreements between and among nation-states are one way in which relations of authority and force are codified and institutionalized on a higher, more general level. International trade agreements have long existed, but now they are tending to create truly global forms of authority. The World Trade Organization (WTO) is perhaps the most visible example of such a global institution. The WTO is a real forum for the global aristocracy, in which we see expressed clearly all the antagonisms and contradictions among nation-states, including their conflicting interests, their unequal powers, and their tendency to align along north-south divisions. This second level is the realm in which we can recognize most clearly the interregnum halfway on the path from national and international law to global or imperial law, where a new global governance is supported by a vast array of legal authorities, normative systems, and procedures. In the contradictory new global economic order that is emerging through international agreements, there are woven together both globalizing tendencies and resurgent nationalist elements, both liberal proposals and self-interested perversions of liberal ideals, both regional political solidarities and neocolonial operations of commercial and financial domination. We can recognize the resurgent economic nationalism, for example, in the way the most powerful countries impose protectionist measures as soon as an important sector of their own national economy, such as steel production or agriculture, is affected adversely by global markets. The self-interested perversions of liberal ideals can be seen in the way that antitrust laws, adopted by the most dominant countries, aimed at defending competition in the national economy are weakened and subverted in order to allow monopoly practices and destroy competition on the international level. With regard to financial domination, one need only look at the restrictive monetary policies imposed on various regions, such as those dictated by the euro in Eastern Europe and by the Latin American currency boards that link national currencies to the dollar. Despite the coexistence of these contradictory elements, the tendency toward the formation of a global economic order is irreversible. Precisely in this regard, some scholars have recognized that the transformations of sovereignty imposed by globalization have given rise not to a simple subtraction of power from the nation-states but rather a global sovereignty that is more "complex."[86]

Finally, at a third level we find the most clearly institutionalized elements of the regulatory apparatus of the global economy. Many of these institutions, such as the World Bank, the International Monetary Fund (IMF), and the economic development organizations of the United Nations, were created at the end of the Second World War to regulate the old international order, but they have gradually transformed their functions to match the needs of the changing economic order. These supranational economic institutions are governed by representatives of the member states but not with equal voting power. Whereas in the WTO each nation has one vote, the World Bank and IMF have a strange "one dollar, one vote" system, such that voting rights are proportional to monetary contributions. In 2003, for example, the United States controlled more than 17 percent of the total votes in the IMF, which has 183 member countries, and the other G7 countries together a total of more than 46 percent.[87] The proportions of votes in the World Bank are roughly the same. And yet the institutions are not completely controlled by the voting member states, which not infrequently leads to expressions of irritation from powerful members such as the United States. Like all large bureaucracies, they develop a limited autonomy and function as not international but properly global institutions. At this global level, the sources of legitimation are internal to the system, which is to say, the economic, political, and legal decisions tend to coincide with one another. The principal supranational institutions, of course, do have very different functions and divergent institutional cultures, which can at times lead to conflict and criticism among the agencies. In general terms, one could say that the IMF is dominated by economic technicians whereas many working at the World Bank and the UN aid agencies have an ethics of social welfare close to that of the NGO community.[88] Despite such differences, however, we will argue, these supranational institutions exercise common and coherent economic and political controls.

The IMF is perhaps the most ideologically coherent of the supranational economic institutions. It was founded at Bretton Woods in 1944 to regulate international monetary cooperation and to preserve the stability of international financial markets between the victors and the vanquished of the Second World War, and thus its mandate was explicitly to avoid the monetary disaster that resulted from the peace of Versailles. In the final decades of the twentieth century, however, the IMF substantially modified its mission along three primary axes: globalization of trade, financialization of markets, and global integration of the circuits of production. The IMF is thus charged with developing a way to govern the new forms of global social production (which are now post-Fordist, postmodern, and defined by the biopolitical condition of the multitude) through financial mechanisms. The basic project of the IMF has become forcing states to abandon Keynesian social programs and adopt monetarist policies. It dictates for ailing and poor economies a neoliberal formula that includes minimal spending on public welfare, privatization of public industry and wealth, and the reduction of public debt. This formula, which has come to be known as the "Washington Consensus," has always been criticized from outside and also from within the supranational economic institutions.[89] Some object on economic grounds, for example, to the way that the policies have been applied as an invariable model in different countries without regard for national specificity and without accounting for the relationship between monetary policies and social dynamics. Others object more generally to the political agenda of the Washington Consensus model: a monetary policeman is never neutral and always supports a specific political regime. After the economic disasters in Southeast Asia in 1997 and Argentina in 2000, which have been largely blamed on the IMF, the model has been even more widely criticized. And yet, despite the criticism and the economic failures, the IMF continues to dictate neoliberal monetarist policies that are largely unchanged.

At the other end of the spectrum of the global institutions, the World Bank continually announces projects dedicated to social welfare, aimed at problems such as global poverty and hunger. The World Bank was created together with the IMF in 1944 and charged with supporting the economic development of the subordinated countries, primarily through loans for specific projects. In the course of its history, and particularly during the tenure of Robert McNamara from 1968 to 1981, the Bank has focused increasing attention on poverty.[90] There are indeed numerous individuals working in the World Bank and various UN umbrella organizations, such as the Food and Agriculture Organization (FAO), who are doing their utmost to reduce global poverty and lessen the divisions of global apartheid. No one should deny their convictions or minimize the good that comes of their efforts, but neither should we ignore the real limitations that frustrate them every day. One of the greatest restrictions from the perspective of those working in these institutions is that they are forced to work with and funnel money through state governments. All the corruption, political divisions, and economic, racial, and gender hierarchies of these states thus become necessarily part of the development or aid projects, often distorting or destroying their intended effects. Many wish they could work directly with the populations and circumvent the states, but the mandate of all these international agencies requires that they work only with states and not interfere with their internal political affairs. The only solution they have is to bind these states by putting conditions on aid—limiting corruption by undermining state sovereignty. Even when the World Bank does confront social problems such as poverty or migration, it has to make these projects consistent with and supportive of the global order. As a result, as we will see in part 3, many criticize the types of projects that the World Bank encourages and lament the debts that it leaves for states to repay.

We need to take a step back from the differences and the family squabbles among the IMF, the World Bank, and the other supranational agencies to see the general design that, despite these conflicts, unites the institutions. The fact of having different functions and even different institutional cultures does not mean that these institutions act in ways that are contradictory one to the other. A general constraint in the final instance determines and unites the activities of all these institutions, since their legitimacy resides ultimately in the ends of their political design, that is, at a most basic level, the project to establish a liberal order for the global capitalist market. Consider a hypothetical example: if two countries have economies that are equally in crisis and performing equally badly, the IMF may impose strict terms of austerity to the one that is more a threat to the global neoliberal order (one where perhaps the elements of class struggle are strong, such as Argentina) and not apply those dictates to the one that is a necessary element in the maintenance of global order (such as Turkey, which serves now as an essential piece in the construction of imperial order in the Middle East). Consequently, the World Bank and the WTO will provide more financial assistance and more commercial advantages for the latter than the former. The norms and regulations dictated by these institutions are, of course, not always uniform and continuous, but despite obstacles and conflicts they do operate within a general band of agreement.

At this point we can begin to see the general design in which the three levels of regulatory apparatuses work together in a combined structure of capitalist market forces and legal-political institutions to form a quasi-global government or a global quasi-government. The first level is the self-regulation of capitalist interactions in the interest of guaranteeing profits; the second involves mediations among nation-states that build consensus at an international level; and the third is the constituent project of the creation of a new global authority. The contractual agreements of the new global *lex mercatoria*, the national and regional trade policies and agreements, and the supranational economic institutions coordinate with each other to legislate the global economy to preserve and reproduce the current order. They must all, for example, strive to create and maintain the market conditions necessary to guarantee contracts between corporations. The interests of the most wealthy and powerful corporations and nations, despite conflicts, must be addressed without fail. What they together must preserve at the most basic level are the global divisions of labor and power, the hierarchies that define the global political body. That is why the image of cozy personal encounters in snow-covered Davos is such a useful standpoint from which to understand the system. Corporate leaders cannot do it on their own, neither can national officials or supranational bureaucrats. They need to work together.

Some who protest against the supranational economic institutions, as we will see in part 3, demand that they be reformed or even abolished because they serve to maintain the divisions and hierarchies of wealth and power in the world. We need constantly to keep in mind, however, how these institutions function together with the other two levels of global economic regulation. From the perspective of this complex whole we can see that eliminating the IMF or the World Bank would not lessen the global hierarchies. Another organism or institution would have to rise to fill its role in the overall structure, or, worse, there would simply be less regulation of the dominant businesses and states—a dangerous situation for capital and a certain disaster for the rest of us. Reforming the supranational institutions, furthermore, is possible only within certain limits because, as we said, they are constrained to reproduce the current global order. More important ultimately, then, are the systemic limitations that will block any substantial reform. The supranational economic institutions must work along with national officials and business leaders to reproduce the global economic order along with its internal hierarchies, and the margin of flexibility on this point is small. This is the hard rock that will crush any serious effort of reform.

BIG GOVERNMENT IS BACK

Big government actually never went away, but certainly it has become more clearly evident in recent years, especially since September 11, 2001. The various military and legal projects for global security led primarily by the United States since that date, for example, are oriented in part toward stabilizing and guaranteeing the global economic order. In some respects, after September 11 the private forms of authority over the global economy, such as the new *lex mercatoria,* along with all the mechanisms of international trade and the macroeconomic equilibria that make them possible, went into crisis. The dominant nation-states had to intervene to guarantee all levels of economic interactions—financial transactions, insurance relationships, air transportation, and so forth. The crisis gave a quick reminder of just how much capital needs a sovereign authority standing behind it, a truth that rises up into view every time there are serious cracks in the market order and hierarchy.

The big government that guarantees market order must be in part a military power. Capital occasionally has to call on an army to force open unwilling markets and stabilize existing ones. In the early nineteenth century, for example, British capital needed the British military to open up the Chinese market with its victory in the Opium War. This is not to say, however, that all military actions are explained by specific economic interests. It is not adequate to think, for example, that the U.S.-led military actions in recent decades—Afghanistan and Iraq, much less Somalia, Haiti, and Panama—were primarily directed at a specific economic advantage, such as access to cheap oil. Such specific goals are secondary. The primary link between military action and economic interest exists only at a much more general level of analysis, abstract from any particular national interest. *Military force must guarantee the conditions for the functioning of the world market,* guaranteeing, that is, the divisions of labor and power of the global political body. This effort is paradoxical, however, because the relationship between security and profits cuts two ways. On one hand, the deployment of state military power is necessary to guarantee the security of the global markets but, on the other hand, the security regimes tend to raise national borders and obstruct the global circuits of production and trade that had been the basis of some of the greatest profits. The United States and other military powers must discover a way to make the interests of security and economic profits compatible and complementary.

We should be clear that the newly prominent need for a big government to support the economy, especially since September 11, does not represent in any way a return to Keynesianism. Under Keynesianism the nation-state supported the stability and growth of the economy by providing mechanisms to mediate the conflicts and interests of the working class and in the process expanded the social demand for production. The forms of sovereignty we see now, on the contrary, reside completely on the side of capital without any mediatory mechanisms to negotiate its conflictual relationship with labor. It is interesting in this regard how ambivalent the position of capital is when risk is the dominant characteristic of economic activity and development, and indeed of all social interaction. The world is a dangerous place, and the role of big government and military intervention is to reduce risks and provide security while maintaining the present order.

Big government is also necessary for economic regulation, but in the present context this turns out to be just as paradoxical as its military role. Just as September 11 was a brutal reminder of the need for security, the Enron scandal was a reminder of the need for big government to combat corruption. The Enron scandal was significant not only because so many investors were affected and such prominent politicians had close ties to the corporation but also and most important because the corrupt business practices were widely seen not as an isolated case but rather a generalized phenomenon that implicated a common way of doing business. The Enron executives and the Arthur Andersen auditors are certainly not the only ones to engage in such forms of strategic misrepresentation. It is perhaps not surprising that in this period of interregnum corruption would become generalized. The weakening of national legal regulations, the preeminence of unwritten rules over codified norms, and the weak form of governance make it open season for the profit hunters. Anytime there is a passage from one regime to another, where the old rules no longer hold and the new have not solidly taken effect, corruption triumphs. The task of big government fighting corruption becomes paradoxical, however, when the regulation disrupts the normal business practices that are basic to profits. The Enron disaster was not just a matter of falsified accounts but also the risky practice of financial speculation with energy futures, which had direct and disastrous consequences for the California energy market. This accepted practice is a form of corruption. One might think of inflated stock market values as another kind of corruption that states are charged with combating. The chairman of the Federal Reserve and the central bankers have to calm the irrational exuberance of the markets without undermining economic profits. As Tacitus says, when the republic is at its most corrupt, the laws are most numerous, but, we should add, these laws, numerous as they are, cannot prevent the corruption because it is essential to the system.

The issue of corruption becomes even more contradictory when it is combined with military actions in projects of "democratic transitions" and "nation building." The task of these projects is not only to create a stable and peaceful regime but also a regime that functions (usually in very subordinate fashion) within the global economic and political system, as an organ of the global body politic. The example that stands behind all the contemporary projects of nation building in this regard is the integration of the former Soviet Union into the global capitalist market. As the former Soviet economies were transformed to adapt to the global divisions of labor and power, privatized state industries and exclusive import-export licenses were transferred according to family and political connections to create the enormous fortunes of the new oligarchs. At the same time powerful Russian mafias emerged in control of a wide range of criminal activities. "Democratic transition," we learned, is a code phrase for corruption. Such corruption may conflict with the need for a stable national political regime but at the same time facilitate integration into the global economic market. There is no need to be surprised, in any case, when such forms of corruption emerge during the long processes of nation building in Afghanistan and Iraq.

LIFE ON THE MARKET

One of the fundamental tasks of big government is the protection of private property. Ever since there was property there was theft, counterfeiting, corruption, sabotage, and other like transgressions. It is obvious that all mobile forms of material property, such as cars and jewelry, are constantly in danger of being stolen. Immobile forms of material property too run the risk of being damaged through sabotage or simple vandalism. Even land, that most secure form of property, suffers from insecurity. All private property, in other words, has always required police protection, but in the paradigm of immaterial production there is an expansion of immaterial property, which is even more volatile and uncontrollable, posing new security problems. As property becomes ethereal, it tends to slip through the grasp of all the existing mechanisms of protection, requiring expanded protection efforts on the part of the sovereign authority.

The new and increased security risks of immaterial property are due primarily to the very same qualities that make these goods useful and valuable in the first place. Computer programs and data banks, for example, are made vulnerable to destruction and corruption by the general connectivity of computer systems. Computer viruses, worms, and the like function as a form of sabotage, since, like the wooden clog thrown in to break the mechanical gears of the machine, they too use the machine's own functioning for its destruction, but they present significantly greater difficulties for security than other forms of sabotage because they do not require physical proximity. Computer sabotage only requires virtual access.

A more significant security problem than the destruction or corruption of immaterial property through connectivity is reproducibility, which does not threaten the property itself but simply destroys its private character. Many forms of illicit reproduction of immaterial products are quite obvious and simple—reproducing written texts, computer software, or audio and video property. They are so obvious because the social and economic utility of these immaterial forms of property depend precisely on their being easily reproducible at low cost, through techniques from the printing press and photocopy machine to digital recording. *The reproducibility that makes them valuable is exactly what threatens their private character*. Reproduction is, of course, very different from traditional forms of theft, because the original property is not taken away from its owner; there is simply more property for someone else. Private property is traditionally based on a logic of scarcity—material property cannot be in two places at once; if you have it I cannot have it—but the infinite reproducibility central to these immaterial forms of property directly undermines any such construction of scarcity.[91] The Napster experience is an interesting example because it poses the issue of reproduction in such a social form. The Napster Web site provided the platform for numerous users to freely share and copy recorded music in the form of mp3 files. In the exchanges among users the recorded music no longer functioned as private property in that it became common. This is an extension well beyond the traditional conceptions of theft or piracy in the sense that it is not merely the transfer of property from one owner to another but a violation of the private character of the property itself—perhaps a kind of social piracy. The Napster site was eventually closed down on the grounds that it facilitated the infringement of copyright, but there are innumerable other examples on the Web of texts, information, images, and other immaterial forms of private property that are illegally made freely accessible and reproducible. Such examples point toward some of the enormous new difficulties of policing private property.

Police activity and force, however, are really secondary in the establishment and preservation of private property; the primary force of big government to protect private property must be not might but right, that is, a legal structure that legitimates private ownership. New forms of property, especially immaterial forms, require new and expanded legal mechanisms for legitimation and protection. Many forms of immaterial property appear immediately to be unjust with respect to the accepted norms and thus require dramatic legal innovations. We can see this clearly, for example, in the case of "bioproperty," that is, life-forms that have become private property. Individual living beings, of course, have long been eligible for private ownership, but at question here is a more general form of bioproperty. Traditionally one can own one or ten or a hundred Holstein cows or Macintosh apple trees, but one cannot own Holstein cow or Macintosh apple tree as a life-form. The general form has traditionally been conceived to be part of nature and thus not eligible for ownership. Perhaps the most celebrated and controversial new example of such bioproperty is OncoMouse, the only animal type to date that has been patented. Du Pont laboratories together with Harvard University created OncoMouse by transplanting a human cancer-producing gene into a mouse. The mouse is predisposed to developing cancerous tumors and is thus useful for oncological research.[92] Du Pont sells individual mice as research tools, but the novel aspect here is that Du Pont does not merely own individual mice but the type of mouse as a whole.

The legal path for the private ownership of types of living organisms was opened in the United States by a 1980 Supreme Court decision that allowed a patent to be issued not only on the process for making a novel organism but on the organism itself. In 1972, a microbiologist filed a patent in the name of General Electric Company for bacteria that broke down crude oil and thus were useful in treating oil spills. The U.S. Patent and Trademark Office granted his patents both for the process of producing the bacteria and for the method of carrying the bacteria in straw floating on the water, but it refused his patent on the bacteria themselves. The office reasoned that microorganisms are products of nature and thus not patentable. The Supreme Court, however, ruled that the microbiologist's bacteria do not fall under that category because "his claim is not to a hitherto unknown natural phenomenon but to a nonnaturally occurring manufacture or composition of nature—a product of human ingenuity. . . ."[93] The Supreme Court reasoned in this case that the bacteria do not belong to nature because they are the result of human labor, and the exact same logic later established the basis for the patent of other life forms such as OncoMouse.

The legal innovation to protect such immaterial private property rests on a recognition of immaterial labor; in other words, what we previously considered part of nature and thus common property, the argument goes, is really the product of human labor and invention, and thus eligible for private ownership. This kind of innovation and expansion of the legal protection of private property applies to a wide range of new forms of property. One of the most complex and contested areas involves the ownership of genetic information. It is worth recounting as illustration one of the most widely discussed cases over the ownership of human genetic information that is valuable for medical treatment and research. In 1976 a patient at the University of California medical center began treatment for hairy-cell leukemia. The doctors recognized that his blood might have special properties for the treatment of leukemia and, in 1981, they were granted a patent in the name of the University of California on a T-cell line—that is, a sequence of genetic information—developed from the patient's blood; the potential value of the products derived for it was estimated at three billion dollars. The patient sued the university for ownership of the T cells and the genetic information, but the California

Supreme Court ruled against him. The court reasoned that the University of California was the rightful owner of the cell line because a naturally occurring organism (on which his claim rests) is not patentable, whereas the information scientists derive from it is patentable because it is the result of human ingenuity.[94]

Cases regarding ownership of the genetic information of plants, and thus ultimately the private ownership of seed and plant varieties, are decided according to the same legal logic and similarly rest on the basis of immaterial labor. Consider, for example, the "seed wars," in which the private ownership of seeds and plant varieties have been contested along the global north-south divide.[95] The global north is genetically poor in terms of varieties of plants, and yet the vast majority of patented plant varieties are owned in the north; the global south is genetically rich in terms of plant varieties but poor in patents. Moreover, many of the patents owned in the north are based on information derived from the genetic raw material found in plants in the south. The wealth of the north generates profits as private property, whereas the wealth of the south generates none since it is considered the common heritage of mankind. The legal basis for the private ownership of plant varieties is fundamentally the same one operative in the case of other living organisms, such as the oil spill bacteria and Oncomouse, and refers explicitly to labor. The plants, plant varieties, and germplasm (that is, the genetic information encoded in the seed) are eligible for private ownership if they are products of human labor and thus not part of nature.[96]

This question of ownership seems to us the central issue in the current debates over genetically modified foods. Some have sounded the alarm that genetically modified Frankenfoods are endangering our health and disrupting the order of nature. They are opposed to experimenting with new plant varieties because they think that the authenticity of nature or the integrity of the seed must not be violated.[97] To us this has the smell of a theological argument about purity. We maintain, in contrast, as we have argued at length already, that nature and life as a whole are always already artificial, and this is especially clear in the era of immaterial labor and biopolitical production. That does not mean, of course, that all changes are good. Like all monsters, genetically modified crops can be beneficial or harmful to society. The best safeguard is that experimentation be conducted democratically and openly, under common control, something that private ownership prevents. What we need most today in this regard are mobilizations that give us the power to intervene democratically in the scientific process. Just like in the early days of the AIDS pandemic, activists from groups like ACT-UP became specialists and challenged the right of scientists to maintain exclusive control of research and policy, so too today activists need to become specialists in genetic modification and its effects in order to open the process up to democratic control.[98] Furthermore, genetic modification has led to a flood of patents that transfer control from the farmers to the seed corporations. This functions as a key lever in the concentration of control over agriculture that we discussed earlier. The primary issue, in other words, is not that humans are changing nature but that nature is ceasing to be common, that it is becoming private property and exclusively controlled by its new owners.

The same logic of immaterial labor also serves as the legal basis finally in the property disputes involving traditional knowledge. Consider, first, the often-cited case of the neem tree in India. For centuries farmers in India have ground the seeds of the neem tree and scattered them on their fields in order to protect the crops from insects. Neem is a natural, nontoxic pesticide that is not harmful to plants. In 1985, W. R. Grace and Company, a multinational chemical corporation, applied for and was granted a patent for a neem-based pesticide that it marketed as organic, nontoxic, and so forth. That patent was unsuccessfully challenged in U.S. courts. In fact, between 1985 and 1998, forty patents were awarded to products based on the neem tree, some of them to Indian organizations and some not.[99] In a very similar case, the University of Mississippi Medical Center was granted a patent in 1995 on the "Use of Turmeric in Wound Healing." In India, turmeric powder is a traditional remedy for healing scrapes and cuts and had been used for generations. In 1996 the Council of Scientific and Industrial Research of India challenged the patent, and it was revoked. The patent was not revoked for the simple reason of its common usage in India. U.S. legal authorities are not required to accept the evidence of traditional knowledge produced outside the United States unless they are recognized and cited in scientific journals.

The turmeric patent was revoked, then, because its prior use had been documented in scientific publications. One interesting aspect of the case, of course, is that it reveals different standards for traditional and scientific knowledges. One might say that the legal system recognizes as labor only formal scientific activity and thus only its products are eligible for property; traditional forms of the production of knowledge are not recognized as labor and thus their products are regarded as the common heritage of humanity.[100]

In all of these cases, the right to the new forms of property—microorganisms, animals, plants, seed, and traditional knowledges—are dependent on the claim that they are produced and that they are produced, specifically, as knowledge, information, or code. Bioproperty, that is, the ownership of life-forms, relies on the production of the codes that define life. This is a two-step legal logic: since life-forms are defined by code and code is produced, then the one who produced the code has the right to own the life-forms.

Some of the most powerful critiques of today's enormous expansion of immaterial property and bioproperty claim that making the common private runs counter to the social good. One of the traditional arguments for protecting immaterial goods such as ideas as private property is to encourage creativity. Thomas Jefferson, for example, famously authored U.S. patent law in order to support technological innovation, and, in our own time, the mandate of the UN-sponsored World Intellectual Property Organization is to foster creativity and innovation by protecting intellectual property.[101] Increasingly today, however, private ownership that limits access to ideas and information thwarts creativity and innovation. Scholars and practitioners of Internet technologies have long insisted that whereas the early creativity of the cybernetic revolution and the development of the Internet were made possible by an extraordinary openness and access to information and technologies, all of this is now being progressively closed at all levels: physical connections, code, and content. The privatization of the electronic "commons" has become an obstacle to further innovation.[102] When communication is the basis of production, then privatization immediately hinders creativity and productivity. Scientists in microbiology, genetics, and adjacent fields similarly argue that scientific innovations and the advancement of knowledge is based on open collaboration and the free exchange of ideas, techniques, and information. Scientists are not generally driven to innovate by the potential of riches from patents, although the corporations and universities that employ them certainly are. The private ownership of knowledge and information is only an obstacle to the communication and cooperation at the base of social and scientific innovation.

It is no coincidence that so many scholars of intellectual property and the Internet use terms like an electronic and creative *commons* or the *new enclosures* of the Internet, because the current processes recall the earliest period of capitalist development. If the processes of neoliberal privatization continue, in fact, our era could end up resembling the Baroque, the period that emerged from the crisis of the European Renaissance. The rational lucidity and the passionate realism of the "new humanity" of the Renaissance had been exhausted and for expression—that is, for communicating and creating the beautiful—the Baroque had to resort to hyperbole and falsification. Behind the transformations of style and fashion, the mystifications of language, and the betrayal of the ontological foundations of knowledge, a more profound historical drama was taking place: the crisis of the first developments of manufacturing, the precipitous decline of the productivity of labor, and, most important, the refeudalization of agriculture along with the definitive privatization of the commons. The happy beginnings of the manufacturing bourgeoisie and its "virtue" were reduced, in the Baroque, to the "fortune" of the few, and the outlook for the future was clouded by a general fear of the new classes of producers, which bourgeois development itself had created. There is a distinct Baroque, neofeudal flavor to today's privatizations—the privatization of knowledges, information, communications networks, affective relationships, genetic codes, natural resources, and so forth. The rising biopolitical productivity of the multitude is being undercut and blocked by the processes of private appropriation.

The logic of the early period of capitalist development leads to a second type of challenge to the expansion of immaterial property and bioproperty, one that addresses who has the right to ownership. Traditional capitalist property law is based on labor: the one whose labor creates a good has the right to own it. I build a house and therefore it is mine. This labor logic remains fundamental, as we have seen, in the new property disputes: when a judge rules that bacteria, a seed, or an animal type is rightfully owned by the scientist who created it, the labor logic of property is at work. There is indeed a necessary relation between the fact that human labor in the realm of immaterial production increasingly directly produces life-forms and knowledges and the fact that ever more life-forms and knowledges become private property. (The increasing importance of immaterial property thus supports our earlier claim of a hegemony of immaterial labor.) In this entire field of immaterial production, however, the right or title to property is undercut by the same logic that supports it because the labor that creates property cannot be identified with any individual or even group of individuals. Immaterial labor is increasingly a common activity characterized by continuous cooperation among innumerable individual producers. Who, for example, produces the information of genetic code? Or who, alternatively, produces the knowledge of a plant's beneficial medical uses? In both cases, the information and knowledge is produced by human labor, experience, and ingenuity, but in neither case can that labor be isolated to an individual. Such knowledge is always produced in collaboration and communication, by working in common in expansive and indefinite social networks—in these two cases in the scientific community and the indigenous community. Scientists themselves once again give the most eloquent testimonies to the fact that knowledge and information are produced not by individuals but collectively in collaboration. And this collaborative, communicative, common process of knowledge production characterizes equally all the other realms of immaterial and biopolitical production. According to John Locke, labor creating private property is an extension of the body, but today that body is increasingly common. The legal justification of private ownership is undermined by the common, social nature of production. When the traditional capitalist right or title to property declines, then there tends to be nothing left to protect private property except violence.

The current paradoxes of immaterial property seem to make new again the young Marx's humanist invectives against private property. "Private property has made us so stupid and one-sided," he writes, that we denigrate all forms of *being* for the simple sense of *having*.[103] All human senses, including knowing, thinking, feeling, loving—in short, all of life—is corrupted by private property. Marx makes clear, however, that he does not want to go back to any kind of primitive communal ownership. He focuses rather on the contradiction in the logic of capital that points toward a new future resolution. On the one hand, as we have seen, capitalist private property rights are based on the individual labor of the producer, but on the other hand capital continually introduces more collective and collaborative forms of production: the wealth produced collectively by the workers becomes the private property of the capitalist. This contradiction becomes increasingly extreme in the realm of immaterial labor and immaterial property. Private property makes us stupid in part by making us think that everything valuable must be owned privately by someone. Economists never tire of telling us that a good cannot be preserved and utilized efficiently unless it is owned privately. The truth is, however, that the vast majority of our world is not private property, and our social life functions only thanks to that fact. As we have seen in this chapter, in addition to traditional forms of property such as land, industries, and railroads, new goods, such as genetic information, knowledges, plants, and animals, are becoming private property. This is an example of what we called earlier the expropriation of the common. Still, we could not interact and communicate in our daily lives if languages, forms of speech, gestures, methods of conflict resolution, ways of loving, and the vast majority of the practices of living were not common. Science would come to a standstill if our great accumulations of knowledge, information, and methods of study were not common. Social life depends on the common. Perhaps some day in the future we will look back and see how stupid we were in this period to let private property monopolize so many forms of wealth, posing obstacles to innovation and corrupting life, before we discovered how to entrust social life entirely to the common.

2.3 TRACES OF THE MULTITUDE

> The question of whether humanity has a predilection to-
> ward the good is preceded by the question whether there
> exists an event that can be explained in no other way than
> by that moral disposition. An event such as revolution.
> Kant says that this phenomenon [of revolution] can no
> longer be ignored in human history because it has re-
> vealed the existence in human nature of a disposition and
> a faculty toward the good, which until now no politics has
> ever discovered in the course of events.
>
> —FRIEDRICH NIETZSCHE

We saw in the last chapter how common productive flesh of the multitude
has been formed into the global political body of capital, divided geographically by hierarchies of labor and wealth, and ruled by a multilevel
structure of economic, legal, and political powers. We studied the physiology and anatomy of this global body through the topology and topography of exploitation. Our task now is to investigate the possibility that the
productive flesh of the multitude can organize itself otherwise and discover an alternative to the global political body of capital. Our point of
departure is our recognition that the production of subjectivity and the
production of the common can together form a spiral, symbiotic relationship. Subjectivity, in other words, is produced through cooperation and
communication and, in turn, this produced subjectivity itself produces
new forms of cooperation and communication, which in turn produce
new subjectivity, and so forth. In this spiral each successive movement
from the production of subjectivity to the production of the common is
an innovation that results in a richer reality. Perhaps in this process of
metamorphosis and constitution we should recognize the formation of the
body of the multitude, a fundamentally new kind of body, a common

body, a democratic body. Spinoza gives us an initial idea of what the anatomy of such a body might be. "The human body," he writes, "is composed of many individuals of different natures, each of which is highly composite"—and yet this multitude of multitudes is able to act in common as one body.[104] If the multitude is to form a body, in any case, it will remain always and necessarily an open, plural composition and never become a unitary whole divided by hierarchical organs. The traces of the multitude will present the same disposition and faculty toward the good that Kant finds in the revolutionary event.

THE MONSTROSITY OF THE FLESH

Postmodern society is characterized by the dissolution of traditional social bodies. Both sides in the debate between "modernists" and "postmodernists," which until recently inflamed academic and cultural discussions, recognize this dissolution. What really divides them is that modernists want to protect or resurrect the traditional social bodies and postmodernists accept or even celebrate their dissolution.[105] In the United States, for example, many authors, facing the breakdown of traditional social organizations and the threat of a fragmented individualistic society, evoke nostalgia for past social formations. Such projects of restoration—often based on family, church, and country—have long been a staple of the vision of the Right, but the most interesting and passionate recent pleas have emerged from the mainstream Left. Consider, for example, Robert Putnam's widely read account of the decline of civic and community organizations in the United States. Bowling clubs, bridge clubs, religious organizations, and the like used to provide a basic means of social aggregation, forming social groups and a cohesive society. The decline of such civic and community groups is a symptom of the general decline of all forms of social aggregation in the United States, Putnam argues, leaving the population not only bowling alone but living alone in a wide variety of ways.[106] A similar tone of nostalgia and regret for lost community dominates a series of popular studies about the recent changes in work. Traditional forms of labor, such as factory labor and even more so craft work, provided stable employment and a set of skills that allowed workers to develop and take pride in a coherent, lifelong career with a durable social connection centered on their jobs. The passage from Fordist to post-Fordist labor arrangement, with the rise of service labor and "flexible," "mobile," unstable types of employment, has destroyed these traditional forms of work, along with the forms of life they generated. Instability, they lament, undermines character, trust, loyalty, mutual commitment, and family bonds.[107] Such accounts of the decline of traditional social forms and communities, tinged with nostalgia and regret, also correspond to a certain extent with calls to patriotism from one stream of the U.S. Left, which predated September 11, 2001, but was strongly reinforced by the events of that day. For these authors, love of country is another (and perhaps the highest) form of community that will—in addition to guaranteeing the defeat of enemies abroad—hold at bay the anomie and individualistic fragmentation that threatens our society at home.[108] In all of these cases, civic associations, work, family, and country, the ultimate object is the reconstruction of the unified social body and thus the re-creation of the people.

The mainstream European Left shares this sense of nostalgia for traditional social forms and communities, but in Europe it is most often expressed not in laments of our current state of isolation and individualism but in sterile repetitions of worn-out community rites. Community practices that used to be part of the Left now become empty shadows of community that tend to lead to senseless violence, from rabid soccer-fan clubs to charismatic religious cults and from revivals of Stalinist dogmatism to rekindled anti-Semitism. The parties and trade unions of the Left, in search of the strong values of old, seem too often to fall back on old gestures like an automatic reflex. The old social bodies that used to sustain them are no longer there. The people is missing.

Even when something that resembles the people does emerge on the social scene in the United States, Europe, or elsewhere, it appears to the leaders of the institutional Left as something deformed and threatening. The new movements that have arisen in the last decades—from the queer politics of ACT-UP and Queer Nation to the globalization demonstrations at Seattle and Genoa—are incomprehensible and threatening to

them, and thus monstrous. It is true, in fact, that with modern instruments and models today's social forms and even economic developments
can only appear chaotic and incoherent. Events and facts seem to flash in
discrete, disconnected images rather than unfold in a coherent narrative.
With modern eyes perhaps postmodernity is indeed characterized by the
end of grand narratives.

One should do away with all this nostalgia, which when not actually
dangerous is at best a sign of defeat. In this sense we are indeed "postmodernists." Looking at our postmodern society, in fact, free from any
nostalgia for the modern social bodies that have dissolved or the people
that is missing, one can see that what we experience is a kind of social
flesh, a flesh that is not a body, a flesh that is common, living substance.
We need to learn what this flesh can do. "The flesh," Maurice Merleau-
Ponty writes in a more philosophical register, "is not matter, is not mind,
is not substance. To designate it, we should need the old term "element,"
in the sense it was used to speak of water, air, earth, and fire."[109] The flesh
of the multitude is pure potential, an unformed life force, and in this
sense an element of social being, aimed constantly at the fullness of life.
From this ontological perspective, the flesh of the multitude is an elemental power that continuously expands social being, producing in excess of
every traditional political-economic measure of value. You can try to har-
ness the wind, the sea, the earth, but each will always exceed your grasp.
From the perspective of political order and control, then, the elemental
flesh of the multitude is maddeningly elusive, since it cannot be entirely
corralled into the hierarchical organs of a political body.

This living social flesh that is not a body can easily appear monstrous.
For many, these multitudes that are not peoples or nations or even communities are one more instance of the insecurity and chaos that has resulted from the collapse of the modern social order. They are social
catastrophes of postmodernity, similar in their minds to the horrible results of genetic engineering gone wrong or the terrifying consequences of
industrial, nuclear, or ecological disasters. The unformed and the un-
ordered are horrifying. The monstrosity of the flesh is not a return to the
state of nature but a result of society, an artificial life. In the previous era
modern social bodies and modern social order maintained, at least ideo-

logically, despite constant innovation, a natural character—the natural identities, for example, of the family, the community, the people, and the nation. In modernity the philosophies of vitalism could still protest against the damaging effects of technology, industrialization, and the commodification of existence by affirming the natural life force. Even in Martin Heidegger's critique of technology, when vitalism has become a kind of nihilism and aesthetics, there are echoes of the long tradition of existentialist resistance.[110] Every reference to life today, however, has to point to an artificial life, a social life.

The vampire is one figure that expresses the monstrous, excessive, and unruly character of the flesh of the multitude. Since Bram Stoker's Count Dracula landed in Victorian England, the vampire has been a threat to the social body and, in particular, to the social institution of the family.[111] The threat of the vampire is, first of all, its excessive sexuality. Its desire for flesh is insatiable, and its erotic bite strikes men and women equally, undermining the order of heterosexual coupling. Second, the vampire undermines the reproductive order of the family with its own, alternative mechanism of reproduction. New vampires are created by the bite of both male and female vampires, forming an eternal race of the undead. The vampire thus functions in the social imagination as one figure of the monstrosity of a society in which the traditional social bodies, such as the family, are breaking down. It should come as no surprise, then, that vampires have become so prevalent in recent years in popular novels, film, and television.[112] Our contemporary vampires turn out to be different. The vampires are still social outsiders, but their monstrosity helps others to recognize that we are all monsters—high school outcasts, sexual deviants, freaks, survivors of pathological families, and so forth. And more important, the monsters begin to form new, alternative networks of affection and social organization. The vampire, its monstrous life, and its insatiable desire has become symptomatic not only of the dissolution of an old society but also the formation of a new.

We need to find the means to realize this monstrous power of the flesh of the multitude to form a new society. On one hand, as Merleau-Ponty makes clear, the flesh is common. It is elemental like air, fire, earth, and water. On the other hand, these various monsters testify to the fact that we are all singular, and our differences cannot be reduced to any unitary social body. We need to write a kind of anti–*De Corpore* that runs counter to all the modern treatises of the political body and grasps this new relationship between commonality and singularity in the flesh of the multitude. Once again, Spinoza is the one who most clearly anticipates this monstrous nature of the multitude by conceiving of life as a tapestry on which the singular passions weave a common capacity of transformation, from desire to love and from the flesh to the divine body. The experience of life is for Spinoza a search for truth, perfection, and the joy of God.[113] Spinoza shows us how today, in postmodernity, we can recognize these monstrous metamorphoses of the flesh as not only a danger but also a possibility, the possibility to create an alternative society.

The concept of the multitude forces us to enter a new world in which we can only understand ourselves as monsters. Gargantua and Pantagruel, in the sixteenth century, in the midst of that revolution that created European modernity, were giants that served as emblems for the extreme powers of liberty and invention. They strode across the revolutionary terrain and proposed the gigantic endeavor of becoming free. Today we need new giants and new monsters to put together nature and history, labor and politics, art and invention in order to demonstrate the new power that is being born in the multitude. We need a new Rabelais or, rather, many.[114]

INVASION OF THE MONSTERS

In the seventeenth century, alongside erudite libraries and laboratories of fantastic inventions, arose the first cabinets of monstrosities. These collections had all kinds of strange objects, from malformed fetuses in jars to the "human-chicken" of Leipzig—all the kinds of things that could feed the imagination of Frederik Ruysch in Amsterdam to create his spectacular allegorical assemblages. Even in the absolutist kingdoms it became common practice to create cabinets of natural history, full of curiosities. Peter the Great, after having constructed the city of Saint Petersburg in an extraordinarily brief time through the suffering and sacrifice of millions of workers, bought Ruysch's col-

lection and on the basis of it constructed a natural history museum in Saint Petersburg. Why such an invasion of monsters?[115]

The rise of monsters in the seventeenth and eighteenth centuries coincided with the crisis of the ancient eugenic beliefs and served to undermine the old teleological assumptions in the emerging natural sciences. By eugenic beliefs we mean the philosophical framework that identifies both the origins of the cosmos and the ethical order in a metaphysical principle: "He who is born well will rule happily." This Greek principle infiltrated the Judeo-Christian creationist worldview through thousands of paths. As for the teleological assumptions, these view every creature and its development as determined by the ends or finalities that link it to the order of the cosmos. It is no coincidence that eugenics and finalism would in the course of "Western civilization" be united: fixed origins and ends maintain the order of the world. But in the seventeenth and eighteenth centuries this old order of civilization was open to question. While the great wars that founded modernity wrought indescribable suffering, monsters began to incarnate the objections to the order determined by eugenics and finalism. The effects were even stronger in politics than in metaphysics: the monster is not an accident but the ever present possibility that can destroy the natural order of authority in all domains, from the family to the kingdom. Various modern luminaries, from Count de Buffon and Baron D'Holbach to Denis Diderot, investigated the possibility of new normative figures in nature or, really, the relationship between causality and error and the indeterminacy of order and power. The monsters even infected the most enlightened ones! This is where the real history of modern European scientific method begins. Before this point, as D'Holbach charges, the dice were loaded, and the orderly results we saw in the development of nature were fake; now the game is finally no longer rigged. That is what we owe to monsters: the break with teleology and eugenics opens the problem of what the source of creation is, how it is expressed, and where it will lead.

Today, when the social horizon is defined in biopolitical terms, we should not forget those early modern stories of monsters. The monster effect has only multiplied. Teleology now can only be called ignorance and superstition. Scientific method is defined increasingly in the realm of indetermination and every real entity is produced in an aleatory and singular way, a sudden emergence of the new. Frankenstein is now a member of the family. In this situation, then, the discourse of living beings must become a theory of their construction and the possible futures that await them. Immersed in this unstable reality, confronted by the increasing artificiality of the biosphere and the institutionalization of the social, we have to expect monsters to appear at any moment. "Monstrum prodigium," as Augustine of Hippo said, miraculous monsters. But today the wonder comes every time we recognize that the old standards of measure no longer hold, every time old social bodies decompose and their remains fertilize the new production of social flesh.

Gilles Deleuze recognizes the monster within humanity. Man is the animal, he claims, that is changing its own species. We take this announcement seriously. The monsters are advancing, and scientific method has to deal with them. Humanity transforms itself, its history, and nature. The problem is no longer deciding whether to accept these human techniques of transformation but learning what to do with them and discerning whether they will work to our benefit or detriment. Really, we have to learn to love some of the monsters and to combat others. The great Austrian novelist Robert Musil poses the paradoxical relation between madness and surplus desire in the figure of Moosbrugger, a monstrous criminal: if humanity were able to dream collectively, he writes, it would dream of Moosbrugger. Musil's Moosbrugger can serve as the emblem for our ambivalent relation to monsters and for our need to enhance our excessive powers of transformation and attack the monstrous, horrible world that the global political body and capitalist exploitation have made for us. We need to use the monstrous expressions of the multitude to challenge the mutations of artificial life transformed into commodities, the capitalist power to put up for sale the metamorphoses of nature, the new eugenics that support the ruling power. The new world of monsters is where humanity has to grasp its future.

PRODUCTION OF THE COMMON

We have seen that the flesh of the multitude produces in common in a way that is monstrous and always exceeds the measure of any traditional social bodies, but this productive flesh does not create chaos and social disorder. What it produces, in fact, is *common*, and that common we share serves as the basis for future production, in a spiral, expansive relationship. This is perhaps most easily understood in terms of the example of communication as production: we can communicate only on the basis of languages, symbols, ideas, and relationships we share in common, and in turn the results of our communication are new common languages, symbols, ideas, and relationships. Today this dual relationship between production and the common—the common is produced and it is also productive—is key to understanding all social and economic activity.

One resource in modern philosophy for understanding the production and productivity of the common can be found in American pragmatism and the pragmatic notion of *habit*. Habit allows the pragmatists to displace the traditional philosophical conceptions of subjectivity as located either on the transcendental plane or in some deep inner self. They seek subjectivity rather in daily experience, practices, and conduct. Habit is the common in practice: the common that we continually produce and the common that serves as the basis for our actions.[116] Habit is thus halfway between a fixed law of nature and the freedom of subjective action—or, better, it provides an alternative to that traditional philosophical binary. Habits create a nature that serves as the basis of life. William James refers to them as the enormous flywheel of society, which provides the ballast or inertia necessary for social reproduction and living day to day. Marcel Proust's great novel, in a rather different register, meditates at length on the necessity of habits for life and the significance they give the small deviations from them: the late goodnight kiss from mother, dinner one hour earlier on Sunday, and so forth. Habits are like physiological functions, such as breathing, digesting, and circulating blood. We take them for granted and cannot live without them. Unlike physiological functions, however, habits and conduct are shared and social. They are produced and reproduced in interaction and communication with others.[117] Habits are thus never really individual or personal. Individual habits, conduct, and subjectivity only arise on the basis of social conduct, communication, acting in common. Habits constitute our social nature.

Habits look not only backward but also forward. If habits were simply rote repetition of past acts, following the grooved ruts in which we walk every day, they would be merely dead encumbrances. "We may think of habits as means, waiting, like tools in a box, to be used by conscious resolve," John Dewey wrote. "But they are something more than that. They are active means, means that project themselves, energetic and dominating ways of acting."[118] Habits are living practice, the site of creation and innovation. If we look at habits from an individual standpoint, our power to change may appear small, but as we said habits are not really formed or performed individually. From the social standpoint, in contrast, from the standpoint of social communication and collaboration, we have in common enormous power to innovate. Really the pragmatists give priority to neither the individual nor the social. The motor of production and innovation lies between the two, in communication and collaboration, acting in common. Habits are not really obstacles to creation but, on the contrary, are the common basis on which all creation takes place. Habits form a nature that is both produced and productive, created and creative—an ontology of social practice in common.

We can already recognize a concept of the multitude emerging from this pragmatic notion of habit. Singularities interact and communicate socially on the basis of the common, and their social communication in turn produces the common. The multitude is the subjectivity that emerges from this dynamic of singularity and commonality. The pragmatists' notion of social production, however, is so linked to modernity and modern social bodies that its utility today for the multitude is necessarily limited. John Dewey's work, more than that of any of the other pragmatists, develops fully the relationship between pragmatism and modern social reform but also makes clear how it is limited to modernity. Dewey is best known for his efforts in education reform, but he was also actively engaged in efforts to reform the U.S. political system, particularly in the 1920s and 1930s.[119] Dewey claimed that industrial modernization and corporate capital have created not only economic disaster but also a disastrous political situation in which the public cannot participate actively in government. He even polemicized against Roosevelt's New Deal reforms because they did not go far enough: rather than a planned economy, Dewey advocated what might be called a planning democracy.[120] He insisted, in other words, on separating the political from the economic in order to enact a pragmatic political reform. Whereas the economic realm for Dewey is condemned to instrumentality—in modern industry habit only appears as dumb repetition—the political is the realm in which communication and collaboration can fulfill the democratic promise of the pragmatic notions of habit and social conduct. Dewey thus demonstrates both the applicability of pragmatism to modern political reform and its limitation to modernity. What we need to recognize today instead is a notion of the production and productivity of the common that extends equally from the political to the economic and all the realms of biopolitical production. The productivity of the common furthermore must be able to determine not simply the reform of existing social bodies but their radical transformation in the productive flesh of the multitude.

There are indeed numerous theories that accomplish this transformation to the conditions of postmodernity, and we can summarize them well in the conceptual shift from *habit* to *performance* as the core notion of the production of the common. Examples include the feminist and queer theories of performativity that mark a postmodern *anthropological* transformation.[121] These new theories of the body that emerged in the 1990s go beyond the old adage that we should "remember the body," because leaving the body out and failing to recognize sexual difference, as philosophy and politics have traditionally done, assumes the male body as the norm, perpetuating and masking the subordination of women. Feminism has a necessarily contradictory relation to the body, since, on the one hand, the body is the site of the oppression of women, and, on the other, women's bodily specificity is the basis of feminist practice. The new theories of the body seem to resolve this paradox insofar as they are really *against* the body and *for* the common performativity of queer social flesh—and here we can begin to glimpse the connection to pragmatism and its notion of social life in common. Judith Butler articulates the richest and most sophisticated theory against the body and also develops clearly the performative processes of constitution. Butler attacks the natural conception of sexual difference, the traditional feminist conception, in other words, that gender is socially constructed whereas sex is natural. The natural conception of sex or the social and political body of "woman," she maintains, subordinates the differences among women in terms of race and sexuality. In particular, the natural conception of sex brings with it heteronormativity, subordinating the position of the homosexual. Sex is not natural and neither is the sexed body of "woman," Butler explains, but rather like gender they are performed every day, the way that women perform femininity and men masculinity in their daily lives, or the way some deviants perform differently and break the norms. Against critics who charge that her notion of gender performativity credits the individual subject with too much volition and autonomy, as if each of us could decide each morning what to perform that day, Butler has to insist repeatedly that such performances are constrained by both the weight of past performances and social interactions. Performance, like habit, involves neither fixed immutable nature nor spontaneous individual freedom, residing instead between the two, a kind of acting in common based on collaboration and communication. Unlike the pragmatists' notion of habit, however, queer performativity is not limited to reproducing or reforming the modern social bodies. The political significance of the recognition that sex along with all other social bodies is produced and continuously reproduced through our everyday performances is that we can perform differently, subvert those social bodies, and invent new social forms. Queer politics is an excellent example of such a performative collective project of rebellion and creation. It is not really an affirmation of homosexual identities but a subversion of the logics of identity in general. There are no queer bodies, only queer flesh that resides in the communication and collaboration of social conduct.

Another example of the new role of performativity is provided by the linguistic theories that grasp the postmodern *economic* transformation. When Dewey confronted the modern industrial paradigm he viewed the characteristics of factory labor as running counter to democratic exchange and tending to form a silent and passive public. Today, however, post-Fordism and the immaterial paradigm of production adopt performativity, communication, and collaboration as central characteristics. Performance has been put to work.[122] Every form of labor that produces an immaterial good, such as a relationship or an affect, solving problems or providing information, from sales work to financial services, is fundamentally a performance: the product is the act itself. The economic context makes clear that all of these discussions of habit and performance have to be given the sense of doing or making, linking them to the creative capacities of the laboring subject. Paolo Virno captures the nature of the new economic paradigm by using linguistic performance as both metaphor and metonym for the new aspects of contemporary production. Whereas factory labor is mute, he claims, immaterial labor is loquacious and gregarious: it often involves linguistic, communicational, and affective skills, but more generally, it shares the primary characteristics of linguistic performance. First of all, language is always produced in common: language is never the product of an individual, but rather is always created by a linguistic community in communication and collaboration. Second, linguistic performance relies on the ability to innovate in changing environments based on past practices and habits. Whereas factory labor tended toward specialization and fixed, determinate activities repeated over extended periods, immaterial labor requires the ability to adapt constantly to new contexts—according to the flexibility and mobility we spoke of earlier—and perform in these unstable and indeterminate contexts: solve problems, create relationships, generate ideas, and so forth. The faculty of language, that is, the generic power to speak, the indeterminate potential prior to any specific thing that is said, is according to Virno not only an important component of immaterial labor but key to understanding all of its forms. "The contemporary organization of labor," Virno writes, "mobilizes generic human linguistic competence: in the execution of innumerable tasks and functions it is not so much a matter of familiarity with a determinate class of enunciations, but the aptitude to produce various sorts of enunciations; not so much what is said but the pure and simple power-to-say."[123] The link Virno establishes between linguistic and economic performativity highlights once again the triple relation to the common: our power to speak is based in the common, that is, our shared language; every linguistic act creates the common; and the act of speech itself is conducted in common, in dialogue, in communication. This triple relation to the common illustrated by language characterizes immaterial labor in general.

Needless to say, that life in common tends to characterize the performance of immaterial production does not mean that we have realized a free and democratic society. As we argued earlier in this chapter, exploitation today tends to act directly on our performances through the control of the common by capital. The most we can say at this point is that the wide social diffusion and economic centrality of these practices of the common in our world provide conditions that make *possible* a project for the creation of a democracy based on free expression and life in common. Realizing that possibility will be the project of the multitude.

BEYOND PRIVATE AND PUBLIC

Before moving on we should make this philosophical discussion about the production of the common a little more concrete by relating it to legal theory and practice. Law has always been a privileged domain for recognizing and establishing control over the common. The production of the common, as we have seen in philosophical terms, tends to displace the traditional divisions between individual and society, between subjective and objective, and between private and public. In the legal realm, especially in the Anglo-American tradition, the concept of the common has long been hidden by the notions of public and private, and indeed contemporary legal trends are further eroding any space for the common. On one hand, in recent years we have witnessed numerous legal developments that increase the powers of social control by eroding "privacy rights" (which are called "subjective rights" in Continental legal theory and what we would call "rights of singularity"). In the United States, for example, women's right to legal abortion and homosexuals' legal rights have been argued and sustained primarily in the name of privacy, by the insistence that these acts and decisions are outside the public domain and thus outside of government control. The forces against abortion and homosexual rights work against this privacy and the protections it affords. The attacks on the private, furthermore, have grown exponentially with the war on terrorism. Legislation in the United States, such as the USA Patriot Act, and in Europe has greatly expanded the right of the government to conduct surveillance over domestic and foreign populations. The capacities for surveillance have also been increased by new technological systems, such as Echelon, the secretive project of intelligence agencies of the United States and other governments to monitor global electronic communications, including telephone, e-mail, and satellite communication. All of this reduces the division that separates and protects the private. In the logic of antiterrorism and counterinsurgency, in fact, since security must in the final instance come before all else, there really is no "private." Security is an absolute logic of the common or, really, a perversion that conceives the entire common as the object of control.

On the other hand, we have already discussed examples in the economic realm of legal attacks on the public. Privatization is a central component of the neoliberal ideology that determines the strategy of the major powers that rule over the global economy. The "public" that is privatized by neoliberalism are generally property and business enterprises previously controlled by the state, from railroads and prisons to parklands. We have also discussed in this chapter the great expansion of private property into realms of life that were previously held in common, through patents, copyright, and other legal instruments. At the extreme point of this logic, economists go so far as to claim that every good should be privately owned in order to maximize its productive use. In the social, in other words, the tendency is to make everything public and thus open to government surveillance and control; and in the economic, to make everything private and subject to property rights.

We cannot understand this situation without clarifying the confusions created by the terminology. The "private" is understood to include the rights and freedoms of social subjects together with the rights of private property, blurring the distinction between the two. This confusion results from the ideology of "possessive individualism" in modern legal theory, particularly its Anglo-American version, that conceives every aspect or attribute of the subject, from its interests and desires down to its soul, as "properties" that are owned by the individual, reducing all facets of subjectivity to the economic realm.[124] The concept of the "private" can thus lump together all our "possessions," both subjective and material. The "public" too blurs an important distinction between state control and what is held and managed in common. We need to begin to imagine an alternative legal strategy and framework: a conception of privacy that expresses the singularity of social subjectivities (not private property) and a conception of the public based on the common (not state control)—one might say a postliberal and postsocialist legal theory. The traditional legal conceptions of private and public are clearly insufficient for this task.

The best example of contemporary legal theory based on singularity and commonality that we know of is the "postsystems theory" school, which articulates the legal system, in highly technical terminology, as a transparent and democratic self-organizing network of plural subsystems, each of which organizes the norms of numerous private (or, really, singular) regimes. This is a molecular conception of the law and the production of norms that is based, in our terms, on a constant, free, and open interaction among singularities, which through their communication produces common norms.[125] This notion of singularity rights might be understood better as an expression of the ethical notion of performativity we discussed earlier: they are produced by the common, in social communication, and in turn they produce the common. The fact that this notion of rights is based on the common, we should point out, does not mean that it is a "communitarian" conception of rights or in any way dictated by the community. The term *community* is often used to refer to a moral unity that stands above the population and its interactions like a sovereign power. The common does not refer to traditional notions of either the community or the public; it is based on the *communication* among singularities and emerges through the collaborative social processes of production. Whereas the individual dissolves in the unity of the community, singularities are not diminished but express themselves freely in the common. In this framework, then, to return to our earlier examples, our freedom of sexual and reproductive practices must be guaranteed not because they are private or individual but because they are singular and exist in open communication with others that form the common. This is not to say, of course, that all practices are acceptable (sexual violence, for example) but rather that the decision to determine legal rights is made in the process of communication and collaboration among singularities.

Up to this point, however, we have still only posed the question in formal legal terms. We need to recognize how the "common" can be constructed politically in our contemporary world. How can the singularities that cooperate express their control over the common, and how can this expression be represented in legal terms? Here we need to confront the legal frameworks that the neoliberal regimes have established and against which the movements of the multitude struggle. These legal frameworks support the project of the privatization of public goods (such as water, air, land, and all the systems for the management of life, including health care and pensions that were previously made state functions during the period of welfare) and also, perhaps more important, the privatization of public services (including telecommunications and other network industries, the postal service, public transportation, energy systems, and education). These public goods and services, one should remember, were the very basis of modern sovereignty in the hands of the nation-state. How can we conceive of resisting the privatization of common goods and services without falling into the old opposition between private and public?

The first task of a juridical or legal theory of the common in this situation is a negative one: to demonstrate the falsity of the neoliberal principle that "everything is determined by the market." Not even the most fanatical neoliberal ideologue (or libertarian, for that matter) can claim that this principle is really all-inclusive: anyone must admit that the liberalization of public goods and services does not necessarily lead to their complete privatization and that the "general interest" or "public interest" must in some way be maintained by law, even if only according to formal codes that guarantee the availability and use of public services. (Even those most devoted to the deregulation and privatization of the energy industries, for example, must recognize the public need to guarantee reliable energy services.) This initial limitation to the right of private property, however, and this possible opening toward public (or, really, state) legal control is not sufficient.

What is necessary here, and this is the second task of a legal theory of the common, is to displace the concept of "general interest" or "public interest" with a framework that allows for a common participation in the management of these goods and services. We thus believe that the legal problem, which is linked to the postmodern transformation of biopolitical production, does not lead from the public interest back toward private control based on different social identities but rather leads forward from the public interest toward a common framework of singularities. The common interest, in contrast to the general interest that grounded the legal dogma of the nation-state, is in fact a production of the multitude. The *common interest*, in other words, is a general interest that is not made abstract in the control of the state but rather reappropriated by the singularities that cooperate in social, biopolitical production; it is a public interest not in the hands of a bureaucracy but managed democratically by the multitude. This is not simply a legal question, in other words, but coincides with the economic or biopolitical activity we analyzed earlier, such as the commonality created by positive externalities or by the new informational networks, and more generally by all the cooperative and communicative forms of labor. In short, the common marks a new form of sovereignty, a democratic sovereignty (or, more precisely, a form of social organization that displaces sovereignty) in which the social singularities control through their own biopolitical activity those goods and services that allow for the reproduction of the multitude itself. This would constitute a passage from *Res-publica* to *Res-communis*.

It should be obvious that our insistence on a legal conception of the common *against* both the private and the public diverges fundamentally from the tradition and constituent experiences of Jacobinism and socialism as they unfolded in the nineteenth and twentieth centuries. In effect the modern patrimonial concept of the disciplinary state (which developed in monarchical absolutism) was translated entirely into the juridical forms and legal structures of the republican state, both in its Jacobin and socialist versions. The concepts of public goods and services were thus developed in the light of a legal theory that considered the public as patrimony of the state and the principle of general interest as an attribute of sovereignty. When the concept of the common arises—not as a preconstituted entity and not as an organic substance that is a byproduct of the national community, or gemeinschaft, but rather as the productive activity of singularities in the multitude—it breaks the continuity of modern state sovereignty and attacks biopower at its heart, demystifying its sacred core. All that is general or public must be reappropriated and managed by the multitude and thus become common. This concept of the common not only marks a definitive rupture with the republican tradition of the Jacobin and/or socialist state but also signals a metamorphosis in the law, its nature and structure, its matter and form.

This theory of the common also implies a profound passage in the field of international law. Whereas in the tradition of domestic law the originary contract was between the private individual and the state and on the traditional Westphalian terrain of international law the contract was among nation-states, today the relation among subjects tends to be defined immediately by the common. As we have argued in this book and elsewhere, the contractual paradigm of international law that governed relations among nation-states is now being undermined and transformed by a new form of global order and imperial sovereignty that assumes (and immediately tries to mystify) a principle of commonality. The fact that this process or tendency continues and develops is not a bad thing, in our view, insofar as it undermines the modern paradigm of state sovereignty in which each state functioned as a "private contractual subject" on the international scene. In the absence of sovereign state subjects there is no other basis for the production of norms but the common. From the traditional perspective this "common" appears merely as a lack, but it is in fact filled by biopolitical production. We will see in part 3 when we speak of global democracy that this connection between biopolitical production and the common opens up possibilities for alternative social relationships, based on new legal relationships, multiple figures of normative production at local and global levels, and variety of competing legal procedures. Once again, this is clearly not only a legal question but also immediately economic, political, and cultural.

The imperial transformation of international law tends to destroy both the public and the private. This paradoxical development, in fact, was already glimpsed in all the modern utopias of cosmopolitan law from Abbé de Saint Pierre to Hans Kelsen, which had the curious result that although many of these authors had reactionary views on domestic law they became surprisingly democratic when imagining a global legal framework, a cosmopolitan *jus condendum*. The fact is that when we touch on global relationships, legal questions tend no longer to be linked only to the exercise of power but must take into account all the values that pertain to the global common. In the present phase, when law appears not as a consolidated normative result but as a process, not as an archaeology but a genealogy in action, when law regains a constituent element and confronts what is new in our world, then the common becomes the only basis on which law can construct social relationships in line with the networks organized by the many singularities that create our new global reality. This path, of course, is not linear, but it does seem to us the only way forward. Just as the concepts of singularity and the common in domestic law contribute to renewing the legal framework of social relations beyond the private and the public, providing for the cooperation of multiple singularities in freedom and equality, so too singularity and the common in international law furnish the only possible basis for our peaceful and democratic cohabitation of the planet. These are some of the conditions, as we will see in more depth in the final part of our book, for the creation of a democracy of the multitude.

CARNIVAL AND MOVEMENT

The notion of the multitude based on the production of the common appears to some as a new subject of sovereignty, an organized identity akin to the old modern social bodies such as the people, the working class, or the nation. To others, on the contrary, our notion of the multitude, composed as it is of singularities, appears as mere anarchy. Indeed as long as we remain trapped in the modern framework defined by this alternative—either sovereignty or anarchy—the concept of multitude will be incomprehensible. We need to break free of this old paradigm and recognize a mode of social organization that is not sovereign. A literary detour can help us accomplish this paradigm shift, a passage through the concept of carnival in Mikhail Bakhtin's Problems of Dostoyevsky's Poetics.

Bakhtin's argument, which is presented in the highly academic form of a critique of the previous literary criticism of Dostoyevsky's novels, has two principle theoretical goals. The book is first of all a declaration of war against

Russian formalism, the then-reigning tradition of literary criticism. Bakhtin conducts this battle from a materialist perspective, that is, from a standpoint that privileges speaking subjects and their forms of expression as the key to the history of sign systems.[126] *Materialist literary criticism here is a matter not of reducing poetic forms to economic, political, or social conditions, but rather of recognizing how literature as linguistic production is a part of this reality and grasping the expressive subject within this world of relations. Bakhtin poses the aesthetic limits of formalism by demonstrating its immobility and its lifeless circularity, and for him these limits directly betray the fact that it is impossible to construct a world in which each subject is not based on its recognition of others. This is where it becomes clear why Bakhtin conducts this polemic with reference to Dostoyevsky's novels, because in Dostoyevsky, he explains,* narration is always dialogical, *even between the protagonist and his cat. Each Dostoyevsky novel seems not to have a single author (in monologue) but rather several author-thinkers in dialogue, such as Raskolnikov, Porfiry Petrovich, and Sonia Marmeladov or Ivan Karamazov and the Great Inquisitor. This is an unending dialogue that constantly enriches every subject drawn into it, imposing on them an anthropological revolution. Dialogue, however, is not simply a conversation between two or three persons; it can become an open apparatus in which every subject has equal force and dignity with respect to all others. Dostoyevsky's novels are thus great* polyphonic *apparatuses that create a world in which an open, expansive set of subjects interact and seek happiness.*

At this point Bakhtin turns from his attack on formalism to his second principle focus of the book and uses Dostoyevsky's polyphonic narrative to challenge monologic or monophonic literature. This opposition between the polyphonic and the monologic, Bakhtin adds, runs throughout the history of European literature. We thus have to go back to a theory of literary genre and plot to understand the singularity of Dostoyevsky's work. "Neither the hero, nor the idea, and nor the very polyphonic principle for structuring a whole can be fitted into the generic and plot-compositional forms of a biographical novel, a socio-psychological novel, novels of everyday life or a family novel, that is, into the forms dominant in the literature of Dostoyevsky's time. . . . Dostoyevsky's work clearly belongs to a completely different generic type, one quite foreign to them."[127] *What is this other literary tradition to which Dostoyevsky belongs? Bakhtin explains that dialogical narration and polyphonic structure derive from the folklore of carnival and from the* carnevalesque vision of the world.

Already in his book on Rabelais, Bakhtin had demonstrated the centrality of carnival in European literature, but how could he claim to have found Dostoyevsky among the nomadic troops of the carnival? How could he pose the tragedies of Crime and Punishment *and* The Brothers Karamazov *as carnevalesque? When we look back at Bakhtin's notion of the carnevalesque in his other writings we find that he really uses it to describe the power of human passions. The carnevalesque is the prose that opposes the monologue and thus refuses to claim an already completed truth, producing instead contrast and conflict in the form of narrative movement itself. The carnevalesque thus sets in motion an enormous capacity for innovation—innovation that can transform reality itself. The carnevalesque, dialogue, and polyphonic narration, of course, can easily take the form of a crude naturalism that merely mirrors daily life, but it can also become a form of experimentation that links the imagination to desire and utopia. Beside Rabelais, from this perspective, stand Swift, Voltaire, and, in a different but important sense, Cervantes. Carnevalesque literature thus becomes a universal genre when dialogue and polyphony, even in the most vulgar forms, create a new world. Yes, of course, Dostoyevsky's novels are tragic, but this tragedy, read in this light of the narrative genre of the carnevalesque, has nothing to do with the tragic internal angst of twentieth century existentialist monologues. Dostoyevsky's dialogical apparatus takes on the determinate crisis of Russian society and represents the impasse in which intellectuals and workers find themselves: it is a material tragedy that seems to take characters from Gogol and crush them under the ferocious and frustrating pressures of modernization. In this sense, Dostoyevsky's tragedies simply stage the unresolvable contradictions of bourgeois life and culture in late-nineteenth-century Russian society. The unbelievable becomes real, as in a carnevalesque ritual, and the suffering of life is exposed to the laughter and tears of the spectator.*

There is another element of carnevalesque narration, however, that is even more important for describing and constructing reality. The polyphonic character of carnevalesque language, which is capable of both Rabelais's laughter and Dostoyevsky's tears, has great constructive power itself. In a polyphonic conception of narrative there is no center that dictates meaning, but rather meaning arises only out of the exchanges among all the singularities in dialogue. Singularities all express themselves freely and together through their dialogues create the common narrative structures. Bakhtin's polyphonic narration, in other words, poses in linguistic terms a notion of the production of the common in an open, distributed network structure.

This allows us finally to come back to the concept of the multitude and the difficulties of understanding it as a form of political organization. It is easy to recognize the performative, carnevalesque nature of the various protest movements that have arisen around questions of globalization. Even when they are ferociously combative, the demonstrations are still highly theatrical, with giant puppets, costumes, dances, humorous songs, chants, and so forth. The protests, in other words, are also street festivals in which the anger of the protesters coexists with their joy in the carnival.[128] *The protests are carnevalesque, however, not only in their atmosphere but also in their organization. This is where Bakhtin comes in. In political organization as in narration, there is a constant dialogue among diverse, singular subjects, a polyphonic composition of them, and a general enrichment of each through this common constitution. The multitude in movement is a kind of narration that produces new subjectivities and new languages. Certainly other political movements, those of the 1960s and 1970s, in particular, succeeded in constructing such a polyphonic narration, but it often seems that all that is left of them today is the monologic history of them told by the ruling powers, the police, and the judges. Today's new and powerful movements seem to elude any attempt to reduce them to a monologic history; they cannot but be carnevalesque. This is the logic of the multitude that Bakhtin helps us understand: a theory of organization based on the freedom of singularities that converge in the production of the common. Long live movement! Long live carnival! Long live the common!*

MOBILIZATION OF THE COMMON

Throughout this part we have highlighted the emergence of the common and the singular—the becoming common of singular forms of labor, the singularity of local human contexts in a common global anthropology, and the common condition of poverty and productivity. This commonality and singularity defines what we called the flesh of the multitude. These, in other words, are the conditions of possibility for the formation of the multitude. We have also focused, however, on the forces that constantly constrain this multitudinous flesh to form a political body, transforming its singularities into divisions and hierarchies, reducing the common to a means of global control, and expropriating the common as private wealth. One fact that should be obvious in all this is that the multitude does not arise as a political figure spontaneously and that the flesh of the multitude consists of a series of conditions that are ambivalent: they could lead toward liberation or be caught in a new regime of exploitation and control.

The multitude needs a political project to bring it into existence. Once we have examined the conditions that make the multitude possible, then, we also have to investigate what kind of political project can bring the multitude into being. We have already noted how antagonism results from every relationship of exploitation, every hierarchical division of the global system, and every effort to control and command the common. We have also focused on the fact that the production of the common always involves a surplus that cannot be expropriated by capital or captured in the regimentation of the global political body. This surplus, at the most abstract philosophical level, is the basis on which antagonism is transformed into revolt. Deprivation, in other words, may breed anger, indignation, and antagonism, but revolt arises only on the basis of wealth, that is, a surplus of intelligence, experience, knowledges, and desire. When we propose the poor as the paradigmatic subjective figure of labor today, it is not because the poor are empty and excluded from wealth but because they are included in the circuits of production and full of potential, which always exceeds what capital and the global political body can expropriate and control. This common surplus is the first pillar on which are built struggles against the global political body and for the multitude.

Revolts mobilize the common in two respects, increasing the intensity of each struggle and extending to other struggles. Intensively, internal to each local struggle, the common antagonism and common wealth of the exploited and expropriated are translated into common conduct, habits, and performativity. Any time you enter a region where there is a strong revolt forming you are immediately struck by the common manners of dress, gestures, and modes of relating and communicating. Jean Genet, for example, remarked that what characterized the Black Panthers was primarily a *style*—not just the vocabulary, the Afros, and the clothes, but also a way of walking, a manner of holding their bodies, a physical presence.[129] These elements of style, however, are really only symptoms of the common dreams, common desires, common ways of life, and common potential that are mobilized in a movement. This new common mode of life always forms in dialogue with local traditions and habits. Consider, for example, how the EZLN in the Lacadon jungle of Chiapas mixes elements of national history, such as the figure of Zapata and the legacy of peasant revolts, with local indigenous Tzeltal mythology and forges them together with network relationships and democratic practices to create a new life in common that defines the movement.[130] The mobilization of the common gives the common a new intensity. The direct conflict with power, moreover, for better or for worse, elevates this common intensity to an even higher level: the acrid smell of tear gas focuses your senses and street clashes with police make your blood boil with rage, raising intensity to the point of explosion. The intensification of the common, finally, brings about an anthropological transformation such that out of the struggles come a new humanity.

Extensively, the common is mobilized in communication from one local struggle to another. Traditionally, as we have noted elsewhere, the geographical expansion of movements takes the form of an *international cycle of struggles* in which revolts spread from one local context to another like a contagious disease through the communication of common practices and desires.[131] Slave revolts spread throughout the Caribbean in the early nineteenth century, revolts of industrial workers expanded throughout Europe and North America in the late nineteenth and early twentieth centuries, and guerrilla and anticolonial struggles blossomed across Asia, Africa, and Latin America in the mid-twentieth century. In each of these cycles of struggles, the common that is mobilized extensively and communicates across the globe is not only the commonly recognized enemy—such as slavery, industrial capital, or colonial regimes—but also common methods of combat, common ways of living, and common desires for a better world. It should come as no surprise, given our discussion earlier, that the surplus that is expressed in each cycle of struggles appears monstrous, especially to those in power. The governors and captains of English colonial expansión in the seventeenth and eighteenth centuries, for example, described the cycle of revolts of sailors and slaves by referring to the myth of Hercules and the many-headed hydra. The rebellions were monstrous and, despite their Herculean efforts, whenever one was put down two more would spring up.[132] Each cycle does, in fact, destroy traditional social and political bodies and create in their stead something new and aberrant, a monster.

After the 1968 global explosion of struggles of industrial workers, students, and anti-imperialist guerrilla movements, decades passed with no new international cycle of struggles. This is not to say there were no significant instances of revolt during these years, because indeed there were and many of them extremely violent—the anti-Apartheid struggle in South Africa, the continuing rebellion against British rule in Northern Ireland, the Palestinian Intifada, feminist movements, Stonewall and the gay and lesbian movements, and numerous less-publicized local and national revolts by industrial workers, agriculturists, and oppressed populations. None of these revolts, however, formed a cycle of struggles in which the common was mobilized extensively across the globe. We should not minimize, of course, the numerous more limited instances of communication among struggles. One of the most fascinating contemporary examples is the Justice for Janitors movement, one of the most successful and creative union organizing efforts in the United States. The organizers face challenges that traditional unions have not been able to address: a mobile population, predominantly very recent immigrants, many of whom do no speak English, possessing few marketable skills. One of the secrets of the success may be that, at least in the Los Angeles region, where the movement won its first victories, many of the leading figures are veterans of the FMLN who fought in the civil war against the government of El Salvador. They carried their revolutionary desire with them from the mountains of Morazán to the skyscrapers of Los Angeles and infected others with it, transposing the struggle from guerrilla warfare to union organizing. This is a real and powerful extension of the common.[133]

A new international cycle finally emerged around the issues of globalization in the late 1990s.[134] The coming-out party of the new cycle of struggles were the protests at the WTO summit in Seattle in 1999. The Seattle protests not only initiated a series of protests at the summit meetings of the representatives of global power that would extend in the subsequent years across North America and Europe, but also revealed the real origins of the cycle in the innumerable struggles in the global south that had already taken place against the IMF, the World Bank, North American Free Trade Agreement (NAFTA), and other institutions of the new global power structure. Suddenly the riots against IMF austerity programs in one country, protests against a World Bank project in another, and demonstrations against NAFTA in a third were all revealed to be elements of a common cycle of struggles. The cycle of struggles has been consolidated in a certain sense at the annual meetings of the World Social Forum and the various regional social forums. At each of these social forums activists, NGOs, and intellectuals meet to exchange views on the problems of the present form of globalization and the possibilities for an alternative form. Each social forum also functions as a celebration of the commonality that extends throughout the various movements and revolts across the globe that form this cycle. The pinnacle of this cycle of struggles thus far, at least in quantitative terms, were the coordinated protests against the U.S.-led war in Iraq on February 15, 2003, in which millions of people marched in cities throughout the world. The war represented the ultimate instance of the global power against which the cycle of struggles had formed; the organizational structures and communication that the struggles had established made possible a massive, coordinated mobilization of common expressions against the war. We should emphasize, once again, that what the forces mobilized in this new global cycle have in common is not just a common enemy—whether it be called neoliberalism, U.S. hegemony, or global Empire—but also common practices, languages, conduct, habits, forms of life, and desires for a better future. The cycle, in other words, is not only reactive but also active and creative. In chapter 3.2 below we will detail some of the common grievances and proposals that animate these movements.

The global mobilization of the common in this new cycle of struggles does not negate or even overshadow the local nature or singularity of each struggle. The communication with other struggles, in fact, reinforces the power and augments the wealth of each single one. Consider, for example, the revolt that broke out in Argentina on the nineteenth and twentieth of December 2001 in the midst of economic crisis and has continued in different forms, with successes and failures, ever since. The crisis and the revolt are in many respects specific to Argentina and its history. In Argentina there already existed a generalized institutional crisis and a crisis of representation due in part to both public and private corruption that proved to be a strong obstacle to conventional political strategies to manage the crisis, such as creating a constitutional alliance between classes under the hegemony of the bourgeoisie. The protesters banging pots and pans shouted, "Que se vayan todos," that they all go, the entire political class. The financial crisis, however, also links the Argentine crisis clearly to the global system and the general instability of the global political body, especially as a result of the neoliberal policies of the IMF. With the currency crisis, Argentina's foreign debt suddenly became unpayable, and its celebrated middle class was thrust into the common situation of the populations of many of the poor countries in the world: savings became worthless, job security evaporated, unemployment skyrocketed, and all social services broke down. The response of the Argentine population was immediate and creative: industrial workers refused to let their factories close and took over managing the factories themselves, networks of neighborhood and city assemblies were formed to manage political debates and decisions, new forms of money were invented to allow for autonomous exchange, and the *piqueteros*, the movements of unemployed we mentioned earlier, experimented with new forms of protest in their conflicts with police and other authorities. All of this is clearly specific to the national situation, but it is also, at the same time, common to all those who suffer and struggle against the exploitation and hierarchy of the global system. The revolt of Argentina was born with the common heritage of the global cycle of struggle at its back, and, in turn, ever since December 2001, activists from elsewhere have looked to Argentina as a source of innovation and inspiration.[135]

The global cycle of struggles develops in the form of a distributed network. Each local struggle functions as a node that communicates with all the other nodes without any hub or center of intelligence. Each struggle remains singular and tied to its local conditions but at the same time is immersed in the common web. This form of organization is the most fully realized political example we have of the concept of the multitude. The global extension of the common does not negate the singularity of each of those who participates in the network. The new global cycle of struggles organizes and mobilizes the multitude.

To grasp fully the novelty of the multitude's network form of organization it helps to contrast it with the dominant organizational forms of our recent past. In the latter part of the twentieth century, protest movements and revolts followed two primary models. The first and more traditional form of organization is based on the identity of the struggle, and its unity is organized under central leadership, such as the party. There might be other axes of conflict important to those in the movement on the basis, for example, of minority status, but these must be subordinated in the name of unity to the primary struggle. The history of working class politics is full of such models. The second dominant model, which stands in direct opposition to the first, is based on the right of each group to express its difference and conduct its own struggle autonomously. This difference model developed primarily through struggles based on race, gender, and sexuality. The two dominant models posed a clear choice: either united struggle under the central identity or separate struggles that affirm our differences. The new network model of the multitude displaces both of these options—or, rather, it does not so much negate the old models as give them new life in a different form. At the 1999 Seattle protests, for example, which we will discuss in more detail later, what most surprised and puzzled observers was that groups previously thought to be in opposition to each other—trade unionists and environmentalists, church groups and anarchists, and so forth—acted together without any central, unifying structure that subordinates or sets aside their differences. In conceptual terms, the multitude replaces the contradictory couple identity-difference with the complementary couple commonality-singularity. In practice the multitude provides a model whereby our expressions of singularity are not reduced or diminished in our communication and collaboration with others in struggle, with our forming ever greater common habits, practices, conduct, and desires—with, in short, the global mobilization and extension of the common.

This new global cycle of struggles will inevitably appear monstrous to many, since, like every such struggle, it is based on a condition of surplus, mobilizes the common, threatens conventional social and political bodies, and creates alternatives. Many media commentators, in fact, especially those who felt most threatened by these movements, were quick after the September 11 attacks to equate the monstrosity of the globalization protest movements with the monstrosity of the terrorist attacks: they both use violent means to attack the ruling global power structure.[136] It is absurd, of course, to equate the violence of breaking the windows of McDonald's at a demonstration with the violence of murdering nearly three thousand people, but we will set aside the question of violence until we have the chance to treat it properly in chapter 3.3. Here instead we should simply emphasize the divergent organizational forms. The new global cycle of struggles is a mobilization of the common that takes the form of an open, distributed network, in which no center exerts control and all nodes express themselves freely. Al-Qaeda, experts say, is also a network, but a network with the opposite characteristics: a clandestine network with strict hierarchy and a central figure of command.[137] Finally, the goals too are diametrically opposed. Al-Qaeda attacks the global political body in order to resuscitate older regional social and political bodies under the control of religious authority, whereas the globalization struggles challenge the global political body in order to create a freer, more democratic global world. Clearly, not all monsters are the same.

The mobilization of the common demonstrates, finally, that the movements that form part of this global cycle of struggles are not merely protest movements (although this is the face that appears most clearly in the media) but also positive and creative. So far we have described this positive and creative face only in terms of the production and extension of the common within the movements themselves. The mobilization of the common and the political project to create the multitude need to be extended much more widely across society and established more solidly. We believe that the creation of democracy is the only way to consolidate the power of the multitude and, conversely, that the multitude provides us with a social subject and a logic of social organization that make possible today, for the very first time, the realization of democracy. This project for a democracy of the multitude is the focus of our next and final part of this book.

Excursus 2: Organization: Multitude on the Left

The Left has now been in crisis for decades. Not only have the parties of the Right dominated national elections in most countries throughout the world and right-wing policies guided the formation of the new global order, but also many of the remaining major parties of the Left have drifted so far past the center that they tend to become indistinguishable from the Right, cutting welfare, attacking unions, supporting and conducting foreign wars. The social base in labor unions and the industrial working class is no longer powerful enough to support the Left political parties. Indeed all the social bodies that used to form "the people of the Left" seem to have dissolved. Most central, however, it seems to us, is *the conceptual lack* concerning what the Left is and what it can become. The primary old models are thoroughly discredited and rightly so, both the Soviet-style state socialism and the welfare model of social democracy. Some who are nostalgic for old times accuse academic radicals of hijacking the Left, abandoning the practical work of reasonable reform proposals and making political discussion so obscure that only other academics can puzzle its intricacies. Others accuse the forces of multiculturalism and identity politics of undermining the central public role of the Left and focusing attention on merely cultural issues to the exclusion of properly political and economic ones.[138] Such accusations are significant symptoms of defeat, symptoms of the fact that no new ideas have emerged that are adequate to address the crisis. If the Left is to be resurrected and reformed it will only be done on the basis of new practices, new forms of organization, and new concepts.

In order to speak of a *new* Left today one has to speak, on one hand, in terms of a postsocialist and postliberal program, based on a material and conceptual rupture, an ontological break with the ideological traditions of the industrial workers movements, their organizations, and their models for the management of production. On the other hand, one also has to deal with the new anthropological reality, with new agents of production and subjects of exploitation that remain singular. One must consider the activity of the singular agents as the matrix of the freedom and multiplicity of everyone. Here democracy becomes a direct object. Democracy can no longer be evaluated in the liberal manner as a limit of equality or in the socialist way as a limit of freedom but rather must be the radicalization without reserve of both freedom and equality. Perhaps some day soon we will have arrived at the point when we can look back with irony at the barbaric old times when in order to be free we had to keep our own brothers and sisters slaves or to be equal we were constrained to inhuman sacrifices of freedom. In our view, freedom and equality can be the motors of a revolutionary reinvention of democracy.

The multitude is one concept, in our view, that can contribute to the task of resurrecting or reforming or, really, reinventing the Left by naming a form of political organization and a political project. We do not propose the concept as a political directive—"Form the multitude!"—but rather a way of giving a name to what is already going on and grasping the existing social and political tendency. Naming such a tendency is a primary task of political theory and a powerful tool for further developing the emerging political form. To clarify the concept it seems useful to enumerate and respond to some of the criticisms of the multitude that have likely already arisen in many readers' minds by this point, similar to the way Marx and Engels catalog the attacks on the communists in the second section of the *Manifesto*. This will allow us to correct mistaken impressions and also highlight problems that need to be addressed further.

We should note before turning to the criticisms that we have used the concept of multitude in this book and elsewhere in two different ways to refer to different temporalities. The first is the multitude *sub specie aeternitatis*, the multitude from the standpoint of eternity. This is the multitude that, as Spinoza says, through reason and passions, in the complex interplay of historical forces, creates a freedom that he calls absolute: throughout history humans have refused authority and command, expressed the irreducible difference of singularity, and sought freedom in innumerable revolts and revolutions. This freedom is not given by nature, of course; it comes about only by constantly overcoming obstacles and limits. Just as humans are born with no eternal faculties written in their flesh, so too there are no final ends or teleological goals written in history. Human faculties and historical teleologies exist only because they are the result of human passions, reason, and struggle. The faculty for freedom and the propensity to refuse authority, one might say, have become the most healthy and noble human instincts, the real signs of eternity. Perhaps rather than eternity we should say more precisely that this multitude acts always in the present, a perpetual present. This first multitude is *ontological* and we could not conceive our social being without it. The other is the historical multitude or, really, the not-yet multitude. This multitude has never yet existed. We have been tracking in part 2 the emergence of the cultural, legal, economic, and political conditions that make the multitude possible today. This second multitude is *political*, and it will require a political project to bring it into being on the basis of these emerging conditions. These two multitudes, however, although conceptually distinct, are not really separable. If the multitude were not already latent and implicit in our social being, we could not even imagine it as a political project; and, similarly, we can only hope to realize it today because it already exists as a real potential. The multitude, then, when we put these two together, has a strange, double temporality: always-already and not-yet.

The first pair of criticisms, and perhaps the most important ones, accuse the multitude of being either a spontaneous conception of political organization or a new kind of vanguardism. The first critics say to us, "You are really just anarchists!" This comes especially from those who can conceive political organization only in terms of the party, its hegemony, and central leadership. The concept of the multitude rests on the fact, however, that our political alternatives are not limited to a choice between central leadership and anarchy. We have tried to describe in the course of this chapter how the development of the multitude is not anarchic or spontaneous but rather its organization emerges through the collaboration of singular social subjects. Like the formation of habits, or performativity or the development of languages, this production of the common is neither directed by some central point of command and intelligence nor is the result of a spontaneous harmony among individuals, but rather it emerges in the space *between*, in the social space of communication. The multitude is created in collaborative social interactions.

From the opposite side, others charge the concept of the multitude with vanguardism and see it as a new identity that seeks to rule over others. "You are really just Leninists!" they say. Why else would we insist on referring to "the multitude" instead of "multitudes"? Perhaps some will see our privileging the global protest movements in our discussion of the multitude, for example, as a proposition of a new vanguard. Concern for the free expression of differences, which is behind this criticism, is certainly an important principle to which we hold strongly. We have tried to argue in conceptual terms, however, that singularity is not diminished in the common and, in more practical terms, that becoming common (the becoming common of labor, for instance) does not negate real, local differences. Our concept of the multitude thus attempts to break this numerical alternative between the single and plural. Like the Geresene demoniac whose name is legion, the correct terms here are both *multitude* and *multitudes*. That is the demonic face of the multitude. When we enter into political considerations, however, we do insist on thinking of "the multitude" rather than "multitudes" because we maintain that in order to take a constituent political role and form society, the multitude must be able to make decisions and act in common. (We will explore the multitude's decision-making capacity later in chapter 3.3.) The single grammatical formulation, "multitude," emphasizes for us not any unity but rather the common social and political capacity of the multitude.

A second pair of criticisms, which relate closely to the first, focus on the economic conception of the multitude. On the one hand, some are sure to understand the multitude as an attack on the industrial working class, despite our protestations to the contrary. "You are really against the workers!" they say. Our analysis, of course, does not claim that there is no more industrial working class or even that its numbers globally have decreased. Our argument rather, to repeat what we said earlier in this chapter, is that industrial labor has been displaced from its hegemonic position over other forms of labor by immaterial labor, which now tends to transform all sectors of production and society itself in line with its qualities. Industrial workers remain important, then, but within the context of this new paradigm. Here arises, then, the second criticism of this pair, that our argument of the hegemony of immaterial labor replaces the old vanguard of industrial workers with a new vanguard of immaterial workers— Microsoft programmers leading us on the shining path! "You are just postmodern Leninists in sheep's clothing!" they cry. No, the hegemonic position of a form of production in the economy should not imply any political hegemony. Our argument about the hegemony of immaterial labor and the becoming common of all forms of labor is aimed instead at establishing that contemporary conditions are tending to form a general communication and collaboration of labor that can be the basis of the multitude. The concept of the multitude, in other words, does contradict those who still maintain that the industrial working class, its representatives, and its parties must lead all progressive politics, but it also denies that any single class of labor can occupy that position. One can see clearly therefore how these economic criticisms map back to the first pair, the political charges of spontaneism and vanguardism.

The economic question also reveals a much more substantial criticism that charges our concept of the multitude with economism, since it fails to consider the dynamics of other axes of social difference and hierarchy, such as race, gender, and sexuality. "You only care about labor and workers!" they say. We should emphasize once again, on one hand, that in the context of biopolitical production the divisions between the economic, the social, and the cultural tend to blur. A biopolitical perspective is always necessarily beyond and broader than an economic perspective in any strict sense. We should also recognize, on the other hand, that the focus on labor is an important limitation of our analysis in this book. We explained earlier (and it is worth repeating) that our focus on labor and socioeconomic class as basis for our analysis of the multitude can serve as a corrective to the relative lack of recent scholarship on class. We also noted that strong traditions of race and gender politics, however, already contain a desire for the multitude, when feminists, for example, pose the goal as not a world without gender difference but one in which gender does not matter (in the sense that it does not form the basis of hierarchies); or when antiracist activists similarly struggle not for a world without race but one in which race does not matter—in short, a process of liberation based on the free expression of difference. This is the notion of singularity and commonality at the heart of the multitude. That said, in any case, if the concept of the multitude is to play a significant political role, it will have to be investigated and developed from these various standpoints.

A third pair of criticisms challenge the philosophical validity of the concept. One criticism, the Hegelian criticism, sees the multitude as merely another version of the traditional dialectic relation between the One and the Many, especially when we pose the primary dynamic of contemporary global politics as a struggle between Empire and the multitude. "You are really just failed or incomplete dialecticians!" they say. If this were the case, then the autonomy of the multitude would be severely limited, since it could not exist without Empire, its dialectical support. We have tried to argue in philosophical terms, however, that the dynamic of singularity and multiplicity that defines the multitude denies the dialectical alternative between the One and the Many—it is both and neither. And we will argue in political terms in part 3 that Empire and the multitude are not symmetrical: whereas Empire is constantly dependent on the multitude and its social productivity, the multitude is potentially autonomous and has the capacity to create society on its own. The second in this pair of philosophical criticisms, the deconstructionist criticism, poses the dialectic on the other side, that is, on the side of the expansive nature of the multitude and challenges the claim that the multitude is all-inclusive. "You forget about the subaltern!" they say. The dialectic here, in other words, is between the multitude and those excluded from it. Every identity, such critics say, even the multitude, must be defined by its remainder, those outside of it, call them the excluded, the abject, or the subaltern. We could return to the philosophical point here that the multitude transposes the exclusive and limiting logic of identity-difference into the open and expansive logic of singularity-commonality, but it may be more useful to point as illustration to the unlimited and indefinite nature of distributed networks. There can certainly be points or nodes outside a network but none are *necessarily* outside. Its boundaries are indefinite and open. Furthermore, we should remember that the multitude is a project of political organization and thus can be achieved only through political practices. No one is necessarily excluded but their inclusion is not guaranteed: the expansion of the common is a practical, political matter.

This philosophical challenge to the potentially all-inclusive nature of the multitude leads immediately to an important political criticism that the multitude is a concept only applicable to the dominant parts of the world and their social conditions, roughly the global north, and cannot apply to the subordinate regions in the global south. "You are really just elite philosophers from the global north pretending to speak for the entire world!" they say. We have tried to respond to this concern with our analyses of peasants, the poor, and migrants earlier in this part by demonstrating that there is a tendency toward common conditions of labor and production. We are very conscious, however, and this was the point of our analysis of the global political body and the topography of exploitation, that the situations across the world are very different and they are divided by dramatic hierarchies of power and wealth. Our claim is that a common political project is *possible*. This possibility, of course, will have to be verified and realized in practice. We refuse to accept, in any case, any vision that poses linear stages of development for political organization, pretending that those in the dominant regions may be ready for democratic forms of organization such as the multitude whereas those in the subordinate regions are condemned to older forms until they mature. We are all capable of democracy. The challenge is to organize it politically.

Finally, our notion of the multitude is likely to strike many as unrealistic: "You are really just utopians!" We have taken pains to argue that the multitude is not merely some abstract, impossible dream detached from our present reality but rather that the concrete conditions for the multitude are in the process of formation in our social world and that the possibility of the multitude is emerging from that tendency. That said, it is important always to remember that another world is possible, a better, more democratic world, and to foster our desire for such a world. Multitude is an emblem for that desire.

3. DEMOCRACY

3.1 THE LONG MARCH OF DEMOCRACY

A pure democracy may possibly do, when patriotism is
the ruling passion; but when the State abounds with ras-
cals, as is the case with too many at this day, you must
suppress a little of that popular spirit.

—EDWARD RUTLEDGE TO JOHN JAY,
NOVEMBER 24, 1776

Al Smith once remarked that "the only cure for the evils
of democracy is more democracy." Our analysis suggests
that applying that cure at the present time could well be
adding fuel to the flames. Instead, some of the problems
of governance in the United States today stem from an
excess of democracy. . . . Needed, instead, is a greater degree of moderation in democracy.

—SAMUEL HUNTINGTON, 1975

CRISIS OF DEMOCRACY IN THE ERA OF ARMED GLOBALIZATION

The end of the cold war was supposed to be the ultimate victory of democracy, but today the concept and practices of democracy are everywhere in
crisis. Even in the United States, the self-proclaimed global beacon of
democracy, such central institutions as electoral systems have been seriously drawn into question, and in many parts of the world there is barely
the pretense of democratic systems of government. And the constant global
state of war undermines what meager forms of democracy exist.

Throughout much of the twentieth century the concept of democracy was both reduced and bolstered by cold war ideology. On one side of the cold war divide, the concept of democracy tended to be defined strictly in terms of anticommunism so as to be synonymous with the "free world." The term *democracy* thus had little to do with the nature of government: any state that stood as part of the bulwark against what was considered to be communist totalitarianism could be labeled "democratic" regardless of how democratic it really was. On the other side of the cold war divide, socialist states similarly claimed to be "democratic republics." This claim too had little to do with the nature of government and instead referred primarily to the opposition to capitalist control: any state that formed part of the bulwark against what was considered to be capitalist domination could claim to be a democratic republic. In the post–cold war world, the concept of democracy has been unanchored from its rigid cold war moorings and set adrift. Perhaps for that reason, it has some hope of regaining its previous significance.

The crisis of democracy today has to do not only with the corruption and insufficiency of its institutions and practices but also with the concept itself. Part of the crisis is that it is not clear what democracy means in a globalized world. Certainly global democracy will have to mean something different than what democracy meant in the national context throughout the modern era. We can get a first index of this crisis of democracy from the voluminous recent scholarly writings on the nature of globalization and global war in relation to democracy. Support for democracy remains a presupposition among scholars, but they differ widely on the question of whether the present form of globalization increases or decreases the powers and possibilities of democracy across the world. Furthermore, since September 11 the increased pressures of war have polarized the positions and, in the minds of some, subordinated the need for democracy to concerns of security and stability. For the sake of clarity let us sort out these positions according to their stance on the benefits of globalization for democracy and on their general political orientation. This gives us four logical categories dividing those who think that globalization fosters democracy from those who think it is an obstacle, on the left and the right. Keep in mind, of course, that there is a great deal of slippage in these various discussions about what is meant by globalization in addition to what is meant by democracy. Designations of right and left are only approximate, but useful nonetheless for sorting the various positions.

Consider first the *social democratic* arguments that claim democracy is debilitated or threatened by globalization, defining globalization usually in strictly economic terms. These arguments maintain that in the interest of democracy nation-states should withdraw from the forces of globalization. Some arguments that fit into this category claim that economic globalization is actually a myth, but a powerful myth with antidemocratic effects.[1] Many such arguments hold, for example, that today's internationalized economy is not unprecedented (the economy has long been internationalized); that genuinely transnational corporations (in contrast to multinational corporations) are still rare; and that the vast majority of trade today is not really global but takes place merely among North America, Europe, and Japan. Despite the fact that globalization is a myth, they say, its ideology serves to paralyze democratic national political strategies: the myth of globalization and its inexorability is used to argue against national efforts to control the economy, and it facilitates neoliberal privatization programs, the destruction of the welfare state, and so forth. These social democrats argue instead that nation-states can and should assert their sovereignty and take greater control of the economy at national and supranational levels. Such action would restore the democratic functions of the state that have been eroded, most importantly its representative functions and its welfare structures. This social democratic position is the one that was most seriously undermined by the events from the September 11 attacks to the war on Iraq. The state of global war seems to have made globalization inevitable (especially in terms of security and military affairs) and thus any such antiglobalization position untenable. In the context of the state of war, in fact, most social democratic positions have tended to migrate toward one of the two proglobalization positions outlined below. The policies of Schröder's Germany are a good example of how the social democratic defense of national interests has come to rely fundamentally on multilateral cosmopolitan alliances; and Blair's Britain is the prime illustration of the way national interests are thought best served by lining up in support of the United States and its global hegemony.

Opposed to the social democratic critiques of globalization, but still maintaining a left political position, stand the *liberal cosmopolitan* arguments that view globalization as fostering democracy.[2] We do not mean to suggest that these authors have no critique of the contemporary forms of globalization, because indeed they do, especially the most unregulated activities of global capital. These are not, however, arguments against capitalist globalization as such but rather arguments for the better institutional and political regulation of the economy. These arguments generally emphasize that globalization brings positive effects in economic and political terms, as well as means of addressing the global state of war. In addition to greater economic development they envision globalization bringing a great democratic potential primarily due to a new relative freedom *from* the rule of nation-states—and in this respect their contrast to the social democratic positions is clear. This is particularly true, for example, in discussions that focus on the question of human rights, which has in many ways taken a greater role against or despite the power of nation-states. Notions of a new cosmopolitan democracy or global governance similarly rely on the relative decline of the sovereignty of nation-states as their condition of possibility. The global state of war has made liberal cosmopolitanism into a major political position and seemingly the only viable alternative to U.S. global control. Against the reality of unilateral U.S. actions, multilateralism is the primary method of cosmopolitan politics and the United Nations its most powerful instrument. We might also include at the limit of this category those who argue simply that the United States cannot "go it alone" and must share its global ruling powers and responsibilities with other major powers in some sort of multilateral arrangement in order to maintain global order.[3]

The various right-wing arguments that focus on the benefits and necessity of *U.S. global hegemony* agree with the liberal cosmopolitans that globalization breeds democracy, but they do so for very different reasons. These arguments, which are omnipresent in the mainstream media today, generally assert that globalization fosters democracy because U.S. hegemony and the expansion of the rule of capital themselves imply necessarily the expansion of democracy. Some argue that the rule of capital is inherently democratic, and thus the globalization of capital is the globalization of democracy; others hold that the U.S. political system and the "American way of life" are synonymous with democracy and thus the expansion of U.S. hegemony is the expansion of democracy, but usually these turn out to be two sides of the same coin.[4] The global state of war has given this position a newly exalted political platform. What has become known as neoconservative ideology, which has been a strong foundation for the Bush administration, seeks for the United States actively to remake the political map of the world, overthrowing rogue regimes that pose potential threats and creating good ones. The U.S. government emphasizes that its global interventions are not based merely on national interests but rather on the global, universal desires for freedom and prosperity. It must for the good of the world act unilaterally without the constraints of multilateral agreements or international law.[5] There is a minor debate among these proglobalization conservatives between some, generally British authors, who view current U.S. global hegemony as the rightful heir to the benevolent European imperialist projects and others, predictably U.S. authors, who view U.S. global rule as a radically new and exceptional historical situation. One U.S. author, for example, is convinced that U.S. exceptionalism has unprecedented benefits for the entire globe: "For all our fumbling, the role played by the United States is the greatest gift the world has received in many, many centuries, possibly all of recorded history."[6]

Finally, *traditional-values conservative* arguments contest the dominant right wing view that unregulated capitalism and U.S. hegemony necessarily bring democracy. They agree instead with the social democratic view that globalization hinders democracy, but for very different reasons—primarily because it threatens traditional, conservative values. This position takes rather different form inside and outside the United States. Conservative thinkers outside the United States who view globalization as a radical expansion of U.S. hegemony argue, in common with the social democrats, that economic markets require state regulation, and the stability of markets is threatened by the anarchy of global economic forces. The primary force of these arguments, however, focuses on the cultural, not the economic, realms. Conservative critics outside the United States claim, for instance, that U.S. society is so corrupt—with its weak social cohesion, its decline of family structures, its high rates of crime and incarceration, and so forth—that it does not have the political strength or the moral fortitude to rule over other countries.[7] Conservative traditional-values arguments within the United States see the growing U.S. involvement in global affairs and the increasing unregulated rule of capital as detrimental to the moral life and traditional values of the United States itself.[8] In all these cases, traditional values or social institutions (or what some call civilization) need to be protected and the national interest preserved against the threats of globalization. The global state of war and its pressure to accept globalization as a fact has quieted but not eliminated expressions of this position. Traditional-values conservatism now generally takes the form of a skepticism about globalization and a pessimism about the benefits that U.S. hegemony claims to bring its own nation and the world.

None of these arguments, however, seem sufficient for confronting the question of democracy and globalization. What is clear, rather, from all of them—from right and left, proglobalization and antiglobalization—is that globalization and global war put democracy in question. Democracy, of course, has been declared to be "in crisis" many times in the last few centuries, usually by liberal aristocrats afraid of the anarchy of popular power or by technocrats disturbed by the disorder of parliamentary systems. Our problem of democracy, however, is different. First of all, democracy is confronted today by a leap of scale, from the nation-state to the entire globe, and thus unmoored from its traditional modern meanings and practices. As we will argue later, democracy must be conceived and practiced differently in this new framework and this new scale. This is one reason why all four categories of arguments outlined above are insufficient: because they do not confront adequately the scale of the contemporary crisis of democracy. A second, more complex, and substantial reason that these arguments are insufficient is that even when they speak of democracy they always undercut or postpone it. The liberal aristocratic position today is to insist on liberty first and democracy perhaps sometime later.[9] In vulgar terms the mandate for liberty first and democracy later often translates into the absolute rule of private property, undermining the will of everyone. What the liberal aristocrats do not understand is that in the era of biopolitical production liberalism and liberty based on the virtue of the few or even the many is becoming impossible. (Even the logic of private property is being threatened by the social nature of biopolitical production.) The virtue of everyone is becoming today the only basis for liberty and democracy, which can no longer be separated.

The enormous protests against political and economic aspects of the global system, including the current state of war, which we will consider in detail later, should be seen as powerful symptoms of the crisis of democracy. What the various protests make clear is that democracy cannot be made or imposed *from above*. The protesters refuse the notions of democracy from above promoted by both sides of the cold war: democracy is neither simply the political face of capitalism nor the rule of bureaucratic elites. And democracy does not result from either military intervention and regime change or from the various current models of "transition to democracy," which are generally based on some form of Latin American *caudillismo* and have proved better at creating new oligarchies than any democratic systems.[10] All of the radical social movements since 1968 have challenged these corruptions of the concept of democracy that transform it into a form of rule imposed and controlled from above. Democracy, instead, they insist, can only arise *from below*. Perhaps the present crisis of the concept of democracy due to its new global scale can provide the occasion to return it to its older meaning as the rule of everyone by everyone, a democracy without qualifiers, without ifs or buts.

THE UNFINISHED DEMOCRATIC PROJECT OF MODERNITY

Today's crisis of democracy throws us back to the early period of European modernity, and particularly to the eighteenth century, because then too the concept and practices of democracy were put in crisis by a leap of scale and had to be reinvented. At the end of modernity reappear the unresolved problems of its beginnings. Advocates of democracy in early modern Europe and North America were confronted by skeptics who told them that democracy may have been possible in the confines of the Athenian polis but was unimaginable in the extended territories of the modern nation-states. Today, advocates of democracy in the age of globalization are met by skeptics who claim that democracy may have been possible within the confines of the national territory but is unimaginable on a global scale.

The eighteenth-century democratic revolutionaries, of course, did not simply repropose democracy in its ancient form. Instead their task, aimed in part at addressing the question of scale, was to reinvent the concept and create new institutional forms and practices. Representation, as we will see in detail shortly, was central to the modern attempt to address the crisis of democracy. That an old problem reappears, however, does not mean that the old solution will be adequate. Modern forms of representation, in other words, will not necessarily be able to be expanded to respond successfully to our new problems of scale. (This will be a theme of chapter 3.2 below.) Rather, like the revolutionaries of the early modern period, we will once again have to reinvent the concept of democracy and create new institutional forms and practices appropriate to our global age. That project of conceptual and practical invention is the primary object of the remainder of our book.

The problem of democracy in a global world appears together, as we said, with the problem of war, another unresolved problem of modernity. As we saw in part 1, one face of globalization reveals that war is again a problem today—or, rather, disorganized and illegitimate violence poses a problem for the existing forms of sovereignty. We are faced with a global state of war in which violence can erupt anywhere at any time. And most important from the perspective of sovereignty, there is no secure means of legitimating the use of violence today and no stable groupings of that violence into friend and enemy camps. The theory and practices of modern sovereignty were born by confronting this same problem, the problem of civil war—and here we are thrown back primarily to the seventeenth rather than the eighteenth century. Hobbes's reflections on the civil wars in England and Descartes's meditations on the Thirty Years' War in Germany are founding moments of the dominant stream of modern European thought. Civil war is the negative instance against which the modern notion of political order is buttressed. The violent state of nature—the war of all against all—is really just a distilled, philosophical conception of civil war, projected back either into prehistory or into human essence itself. Modern sovereignty is meant to put an end to civil war.[11]

We should keep in mind, however, that Hobbes's solution to the problem of civil war is an ambivalent, incomplete one. On one hand, Hobbes states that the central objective of his Leviathan is putting an end to England's long civil wars and thus the sovereign power he proposes will be constituent, producing and reproducing the people as a peaceful social order and bringing an end to the war of all against all that is synonymous with social and political chaos. On the other hand, war—the violent state of nature, the forces of civil war, and the threat of foreign war—necessarily remains as an ever present possibility for Hobbes, in part because that threat of war and death is the primary weapon used to coerce the multitude to obey the rule of the sovereign: *protego ergo obligo*, that is, protection is the basis of obligation to the sovereign. Modern sovereignty, we should be clear, does not put an end to violence and fear but rather puts an end to civil war by organizing violence and fear into a coherent and stable political order. The sovereign will be the only legitimate author of violence, both against its own subjects and against other sovereign powers. This is how the sovereign nation-state serves modernity as an answer to the problem of civil war.

Today the problem of civil war reappears on a much larger, global scale. The current state of war, which has become continuous police activity that supports the regulative foundation of administration and political control, similarly demands the obedience of subjects who are plagued by violence and fear. That the problem is similar, once again, does not mean that the same solution will be effective. The reenforced sovereignty of nation-states will not succeed in putting an end to the global state of war. A new global form of sovereignty is instead necessary. This is the object, for example, of Samuel Huntington's proposed paradigm of global civilizational conflict that we discussed earlier. Recognizing how the cold war succeeded in organizing global violence into coherent blocs and a stable order of power, Huntington seeks a similar ordering function for civilizations: civilizations will make global conflict coherent and divide nation-states into stable groups of friend and enemy. The "war on terrorism" too seeks, along somewhat different lines, to organize global violence. The so-called alliance of the willing and the axis of evil designate strategies for grouping nation-states into blocs and thus making their violence coherent. (As we saw in chapter 1, however, the definition of terrorism used here varies greatly depending on the perspective of the one making the accusation.) None of these solutions seems to us adequate, but they at least address the problem that global civil war poses for imperial power. Once again, from this perspective, putting an end to civil war does not mean putting an end to violence and fear but rather organizing them into a coherent order and gathering them into the hands of the sovereign.

The fact that contemporary problems of democracy and war bear similarities to those faced in the early modern period, we should repeat, does not mean that the old solutions will prove successful again. When we look back at the early modern conceptions of democracy we should appreciate both what a radical process of invention they accomplished and also how that modern project of democracy remained unfinished. Eighteenth-century revolutionaries in Europe and the United States understood democracy in clear and simple terms: the rule of everyone by everyone. The first great modern innovation on the ancient concept of democracy, in fact, is this universal character, this absolute extension to everyone. Remember, for example, how Pericles had defined democracy in ancient Athens as the rule of the many, in contrast to the rule of the few (in aristocracy or oligarchy) and the rule of the one (in monarchy and tyranny).[12] In modern Europe and North America between the seventeenth and eighteenth centuries this inherited notion of the democracy of the *many* was transformed into the democracy of *everyone*. The ancient notion of democracy is a limited concept just as are monarchy and aristocracy: the many that rule is still only a portion of the entire social whole. Modern democracy, in contrast, has no limits and this is why Spinoza calls it "absolute."[13] This move from the *many* to *everyone* is a small semantic shift, but one with extraordinarily radical consequences! With this universality come equally radical conceptions of equality and freedom. We can only all rule when we do so with equal powers, free to act and choose as each of us pleases.

We should note, parenthetically, that the "democracy of everyone" should not be confused with the concept of ochlocracy, that is, the power of all or the whole, which has continually been denounced in the history of political theory as a false derivative of the power expressed by everyone. The critiques of totalitarianism that emerged in the mid-twentieth century rightly protested against any such confusion.[14] These critiques, however, even when they denounced tyranny (grounding their analyses in the ancient Greek notion of the corruption of the forms of government in the polis), never managed to arrive at the point where they could support democracy as a paradigm of good government. The dominant European tradition has certainly been against tyranny but almost always from an aristocratic standpoint; against totalitarianism but also against the expression "of everyone," that is, the democracy of singularities and the multitude.

Modern revolutions did not immediately institute the universal concept of democracy even within the national space. The exclusion of women, the propertyless, the nonwhite, and others negated the universal pretext of "everyone." In fact, this universal notion of democracy has never yet been instituted, but it has served notwithstanding as a goal toward which modern revolutions and struggles have tended. One can read the history of modern revolutions as a halting and uneven but nonetheless real progression toward the realization of the absolute concept of democracy. It is a North Star that continues to guide our political desires and practices.

The second great innovation of the modern concept of democracy is its notion of representation. Representation was thought to be the distinctively modern practical mechanism that would make republican government feasible in the extensive territories of the nation-state.[15] Representation fills two contradictory functions: it links the multitude to government and at the same time separates it. Representation is a *disjunctive synthesis* in that it simultaneously connects and cuts, attaches and separates.[16] Many of the great eighteenth-century revolutionary thinkers, we should note, were not only reserved about democracy but actually feared and opposed it in explicit and concrete terms. Representation serves them as a kind of vaccine to protect against the dangers of absolute democracy: it gives the social body a small controlled dose of popular rule and thereby inoculates against the fearsome excesses of the multitude. Often these eighteenth-century authors will use the term *republicanism* to mark this distance from democracy.

Jean-Jacques Rousseau, for example, in his *Social Contract* treats democracy and representation in a complex, ambivalent way. On one hand, the people of a republic, he claims, must be absolutely sovereign and everyone must participate in an active and unmediated way in founding and legislating political society. On the other hand, this full political participation is tempered by the fact that only in some special cases is democracy the appropriate form of government to execute the will of the sovereign people. Different forms of government are suited to different nations, but elective aristocracy is in his view the best and most natural political order.[17] "If there were a nation of gods, it would be governed democratically," Rousseau claims. "So perfect a government is unsuited to men."[18] So, at least on first reading, whereas representation is not admissible in the realm of sovereignty for Rousseau, in the realm of government representation it is acceptable and even in most cases preferable.

And yet on closer inspection we can see that, despite Rousseau's insistence to the contrary, his notion of sovereignty too contains a strong conception of representation. This is most clear in Rousseau's explanation that only the "general will" of the people is sovereign, not the "will of all." The will of all is the plural expression of the entire population, which Rousseau considers to be an incoherent cacophony, whereas the general will stands above society, a transcendent, unified expression.[19] We should recognize in Rousseau's conception that the general will itself is a representation that is simultaneously connected to and separated from the will of all. This relationship of unity, transcendence, and representation is illustrated by Rousseau's distinction between the people and the multitude. The people is only sovereign for Rousseau when it is unified. The people, he explains, is constructed by maintaining or creating unitary habits, customs, and views such that the population speaks with one voice and acts with one will. Difference is an enemy of the people. A population, however, can never really eliminate difference and speak with one voice. The unity of the people can be created only through an operation of representation that separates it from the multitude. Despite that the people all meet in person to exercise sovereignty, then, the multitude is not present; it is merely represented by the people. The rule of everyone in Rousseau is thus paradoxically but nonetheless necessarily reduced to the rule of one through the mechanism of representation.

The authors and defenders of the U.S. Constitution were much more explicit than Rousseau in their fear of democracy and the need for the separation provided by representation. For James Madison, for example, coauthor of *The Federalist*, the concept of democracy is defined, as popular sovereignty was for Rousseau, by the fact that "the people meet and exercise the government in person" such that all the people govern directly, freely, and equally.[20] Madison considers such democracy dangerous because, like Rousseau, he fears that there will be differences within the people—not only individual differences, which can be easily controlled, but collective differences, that is, factions. A minority faction, Madison reasons in *Federalist*, no. 10, does not pose a serious problem for a democracy because the majority can control it, but democracy has no mechanism to control a majority faction. The democratic multitude itself, in Madison's view, has no mechanism of intelligence, prudence, or virtue that could organize differences: differences are immediately and inevitably expressed as conflict and oppression. Madison argues that the representative schema of the U.S. Constitution is an effective guarantee against the oppression of the majority in a republic.

Here the question of scale becomes primary. Democracy may have been feasible in the limited spaces of the ancient city-states, the argument goes, but the practical demands of the size of modern nation-states require that democracy be tempered with mechanisms of representation: democracy for small populations; representation for extensive territories and populations.[21] Many of the anti-Federalist writers in the eighteenth-century United States use this opposition between democracy and representation as an argument against the proposed Constitution and against a strong federal government. They favor small sovereign states because the small scale provides the conditions for democracy or, at least, representation of small proportions, where each delegate represents relatively few people.[22] The Federalists agree that representation is an obstacle to democracy—to the universal, equal, and free rule of everyone—but support it for that very reason! The enormous size of the modern nation-states, the United States in particular, is not an impediment to good government but instead a great advantage! Representatives who are too close to the represented do not provide an adequate protective barrier against democracy; representation has to be distant enough to hold the dangers of democracy at bay and yet not so distant that representatives have no contact with the represented. It is not necessary that representatives have detailed local knowledge of the represented (*Federalist*, no. 56); rather, what is most important is "to obtain for rulers men who possess most wisdom to discern, and most virtue to pursue, the common good of society."[23] Madison insists that this representative schema whereby the few rule is neither an oligarchy (no. 57) nor an aristocracy in the British style (no. 63). We might characterize it best perhaps by what Rousseau calls an elective aristocracy, as opposed to natural or hereditary forms of aristocracy. Madison certainly agrees with Rousseau's view that "it is the best and most natural order of things that the wisest should govern the multitude."[24] Once again in these discussions we can recognize the essence of representation: it connects the citizens to government and at the same time separates them from it. The new science is based on this disjunctive synthesis.

One element that is refreshingly lucid about these eighteenth-century deliberations is that they recognize so clearly that democracy and representation stand at odds with one another. When our power is transferred to a group of rulers, then we all no longer rule, we are separated from power and government. Despite this contradiction, however, already in the early nineteenth century representation came to define modern democracy to such an extent that since then it has become practically impossible to think democracy without also thinking some form of representation. Rather than a barrier against democracy, representation came to be viewed as a necessary supplement. Pure democracy may be beautiful in theory, the argument goes, but it is relatively weak in practice. Only when democracy is mixed with representation does it form a sufficiently strong, resistant substance, as iron is mixed with carbon to make a steel alloy. The "new science" that the Federalists announced as their contribution to the new nation and the new era became something like a theory of modern metallurgy. By the 1830s Alexis de Tocqueville could call "democracy" in America the same representative schema that the founders, fifty years before, had conceived as a bulwark against the dangers of democracy. Today the dominant notion of democracy is even more distant. Consider, for example, the definition given recently by Joseph Nye, a leading liberal political thinker: "Democracy is government by officials who are accountable and removable by the majority of people in a jurisdiction."[25] How far we have strayed from the eighteenth-century conception!

Since representation has come to monopolize the field of political thought to such an extent, it is useful in summary fashion to distinguish the different types of representation. Following Max Weber, we can distinguish three basic types according to the degree of separation between the representatives and the represented: appropriated, free, and instructed.[26]

Appropriated representation (appropriierte Repräsentation) is the form with the weakest link and the strongest separation between the representatives and the represented. In this type the representatives are not selected, appointed, or controlled in any direct way by the represented; rather the representatives merely interpret the interest and will of the represented. Weber calls this form of representation appropriated because the representatives appropriate all decision-making powers for themselves. We should point out that these representatives are not completely autonomous because representation, like all relations of power, is two-sided, and the represented always have some means to refuse or modify the relationship, but in this case their means are the most indirect and distant. We can also call this type *patriarchal representation* because it defines the sense in which a feudal lord represented the peasants of the estate. This is similar, in fact, to how black slaves, women, and children were thought to be represented in the U.S. Constitution.[27] In a rather different context, patriarchal or appropriated representation also defines the way that today supranational organizations like the IMF and the World Bank represent the interests of nations like Thailand and Argentina, as we will see later. In all these cases, the representatives stand clearly separate from, and interpret the interests of, the represented, who can exercise only weak and indirect forms of influence.

Free representation (freie Repräsentation) stands in the middle position, typical of parliamentary systems, in which the represented have some direct connection to the representatives but their control is constrained or limited. In most electoral systems, for example, the choice or control that the represented exert is limited primarily in temporal terms, since the represented exercise their connection only every two or four or six years. Between elections representatives act relatively independently without the instruction or consultation of the represented, and thus Weber calls this form "free" to emphasize the relative autonomy of the representatives. The freedom of the representatives, of course, is inversely related to the degree of choice or control of the represented. The power of the represented is also limited, for example, by a constrained range of representatives to choose from. Their power is increasingly limited or partial too, of course, and the representatives correspondingly are more free with every additional degree of separation from the represented, the way a political appointee, for example, represents those who elected the appointing official. The delegates to the General Assembly of the United Nations might thus be said to represent the various national populations with a second degree of separation. The more limited or partial the representation becomes and the stronger the separation between representatives and the represented, the more it approaches a form of patriarchal or appropriated representation.

When the represented constantly control the representatives, the system is defined by what Weber calls *instructed representation* (gebundene Repräsentation). The various mechanisms that create stronger connections and bind the representatives to obey constantly the instructions of the represented all serve to lessen the autonomy of the representatives.[28] Frequent elections, for example, or even the constant revocability of delegates undercut the temporal limitation imposed on electors by periodic elections. Expanding the possibility of all members of the society to serve as representatives also lessens the limitations on the power of the represented. Finally, increasing the opportunities for all citizens to participate in governmental decisions reduces the separation of representation. The participatory procedures for determining budget allocations in some Brazilian cities, such as Porto Alegre and Belem, is one example of such a mechanism to reduce separation.[29]

This Weberian typology of representation might immediately suggest a political task: work to transform all patriarchal or appropriated forms of representation into limited, liberal forms, and transform those limited forms into more directly instructed ones, making ever stronger the connection between the represented and their representatives. Such attempts can undoubtedly improve our contemporary political situation but they can never succeed in realizing the promise of modern democracy, the rule of everyone by everyone. Each of these forms—appropriated, free, and instructed—brings us back to the fundamental dual nature of representation, that it simultaneously connects and separates. The three forms designate different proportions of the two functions, which are necessary for sovereignty. The institutions of political representation must allow (at least some) citizens to express their plural desires and demands while at the same time allowing the state to synthesize them as one coherent unity. The representative is thus, on one hand, a servant of the represented and, on the other, dedicated to the unity and effectiveness of the sovereign will. As we will see in more detail later, according to the dictates of sovereignty, in the final analysis only the one can rule. Democracy requires a radical innovation and a new science.

DEBTORS' REBELLION

Abigail Adams, wife of John Adams, was furious with Thomas Jefferson. It was easy for him to write such pretty phrases while away in France. Back home in Massachusetts things were a mess.

The young United States was undergoing its first serious domestic rebellion. In the summer of 1786 the Court General of the state of Massachusetts began to foreclose on the property of indebted farmers in Hampshire County, seizing their cattle and their land. The farmers called on Massachusetts to print more money as Rhode Island had done to relieve their debt, but the state legislature was deaf to their demands. A militia of fifteen hundred armed farmers, many of who were veterans of the Revolutionary War, blocked the courts from meeting and taking away their property; in the town of Great Barrington they broke open the county jail and set free the debtors. Daniel Shays, a former captain in the Continental Army, eventually became known as its leader.

Abigail Adams wrote from London to her friend Thomas Jefferson, who was serving as ambassador to France, and described in dramatic terms the tumults created by the debtors in her native state: "Ignorant, restless desperadoes, without conscience or principles, have led a deluded multitude to follow their standard, under pretense of grievances which have no existence but in their imaginations." Thomas Jefferson was untroubled by the events and responded, to Abigail Adams's great consternation, in high-minded terms: "The spirit of resistance to government," Jefferson wrote, "is so valuable on certain occasions, that I wish it to be always kept alive. . . . I like a little rebellion now and then."[30] Abigail Adams broke off her regular correspondence with Jefferson for several months after that, and the rebellion indeed ended badly for everyone involved. The Massachusetts legislature suspended habeas corpus and allowed indefinite imprisonment without trial to facilitate the suppression of the rebellion. Over the course of the next year the rebel farmers were pursued, many of them arrested, and a dozen executed. Thomas Jefferson's positive view of the rebellion, however, was undiminished by news of the violence. To Colonel Smith, the Adamses' son-in-law, Jefferson wrote, "The tree of liberty must be refreshed from time to time, with the blood of patriots and tyrants. It is a natural manure."[31]

We do not have such a positive view of bloodshed and rebellion under any and all circumstances as Jefferson seems to in these letters. Indeed there is no reason to celebrate Shays's militia of armed farmers as a force for democracy in the young republic. What is more useful, instead, is to recognize the rebellion as a symptom of an economic contradiction immanent to the United States from its beginning. The rebellion, after all, was about debt—debts that the farmers could never hope to repay. The United States, despite all its rhetoric of equality, was a society divided along class lines, and its constitution was designed in many respects to maintain the wealth of the rich.[32] The rebellion of the indebted farmers was a powerful symptom of this contradiction.

This is one instance in which the formation of the global system today is re-

peating elements of the history of the formation of the United States. One of the contradictions of the global system today is that the poorest countries, including most of sub-Saharan Africa, suffer from the burden of national debts that they can never hope to repay. Debt is one of the factors that keeps the poor poor and the rich rich in the global system. It is not impossible to imagine that someday soon this contradiction could inspire something like a Shays' Rebellion of debtors on a global scale that would not only horrify the likes of Abigail Adams but also wreak enormous destruction. Perpetual indebtedness in an economic system designed to maintain the divisions of wealth is a perfect recipe for desperate, violent acts. One would be hard pressed to muster any Jeffersonian optimism about such a possibility. The spilled blood of such a conflagration is not likely to nurture the tree of liberty. We would be much better served by searching for other means to address the systematic inequalities and contradictions of our global system before any such violent event arises.

THE UNREALIZED DEMOCRACY
OF SOCIALISM

Socialist political representation has run parallel to liberal and constitutional representation in the history of modernity and finally failed in a similar way. Despite various efforts socialism did not succeed in constructing independent and original ideas or practices of political representation to avoid the unhealthy mystifications that plagued representative institutions throughout the history of modern sovereignty. There were certainly from the beginning promising elements in the socialist tradition. First of all, socialist movements criticized the notion of the "autonomy of politics" that supported the bourgeois conception of the state. Democracy would have to be constructed from below in a way that could neutralize the state's monopoly of power. Second, socialist movements recognized that the separation between political representation and economic administration was a key to the structures of oppression. They would have to find a way to make the instruments of political power coincide democratically with the economic management of society. Despite these promising beginnings, however, the history of socialist politics often led down different, less auspicious avenues.

In the late nineteenth and early twentieth centuries, socialists and communists, social democrats and Bolsheviks, in different but corresponding ways, proposed the idea of the party as an alternative to the traditional forms of institutional representation. They conceived the modern state, even in its representative forms, as a dictatorship of the ruling class, a political apparatus designed to dominate the working class. The party was to be a vanguard, an organization that could bring together the working class with intellectuals and activists outside the working class to form a political power to compensate for the workers' lack of representation and address their miserable condition. The party was to represent those who lacked representation. The party was thus thought to be separate from the working class and outside the logic of both the capitalist economy and the bourgeois social order narrowly understood. This conception of the vanguard party clearly links socialism and communism with the Jacobin tradition insofar as they re-created the guiding role of the elite that the radical and progressive part of the bourgeoisie had expressed in Jacobinism. The party of the working class, from this perspective, had to raise the flag of Jacobinism, stripping it of its bourgeois class interests and making it coherent with the new interests of the proletariat: power to the proletarians, the state to the communists!

The most radical segments of the socialist, communist, and anarchist traditions in the late nineteenth and early twentieth centuries were united in their critique of parliamentary representation and their call to abolish the state. Instead of parliamentary representation, they proposed more complete, instructed forms of representation and even forms of direct democracy. The 1871 Paris Commune was the primary example of a new democratic experiment of government for Marx, Lenin, and many others. The Commune was still, of course, a representative government, but what inspired Marx so much were the mechanisms it instituted to reduce the separation between the representatives and the represented: the Commune's declaration of universal suffrage, for example, the fact that representatives to the Commune could be revoked by their electors at any time, that they were paid the same wages as workers, and the Commune's proposition of free and universal education.[33] Every step that narrows the separation between representatives and represented was thought to be a step toward the abolition of the state, that is, *the destruction of the separation of sovereign power from society*. We should note that the conceptions of representation and democracy inspired by the Commune were not really fundamentally different than those of the eighteenth-century revolutionaries. In fact, one of the most striking elements of Marx's and Lenin's writings on the Paris Commune in retrospect is how similar their rhetoric of democracy is to that of the earlier period. Marx hailed the Commune, for example, as a government "of the people by the people" and Lenin saw it as a step toward a "fuller democracy" in which the representatives are "directly responsible to their electorate."[34]

Another avenue for finding new modes of political representation involved creating mechanisms to give the proletariat a *direct* role in economic management and social administration. The most important experiments of this kind of democratic representation in the socialist and communist traditions were the various "council" forms of management and government, including the soviets and the so-called Rat forms.[35] The councils and soviets were conceived as mechanisms to increase dramatically the multitude's connection to and participation in government. The industrial workers, the soldiers, and the peasants would all be represented by their soviets. Both in the social democratic experience, stuck between corporative labor organizations and the illusions of self-government, and the Bolshevik experience, constantly struggling for economic and political survival, the councils never really succeeded in constructing a new model of representation. In the council or soviet the social base was called to make greater sacrifices for the factory, society, and the state, and in return were promised greater participation in their management, but that participation was always kept separate, at a distance from sovereign authority, and in time the participation and representation became even more ephemeral. The antiauthoritarian initiatives and demands of direct democracy of socialist and communist movements were thus ground down.

We should note that the demands for direct democracy and self-management were strongest in the socialist and communist movements during the phase of industrial development when the professionalized industrial worker occupied a hegemonic position in the organization of capitalist production, roughly from the late nineteenth to the early twentieth centuries. The industrial workers then knew each aspect of the productive process and understood the entire cycle of production because they were its pivot. As the industrial revolution continued in the twentieth century, as assembly lines were introduced and workers were progressively deskilled, the call for worker self-management seemed almost naturally to evaporate. The project of self-management thus gave way to the notion of planning, which was a mechanism to correct (but not displace) the capitalist organization of labor and the market.

As the twentieth century developed, the democratic socialist parties, in Europe and elsewhere, integrating themselves into the capitalist system, abandoned even the pretense of representing or defending the working class. The majority of communists, for their part, were swept up in the new proletarian states; leading the way was the Soviet Union, which, to guarantee its own legitimacy, pretended to represent all people and the future of humanity as a whole. Listen, for example, to the hopes of a utopian communist future the Soviet Union inspired in the French poet Louis Aragon. Walking the streets of Moscow, Aragon writes, "ici j'ai tant rêvé marchant de l'avenir / qu'il me semblait parfois de lui me souvenir." (I dreamed so much of walking in the future here / that sometimes I seemed to have remembered it.)[36] In the Soviet Union and other socialist states, however, representation did not even remain at the level of the bourgeois tradition but was in the course of time degraded and reduced to a fiction of demagogic control and populist consensus, drained even further of its elements of connection to the multitude. This degradation of representation was one important factor that contributed to the bureaucratic implosion of the Eastern European socialist regimes in the late 1980s. This failure was due to not only historical circumstances but also a conceptual lack. Even in their most radical expressions, socialism and communism did not develop fundamentally different conceptions of representation and democracy, and as a result they repeated the founding nucleus of the bourgeois concept of sovereignty, trapped paradoxically in the need for the unity of the state.[37]

We do not mean to suggest that communism and socialism did not contain profoundly democratic strains or that these were not often expressed in powerful and tragic ways. In the early years of the Soviet Union, for example, there were numerous social, political, and cultural experiments that imagined the creation of a new and more democratic society, particularly in terms of women's liberation, transformation of the peasant world, and artistic innovation.[38] Early Soviet legal theorists, such as Eugeny Pashukanis, saw the possibility of going beyond private law and transforming public law into an institutional system based on the common.[39] In China and Cuba too there were numerous similar examples. In various different periods each of these countries witnessed new experiments in the democratic management of production and society that rejected the bureaucratic, Stalinist model. They also created projects of technical and economic assistance to struggles against colonialism and imperialism throughout the Third World. Long before most of today's humanitarian NGOs, Cuban doctors were treating tropical diseases all over Latin America and Africa. The utopian desires of communism and socialism at times guided the institutions of the socialist regimes and forced them to make social justice the primary criterion of government. And more generally, communist and socialist movements and parties often defended democracy—both in Europe and the Americas as well as in Asia and Africa, and on both sides of the iron curtain—from fascist and reactionary attacks, from Stalinism and McCarthyism. In the end, however, the dreams of socialist and communist representation proved to be an illusion. Once again, Aragon: "On sourira de nous d'avoir aimé la flame / au point d'en devenir nous même l'aliment. (They will laugh at us for having loved the flame / to the point of being consumed by it.)"[40]

Max Weber, for one, perfectly understood that the socialist organization of labor would end up having the same laws as the capitalist one and that they would correspond to analogous concepts of representation.[41] This analogy was not merely grounded on his observation of the convergent models of the organization of parties and their bureaucratic legacies (an observation of Robert Michels, which Weber certainly shared). Weber's insight went to a much deeper level of the problem and sprung from the fact that, according to him, one cannot speak of politics (and democratic representation) without speaking of social politics and thus representation remained an essential organ of the mediation and expression of social interests in every complex system of the management of society, either socialist or bourgeois. Socialism, in every form, thus necessarily involves the *management of capital*—perhaps in a less privatist or individualist way, but always within the same relentless dynamic of the instrumental rationalization of life. Since the modern concept of representation necessarily corresponds to that dynamic of rationalization, socialism could not do without it. Neither could it substitute for it a form of labor representation based on trade unions or councils. In the framework of the management of capital, Weber concludes the contradiction between worker democracy and representative democracy could only be solved in favor of the latter. That said, despite this impossibility we can also recognize in Weber a kind of nostalgia for that fantastic power of social transformation contained in the Russian Revolution and the entire socialist tradition.

Weber's critique of socialism and its mechanisms of representation because it helps us see how the various right-wing forms of populism have sprung, perversely, from the socialist tradition. A stream of the modern tradition of democratic representation breaks off and ends up in a swamp. Various elements of the authoritarian right, from the National Socialists in Germany and the Peronists in Argentina to France's Front nationale and Austria's Freedom Party, attempt to resolve the contradictions of the socialist idea of representation in populist fashion by imposing on it the most traditional theories of sovereignty. Here, on the right, the construction of representation as an external function, as a complete delegation of one's rights, reaches an extreme point. Political consciousness is entirely grounded in and nourished by tradition, and mass participation is invoked on the basis of a defensive and redemptive identification. All of these right-wing projects, be they aristocratic, clerical, or sectarian, imagine an identification of minds or spirits that legitimates its form of representation on the basis of tradition. Carl Schmitt indeed demonstrates how the reactionary idea of representation from Juan Donoso Cortés to Georges Sorel is constructed on the identitarian and traditionalist idea of sovereign legitimacy. This is how all fundamentalisms are born. Such contemporary forms of right-wing populism and fascism are deformed offsprings of socialism—and such populist derivatives of socialism are another reason for which we have to search for a postsocialist political alternative today, breaking with the worn-out socialist tradition.

It is strange now to have to recall this amalgam of ideological perversions that grew out of the socialist concept of representation, but today we can finally preside over its funeral. The democratic hopes of socialist representation are over. And while we say our farewells we cannot but remember how many ideological by-products, more or less fascist, the great historical experiences of socialism were condemned to drag in their wake, some merely useless sparks and others devastating infernos. There is no longer any possibility of going back to modern models of representation to create a democratic order. We need to invent different forms of representation or perhaps new forms of democracy that go beyond representation.

REVOLT, BERLIN 1953

If we now have a socialist regime, the Berlin workers reasoned, then we should no longer suffer under the weight of production quotas. When Benno Sarel recounts the revolts of the construction workers along Stalinallee and throughout Berlin, which on June 16 and 17, 1953, spread to the big factories, the workers' neighborhoods, and then the suburbs and countryside of East Germany, he emphasizes that the most important demand of the factory worker was to abolish the production quotas and destroy the structural order of command over labor in the factories. Socialism, after all, is not capitalism! [42]

In spring 1953, in the newborn German Democratic Republic, the socialist regime developed a long-term plan and proposed the intensification of work in the factories and all other work sites. It was a matter of reconstructing Berlin and founding a socialist state. On a four-kilometer stretch of the great boulevard Stalinallee, the old Frankfurterallee, there was an enormous concentration of construction workers and their workshops. They had already cleaned up the rubble from the war, working day and night by the light of electric flood lamps to reconstruct their city. After the planning decisions were announced in spring 1953, production quotas were raised. In the first trimester of the year, in fact, the construction industries had met only 77 percent of what the plan required. Now the timekeepers assiduously controlled the workers, and the party activists and foremen actively supported raising the production quotas, often passing them off as voluntary.

Resistance began in the workshops. The rise of production quotas was accompanied by a cut in salaries. Friday was payday, and the first Friday in June there were conflicts, protests, and numerous incidental acts of resistance. Faced with this growing unrest, the party bureaucrats and the management bureaucrats, who in the workshops were often the same people, reacted only with more discipline: they promised individual punishment and collective sanctions for those who disobeyed. The workers responded by threatening strikes. The party rank and file, who had the pulse of the workers' sentiments, tried quickly to find a compromise, and many of them moved over to the workers' side. June 12, the second payday after the raise of the production quotas, salaries were lowered even further. Worker assemblies were formed to express their outrage.

Monday, June 15, central leaders of the party's union visited the workshops to open discussions. The workers, however, organized a delegation to protest directly in front of the House of Ministers. A small demonstration of about three hundred workers was led by a banner that called for an end to the production quotas. The demonstrators passed in front of other workshops and called the workers to join them. The original three hundred was quickly transformed into a flood of thousands. On the following day and late into that night workers' committees blocked production in the workshops and went through the neighborhoods to explain their demands. The Berlin metallurgy and chemical factories quickly joined the struggle. As news of the Berlin revolt spread to the other industrial cities of East Germany the strikes spread too—Brandenburg, Halle, Bitterfeld, Merseberg, the great industrial centers of Saxony, and finally Leipzig and Dresden.

Why were those trade union and party leaders, many of whom had been part of the heroic resistance against the Nazi regime and who now claimed to be representing a socialist, worker republic, unable to convince or even reason with those workers who shared their common history and emancipatory project?

When, in front of the House of Ministers, the Minister of Industry, Selbmann, a former worker himself with calloused hands, referred to the strikers as "comrades," they responded, "We are not your comrades!" Why was there such a lack of solidarity? We know the history of how the political system of East Germany later developed into a kind of police state, but at this point in 1953 that had not yet happened. This was an instance of class struggle in the construction of a "workers' state" in which representation should have resembled a direct form of democracy. Why instead did the representatives not represent anything but the authority and quotas of the plan? When President Grotewohl declared during the strikes that "we are flesh of the flesh of the working class," no one disputed the fact. Why then had the faith in representation so quickly and completely evaporated?

The morning of June 17 demonstrators converged on the House of Ministers. The general population joined the workers, and the revolt transformed into an insurrection that involved many of the cities of East Germany. In Berlin the police blocked the demonstrators in front of the House of Ministers, and the multitude quickly found a new symbolic convergence point: Marx-Engelsplatz. At 1:00 p.m. the Soviet leadership in Moscow declared a state of siege. Late into the evening the rebels desperately fought against armored vehicles with nothing but their bare hands. Worker delegates were sent from the Eastern sector of Berlin to the Western sector, knocking on the doors of the West German administration asking for assistance, arms, and strikes in solidarity, but to no avail. The worker revolt in Berlin thus came to an end, the first of many often silent worker revolts against socialist regimes.

We do not know what reduced representatives in the German Democratic Republic to a parody of that communist dream of democratic representation, what corrupted them to the point of becoming merely emissaries of disciplinary power, not much different from the agents of bourgeois sovereignty, as the old communist militants would say. (Those who had no illusions about the fact that "really-existing socialism" had in its closet the skeleton of capitalism call this an example of socialism as a form of state capitalism.) And yet, faced with the decline of the revolutionary utopia and its constituent power, a revolt emerged that pointed toward the future. The workers sang the verses of the old hymn: "Brothers toward the light! Toward freedom!" This hymn was part of the practices of resistance, the strikes, and the barricades erected against the bureaucratic regimes in the name of a future democracy. In the case of Berlin 1953 the new form of organization was the strike committee. The strike committee united the trade union function of managing labor (immediately taking command of the factory) with the political function of the organization of the revolt. As the hegemony of the working class spread in society they called on other social groups to join the rebellion. They demanded a democracy of the workers by the workers, everywhere. The members of the strike committee were a broad social mixture: there were those workers in the workshops who were the first to express their indignation and organize the resistance, there were those communists who from the beginning stood by the mass of workers, and there were those intellectuals, students, Protestant pastors, and antifascist veterans who had been woken up by the call for justice. How the members of the strike committee were chosen is perhaps not the most important element of the story. Central instead was their insistent call for freedom and democracy. No more production quotas! If labor is not free, then there can be no communism! This is the essence of Berlin 1953: they recognized representation *to be a capitalist function of command over the working class and they said no. In response they affirmed the communist expression of desire through the multitude.*

FROM DEMOCRATIC REPRESENTATION TO GLOBAL PUBLIC OPINION

Public opinion has in many respects become the primary form of representation in contemporary societies. The Monday after a weekend of massive demonstrations against the U.S. war in Iraq in February 2003, with millions of people in the streets of major cities throughout the world, the *New York Times* proclaimed in a front-page story that there are now two superpowers in the world: the United States and global public opinion.[43] Public opinion, it seems, has finally arrived on the grandest of political stages. Public opinion, however, if it is to be considered a superpower, must be a political subject of a nature very different than a nation-state such as the United States. It is unclear, moreover, whom public opinion represents and how it represents them. It will be useful for us to take a step back at this point to consider the history of public opinion and the various theories that have sought to characterize its form of representation. We will find that public opinion is in fact neither representative nor democratic.

Although "the public" and "opinion" are notions that stretch back to the ancients, public opinion is essentially an eighteenth-century invention, born, not coincidentally, in the same period as the "new science" of democratic representation. Public opinion was conceived as the voice of the people, and thus it was thought to fill the role for modern democracy that the assembly filled for the ancient democracy: the site where the people express themselves in public affairs. Public opinion was thought to function through representative institutions such as electoral systems but go well beyond them; in it the popular will is imagined to be constantly present. Public opinion was thus from the beginning intimately related to notions of democratic representation, both as a vehicle that completes representation and as a supplement that compensates for its limitations.

This notion of public opinion quickly divides in modern political thought according to two opposing views: a utopian vision of the perfect representation of the will of the people in government and an apocalyptic vision of manipulated mob rule. Consider, for example, two texts published in 1895: James Bryce's *American Commonwealth* and Gustave Le Bon's *Psychologie des foules* (The Crowd). Bryce, a Scottish scholar and politician who, like Tocqueville before him, celebrates U.S. democracy, sees public opinion as an essential mechanism of democratic representation. The rule of public opinion could be achieved, Bryce writes, "if the will of the majority of citizens were to become ascertainable at all times, and without need of its passing through a body of representatives, possibly without the need of voting machinery at all. . . . this informal but direct control of the multitude would dwarf, if it did not supersede, the importance of formal but occasional deliverances made at the elections of representatives."[44] Bryce imagines a political system in which the will of all individuals is completely and immediately represented in government, a system that he thought nineteenth-century U.S. politics made possible. Le Bon, in contrast, sees in the public expressions of the masses not many rational individual voices but one indifferent and irrational voice. In the crowd, according to Le Bon, "the heterogeneous is swamped by the homogeneous and the unconscious qualities obtain the upper hand."[45] Crowds are fundamentally irrational and susceptible to external influence; they naturally and necessarily follow a leader whose control maintains their unity through contagion and repetition. In fact, panic might be thought of as the primary emotion of the crowd. The Greek god Pan, from whose name the term derives, leads the masses and drives them insane: innocent people are lynched by mobs, markets collapse, currencies crumble, wars begin.[46] Public opinion is so dangerous according to this second, apocalyptic vision, then, because it tends to be both unified and susceptible to manipulation.

Between these two extreme views, public opinion is also conceived in the history of modern political philosophy as a form of mediation that negotiates between the many individual or group expressions and the social unity. G. W. F. Hegel's notion of civil society is fundamental to this conception of mediation.[47] Civil society is the realm of all social, economic, and political organizations and institutions that are not part of the state. Into civil society enter not only individuals but also and more importantly families, civic groups, trade unions, political parties, interest groups, along with all the various other forms of social association. The key to Hegel's notion of civil society is the way it matches perfectly with the capitalist ideology of a society based on exchange relations. Through its political alchemy, civil society transforms the multiple exchanges of capitalist society into the unitary authority of sovereignty; it is both the plural expression of the wills of everyone and their enlightened synthesis in a unified general will. We should note that civil society fills for Hegel the same role that representation serves for modern political thought as a whole: through civil society all members of the society are both linked to and separated from the political realm of sovereignty and the state. Hegel's notion of civil society provides a model for leading the plurality of individual expression in public opinion to a rational unity compatible with sovereignty.

Since at least the middle of the twentieth century, however, public opinion has been transformed by the enormous expansion of the media—newspapers, radio, television, Internet sources, and so forth. The speed of information, the exasperating overlap of symbols, the ceaseless circulation of images, and the evanescence of meanings seem to undermine the notions of public opinion both as multiple individual expressions and as a unified rational voice. Among contemporary theorists of public opinion, Jürgen Habermas most clearly renews Hegel's notion of mediation (drawing primarily on Hegel's early conception of interrelation rather than the later concept of civil society) and links it to the utopian vision of rational individual expression.[48] From Habermas's perspective, public opinion can be conceived in terms of communicative action aimed at reaching understanding and forming a world of values. This public sphere is democratic insofar as it allows for free expression and plural communicative exchanges. For Habermas this lifeworld actively stands as an alternative, outside the system of instrumental reason and the capitalist control of communication. There is, of course, a rationalist and moralistic echo that runs throughout this effort to divide the world of free and ethical communication from the system of instrumentality and domination a sense of indignation against the capitalist colonization of the lifeworld. This is where Habermas's conception of ethical communication in a democratic public sphere appears completely utopian and unrealizable, however, because it is impossible to isolate ourselves, our relationships, and our communication outside the instrumentality of capital and the mass media. We are all already inside, contaminated. If there is going to be any ethical redemption it will have to be constructed inside the system.

In contrast to Habermas, Niklas Luhmann rejects any such moral transcendentalism or utopianism and proposes instead conceiving the public sphere with a functionalist method that makes the networks of social interaction into a motor of social equilibrium.[49] This view renovates the functionalism characteristic of traditional U.S. sociology and couples it with various newer methodological approaches in sociology. Luhmann considers the public sphere an extraordinarily complex but nonetheless self-sustaining system in which all of the various social actors—despite their differences of opinion and belief, and even by expressing these differences—end up contributing to the equilibrium of the system as a whole. To the extent that this conception of public opinion involves democratic representation, this representation rests on a notion of the free interaction of the vast plurality of social differences within the social system; the very complexity of the system is taken as a sign of its representative nature. But this is a very weak notion of representation. Functionalist perspectives such as Luhmann's pose a model of mediation between the plurality of social voices and the synthesis of the social totality, but the accent is firmly placed on the solid, stable unity and equilibrium of the system.

None of these theories of mediation, however, grasp the new role of the media and polling, which are the essential factors in the construction and expression of contemporary public opinion. In the field of media studies, which indeed does confront these new factors, we find once again the old bifurcated view of public opinion as either rational individual expression or mass social manipulation. The utopian view is promoted chiefly by the mainstream media itself: the media present objective information that allows citizens to form their own opinions, which in turn are reflected back to them faithfully by the media's opinion polls. George Gallup, for example, the primary founder of the U.S. model of opinion polls, who was, incidentally, deeply influenced by the work of James Bryce, claims that polls serve to make government more responsive to the will of the people.[50] The scholarly field of media studies tends instead toward the apocalyptic view. Although information and images are omnipresent and superabundant in contemporary society, the sources of information have in certain respects been dramatically reduced. The alternative newspapers and other media that expressed the views of various subordinated political groups in much of the nineteenth and twentieth centuries have all but disappeared.[51] As media corporations merge into huge conglomerates, the information they distribute becomes increasingly homogeneous. Media scholars complain, for example, that during the 2003 war against Iraq the major U.S. newspapers and television networks uniformly reported only the U.S. government version of events with little or no deviation.[52] The corporate media can at times act just as reliably as a mouthpiece for government positions as any state-run system. Scholars also highlight the manipulative effect of opinion polls. There is, of course, something strangely circular in the notion that opinion polls tell us what we think. At the very least, opinion polls have a centripetal psychological effect, encouraging all to conform to the view of the majority.[53] Many on both the left and the right charge that the media and their opinion polls are biased and serve to manipulate and even fabricate public opinion.[54] Once again, public opinion seems to be trapped between the naive utopianism of objective information and rational individual expression and the cynical apocalypticism of mass social control.

In the context of this extreme and untenable alternative, the field of cultural studies, especially the stream that emerged from the work of Stuart Hall and the Birmingham School, provides an important perspective.[55] One fundamental insight of cultural studies is that communication (and thus also public opinion) is two-sided. Although we are all constantly bombarded by the messages and meanings of culture and the media, we are not merely passive receivers or consumers. We constantly make new meanings out of our cultural world, resist the dominant messages, and discover new modes of social expression. We do not isolate ourselves from the social world of the dominant culture but neither do we simply acquiesce to its powers. Rather, from inside the dominant culture we create not only alternative subcultures but, more important, new collective networks of expression. Communication is *productive*, not only of economic values but also of subjectivity, and thus communication is central to biopolitical production. *Public opinion* is not the adequate term for these alternative networks of expression born in resistance because, as we have seen, in the traditional conceptions public opinion tends to present either a neutral space of individual expression or a unified social whole—or a mediated combination of these two poles. We can only understand these forms of social expression as networks of the multitude that resists the dominant power and manage from within it to produce alternative expressions.

Public opinion, finally, is not a unified voice or an average point of social equilibrium. When polls and surveys lead us to think of the public as an abstract subject—the public thinks or wants x or y—that is pure fiction and mystification. Public opinion is not a form of representation or even a modern, technical, statistical substitute for representation. Rather than a democratic subject, public opinion is a *field of conflict* defined by relations of power in which we can and must intervene politically, through communication, cultural production, and all the other forms of biopolitical production. This field of public opinion is not an even playing field but rather radically asymmetrical, since the media are primarily controlled by large corporations. In fact there are no real constitutional guarantees or system of checks and balances that guarantee or regulate access to this field. There have been many attempts in Europe to exert public control over the mechanisms of public opinion, but they have never managed to touch the essential core of the corporate-owned media. In any case, recognizing that public opinion is not a space of democratic representation but a field of conflict does not really provide answers but only clarifies the problem. The conflict on the field of public opinion is a threshold through which the multitude must pass in its process of formation.

Now we can come back to our point of departure: the second superpower that the *New York Times* recognized in the globally coordinated antiwar demonstrations in February 2003. Calling this new superpower global public opinion does grasp that it extends well beyond the political institutions of representation and that its emergence is a symptom, in fact, of *the general crisis of democratic representation in global society*: the multitudes managed to express what their representatives could not. *Global public opinion*, however, is a term completely inadequate to understand the nature and power of such expressions of the networks of the multitude, and referring to them as a superpower is not only premature but also misleading, since their form of power is so dramatically asymmetrical to the one that dominates the global order today. To understand this power of the multitude better we need first to investigate in the next section some of its contemporary expressions—its grievances against the current global system and its proposals for reform—and then in the final section of the book explore how these networks of the multitude can form a real counterpower and make possible a truly democratic global society.

WHITE OVERALLS

The radical democratic movements in Europe found their strongest image during a three- or four-year period of the late 1990s in a group of Italian activists known as the "White Overalls." The White Overalls were born in the "social centers," where activists began in the mid-1990s to reflect on the pro-

found transformations in our society. The Italian "social centers" originated in the 1970s as alternative social spaces.[56] *Groups of young people would take over an abandoned building and create in it a place for themselves, a social center, often complete with collectively run bookstores, cafés, radio stations, spaces for lectures and concerts—everything they needed. In the 1980s the youth in the social centers had suffered and mourned the death of the old working class and the end of the Fordist factory work of their parents, compounding the tragedy with a series of self-inflicted wounds, including heroin, isolation, despair. All of the dominant industrialized countries went through this experience, but since in Italy in the 1970s class struggle had been especially intense, the Italian youth in the 1980s were particularly affected. By the 1990s, however, the mourning was over and the youths in the social centers began to recognize the new paradigm of work that characterized their experiences: the mobile, flexible, precarious work typical of post-Fordism that we described in part 2. Rather than the traditional blue overalls of the old factory workers, white overalls represented this new proletariat.*

The White Overalls movement first appeared in Rome in the mid-1990s when the traditional parties and organizations of the Italian left were becoming increasingly marginalized. The White Overalls, from the beginning, claimed no political affiliation with any other political groups or parties. They claimed they were the "invisible" workers, since they had no fixed contracts, no security, no basis for identification. The whiteness of their overalls was meant to represent this invisibility. And this invisibility that characterized their work would also prove to be the strength of their movement.

Early on they became masters at organizing raves in the big cities. On any given night and in any part of the city they could bring together mountains of sound equipment and a caravan of trucks for huge, carnevalesque dance parties. Thousands of young people seemed to appear from nowhere to dance all night. And the While Overalls mixed this festive vocation with their political activism. In the streets they denounced the miserable conditions of the new precarious workers, protested their poverty, and demanded a "guaranteed income" for everyone. Their demonstrations seemed to erupt from thin air, the way Ariel suddenly appears in The Tempest. *They were transparent, invisible. At a certain point their demonstrations began to expand dramatically in various*

*cities. The White Overalls began to organize demonstrations together with ille-
gal immigrants (other invisible members of society), political refugees from the
Middle East, and other liberation movements.*

*That is when the serious conflicts with the police began, and the White
Overalls came up with another stroke of genius of symbolism. They began to
mimic the police spectacles of repression: when the police put on their riot gear
to look like Robocops behind their Plexiglas shields and armored vehicles, the
White Overalls too dressed up in white knee pads and football helmets and
transformed their dance trucks into monstrous mock battle vehicles. This was a
spectacle of postmodern irony for political activists.*

*The really decisive development in the organization of the White Overalls,
however, came when they first looked outside Europe to Mexico. It seemed to
them that Subcomandante Marcos and the Zapatista rebellion had grasped the
novelty of the new global situation. As the Zapatistas said, they had to walk
forward questioning, "caminar preguntando," in search of new political strategies for the movements. The White Overalls thus joined the support groups for
the Mexican revolt and Zapata's white horse became their symbol too. The Zapatistas are famous for their global Internet communication, but the White
Overalls were not zombies of the net. They wanted to act physically on the international and global terrain through operations that they came later to call
"diplomacy from below." Therefore they made several trips to Chiapas. The
White Overalls served as part of the European escort service protecting the historic Zapatista march from the Lacandon jungle to Mexico City. They found
themselves in the same struggle with the indigenous Mexican population because they were all exploited in the new and violent reality that global capital
had created. In neoliberal globalization spatial mobility and temporal flexibility were essential elements both for the metropolitan workers and for the rural
indigenous populations, who suffered the new laws of the divisions of labor
and power in the new global market. The reawakened European metropolitan
proletariat needed a new politics beyond just the symbolism, and they found it
in the jungles of Chiapas.*

*From Mexico City the White Overalls returned to Europe with a coherent
project, orienting their actions against neoliberal globalization. That is when
Seattle exploded at the 1999 WTO protests, so they went to Seattle and learned
from the U.S. activists techniques of civil disobedience and nonviolent protest*

that had been seldom used in Europe. These aggressive and defensive tactics learned in Seattle added to the ironic and symbolic innovations of the movement. The White Overalls continued their travels, back to Chiapas, north to Quebec, and they were present at every international summit meeting in Europe, from Nice to Prague and Gothenburg.

The final stop for the White Overalls was the Genoa G-8 protests in summer 2001. They were one of the central organizing groups of the protests, which brought together more than three hundred thousand activists. The White Overalls, when allowed to proceed, marched peacefully toward the site of the summit meeting, and they resisted as best they could when the police attacked them with tear gas, clubs, and bullets. Their ironic mimicry was met by the police this time, however, with intense violence, more like low-intensity warfare than police activity. One of the demonstrators, Carlo Giuliani, was killed by the police. The indignation against the violence of the police was extreme in Italy and throughout Europe, and court cases to punish police brutality continued long afterward.

After Genoa the White Overalls decided to disappear. They decided that the time had passed when a group like theirs should act as leaders in the movements of the multitude. They had served a role in organizing the great protests around the international and global summit meetings; they had worked to expand the protest movements and given them political coherence; and they had tried to protect the protesters and direct their aggressiveness away from counterproductive violence and toward more creative—often ironic—forms of expression. What may have been most valuable in the experience of the White Overalls was that they managed to create a form of expression for the new forms of labor—their network organization, their spatial mobility, and temporal flexibility—and organize them as a coherent political force against the new global system of power. Without this indeed there can be no political organization of the proletariat today.

3.2 GLOBAL DEMANDS FOR DEMOCRACY

> I am conscious that an equal division of property is imprac-
> ticable, but, the consequences of this enormous inequality
> producing so much misery to the bulk of mankind, legis-
> lators cannot invent too many devices for subdividing
> property.
> —THOMAS JEFFERSON

> Comrades, let us speak about property relations!
> —BERTOLT BRECHT

CAHIERS DE DOLÉANCES

We need at this point to set aside our theoretical analysis for a brief practical, empirical investigation. Today there are innumerable protests throughout the world against the inequalities, injustices, and undemocratic characteristics of the global system, and these protests are increasingly organized in powerful, sustained movements. The demonstrations at the World Trade Organization (WTO) summit in Seattle in 1999 may have focused international media attention for the first time, but for decades groups in the dominant and subordinated parts of the world have posed grievances against the global system on political, legal, and economic issues. Each of these protests has its own specific message (which often at least immediately falls on deaf ears, like a bottle thrown in the ocean or a seed under the snow waiting for spring), but it is unclear what the various protests amount to as a group. Indeed, taken together, they necessarily appear, at least on first sight, as an incoherent collection of complaints about disparate issues.

Let us try to consider the various protests and demands against the imperial system today as a new version of the *cahiers de doléances* (lists of grievances) that were compiled in France on the eve of the French Revolution. In 1788, faced with a growing financial crisis, King Louis XVI called an assembly for the following year of the Estates General, which had not met since 1614. Custom was that at an assembly of the Estates General the monarch could impose new taxes to raise funds and in exchange would consider grievances from the participants. The king, however, did not expect so many grievances. By the time of the meeting of the Estates General at Versailles in May 1789, more than forty thousand *cahiers de doléances* had been compiled from all over the country. These lists consisted of denunciations and demands that ranged from the most local problems to issues that touched the highest levels of government. The revolutionary forces growing in France absorbed these demands as part of their foundation and read in the concrete grievances the embryo of a new social power. Abbé Sièyes and his comrades, in other words, constructed on the basis of the *cahiers* the figure of the Third Estate as a political subject with the power to topple the ancien régime and carry the bourgeoisie to power. Perhaps we can see the protests against the present form of globalization in the same light today and read in them the potential figure of a new global society.

We should note that the incoherence of today's complaints and demands is different than it was in eighteenth-century France. The thousands of *cahiers de doléances* were extremely varied then but behind them, one might say, stood the coherent, ordered lists of Diderot and D'Alembert's *Encyclopedia*, which seemed to give them a deep, enlightened logical structure. There is no encyclopedic rationality behind today's protests. Today's lists of grievances are more like Jorge Luis Borges's library of Babel, a chaotic, bizarre, unending collection of volumes on everything in the world. If there is a coherence today, in fact, it will only come afterward, from the subjective standpoint of the protesters themselves. Eventually, perhaps, the seismic vibrations of each protest will resonate with the others, amplifying them all in coordination, creating an earthquake of the multitude.

Eventually, despite the variety of the grievances, we will be able to recognize three common points that return repeatedly as conditions for any project of a new, democratic world: the critique of existing forms of representation, the protest against poverty, and the opposition to war. For the moment, however, be patient. Just sit back and listen to some of the clamorous grievances against the contemporary global system. Our list does not pretend to be comprehensive, and the partiality of its selections will undoubtedly reveal our own blindnesses, but it should nonetheless give a sense of the range and depth of today's grievances.[57]

GRIEVANCES OF REPRESENTATION

Most contemporary protests focus, at least in part, on the lack of representation. Although our focus will be on the global system, we have to look briefly first at local and national institutions of representation because the global level rests directly on them. Today indeed one can hear constant and ubiquitous grievances about the domestic institutional systems of representation in every nation of the world. The false and distorted representation of local and national electoral systems has long been a subject of complaint. Voting seems often to be nothing more than the obligation to choose an unwanted candidate, the lesser of two evils, to misrepresent us for two or four or six years. Low levels of voter turnout certainly undermine the representative claim of elections: those who do not vote serve as a silent protest against the system. The U.S. presidential election of 2000, which was decided by the controversial recount of votes and the intervention of the Supreme Court, is only the most visible example of the crisis of representation through electoral institutions.[58] Even the United States, the nation that claims to guarantee democracy for the entire world, makes such a mockery of representation. No other nations have electoral systems that are much more representative, and most significantly less.

Many of the nonelectoral forms of representation at the local and national levels have even less legitimacy. One might say, for example, that, even though they are not elected, the major corporations represent national interests—"What is good for General Motors," as they say, "is good for America." Indeed "corporate irresponsibility," that is, the lack of accountability or representation, is a common refrain in many protests. The most one can say for corporate representation is that we vote with our checkbooks, choosing to support one corporation over another by consuming its goods. Or, in a much more limited sphere, corporations might be said to represent their stockholders. Few of us, however, have the purchasing power or stock holdings to claim significant connection or control. Really, such notions of corporate representation are much more ephemeral, relying on the wisdom of the representatives with no substantial input from the represented. Such claims to representation are finally as insulting as the old notion that the feudal lord represents the peasants of his estate or the slaveholder his slaves.[59]

All of these grievances about the failures of representation at the local and national levels increase geometrically in the processes of globalization. The mechanisms of connection and instruction in the new realms of globalization are much more tenuous than even those of the old patriarchal representation. One result of the current form of globalization is that certain national leaders, both elected and unelected, gain greater powers over populations outside their own nation-states. In many respects, for example, the U.S. president and the U.S. military today wield power that claims to represent all of humanity. What kind of representation is this? If the connection of U.S. voters to these leaders is small, then that of the rest of humanity is infinitesimal. Protests against the United States throughout the world are often not so much expressions of anti-Americanism as they are grievances against this lack of representation. The global population's connection to and control over the dominant corporations, of course, is even more tenuous.

One might think that the lack of representation caused by the power of national economic and political institutions spilling over to the global level would be compensated or at least ameliorated by international and supranational institutions. Such institutions only confirm, however, the depth of the crisis of representation. The World Bank and the IMF, for example, which have in the past decades become the object of increasingly large, clamorous protests, might be said to represent the interests of the entire global economy, and more specifically their loan programs and currency-relief operations are conceived as representing the interests of the host nation or region, but this is almost exclusively what we called earlier a patriarchal form of representation, with minimal input from or control of the nation or region in question. In fact, the common practice of both the IMF and the World Bank is to impose on the recipients of loans or assistance conditions that dictate their economic and political policies, diminishing their national sovereignty.[60] The World Bank and the IMF, one might respond, are governed by their member nations, but that governance, one should keep in mind, is based, as we saw in part 2, on voting rights that are proportional to monetary contributions, which gives disproportional power to the United States and other dominant countries. The skewed voting powers of different members of the IMF and World Bank thus repeat the unrepresentative control exerted by the dominant nation-states in the global system.

The most representative of the primary existing global institutions is undoubtedly the United Nations, which has not, in fact, been the object of large social protests up to this point, but even there we should recognize that the crisis of representation is extreme. First of all, the General Assembly, the United Nations' most democratic forum, can only be as representative as its member nations. In other words, the lack of democracy we recognized at the national level is passed on undiminished to the General Assembly. A representative in the UN General Assembly can be no more representative of a national population than the politician who appointed him or her—in fact, necessarily less so. Representation decreases with each degree of separation. Furthermore, representation in the General Assembly is dramatically skewed with respect to the global population, since each nation has an equal vote in the assembly regardless of population. In the second place, the limited representation of the General Assembly is even further restricted by the powers of the Security Council. The Security Council makes no pretense to being representative, since in addition to rotating members it is constituted by five permanent members who alone have veto power over resolutions: China, France, Russia, the United Kingdom, and the United States. The actions of the Security Council, particularly the vetoes exerted by its permanent members, can effectively negate the global representation (limited as it is) of the General Assembly.

It is not surprising (or unjustified) that so many today protest the lack of representation not only in national governments and national media but also and with even more reason at the global level. These protests highlight not only a crisis of democratic representation but also the corruption of our political vocabulary. In their grievances we can recognize at least three fundamental principles of modern constitutionalism that seem to have been bled of their former meaning: no power without representation, the separation of powers, and the freedom of expression. The arguments of Madison, who thought representation the key to breaking apart any monarchy of power, now seem merely like mystifications; Montesquieu, who advocated the radical division of constitutional powers, has been silenced by the unity of the system; and Jeffersonian free expression has been monopolized by the corporate media. The political lexicon of modern liberalism is a cold, bloodless cadaver. Liberalism never really even pretended to represent all of society—the poor, women, racial minorities, and the rest of the subordinated majority have always been excluded from power by explicit or implicit constitutional mechanisms. Today liberalism tends not even to be able adequately to represent the elites. In the era of globalization it is becoming increasingly clear that the historical moment of liberalism has passed.

GRIEVANCES OF RIGHTS AND JUSTICE

Rights and justice have traditionally been guaranteed by national constitutions, and thus protests have been cast in terms of "civil rights" directed to national authorities. Significant grievances in terms of civil rights continue to be expressed today, particularly among minority groups in the dominant countries, such as struggles to maintain affirmative action for women and people of color in the United States, for the rights of Muslims in France, and for native populations in Canada and Australia. Increasingly, particularly in the subordinated countries, where the nation-state is not capable of guaranteeing rights, protesters appeal directly to international and global authorities, shifting the discussion from "civil rights" to "human rights." Throughout the world today human-rights NGOs express grievances of injustices against women, racial minorities, indigenous populations, workers, fisherman, farmers, and other subordinated groups. It is especially striking how feminist movements over the past twenty years, first in the subordinated countries and then in the dominant ones, have transformed their organizations into NGOs and formulated women's rights as human rights.[61]

The promise of human rights is to guarantee rights universally, with the power both to counter the injustices of national legal systems and to supplement their incompleteness. When the national authorities of Nazi Germany, to cite the classic, extreme example, conducted their project to exterminate the Jews, the universal perspective of human rights mandated overriding and countering the national legal norms and authority. Similar arguments were made by human rights activists in favor of European and U.S. military intervention in the former Yugoslavia and Rwanda in the 1990s. In less dramatic cases too human rights are invoked to defend those whom national systems simply cannot or will not protect. Finally, human rights are also meant to protect those who have been deprived of protection under any national legal system, such as refugees. Human rights are at base, in this sense, the right to have rights, both inside and outside national jurisdictions.[62]

One of the strongest examples of a successful campaign for justice and human rights is the Madres de Plaza de Mayo, the movement of the mothers of those "disappeared" during the dictatorship in Argentina, who, since the mid-1970s, meet every Thursday in the Plaza de Mayo, the square in front of the presidential palace. The mothers wear white headscarves, carry placards of the disappeared, and demand to know what happened to their sons and daughters. The Madres' demand began as an appeal to the government within a national context but quickly became cast as international issue of human rights, with North American and European participation. Their struggle has become the symbol for a general call for justice against the crimes and abuses of power.[63]

The primary frustration for many of those who advocate human rights, however, is that no adequate institutional structure exists to enforce them. The primary power of human rights is moral persuasion. Human rights NGOs and activists can certainly achieve important results by lobbying national governments, often funded by international foundations, backed by political pressure from the dominant nation-states, and reinforced by international media attention, but human rights remains merely a rhetorical device rather than a proper legal framework. Paradoxically, the enforcement of human rights has thus far relied in the most visible cases on the might of the dominant national powers, as, for example, in the 1998 NATO military intervention in Kosovo. One nation might be willing to violate the sovereignty of another in the name of human rights, but it will simultaneously insist on the principle of national sovereignty—especially its own! The universal applicability of human rights clearly cannot be realized as long as it has no legal institutional structure and relies instead on the dominant nation-states.

Some institutions have indeed been formed that strive for or at least allude to a framework of justice beyond the national legal structures. The first level of legal institution beyond national legal structures is constituted by the various truth commissions that have been established at the end of civil wars or conflicts, such as those in South Africa, Guatemala, Chile, and Argentina. These truth commissions are national institutions, but they necessarily stand above the national legal structure because they address in large part crimes of the state regime itself. Many of these truth commissions have limited themselves, however, to revealing the facts of the past while not seeking punishment of the guilty and often even guaranteeing immunity of those who testify. The resulting national discussions in some cases revise history and modify the balance of political forces but in others merely serve as a kind of national therapy or talking cure that puts the troubles in the past and restores the traditional order. In any case, in terms of our discussion here, such truth commissions do not constitute effective institutions of justice.

The international tribunals established after national conflicts to prosecute war crimes and crimes against humanity constitute a second level of legal institutions beyond national legal structures. The Nuremberg Tribunal that prosecuted leaders of the Nazi regime set the precedent, and in the 1990s international criminal tribunals were established to prosecute war crimes in Rwanda and Yugoslavia. These tribunals are clearly very limited in their scope—they consider only the most outrageous crimes committed in a specific country for a delimited period—but they do nonetheless constitute a real institutionalized system of justice beyond the national level. They might be thought of as the first institutions of a global system of justice, even though too often such tribunals function merely as a fig leaf to cover the operations of the victors.

At a third and more general level are the experiments of permanent international criminal courts. The International Court of Justice (ICJ), for example, was established under the UN Charter in 1945 to adjudicate disputes between nation-states. The enforcement powers of the ICJ, however, were extremely weak. Participation of a nation-state in any ICJ proceeding was voluntary, and the court's rulings carried very little weight. In 1986, for example, the ICJ ruled against the United States for damage caused by U.S.-funded military operations in Nicaragua, but the United States simply refused to comply with the decision and the court had no recourse. In 2002, a much more powerful institution, the permanent International Criminal Court (ICC), was established. All the countries that ratify the statute of the court are subject to its rulings. The ICC, in contrast to the criminal tribunals for Rwanda and Yugoslavia, does not have precedence over national courts but rather only considers crimes that extend beyond any national jurisdiction. Despite such limitations, the ICC, more than any other existing institution, indicates the possibility of a global system of justice that serves to protect the rights of all equally.

As soon as one utters such a hopeful sentence, one is brought back to earth by the fact that the United States has refused to ratify the statute of the ICC (or, really, the United States "unsigned" the treaty) because it objects to its citizens, particularly its soldiers and politicians, being subject to the court's rulings.[64] Once again we are confronted by the fact that undercuts all the attempts to institute a supranational or global system of justice: the most powerful nation-states constantly maintain the power to negate any legal actions. If in fact the most powerful nation or nations can be exempt, then suddenly the aspirations to universal justice and universal rights collapse back to something like the rule of the strong over the weak.

We should not have illusions, then, about the effectiveness of these truth commissions, tribunals, and courts or about the justice we can expect from them. Sometimes they just leave us with the bitter taste of the "justice" imposed by the victors; and at other times they function merely to neutralize and pacify conflict rather than create justice. The pretense of justice too often serves merely to mask the machinations of power.

Finally, we should recognize that the injustices that are the subject of so many grievances today point toward not only the lack of international legal structures that guarantee rights but also and more fundamentally the emergence of global legal structures that function against such rights. Many scholars have begun to discuss a new form of *imperial law* that has emerged since the end of the cold war. On one hand, U.S. law has gained such a powerful hegemony that it has been able significantly to influence legislation in all other countries and transform legal structures and codes, particularly with respect to property law. On the other hand, new global imperial legal structures guaranteed by U.S. military power have emerged, constituted in part, for example, by the processes of *lex mercatoria* that we analyzed earlier. Imperial law, according to these legal scholars, is a vehicle of predatory capitalist globalization, which primarily serves the interests of the multinational corporations and dominant capitalist countries. "Ironically," one legal scholar writes, "despite its absolute lack of democratic legitimacy, imperial law imposes as a natural necessity by means of discursive practices branded "democracy and the rule of law" a reactive legal philosophy that outlaws redistribution of wealth based on social solidarity."[65] Recently the neoconservative theory and practice of imperial law has shifted its center of gravity from the focus on commercial law and international business to questions of military intervention, regime change, and nation building—from neoliberal globalization to armed globalization. As the imperial constitution is based ever more on the "right of invention" and human rights are imposed militarily, the function of imperial tribunes has become ever more ambiguous.[66] It should be clear, in any case, that the imperial legal frameworks and structures tend not to serve to promote the rights and justice that are the subject of protests, but on the contrary pose further obstacles to them.

ECONOMIC GRIEVANCES

Economic protests are perhaps the most vocal and evident. Many of the grievances expressed against the contemporary global system—at the massive demonstrations but also in religious groups, nongovernmental organizations (NGOs), and UN agencies—are based on the simple fact that so many people in the world live in dire poverty, many at the limit of starvation. The figures are indeed staggering. The World Bank reports that almost half of the people in the world live on under two dollars a day and a fifth on less than a dollar a day.[67] Such figures are really only a very partial, indirect indication of the state of poverty; real misery is a biopolitical fact that depends of all facets of life and cannot be measured in dollars. Monetary measures can nonetheless serve as a first approximation. The lack of resources does, of course, bring with it a lack of access to health care and education. Such poverty is devastating, thwarting all kinds of opportunities for political and social participation, when it does not threaten life itself. Only the most cynical can ignore their plight by saying it is their own fault or by rationalizing philosophically in Christian tones that the poor will always be with us. Hunger and poverty have always been and continue to be today the world's most powerful grievances.

After recognizing the extent of poverty in the world today, one has to recognize also its uneven geographical distribution. In each nation-state, poverty is distributed unequally along lines of race, ethnicity, and gender. In many countries throughout the world, for example, there are significantly higher rates of poverty among women than men, and many ethnic minorities, such as the indigenous populations throughout the Americas, have significantly higher rates of poverty. Local and national variations in the rate of poverty, however, are dwarfed by the inequalities of wealth and poverty on a global scale. South Asia and Sub-Saharan Africa account for about 70 percent of the global population living on less than a dollar a day, up from about 60 percent ten years ago. The average income of the richest 20 countries is thirty-seven times greater than the average in the poorest twenty—a gap that has doubled in the past forty years.[68] Even when these figures are adjusted for purchasing power—since some basic commodities cost more in rich countries than in poor—the gap is astonishing. The construction of the global market and the global integration of the national economies has not brought us together but driven us apart, exacerbating the plight of the poor.

There are millions of specific expressions across the world of indignation and generosity with respect to the poor, often through courageous acts of charity and self-sacrifice. Nonprofit and religious charity organizations provide enormous assistance for those in need, but they cannot change the system that produces and reproduces poverty. It is impressive, in fact, how so many people who begin in volunteer charity work pass to activism and protest against the economic system.

Some protests against the systemic reproduction of poverty, such as the Jubilee Movement International, focus on the fact that foreign debt obligations serve as a mechanism that keeps the poor countries poor and their populations hungry.[69] It is clear that no matter what economic policies they enact the poorest countries cannot repay their current foreign debts or even keep up with interest payments, perpetuating an inescapable cycle of misery. Furthermore, many claim that these debts were incurred originally through dubious or illegitimate means. It is always the same story: debt serves as a legal mechanism of enslavement.[70] The difference here is that this logic of bondage is applied not merely to the individual indentured worker or even to a specific racial group or indigenous population (where the assumption of a civilizing mission is the basis of debt) but rather to entire nations.

In more general terms many economic grievances against the global system are based on the assumption that the inequalities and injustices of the global economy result primarily from the fact that political powers are less and less able to regulate economic activity. Global capital, the argument goes, since its movement and reach extend well beyond the limits of national space, cannot be effectively controlled by states. Many labor unions, particularly in the dominant countries, protest the fact that the mere threat of the mobility of capital—the threat, for example, of moving production and jobs to another country where state regulations and/or labor costs are lower and more favorable—can convince states to abandon or temper their own regulatory powers. States conform to and even anticipate the needs of capital for fear of being subordinated in the global economic system. This creates a sort of race to the bottom among nation-states in which the interests of labor and society as a whole take a backseat to those of capital. Neoliberalism is generally the name given to this form of state economic policy. Neoliberalism, as we claimed in part 2, is not really a regime of unregulated capital but rather a form of state regulation that best facilitates the global movements and profit of capital. Once again, in the era of neoliberalism, it might be helpful to think of the state as the executive committee assigned the task of guaranteeing the long-term well-being of collective capital. The fundamental task of the neoliberal state, from this perspective, like all forms of the capitalist state, is to regulate capitalist development in the interest of global capital itself.

One central pillar of neoliberal policies is privatization, which, when not adopted by states of their own accord is often dictated by supranational economic organizations, such as the IMF. In certain periods of history privatization has become a kind of feeding frenzy, as it did after the long period of the French Revolution, between the reigns of Louis Philippe and Louis Bonaparte; or after the crisis of the welfare state in Europe in the 1970s; or again after the fall of the Berlin wall, when the old state apparatchiks of the Soviet bloc were reborn as capitalist oligarchs. Today, privatization often involves selling state-run businesses and industries to private hands, but it also involves expanding the realm of property itself. We saw earlier how traditional knowledges, seeds, and even genetic material have increasingly become objects of ownership. Not only railroads, electric companies, and prisons, in other words, but also more and more common realms of life are becoming private and exclusive. When activists of the Movimento Sem Terra, for example, the landless movement in Brazil, invade and destroy a field of soybeans where Monsanto Corporation is experimenting with genetically engineered seeds that it can patent, their grievance is directed in part at such a process of privatization.

Neoliberal policies that restrict political and social regulation of the economy are particularly evident with respect to markets and finance. As markets become increasingly global and neoliberal policies lower political regulation, the power of finance becomes ever stronger.[71] There has been an enormous expansion, in particular, of the role of derivatives, that is, financial instruments whose value derives from the price of an asset, such as a commodity or a currency. Investing in a derivative, for example, does not involve buying grain but rather wagering on the rise or fall of the price of grain. Abstraction is the key to derivatives and financial markets in general. Since the 1970s, in fact, derivatives have come to be based on quantities that are increasingly abstract from specific forms of economic production, such as derivatives based on interest rates or stock market indexes or even the weather.[72] Because of this abstraction a very few key players, the kings of finance, can wield enormous influence over vast markets and also make those markets more susceptible to crises and catastrophic changes. At such a high level of abstraction all changes are multiplied such that a slight shift in the breeze can become a hurricane, bankrupting businesses and collapsing currencies. Especially in the subordinated countries, political leaders have few means to regulate the national economy in the face of these colossal powers of global finance. When protesters rail against neoliberalism and finance, in short, their grievance is with finance's tendency to concentrate wealth in the hands of few, exert control over national and global markets, and destabilize all the economic systems in which they operate.

We should note that finance capital also has another face, a common face that points toward the future. Finance is not really, as some claim, any less productive than other forms of capital. Like all forms, it is simply accumulated labor that can be represented in money. What distinguishes finance is, first, its high level of abstraction that allows it, through money, to represent vast realms of labor and, second, its orientation toward the future. Finance capital, in other words, tends to function as a general representation of our common future productive capacities. All of the strange tricks used in financial markets—such as, in a technical way, using timezone differences as a tool for speculating in different stock markets; or, in a substantial way, investing pension funds in stock markets and risking workers' livelihoods; or, finally, in a managerial way, giving huge stock options to the CEOs and managers—all of these are mechanisms to give finance the power to command and shape the new forms of labor and their future productivity.[73] Since finance capital is oriented toward the future and represents such vast realms of labor, we can perhaps begin to see in it, paradoxically, the emerging figure of the multitude, albeit in inverted, distorted form. In finance the contradiction becomes extreme between the expansive becoming common of our future productivity and the increasingly narrow elite that controls it. The so-called communism of capital, that is, its drive toward an ever more extensive socialization of labor, points ambiguously toward the communism of the multitude.

BIOPOLITICAL GRIEVANCES

We have felt uncomfortable thus far dividing the series of grievances into the conventional categories of politics, rights, justice, and economics, because in step with the processes of globalization in recent decades the divisions among these domains of life and power have progressively broken down, such that economic questions are immediately political and vice versa. We now add to the list the category of biopolitical not as a supplement that gathers up all that has been left out—considering it the merely social or the merely cultural—but rather as the fundamental category that demonstrates how all of the others are mutually implicated. Here there is a sort of whirlpool that pulls down all of common life into the grips of exploitation.

Ecology is one field on which the basic questions of life are clearly immediately political, cultural, legal, and economic. In fact, ecological grievances were perhaps the first to be recognized as necessarily global in scope. There is no way for one country to stop the air pollution, water pollution, or radioactive fallout produced in another from drifting across its borders. We all live on and with the planet, which is one common, interconnected whole. The Greenpeace fleet of ships circulating in the world's oceans is perhaps the best symbol of the fact that ecological protests are just as global as ecological problems. Feminist struggles, antiracist struggles, and struggles of indigenous populations too are biopolitical in the sense that they immediately involve legal, cultural, political, and economic issues, indeed all facets of life. One might consider the 1995 UN World Conference on Women in Beijing and the 2001 UN World Conference on Racism as great syntheses of biopolitical grievances against the current global system.

One very specific example of biopolitical grievances is the Save the Narmada Movement (Narmada Bachao Andolan) that has protested since the 1980s against the building of the enormous Sardar Sarovar dam across the Narmada river in India.[74] Since the dam project was originally funded in part by a loan from the World Bank—and indeed the World Bank encourages governments to take loans for big dams such as this—the protests have been directed against the World Bank in addition to the Indian government. One of the protesters' grievances is the simple fact of being displaced from their land. Big dams each displace tens and sometimes hundreds of thousands of inhabitants, often with little or no compensation. The most dramatic confrontations of the Narmada movement have involved protesters refusing to leave their villages, vowing to drown in the rising waters if the reservoir is filled. The grievances are also ecological and economic. The dam, the protesters charge, endangers fish species by blocking their spawning routes and disrupting traditional farming practices by changing the natural flow of the river. Such grievances might sound like absolute condemnations of all technology that disturbs the order of nature—and indeed some protests do express them in such terms—but the real issue is the use and control of the technology. Dams certainly can provide social benefits, such as electricity, safe drinking water, irrigation, and flood protection. In many cases, however, and this is the fundamental issue in the Narmada protests, the poor bear the major social costs of the dam, and the profits go primarily to the rich. The dam, in other words, functions as a powerful vehicle for privatization, transferring the common wealth of the river and the land to private hands, the hands, for example, of the agribusiness corporation that owns the land and grows the crops that receive the irrigation. This is not a protest against technology, in other words, but against the political powers that decide without the representation of those primarily affected to privatize the common, enriching the few and exacerbating the misery of the many.

Another type of biopolitical struggle involves the control of knowledges. Scientific knowledge has become part of economic production to such an extent that the dominant economic paradigm has shifted from the production of material goods to the production of life itself. When knowledge becomes so identified with production, it should come as no surprise that economic powers would put their brand on knowledges and submit the production of knowledge to the rules of profit. As we saw in the last section, seeds, traditional knowledges, genetic material, and even life-forms are increasingly becoming private property through the use of patents. This is an economic issue first in the sense that it assigns profits and wealth and second in that it often restricts the free use and exchange that is necessary for development and innovation. It is also, however, clearly a political question and a question of justice, in part because the ownership of these knowledges is systematically concentrated in the wealthy countries of the Northern Hemisphere to the exclusion of the global south. Grievances against the pharmaceutical corporations who sued the South African government to prevent the import of cheap copies of their patented AIDS drugs, for example, are fundamentally against the private control of the knowledge to produce the drugs. The contradiction is extreme in this case between the profits of the pharmaceutical corporations and the thousands of lives that could be saved with access to inexpensive drugs.[75]

After September 11, 2001, and the subsequent war on terrorism, all the protests against the global system were trumped temporarily by the global state of war. First of all, in many countries it became almost impossible to protest because the police presence at demonstrations became much larger and more brutal in the name of antiterrorism. Second, against the suffering of war the various grievances seemed to fade in the background and lose their urgency. In effect, during the most intense periods of combat and bombing, all grievances were transformed into the one overriding grievance, the ultimate biopolitical grievance, against destruction and death. As we saw earlier, the protests against the war reached a pinnacle on February 15, 2003, with a massive demonstration coordinated in cities throughout the world. The other grievances have not gone away, and they will all reappear forcefully in time, but now war has been added to each struggle as the common, fundamental grievance. The grievance against war tends, in fact, to become the summary of all the grievances: global poverty and inequality, for example, are exacerbated by war and war prevents any possible solutions. Peace is the common demand and the necessary condition for all projects to address global problems.

Finally, this series of biopolitical grievances allows us to recognize and engage the ontological conditions on which they are all established, something like what Michel Foucault calls the critical interrogation of the present and ourselves. "The critical ontology of ourselves," Foucault writes, "must be considered not, certainly, as a theory, a doctrine, nor even as a permanent body of knowledge" but rather as "the historical analysis of the limits imposed on us and an experiment with the possibility of going beyond them."[76] The legal, economic, and political protests that we have considered are all posed on this ontological foundation, which is crisscrossed by powerful and bitter conflicts over goals that invest the entire realm of life. A democratic project lives in each of these grievances, and the struggles are part of the flesh of the multitude. It is certainly an open question whether the development of this biopolitical fabric will allow us to build sites of liberation or rather submit us to new forms of subjugation and exploitation. We have to decide here, as the ancients used to say, whether to be free men and women or slaves, and precisely this choice is at the basis of the establishment of democracy today. Spinoza would be happy to see the question posed in these terms, in which the problem of democracy invests all of life, reason, the passions, and the very becoming divine of humanity.

CONVERGENCE IN SEATTLE

The Speakeasy Internet Cafe on Second Avenue in Seattle was one of the designated "convergence centers." In the final typically gray days of November 1999, affinity groups of activists met at the Speakeasy to construct huge papier-mâché puppets and plan their protests. Some activists had come from outside the United States and many from other cities on the West Coast, but most were from Seattle. High school teachers had focused their classes on global issues, university students had studied global trade, church groups and political activists had planned street theater and held seminars on nonviolent protest, lawyers had organized teams of observers and legal aid in case of arrests: Seattle was ready.[77] A few blocks from the Speakeasy, delegates and heads of state from 135 countries had gathered for a summit meeting of the World Trade Organization (WTO) to discuss agricultural subsidies, selling products overseas at below cost (known as "dumping"), and other trade issues. In the days that followed, however, the dramatic protests succeeded not only in preventing the WTO delegates from completing their meeting and agreeing to a final dec-laration for the summit but also stole the headlines from the presidents, prime ministers, and official delegates. At center stage in the bright lights of the global media, the streets of Seattle erupted in a battle over the new global order.

Seattle was the first global protest. There had, of course, been numerous protests against economic and political institutions of the global system. There had been protests directed against World Bank projects and policies, such as those we described against the construction of the Sardar Sarovar dam in In-dia; numerous revolts throughout the world had previously responded to aus-terity and privatization programs dictated by the IMF, such as the 1979 protests in Jamaica[78]; and some had targeted regional free trade agreements, such as the Zapatista rebellion, which was born in 1994 in protest of the NAFTA agreement and its negative effects, particularly on the indigenous population in Chiapas. Seattle was the first major protest against the global sys-tem as a whole, the first real convergence *of the innumerable grievances against the injustices and inequalities of the global system, and it opened a cy-cle of similar protests. After Seattle, summit meetings of major international or global institutions—the World Bank, the IMF, the G8, and so forth—would routinely be met with dramatic protests.*

The world media, which had come to Seattle for the summit meeting, were most impressed by the violence of the protests. The Seattle police were initially unprepared for the large numbers of protesters and their insistence on blocking the site of the WTO meetings. The media painted an idyllic, tranquil image of Seattle, the Emerald City, forgetting the violence of its radical past, from the actions of the International Workers of the World in the early twentieth century and the 1919 general strike to the bombings by the George Jackson Brigade in the 1970s. The violence of the protesters at the WTO, however, was relatively minor. The vast majority of protesters, of course, were entirely peaceful and even festive. The most serious acts of violence involved the de-struction of property, such as breaking the storefront windows of symbolic global corporations like McDonald's and Starbucks. No serious injuries were reported as the result of the violence of protesters in Seattle (or in any of the summit meeting protests that followed it to this point either), but the Seattle police, after initial criticism for being too gentle, began attacking the protesters and citizens of Seattle relatively indiscriminately with rubber bullets and tear-

gas: unsuspecting diners in restaurants in one neighborhood were tear-gassed, as were Christmas carolers in another.[79] The police were out of control. At subsequent summit protests police went even further and shot protesters with live ammunition, gravely injuring one in Gothenburg and killing another in Genoa. Many protesters have complained that the violence of a few incites the police, monopolizes the headlines, and eclipses the messages of the many, in addition to creating divisions among the protesters. This is certainly true, but we have to recognize also the unfortunate fact that the media focus on the protests because of the violence. Without the violence they have no story. There is a kind of objective complicity between the media and the small groups of protesters who destroy property and seek clashes with police. The resulting media attention is at best a mixed blessing.

The media attention focused on the protests has certainly had some beneficial effects on those in power. Already during the Seattle events, President Clinton said rather vaguely that he supported the protesters' message. Later other global leaders—from the editorialists of The Economist *to leaders at the World Bank—have said that the protesters have valid concerns about global poverty and the inequalities and injustices of the global system. The real importance of the Seattle events was not to influence global leaders and neither was obstructing the meeting of delegates to the WTO, in itself, a very important accomplishment. The WTO, which is designed to oversee compliance with international trade agreements and settle trade disputes, is by no means the most powerful or the most destructive of international and global institutions, and blocking the 1999 meeting did not do it permanent damage. A few years after the Seattle fiasco, in fact, the WTO managed to move forward on its agenda and recoup lost time at its highly protected summit at the isolated enclave of Doha, but then at the Cancun meetings in 2003 it was blocked again, by a group of twenty-two nations from the global south that objected to agricultural trade policies.[80] For the protesters in Seattle, however, the WTO merely stood in for the global system as a whole.*

For the protesters, both the violence and the sympathetic murmurings of some leaders were all beside the point. The real importance of Seattle was to provide a "convergence center" for all of the grievances against the global system. Old oppositions between protest groups seemed suddenly to melt away. During the protests, for example, the two most prominent groups were the environmentalists and the trade unions, and, to the surprise of most commentators, these two groups, which were thought to have contradictory interests, actually supported each other. Although the leadership of the AFL-CIO did comply with the police and the WTO organizers by leading their march away from the summit site, many of the rank-and-file unionists, particularly steelworkers and longshoremen, deviated from the official labor march to join the street protests, wading in the sea of beautiful green sea turtle puppets and eventually engaging in conflicts with police. The unexpected collaboration of trade unionists and environmentalists, however, was just the tip of the iceberg. Seattle and the following summit protests brought together innumerable other groups expressing their grievances against the global system—those against the practices of the huge agribusiness corporations, those against the prison system, those against the crushing debt of African countries, those against IMF controls of national economic policies, eventually those against the permanent state of war, and so on ad infinitum.

The magic of Seattle was to show that these many grievances were not just a random, haphazard collection, a cacophony of different voices, but a chorus that spoke in common against the global system. This model is already suggested by the organizing techniques of the protesters: the various affinity groups come together or converge not to unite into one large centralized group; they remain different and independent but link together in a network structure. The network defines both their singularity and their commonality. Seattle demonstrated, from a subjective standpoint, from the perspective of the protesters, the coherence of the lists of grievances against the global system. *This is the primary message that was heard around the globe and inspired so many others. Anyone who travels to different parts of the world and meets the various groups involved in the protests can easily recognize the common elements that link them in an enormous open network.*[81]

The new global order has never convened a meeting of the Estates General and invited the various estates of the global population to present their cahiers de doléances. Beginning with Seattle, protesters have started to transform the summit meetings of the global institutions into a kind of impromptu global Estates General and, without being asked, present their lists of grievances.

EXPERIMENTS IN GLOBAL REFORM

Whenever a massive protest movement explodes onto the social scene or whenever there is any organized critique of the global system, the first question asked by the media and sympathetic observers is always, what do you want? Are you just malcontents, or do you have concrete proposals to improve the system? There is, of course, no shortage of specific and concrete reform proposals to make the global system more democratic. Constructing such lists of demands, however, can sometimes be a trap. Sometimes focus on a few limited changes obscures the fact that what is necessary is a much more general transformation of society and the structures of power. This does not mean we should refuse to propose, evaluate, and implement our concrete demands; it means rather that we should not stop there. Every such real institutional reform that expands the powers of the multitude is welcome and useful as long as it is not sacralized as a figure of superior authority and posed as a final solution. We have to construct a method or a set of general criteria for generating institutional reforms, and, more important, we have to construct on the basis of them constituent proposals for a new organization of global society.

There is no conflict here between reform and revolution.[82] We say this not because we think that reform and revolution are the same thing, but that in today's conditions they cannot be separated. Today the historical processes of transformation are so radical that even reformist proposals can lead to revolutionary change. And when democratic reforms of the global system prove to be incapable of providing the bases of a real democracy, they demonstrate ever more forcefully that a revolutionary change is needed and make it ever more possible. It is useless to rack our brains over whether a proposal is reformist or revolutionary; what matters is that it enters into the constituent process. This recognition is widespread not only among progressives but also among conservatives and neoconservatives who see dangers of revolution in even modest reform proposals and respond with radical initiatives in the opposite direction. In some ways, the reactionary theorists of Washington, circa 2000, correspond to those of London and Vienna, circa 1800, from Edmund Burke to Friedrich von Gentz and Franz von Baader, in that they all recognize the emerging constituent power and believe that the forces of order must oppose it actively, posing against the possibilities of reform and revolution a violent counterrevolution.

Like the list of grievances in the last section, the list of democratic reform proposals here will necessarily be incomplete and will also, at least at first sight, compose a disordered, incoherent group. Each proposal points toward a specific way to improve the global system, but it is initially unclear what together they amount to. Once again, we need to enumerate patiently the existing proposals we hear, follow them, and see where they lead. We disagree with elements of many of the proposals, of course, and indeed one should, but our primary intent is not to evaluate them. We want above all to register the enormous desire for global democracy contained in them.[83]

REFORMS OF REPRESENTATION

Let us begin for clarity's sake with a set of reform proposals that turn out *not* to be aimed at democratizing the global system. Many scholars and bureaucrats inside and near the supranational economic institutions, such as the IMF and World Bank, maintain that the institutions must be reformed to be more transparent and accountable.[84] Such proposals could appear to be at first sight aimed at increasing the democratic and representative nature of the institutions, but in fact on closer inspection they prove not to be. Transparency itself, of course, does not necessarily imply any greater representation—tyrants can be perfectly transparent. At best, greater transparency may make the lack of representation more visible and thus easier to protest. The more substantive notion, which is omnipresent in these internal proposals, is "accountability" (which is often paired with the notion of "governance"). The concept of accountability could refer to mechanisms of social representation, but it does not in these proposals. One has to ask, "Accountable to whom?" and then we find that these authors do not propose making global institutions accountable to a global (or even a national) people—"the people," precisely, is missing. They rather seek to make the global institutions accountable to other institutions and especially to a community of experts. If the IMF were more transparent and accountable to economic experts, for example, there would be safeguards against its implementing disastrous policies, such as those dictated by the IMF in Southeast Asia or Argentina in the late 1990s.[85] What is central and most interesting about the use of the terms *accountability* and *governance* in these discussions, finally, is that the terms straddle so comfortably the political and the economic realms. Accountability and governance have long been central concepts in the theoretical vocabulary of capitalist corporations and they carry many characteristics of that domain. With respect to such terms as *responsibility,* for example, *accountability* drains the democratic character of representation and makes it a technical operation, posing it in the realm of accounting and bookkeeping. (Since many other languages have no equivalent for *accountability* and are forced to translate it as *responsibility,* one might get the impression that the term is specific to the world of Anglo-American business.) The notions of accountability and governance in these reform proposals seem to be directed most clearly at assuring economic efficiency and stability, not at constructing any representational form of democratic control.[86] Supranational institutions like the IMF and World Bank are designed, in fact, to be able to make technical economic decisions based on their own expertise, free from the instruction or control of the public, which is presumed less knowledgeable and informed. They are organized, in other words, in a way that is contrary to mechanisms of social or public representation and, furthermore, they do not even conform to the minimal conceptions of bourgeois liberalism and public space. Such a substitution of administration for politics is a general phenomenon that runs counter to democratic legitimacy. This is what leads some more radical authors to advocate that these supranational institutions simply be abolished.[87]

The most significant proposals to reform global systems of representation focus on the United Nations. Many proposals seek to eliminate or reduce the power of the most unrepresentative element of the United Nations, the Security Council, whose five permanent members have veto power. The power of a single member nation to block with a veto a resolution decided by the majority is clearly the most significant element that obstructs the representative functioning of the General Assembly and the United Nations as a whole. One proposal to address this problem is simply to eliminate or phase out the veto power of the five permanent members.[88] Other proposals seek to change the power of the Security Council by changing its membership. Originally, the Security Council was composed of the five permanent members plus six rotating members. In 1965 the number of rotating members was expanded from six to ten. Significant transformation, however, would have to involve changing permanent membership. Since permanent membership in the Security Council is a relic of World War II, composed as it is of the primary victors of that war, some argue that, over a half century after the end of the war, the powerful countries that were defeated, particularly Germany and Japan, should now be granted permanent membership. Others argue that large and populous nations from the Southern Hemisphere, such as Brazil and India, should be added to the group of permanent members to give the Security Council more geographical representation.[89] One could also propose, if the Security Council is deemed necessary, that all the members rotate, thus making it even more representative. (One should keep in mind, however, that reforms to the UN governing structure require approval by two-thirds of the General Assembly and all members of the Security Council. It is hard to imagine that the Security Council would vote away its own privileges.)

Transforming and decreasing the powers of the Security Council would certainly increase the powers of the General Assembly and allow it to exercise its representative functions more fully. We noted earlier, however, that the representative nature of the General Assembly is itself limited in at least two significant regards. First of all, since states appoint representatives to the assembly, the assembly can only be as representative as the member states themselves, and we know the democratic and representative character of nation-states is quite limited.[90] Second, representation in the General Assembly is very disproportionate with respect to population, since it operates on a one state, one vote basis rather than a one person, one vote model. In order to alleviate some of these unrepresentative characteristics of the General Assembly, then, some propose adding a second assembly to the United Nations governing structure, something like a People's

Assembly, that would be based on representation proportional to population and independent of nation-states. Such a two-assembly structure might be conceived as similar to the two houses of the U.S. Congress. Adding a second assembly, of course, would constitute a radical conceptual transformation of the United Nations, since the institution from its foundation has been conceived as a union of nation-states, not individuals, peoples, communities, or other groups. Rather than adding a second assembly to the United Nations, then, others make a similar proposal to construct a global parliament.[91] All such proposals, however, raise the question of how representation can function in a global institution that brings together not nation-states but the global population.

Let us try to imagine how a people's assembly or a global parliament could apply the central element of the modern notion of democratic representation, that is, the electoral process based on a standard of one person, one vote. Imagine, for example, that the global voting population of approximately 4 billion (excluding minors from the total global population more than 6 billion) would be divided into four hundred districts of 10 million people each. North Americans would thus elect about twenty representatives, and the Europeans and Indonesians another twenty each, whereas the Chinese and Indians would elect about one hundred and eighty, respectively. These resulting four hundred representatives would constitute the assembly or parliament. It might be best, furthermore, that these voting districts be drawn so as not to follow the old national borders, so that the new institutions do not simply reproduce the same corrupt and antidemocratic forms that have come to characterize so many nation-states. (Remember that during the French Revolution, in order to avoid repeating the corrupt traditions of the ancien régime, completely new electoral districts were drawn.) Such a global voting scheme would indeed restore the sense of equality central to the modern conception of democratic representation, something that even the UN General Assembly fails to realize. As one articulates such a scheme, however, it quickly becomes clear that it would be unmanageable in practice. The practical challenges of conducting elections with 4 billion voters seem, at least at first sight, insurmountable. Furthermore, the modern concept of representation stretched so thin across the global terrain cannot support a substantial notion of democracy. As James Madison and the U.S. Federalists clearly recognized, representation decreases as the size of population increases with respect to the number of representatives. (Madison thought the ideal proportion was one representative for every thirty thousand inhabitants.[92]) The representative function is clearly reduced to a minuscule level when one delegate represents 10 million voters. And where would they put the global Federal District, the administrative center of the world?

There are some proposals for either a second assembly for the United Nations or a global parliament that do not rely on the one person, vote principle but rather configure representation in terms of already existing organizations or communities. Some, for instance, point to the World Social Forum (WSF) as an instructive example of how NGOs and social movements can be organized as a global body.[93] Since its first meeting in Porto Alegre, Brazil, in 2001, the WSF has held an annual gathering that brings together delegates from NGOs, social movements, and individuals from around the world to exchange information and views about social and political issues related to the processes of globalization. The WSF is also complemented by a series of regional forums that are held at other times of the year. The point is not that the WSF could be conceived as even an embryonic figure of a global governing body—indeed the WSF does not pretend to have any deliberative or ruling powers. The point rather is that the WSF demonstrates that a global set of nonstate actors, such as NGOs, can be brought together for real and substantial discussions, thus indicating the possible lines according to which a global political body is possible.

One might also imagine a global parliament or assembly that is based on peoples, nations, or even civilizations. Such a body might conceive of representation as following racial, ethnic, or religious lines. In such a scheme, for example, indigenous and oppressed peoples who presently have no state could have equal or proportional representation. Alternatively, one could imagine transforming Samuel Huntington's model of civilizational conflict into a representational mechanism. In other words, if one were to accept that the identities of the global population are really defined by the civilizations that Huntington indicates, or some similar civilizations, then the civilizations themselves could serve as a representational basis for a global assembly or parliament.

We should keep in mind, however, that in all of these possibilities we have enumerated of representation based neither on nation-states nor individuals, the representative character of the various organizations or communities is extremely weak. NGO, of course, is a vague term that covers a wide range of organizations, but the vast majority of such organizations make little or no claim to being representative of the population. *Global civil society* is an equally vague term that is often used to name the various non-state organizations or communities, but this too has no real mechanism of representation. And finally, identitarian conceptions based on race, ethnicity, or religion, such as civilizations or peoples, have no claim on representation either.

The major stumbling block for all of the various proposals we have considered to create a new global representative body, such as an assembly or parliament—whether based on the principle of one person, one vote or on existing communities—is the concept of representation itself. All of them rely on the modern concept of representation, which was conceived for the dimensions of the nation-state. Once again, when we move from the national to the global level, the leap of size undermines all the old models of representation. It is not, however, merely a question of scale. The biopolitical nature of contemporary social production, which we analyzed at length in part 2, not only makes impossible old forms of representation but also makes new forms possible. This new biopolitical possibility is what needs to be addressed; as long as it is not, the lack of representation will continue to corrupt global society.

We should point out that a large proportion of the global political reform proposals we have outlined, such as reforms of the UN institutions or the creation of a global parliament, replicate the structure of the U.S. Constitution. Global political reform thus becomes something like making the world power structure more like the United States, expanding the U.S. model to a global scale. Ironically, the United States presents the greatest obstacles to such reforms, since the practices of unilateralism and exceptionalism that we discussed earlier undermine any international or global form of democratic representation. The United States blocks the expansion of the U.S. model. How long can such a contradiction continue?

Finally we should note, at least briefly, a proposal for a new global constitution that does not rely on modern national models but points rather to the experience of the European Union.[94] The global level is, of course, very different from the continental, but, given the violent clashes and cultural conflicts of European history, we can see that the project of a unified European constitution confronts some of the same difficulties that a global constitution would face. The key to the European constitution is its plural, multilevel method of decision making based on multilateral relationships. This multilevel arrangement is, on one hand, not merely a European superstate or, on the other, a union of nation-states, but rather a complex federal system. Some decisions take place on the European level, others at the national level, and others still at subnational and regional levels. The unity of the administrative process results from the overlapping interaction of these various levels. This method, in other words, by creating a multilevel federal system, breaks the traditional conception of a linear, isomorphic relationship among the legal and political forms of the city, the nation, the region, and the world. We should also note here that with this multiplicity of actors and levels there is no longer any "outside" to the system, or, rather, the outside becomes inessential and all the constitutional conflicts become internal. This European constitutional model does indeed provide mechanisms that could contribute to a stable global system, but it does not really address the issue of representation. The multilevel federal model, in fact, seems only to undermine traditional forms of representation without creating new ones.

REFORMS OF RIGHTS AND JUSTICE

The various grievances about the lack of rights and justice in the global system we enumerated earlier make clear that new institutions of justice must be independent from the control of the nation-states, since the dominant nation-states have consistently blocked or distorted previous attempts in their own favor. If universal principles of justice or human rights are to be enacted at a global level, they will have to be grounded in powerful and autonomous institutions. One logical proposal, then, would be to extend the project of the International Criminal Court we described earlier, giving it global jurisdiction and enforcement powers, perhaps tied to the United Nations.

A closely related proposal to institute global justice calls for the creation of a permanent international or global truth commission.[95] Such an institution could build on the various national truth and reconciliation commissions to consider not only national allegations but also large-scale, international claims of injustice and determine penalties and compensation. A global truth commission, for example, would be given the task of adjudicating the many calls for reparations to compensate for historic injustices against peoples and communities. Some cases of reparations have been presented in existing national courts along the lines of class-action suits: Japanese Americans who were unjustly interned in camps in the United States during World War II, for example, and surviving European Jews whose relatives were killed and property stolen. Such cases are complicated enormously, however, both when they stretch spatially across national borders and when the events span long historical periods so that the individuals who directly suffered the injustice have died. What court does one appeal to in cases of conquest, colonialism, and slavery? "Comfort women," for example, who were forced into prostitution by the invading Japanese in Korea, Taiwan, Indonesia, and other parts of East Asia, demand reparations of the Japanese government.[96] In a more general and far-reaching way, the descendents of those who suffered from the slave trade and slavery demand reparations: African American descendents of slaves demand reparations from the U.S. government and the corporations that profited from slavery; black African nations, which were ravaged by the slave trade, demand reparations from the European nations that participated in the slave trade; and former colonies demand reparations from their former colonizers. The united African Ministers, for example, in preparation for the 2001 World Conference on Racism, proposed that "a Development Reparation Fund should be set up to provide resources for the development process in countries affected by colonialism."[97] The specific legal action to be taken is not clear, however, in any of these cases and numerous others like them. Who can be held responsible? Who should pay what and to whom? What institution has the authority to decide? In many cases simply revealing publicly the systematic historic injustice is itself a beneficial development, but recognition and apologies are not enough to address injustice. A global truth commission might be charged with addressing this lack. (We should add, at least parenthetically, however, a note of skepticism about the *gigantism* of such proposals. Global commissions, global institutions, and global agencies are not necessarily adequate solutions to global problems.)

Another enormous question of restitution has to do with economic corruption. Corruption, in this case, means the illegal deviation of public systems for private gain, reducing public goods to private wealth. One obvious example of such corruption is the creation of the enormous fortunes of the so-called Russian oligarchs during the "transition to democracy" through family connections, political influence, and a variety of illegal means. The public wealth of the nation was quickly transmitted into the private hands of the few. Another example of such corruption, on a very different scale and in a different context, was revealed in the Enron scandal. The wealth accumulated by Enron's executives was extorted not only from Enron employees and investors but also energy consumers and the public more broadly. It is clear that national courts are not capable of dealing adequately with such corruption and restituting the stolen wealth, even if a few Russian oligarchs and Enron executives do go to prison. We need a new institutional mechanism not only to prevent corruption but restitute the common that has been stolen. That would require a great institutional innovation.

This current inability to enforce rights and address injustices on the global level, however, is really not just a lack. In recent years, in fact, there has been a clear tendency in the opposite direction. Particularly since September 11, the notion of U.S. exceptionalism coupled with the idea that freedoms have to be sacrificed in the interest of security have seriously undermined institutions of rights and justice. There has been a kind of dual tendency that combines the domestic erosion of civil liberties in the United States (through innovations of the Office of Homeland Security and legislation such as the USA Patriot Act) with the United States's rejection and violation of international agreements regarding rights and justice.[98] The prisoners held indefinitely at the U.S. military base at Guantánamo Bay represent the point of intersection between the two, since their imprisonment violates not only the Geneva Conventions on the treatment of prisoners of war but also U.S. criminal law. This dual tendency to undermine existing systems of justice probably cannot last long, since in time it will inevitably be met by overwhelming indignation and protest. It does make clear, however, that proposals to reform global systems of rights and justice in a democratic direction today face a steep uphill battle.

ECONOMIC REFORMS

One should recognize the sometimes heroic efforts of all those—in religious organizations, NGOs, UN agencies, and supranational institutions like the World Bank—who work to better the lives of the poor. One must also recognize, however, the limitations of all such efforts that leave the system unchanged. In addition to ministering to the pains of the sick we also have to attack the disease, that is, the system that reproduces global poverty. There are indeed numerous reasonable proposals to alleviate the poverty and suffering of the most subordinated in the global economy without making systematic changes to the global system.[99] The most radical and far-reaching of these is perhaps the proposal to eliminate or drastically reduce the foreign debt of the poorest nation-states, since the debt is clearly an important cause of continuing poverty. This proposal is economically feasible because the sums in question are relatively small in the context of the global economy, but many object that simple debt elimination would set a bad precedent for future loans. The World Bank proposes reducing or eliminating the debt of nations affected worst under the supervision of the Bank itself, and according to conditions the Bank would impose on the nation's economic policies. Others propose setting up a new, independent agency to decide which debts should be eliminated or reduced and determine conditions. Some propose, for example, a global, legally binding debt-arbitration agency to deliberate on cases based on the model of domestic bankruptcy laws, such as Chapter 11 and Chapter 9 in the United States.[100] Countries could thus default on loans and go into bankruptcy just as individuals and corporations do now in domestic systems. Debt relief is clearly needed to break the cycle of misery for the most subordinated in the global economy, but such remedies do not address the systemic problems of the global economy that continually produce and reproduce inequality and poverty.

In general most existing propositions of reform of the basic functioning of the global economic system divide between two broad lines of action, which stand opposed to one another: a strategy that gives nation-states more regulatory power and one that strives to undercut control over the economy by either states or economic powers. The two strategies, of course, rely on very different analyses of the root causes of our economic problems. The first points primarily to neoliberal regimes and unregulated capital as the source of problems, whereas the second focuses principally on forms of power, both political and economic, that exert control over production and circulation.

Consider as an example of the first strategy the group ATTAC and its proposal of the Tobin tax, which is a currency transaction tax, first conceived by Nobel laureate James Tobin, that would impose a small tax on all international currency exchanges and contribute the resulting tax revenue to the nation-states. The proponents argue that one benefit of such a tax is that it would help control the volatility of international financial markets and thereby avoid or moderate the financial crises caused in part by rapid currency trading: "Throwing sand in the wheels of global finance" is Tobin's phrase. A second benefit, in the view of proponents, is that the tax would give states not only more control over the value of their currencies but more important, with the added revenues, more control over the economy as a whole.[101] In fact, the fundamental goal of this and similar proposals is to allow nation-states the possibility to act to correct some of the most extreme differences and distortions of wealth and income. State regulation of capital, as opposed to neoliberal regimes that grant capital a maximum autonomy, is thus conceived in these proposals as the primary solution to the problems of the global economy.

One limitation of this strategy, from our perspective, is that it relies so heavily on the beneficial actions of sovereign nation-states. It seems to us that nation-states, both the most powerful ones and the least, do not act consistently to alleviate poverty and inequality. With this in mind, some propose a modification of the Tobin tax that would contribute the revenues from the currency tax not to nation-states but to a democratic global body combining this economic proposal with one of the proposals to reform representative systems we saw above.[102] One could even fund the United Nations or a global parliament with this tax, thereby freeing it from financial reliance on nation-states.

The second general strategy includes proposals that seek to eliminate destructive forms of political and economic control. In the realm of cybernetics and the Internet, for example, as we saw earlier, the control of access, information, and ideas through copyright increasingly thwarts creativity and innovation. We have also cited repeatedly numerous grievances that arise from patents that control pharmaceutical drugs, knowledges, genetic material, and even life-forms. There are many proposals to solve or ameliorate these problems. Some modest proposals, for example, seek to address the expanding controls of copyrights simply by limiting their duration. Copyright was originally conceived as a means to encourage innovation by allowing the author to enjoy a monopoly on the work for a limited time. Copyrighted material can now be controlled, however, for more than 150 years with very little action on the part of the owner, thereby restricting its use in the common public domain. One could improve the system simply by reducing the possible duration of copyright to a much shorter period and require more efforts of the owner to renew the copyright periodically.[103] And more generally, one could limit copyright protection to only the commercial use of material, such that copying texts or music without commercial gain would no longer be restricted.[104] Similarly, one could reduce the kinds of products that are eligible for patents, excluding, for example, life-forms and traditional knowledges. These are very modest proposals that easily fit within the existing legal framework. The open-source movement, which strives to make software free and accessible for modification without copyright, offers a more radical example.[105] Since proprietary software owned by corporations does not expose its source code, the proponents of open source maintain that not only can users not see how the software works but they also cannot identify its problems or modify it to work better. Software code is always a collaborative project, and the more people who can see and modify it, the better it can become. One can certainly imagine doing away entirely with the legal protection of patents and copyright, making ideas, music, and texts free and accessible to everyone. One would have to find, of course, other social mechanisms to compensate the creativity of authors, artists, and scientists, but there is no reason to assume that creativity depends on the promise of great riches. Authors, artists, and scientists are indeed often outraged when corporations get rich off of their creativity, but they are not themselves generally driven to create by the prospect of extraordinary wealth. It should be clear, in any case, that each of these proposals aims to reduce political and economic control, through mechanisms such as patents and copyright, not only because it is unjust to limit access to these goods but also because such controls thwart innovation and restrict economic development.

Some of the most innovative and powerful reform projects, in fact, involve the creation of alternatives to the current system of copyright. The most developed of these is the Creative Commons project, which allows artists and writers a means to share their work freely with others and still maintain some control over the use of the work. When a person registers a work with Creative Commons, including texts, images, audio, and video productions, he or she forgoes the legal protections of copyright that prevent reproduction but is able instead to choose minimal restrictions that apply to its use. Specifically, the author or artist can choose whether reproductions have to include attribution of authorship, whether the work can be used commercially, whether it can be transformed to make derivative works, and whether any use made of it has to be equally open to reproduction.[106] One might say that this alternative system is just a supplement to existing copyright laws that serves those who do not want its restrictions, but really such an alternative is a powerful agent of reform. Its example highlights the inadequacy of the patent system and cries out for change.

Economic reform in general has to be based on a recuperation or creation of the common. There has been a long process of privatization that in the dominant countries corresponded to the dismantling of the welfare state and that in the subordinated countries has often been imposed by global economic institutions such as the IMF. The programs of democratic transition and nation-building, from Russia to Iraq, are also based primarily on privatization. As the catastrophes for social welfare of these processes of privatization accumulate—the British rail system and the U.S. electrical system can serve as two emblematic examples—the need for change will become ever more clear. In our view this will have to be not a return to the *public*, with state control of industries, services, and goods, but a creation of the *common*. This conceptual and political distinction between the public and the common will be one of the elements we will address in the context of democracy in the final section of the book. This notion of the common is the basis for a postliberal and postsocialist political project.

BIOPOLITICAL REFORMS

When we arrive at the question of biopolitical reforms, all the difficulties we saw facing the various political, legal, and economic proposals for the global system seem to be compounded and magnified. The forces against biopolitical reform are enormous, sometimes making it difficult even to imagine ways to make the system more democratic.

It is certainly difficult to imagine a reform proposal that could address the most central biopolitical grievance: our current state of global war. Instead of a reform proposal we might point to an experiment that simply expresses the need for an alternative to the war system. Antiwar activists have begun a dangerous practice of "diplomacy from below," sending delegates to intervene in war zones. Activists from Italy, France, and the United States went to Palestine during the summer 2002 Israeli offensive, and many attempted to enter Iraq before the 2003 war. This "diplomacy from below" demonstrates how the "diplomacy from above" among national leaders, which perpetuates our state of war, is not representative of the populations. The activist-diplomats, of course, are not representative either, but their efforts do give concrete expression to the widespread desire to put an end to this global system of permanent war.

On biopolitical issues other than the war system it is less difficult to imagine global reform proposals. One reform strategy for biopolitical systems has involved international treaties on very specific issues. The 1997 Kyoto Accord on climate change, for example, was designed to address the problem of global warming. Industrialized nations that sign the accord commit to cutting the carbon-rich "greenhouse" gas emissions, which mostly result from burning coal, gas, and oil. The 2001 announcement by the Bush administration that the United States would not sign the accord, however, put its effectiveness in doubt. The 1997 Landmine Ban Treaty has had some success, but its effectiveness too has been put in question by the reluctance of the United States to comply. Similar international treaties to ban the production and destroy stocks of biological, chemical, and nuclear weapons have similar histories of mixed success, and here too the unwillingness of the United States to comply poses an enormous obstacle. Unilateralism or, rather, the exception posed by the United States within the global system, thwarts all these reform proposals.

There are indeed many other proposals that do not rely completely on the United States. Some propose an independent global water agency, for example, that could adjudicate not only international disputes over water rights but also national conflicts, such as those resulting from dam projects. Such an agency would be charged with both guaranteeing the fair distribution of existing water resources and encouraging their increase. Others propose an independent global communications authority that would regulate the global means of communication, something like a global version of the U.S. Federal Communications Commission. The principle task of such an authority would be both to guarantee equal access to the existing means of communication and information and to expand the available means of communication, for example, by requiring all military and commercial satellites to dedicate a certain percentage of their communications capacity to freely accessible public channels. Such proposals, however, suffer from the "gigantism" we referred to earlier. In an effort to democratize relationships, they pose a central authority that serves to undercut democratic participation.

It may not be difficult to imagine such global reforms on these biopolitical issues, but they do not really proceed very far. So many forces are stacked up against them, not the least of which is the U.S. predominance in the international system and its tendency to exempt itself from all multilateral agreements, that it seems useless even to forward a proposal. Once again, it is perhaps more useful for us to cite an experiment here rather than a reform proposal, one in this case that constructs an alternative, more democratic system of communication and information. Indymedia is a network of collectively run Web-based information centers that provide print and video news services on their Web sites. There is, of course, a long tradition of free radio stations and cable television experiments aimed at breaking the monopoly of information that has formed in the hands of the major media corporations. Indymedia, which grows out of this tradition, was first created to provide information about the demonstrations at the WTO summit in Seattle in 1999.[107] Since that time the network of independent media centers has expanded to dozens of cities on six continents. The Indymedia slogan—"Don't hate the media, become the media"—calls for not only breaking the information monopoly of the corporate media but also becoming actively involved in the production and distribution of information. Anyone can submit a story on an Indymedia Web site. Both of these elements—equal access and active expression—are central to any project of democratizing communication and information. The media must be able to speak the truth. It is not a matter of fixing the truth in some global version of political correctness, but on the contrary guaranteeing the differences of expression of the multitude in a democratic process of communication. Indymedia and the numerous independent media projects like it do not provide a model to reform global communications systems. Rather, they are important experiments that demonstrate once again the powerful desire for global democracy.

As these examples indicate, in the realm of biopolitics it may be more productive not to generate reform proposals but to develop experiments for addressing our global situation. Furthermore, the biopolitical perspective can help us, recognize the ontological character of all the movements and identify the constituent motor that drives each of them. We can never arrive at this essential element by enumerating or adding together all the grievances and reform proposals. This constituent motor is a biopolitical fact. It is what will be able to call the multitude into being and thereby develop the more general power to create an alternative society.

BACK TO THE EIGHTEENTH CENTURY!

All of the various reform proposals we enumerated in the previous section are good and useful ideas, even when, as we saw is often the case, the forces mounted against their realization are nearly insurmountable. Simply by considering a proposal one gains a new, critical perspective on the existing structures, something like a cognitive map of the global system. Each proposal, in this sense, is a pedagogical tool. Every person who thinks, "That's a good idea, why can't we do that?" learns an important lesson.

At this point, we need to recognize not only that most of these global-reform proposals are unrealizable as a result of the forces against them but also that the reforms, beneficial as they may be, are not able to sustain democracy on a global scale—and we want nothing less than democracy, real democracy. We aim too high, some are sure to say. In fact, we feel something like the eighteenth-century proponents of democracy who, as we saw earlier, were confronted by skeptics who charged that democracy may have been possible in the small confines of the Athenian polis, but is utterly impossible in the extensive territories of the modern nation-state. Today's proponents of democracy are met by the same skeptical argument: democracy may have been possible in the confines of the modern nation-state, but in the extensive territories of our globalized world it is utterly absurd. Liberal skeptics insist that the sheer size of the world, along with its cultural, religious, and anthropological differences—and why not add, as they used to, the question of climate!—undermine the possibility of a unified global people and the other conditions necessary for a global democracy. Conservative skeptics generally focus rather on the different levels of civilization, with strong racist undertones: talk of democracy might do in Europe and North America, they say, but those elsewhere are not ready for democracy. After they learn from our free markets and our legal systems to gain a respect for private property and a sense of liberty, then maybe they will be capable of democracy.

Well, to all these various skeptics we say, back to the eighteenth century! One good reason to go back to the eighteenth century is that back then the concept of democracy was not corrupted as it is now. The eighteenth-century revolutionaries did not call democracy either the rule of a vanguard party or the rule of elected officials who are occasionally and in limited ways accountable to the multitude. They knew that democracy is a radical, absolute proposition that requires the rule of everyone by everyone. It is also useful to recognize that if the eighteenth-century revolutionaries were utopian, it is simply in the sense that they believed another world was possible. What was indeed utopian and completely illusory in the eighteenth century was to repropose the ancient form of democracy designed for the city-state as a model for the modern nation-state. That is not, of course, what the eighteenth-century revolutionaries did. As we saw earlier, the challenge then was to reinvent the concept of democracy and create new institutions adequate to modern society and the national space. It is useful to go back to the eighteenth century, finally, to appreciate what a radical innovation they accomplished. If they did it, then we can too!

With the reference back to the eighteenth century, then, we can recognize today the limitations of being wedded to old models. Just as it was illusory in the eighteenth century to repropose the Athenian model on a national scale, so too today it is equally illusory to repropose national models of democracy and representative institutions on a global scale. Indeed many of the reform proposals we outlined in the previous section maintain the modern concepts and national institutional models of democracy, simply projecting them in expanded form onto the entire globe. (Hence the tendency toward "gigantism.") Such proposals are based on what scholars in international relations call the "domestic analogy," that is, the analogy between the internal structures of the nation-state and structures of the international or global system. It is striking, in fact, how often domestic U.S. institutions and practices came up as models in the proposals above. We do not mean to suggest that proposals of global representative systems, a global parliament, global federalism, global courts, and global tax schemes are not useful. Indeed the discussion and implementation of many such proposals, we repeat, can certainly ameliorate the injustices and inequalities of our present global system. Our point, rather, is that such reforms will not be sufficient for the creation of a global democracy. What is necessary is an audacious act of political imagination to break with the past, like the one accomplished in the eighteenth century.

We have to find a way to free ourselves of the tenacious ghosts of the past that haunt the present and cripple our imagination, not only because of the question of scale and the fact that modern forms of representation and accountability are diluted and disoriented in the vast global territories, but also because we ourselves have changed. As we argued at length in part 2, not only are the conditions of labor becoming increasingly common throughout the world, our production also tends to be biopolitical. We claimed, in other words, that the dominant forms of production tend to involve the production of knowledges, affect, communication, social relations—in short, the production of common social forms of life. The becoming common of labor, on the one hand, and the production of the common, on the other, are not isolated to software engineers in Seattle and Hyderbad but also characterize health workers in Mexico and Mozambique, agriculturists in Indonesia and Brazil, scientists in China and Russia, and industrial workers in Nigeria and Korea. And yet the new centrality of the common does not in any way diminish the singularity of the various situated subjectivities. This coincidence of the common and singularities is what defines the concept of the multitude. The anthropological difference of the present, the difference marked by the formation of the multitude, also makes it impossible simply to repropose past models. This is one reason why we find it useful to call our present age postmodern, to mark these differences with our modern past. Rather than an archaeology that unearths the models of the past, then, we need something like Foucault's notion of genealogy, in which the subject creates new institutional and social models based on its own productive capacities. "The genealogical project is not an empiricism," Foucault explains, "nor is it a positivism in the ordinary sense of that term. It tries to bring into play local, discontinuous, disqualified, not legitimated knowledges against every unitary theoretical instance that pretends to filter, hierarchize, and order them in the name of a true knowledge. . . . Genealogies are thus not positivist returns to a form of science that is more attentive and more exact; genealogies are more precisely *anti-sciences*."[108]

If it is no longer sufficient to use national institutional models of democracy to defend ourselves against global oppression and tyranny, then we will have to invent new models and methods. As the Federalists said in the eighteenth century, the new times require a "new science" of society and politics in order to stop repeating the old myths of good government and block the attempts to resurrect the old forms of order. Today, given not only the global scale of contemporary society but also the new anthropology and new productive capacities of the multitude, we too need a new science—or, maybe, following Foucault, an anti-science!

A new science of global democracy would not simply restore our political vocabulary from the corruptions it has suffered; it would also have to transform all the primary modern political concepts. From the concept of nation-state and free market to that of socialism, from the notion of political representation to that of soviet and council forms of delegation, and from human rights to the so-called rights of labor, all of these have to be rethought in the context of our contemporary conditions. This will have to be a science of plurality and hybridity, a science of multiplicities, that can define how all the various singularities express themselves fully in the multitude.

There are, of course, important differences between our approach to the multitude and the eighteenth-century new science. One difference is that the French and North American prophets of Enlightenment wanted to create an institutional mirror of society, but an artfully distorted mirror that could create out of the plurality of the multitude a unitary people: *E pluribus unum*, as the banner in the eagle's beak still reads on the back of the one-dollar bill. Today it is not a question of reducing the global multitude to a people. Global society is pervaded by a biopolitical dynamic of the constant, and surplus production of the common and global subjectivities affirm themselves as not only plural but also singular. A new concept of democracy must take account of the constituent dynamic of the multitude and the fact that its plurality refuses to be reduced to an *unum*.

Another important difference between the eighteenth-century new science and the one needed today has to do with the fact that today the basis for political analysis and proposition is not the individual but rather the common, that is, the common set of biopolitical productive relations. Whereas modern political thinkers had to struggle with the contradiction between the individual and the social whole, we today have to grasp the complementarity between the multiple singularities and our common social life, which is constantly negotiated through linguistic cooperation and biopolitical productive networks. In truth, the great eighteenth-century republican innovators were never really individualists. A strong notion of community convention was always an important element in their thought and practice, which was combined, it is true, with a conception of appropriation and possession that did tend to separate and define individual subjects.[109] In any case, today the social coordinates are completely different and, as we claimed earlier, the ontological conditions of society are defined by a common fabric, which is not fixed and static but open, overflowing, and continually constructed in lapidary fashion by the accumulated energies and desires of the multitude. Paradoxically, the world of finance, with its enormous powers of abstraction, gives an excellent expression of the both common social wealth of the multitude and its future potential, but an expression that is distorted by the private ownership and control in the hands of the few. The task is to discover a way in common, involving men, women, workers, migrants, the poor, and all the elements of the multitude, to administer the legacy of humanity and direct the future production of food, material goods, knowledge, information, and all other forms of wealth.

Finally, one more difference with eighteenth-century thought is that the war of all against all and the notion of a violent state of nature, which used to serve as a kind of blackmail against republican projects, are no longer effective weapons of reactionary thought to legitimate the domination of a monarchical sovereign power. We do not mean to suggest that powerful leaders no longer try to use this tactic to gain control over nations, regions, and the global system as a whole. We mean rather that this notion corresponds less and less with our social reality. The notion of a foundational war of all against all is based on an economy of private property and scarce resources. Material property, such as land or water or a car, cannot be in two places at once: my having and using it negates your having and using it. Immaterial property, however, such as an idea or an image or a form of communication, is infinitely reproducible. It can be everywhere at once, and my using and having it does not hinder yours. On the contrary, as Thomas Jefferson says, ideas are enhanced by their communication: when I light my candle from yours they both seem to burn brighter. Some resources do remain scarce today, but many, in fact, particularly the newest elements of the economy, do not operate on a logic of scarcity. Furthermore, when productive mechanisms rely increasingly on expansive open networks of communication and cooperation, then the notion of a basic conflict with everyone tends to seem increasingly unnatural. Our state of nature is indeed what is created in the common networks of the multitude. It is increasingly nonsensical to legitimate a central sovereign power on the basis of a war between "democracy" and other civilizations or to defend "democracy" with a permanent state of war or even to impose "democracy" militarily. The only democracy that makes sense today is one that poses peace as its highest value. Peace, in fact, is not only required for democracy but it is also a fundamental condition of knowledge and more generally of our being in this world.

We have to recognize that democracy is not an unreasonable or unattainable demand. When Spinoza calls democracy absolute he assumes that democracy is really the basis of every society. The vast majority of our political, economic, affective, linguistic, and productive interactions are always based on democratic relations. At times we call these practices of social life spontaneous and at others think of them as fixed by tradition and custom, but really these are the civil processes of democratic exchange, communication, and cooperation that we develop and transform every day. If such democratic interactions were not the basis of our living in common, then society itself would be impossible. That is why for Spinoza other forms of government are distortions or limitations of human society whereas democracy is its natural fulfillment.

The invention of a new science of democracy for the multitude is certainly an enormous task, but the general sense of the project is clear. We can recognize the need for it in the real and urgent grievances and demands of so many throughout the world—and from where would the power to realize such a project come if not from the desires of the multitude? The protesters do not accept the idea of living in a world defined for so many by fear, injustice, poverty, and unfreedom. Even when those who express a guarded skepticism about the possibility of substantial changes in the short term still recognize that these current forms of domination, violence, mystification, alienation, and expropriation cannot continue long in our new reality: the common languages, common practices, and forms of production of our society run counter to the forms of command. In short, our dreams make necessary (if not yet possible) another world. The global scale seems increasingly like the only imaginable horizon for change, and real democracy the only feasible solution.

What we propose today, then, is not repeating old rituals and tired slogans but on the contrary going back to the drawing board, taking up research again, launching a new investigation in order to formulate a new science of society and politics. Conducting such a social investigation is not about piling up statistics or mere sociological facts; it is a matter of calling on ourselves to grasp the present biopolitical needs and imagine the possible conditions of a new life, immersing ourselves in the movements of history and the anthropological transformations of subjectivity. A new science of the production of wealth and political constitution aimed at global democracy can emerge only from this new ontology.[110]

Excursus 3: Strategy: Geopolitics and New Alliances

Most of the contemporary discussions about geopolitics pose a choice between two strategies for maintaining global order: unilateralism or multilateralism. Such discussions do not take into account the power of the movements for global democracy, their grievances, and their proposals. The movements have a constituent effect on geopolitics and the possibilities of global order. We need to go back for a moment to the history of geopolitics to see how it has developed, how today it has been thrown into crisis, and what strategic possibilities this offers the multitude.

THE CRISIS OF GEOPOLITICS

Modern geopolitics was born in Europe as the eminent field of *Realpolitik* in the sense that the European nation-states, closed in their small territories, played out the real relations of power in the vast global spaces. The European political tradition could pretend to cast its politics over the entire world, paradoxically, because it conceived of Europe as a finite horizon, as "the West," where sun set, *finis terrae*. Europe had to escape its own finitude. Spatial elements are always present in Europe's own self-definition, at times in expansive terms and at others in conflictual, tragic, and obsessive ones, from Homer's Aegean to Columbus's Atlantic. Already in the ancient Greeks and Romans we find that controlling the space outside the city is a necessary element for maintaining peace and well-being within the city. In ancient Rome, in fact, this role of external space was transformed into a motor for imperial expansion. Geopolitical space has thus become a trajectory, a directed movement of destiny over foreign territories defined by the dominant imperial classes. Thus was born the national and imperialist *Grossraum*.

The rise of the United States as a global power transformed the European tradition of geopolitics, opening it up from questions of permanent borders and finite spaces to the indefinite outside and open frontiers, focusing on flows and mobile lines of conflict like oceanic currents or seismic faults. Geopolitics in the American key seems to go beyond the fixed spatial horizon and become rather an alternation or dialectic between openings and closures, expansionism and isolationism. This is indeed the contemporary notion of geopolitics we find today. Geopolitics may regard borders as fixed but they are also, at the same time, thresholds or points of passage. Wars, from this perspective, begin when one crosses a border armed with weapons; progress is conceived as crossing these same borders unarmed; and commerce crosses borders both with arms and without. The borders of geopolitics have nothing to do with natural borders, conceived in either geographical, ethnic, or demographic terms. When geopolitics confronts borders posed as natural, in fact, it either uses them instrumentally or undermines them, setting in motion a slide toward expansion, going beyond.

In order to understand the current form of geopolitics (and eventually to challenge it) we must, then, avoid resorting to the naturalist, determinist, or economistic conceptions of borders and limits that characterized the old European geopolitics. We must instead engage the notion of flexible boundaries and thresholds that are continually crossed, which is typical of U.S. ideology. We must, in effect, understand that contemporary geopolitics is based on the crisis of its traditional concepts. When we say crisis we do not mean that geopolitics is on the verge of collapse, but rather that it functions on the basis of borders, identities, and limits that are unstable and constantly undermined. Geopolitics cannot function without such boundaries, but it must also continually displace and overrun them, creating the dialectic between expansionism and isolationism. This is a *geopolitics of crisis*.

Contemporary geopolitics thus demonstrates the same logical schema that defines the contemporary theory of sovereignty and the reality of economic activity: it has two sides that are constantly in contradiction and conflict. This internal crisis, as we said, is not the sign of collapse, but the motor of development. Geopolitical analysis assumes crisis as its foundation and opens the system to the conflict between different political forces that determine the open spaces, the borders, and the closed spaces. Our hypothesis, which is undoubtedly reductive but nonetheless effective, is that these internal conflicts or contradictions within the concept of geopolitics should be recognized as the conflict between the multitude (that is, the forces of social production) and imperial sovereignty (that is, the global order of power and exploitation), between biopolitics and biopower. This hypothesis leads us to view the changing paradigms of geopolitics as *responses* to the challenges posed by the struggles of the multitude. Elsewhere we have argued, for instance, that the transformation of the geopolitical framework in the late twentieth century, after the oil crises and monetary crises in the 1970s and the collapse of the Bretton Woods system, was a response to the anticolonial and antiimperialist struggles in Asia, Africa, and Latin America as well as the massive social struggles in Europe and North America.[111] Today, it seems to us, the crisis of geopolitics is best understood in terms of the struggles against the present global order that we sketched in the previous chapter, from movements against neoliberalism in India, Brazil, Seattle, and Genoa to the movement against the Iraq War. The elements of this crisis can determine the future developments of geopolitics. And we have to see what strategic use the multitude can make of the crisis of geopolitics.

UNILATERAL COMMAND AND THE AXIS OF EVIL

How we can return to the strategies of geopolitics in the twenty-first century and the alternative between unilateralism and multilateralism. The first task of a unilateralist geopolitical strategy today, represented most often by the United States, is furthering the crisis of the institutions of the old international order. In order to govern global politics effectively, for instance, a unilateralist strategy must undermine the political and legal capacities of the United Nations. When the United Nations was formed at the end of the Second World War it brought together the enlightened aspiration for cosmopolitan government with a democratic arrangement among the nation-states that had won the war against fascism. After half century of life, this alliance had clearly been exhausted. After being constrained by the cold war and neutralized by its inability to break the bureaucratic mechanisms within it, the United Nations has now fallen under the rule of the sole remaining superpower. The United Nations, in other words, has become the site in which the global hegemony and unilateral control of the United States can be most clearly expressed. It is also, paradoxically, the site where at least the image of a more distributed form of power, more adequate to the processes of globalization, is still expressed.

With the end of the cold war, then, the form of imperial sovereignty began to redefine the boundaries of the former enemy and organize a single network of control over the world. The politics of containment in the Middle East, which was oriented toward blocking the advance of the social threat, was transformed into operations of "roll back" and military penetration into the former Soviet sphere. What has resulted is a great half moon of imperial command that stretches from the Middle East, to East Asia, from the Arabian Peninsula to the Korean Peninsula, crossing the ex-Soviet territories in central Asia and dipping down to strategic bases in the Philippines and Australia. This half moon configures the new, global geopolitical horizon. Global sovereignty has adopted an imperial figure under the control of the United States and its enormous centralized military apparatus that extends across the world.

This operation, however, is neither fully realized nor free from internal contradictions. There are large zones that are not (and perhaps never can be) directly included in this unilateralist imperial regime. They resist with strong state formations and in some cases global aspirations of their own. The unilateralist strategy is to weaken these resisting powers, close them in a regional axis, and eventually integrate them into the global hierarchy. There are three great strategic competitors, in fact, that cannot be ignored by any unilateralist strategy: Europe, Russia, and China. The United States, from this perspective, must keep pressure on them. Perhaps in this regard we should read the U.S. proclamation of an "axis of evil" not only as a direct warning to the three relatively weak enemy dictatorships, but also, and more important, as an indirect threat to the much more powerful friends that stand near them. Perhaps we can read the Iraq War as an indirect attack against Europe—not only in the political way it was conducted but also in the threat to European industry posed by U.S. control of Iraqi energy resources. Perhaps similarly we should read in the United States warnings to Iran an indirect threat to the southern sphere of Russian control. And, finally, it is not difficult to imagine how the warnings to North Korea can indirectly threaten and weaken Chinese control, providing a strong rationale for a large U.S. military presence in East Asia. This is not to say that the "rogue states" do not pose real threats to those within and outside their countries, but rather that designating these particular states can serve the additional (and perhaps more important) function of challenging and weakening the primary strategic competitors that threaten U.S. unilateral control. This strategic objective could thus fill out the complete arsenal of imperial geopolitics, including the use of preemptive war, the processes of hierarchical organization of nation-states, and the segmentation and eventual isolation of regions or continents in the global system.

CONTRADICTIONS

The unilateralist strategy of imperial power involves a fundamental geopolitical rearrangement organized around three primary elements. The first element is the grouping of world powers into regional formations and the maintenance of hierarchy among them. Unilateralist geopolitical strategy can thus be imagined in the shape of a wheel with the United States as hub with spokes extending to each region of the globe. Each region is defined from this perspective as the group of local powers plus the United States as the dominant element. The North Atlantic region is defined as the Western European states plus the United States; the Latin American region as the Latin American powers plus the United States; the Pacific region as the East Asian states plus the United States; and so forth.

We should take into account, however, the unpredictability of these relations of force in international politics and recognize that regional formations can also act in contradiction with the hierarchical unity of imperial command. The regional model of imperial order is occasionally disrupted by the self-assertion of the various regional powers. Thus the back and forth movements of the European Union, sometimes favorable to the Atlantic alliance with the United States, at others open to the possibility of a continental unification with Russia, and at still others intent on achieving the autonomy of Europe's political will. The ex-Soviet countries similarly vacillate between loyalty to U.S. projects, proposals of greater European alliances, and resurrections of old geopolitical lines (between Russia and India, for example). We could read the creative Chinese experiments in a "democracy of the middle classes" as an assertion of regional autonomy aimed at an Asian-centered globalization. Such regional developments and vacillations are also equally present in other parts of the world, for example, in the emerging Latin American projects of regional autonomy centered on Brazil and Argentina. Could one even imagine a project of regional autonomy in the Middle East? In all of these cases, regional formations play a contradictory, double-edged role in unilateralist imperial geopolitics, both as necessary parts of the unified order and as potentially autonomous forces that can break that order.

The second element of the unilateralist strategy involves economic production and the crisis that the multinational "aristocracies" of imperial order have suffered and continue to suffer. In this case, it is not a matter of contradictions among states but rather of fault lines that have emerged in the conflicts of interest among different factions of the global capitalist class, which rose to the surface especially clearly during the Iraq War. (Consider, for example, the vocal opposition to the war by business leaders such as George Soros.) The global state of war and conflict created by the unilateralist military policies has had strongly detrimental effects on the global circuits of production and trade. One might say, in summary fashion, that the unilateralist armed globalization pursued by the United States has raised new boundaries and obstacles, blocking the kinds of global economic networks that had been created in the previous decades. The most important crisis of the current global economic regime from the perspective of the aristocracies is indicated by the fact that it engages such a small fraction of the productive potential in today's world. Large and growing portions of the global population live in poverty, deprived of education and opportunities. Numerous countries are plagued by national debts that drain vital resources. It is increasingly clear, in fact, that the majority of the world is excluded from the primary circuits of economic production and consumption. From this perspective, then, the aristocratic crisis does not concern only the multinational industrialists but affects all the productive subjects of the global economic order. The symptoms of these fault lines go from the simple expressions of disdain for the unilateralist use of U.S. power and the lack of faith in its justice to attempts to establish rival regional formations. In the period from the attacks of September 11, 2001, to the Iraq War in 2003, the dissolution of previously solid ties of loyalty and common political and economic interest among the world aristocracies has been dramatic. One manifestation of the aristocratic crisis that has a strong effect on geopolitics is the competition among currencies. The passage of the euro from a weak to a strong position, for example, and the first threat that the euro poses to the dollar as the reserve currency of international business represents a minefield and a problem that must be resolved before long within the imperial order.

The third element of unilateralist strategy has to do with the maintenance of order itself, the form of global governance, and the search for security. The United States's unilateralist version of Empire has been imposed by military might, but the U.S. military campaigns in Afghanistan and Iraq are proving incapable of meeting the minimum objectives of security and stability. On the contrary, they are creating increasing conflict and strife. Furthermore, military dominance is not sufficient to guarantee global security. Economic and cultural relations are equally important, as are social conditions of inequality and the extreme conditions of poverty that are too frequently present in large parts of the world. The United States will not succeed in imposing its unilateral command if it cannot establish an agreement with the other major financial powers in the world. Global security will never be possible if the economic development of the poorest countries cannot be assured. And it is obviously not merely an economic question, but also a matter of social, cultural, and political equilibria and conflicts. In effect, the ends of globalization and the forms of geopolitical strategy are still deeply in question.

A NEW MAGNA CARTA?

It is becoming increasingly clear that a unilateral, or "monarchical," arrangement of the global order, centered on the military, political, and economic dictation of the United States, is unsustainable. The United States cannot continue to "go it alone." The crisis of this arrangement presents the opportunity for the "global aristocracies," that is, the multinational corporations, the supranational institutions, the other dominant nation-states, and powerful nonstate actors.

This is the moment of the Magna Carta. Remember from English history that in the early thirteenth century King John could no longer pay for his foreign military adventures and could no longer maintain social peace. When he appealed to the aristocracy for funds and support, they demanded in return that the monarch submit to the rule of law and provide constitutional guarantees, and thus they drafted the Magna Carta. The monarch, in other words, agreed to abandon a strictly unilateralist position and collaborate actively with the aristocracy. Our global "monarch" is faced with a comparable crisis today, unable to pay for its wars, maintain peaceful order, and moreover provide the adequate means for economic production. Today's "aristocracies" are thus in the position, in return for their support, to demand a new social, political, and economic arrangement that goes well beyond contemporary notions of multilateralism—a new global order.

What would be the content of a Magna Carta today? What do the global aristocracies want? Peace and security are obviously important objectives. Putting an end to the unilateralist military adventures and the seemingly interminable state of global war is a fundamental condition. It is also important to the aristocracies to renew global productive forces and bring the entire global population into the circuits of production and exchange. Priorities such as eliminating poverty and absolving the debts of the poorest countries would not in this context be acts of charity but efforts aimed at realizing the productive potential that exists in the world. Another priority would be reversing the processes of privatization and creating common access to necessary productive resources, such as land, seeds, information, and knowledges. Making resources common is necessary for the expansion and renewal of creative and production potentials, from agriculture to Internet technologies.

We can already recognize some movements that can guide the aristocracies on a path to create such a new Magna Carta. At the Cancun meetings of the WTO the demands of the "group of 22" for more equitable agricultural trade policies, for example, is one step toward reforming the global system in this direction. More generally, the international alliances tentatively articulated by Lula's government in Brazil within Latin America and more broadly indicate possible bases for global reconstruction. Taking the lead from the governments of the global south in this manner is one way for the aristocracies to orient their project of the renewal of productive forces and energies in the global economic system.

A second source of orientation for the aristocracies is provided by the multitude of voices that protest against the current state of war and the present form of globalization. As we have detailed at length, these protesters in the streets, in social forums, and in NGOs not only present grievances against the failures of the present system but also provide numerous reform proposals, ranging from institutional arrangements to economic policies. It is clear that these movements will always remain antagonistic to the imperial aristocracies and, in our view, rightly so. It is in the aristocracies' interest, however, to consider the movements as potential allies and resources for formulating today's global policies. Some version of the reforms the movements demand and some means to incorporate the global multitudes as active forces is undeniably indispensable for the production of wealth and security. Along with the most progressive governments of the global south, the globalization protest movements are the most promising existing forces that can orient a project of renewal, creating an alternative to the failed unilateralist regimes and posing the bases for a new Magna Carta.

The global aristocracies, we should be clear, do not in any way *represent* the multitude. The project of the aristocracies, even with a new Magna Carta, is aimed not at democracy but at a different form of imperial control. The multitude is and will remain necessarily antagonistic to these aristocracies. That said, we should still recognize that the crisis of the aristocracies in the face of U.S. unilateralism does provide strategic opportunities on the global horizons for democratic propositions. There are possible alliances, for instance, between industrial aristocracies and the productive multitudes at the weakest and poorest levels of development, on the points of disequilibrium between the productive order and the potentials of existing labor power, and with regard to putting an end to the global state of war.

Here we can begin to see the possibility of alternative strategies of global constitution. Is it possible to propose through alliances with the aristocracies a program of a counter-Empire? Does it make sense to propose on the field of geopolitics tactics and strategies that could be intelligently directed by the multitude toward this end? Many symptoms are beginning to point in that direction. When the movements to flee from poverty are accompanied by rebellion, when migrations open spaces of miscegenation and new anthropological and cultural forms, when the wars of liberation are linked to processes of diplomacy from below, and when the global aristocracies interpret the multilateral elements of world disorder and are constrained to reconsider the subordination of the multitudes and eventually establish alliances with them, then there are new possibilities for subversion of the global order. In short, it seems to us that the powerful contradictions that traverse the geopolitical order of Empire, including the contradictions between the global aristocracies and unilateralist strategies, provide possibilities for the multitude to propose alternative constituent processes that no longer have the face of capitalist command but follow the rhythms of emancipation.

To conclude, let us return to our initial question. Does it still make sense to talk about geopolitics? Geopolitics was traditionally, as we said, a theory of borders. Really it was a paradoxical theory because it pretended to be global, but at every turn of the reasoning and on every limit of perspective it referred to a "center" and an "outside." Today imperial geopolitics has no center and no outside; it is a theory of internal relations in the global system. The public law of Empire takes the place of geopolitics just as the art of war takes the place of the police. Really we have passed from national government to imperial governance, from the hierarchy of fixed national powers to the mobile and multilevel relations of global organizations and networks. Certainly some want to impose unilateral command over it.

The deployments of marines and military bases scattered around the global are not insignificant. And yet this picture, like an Escher drawing, is completely unstable and with a shift of perspective can quickly be inverted. The strength of unilateral deployments is suddenly revealed as weakness; the center it raises up is revealed as a point of maximum vulnerability to all forms of attack. In order to maintain itself Empire must create a network form of power that does not isolate a center of control and excludes no outside lands or productive forces. As Empire forms, in other words, geopolitics ceases to function. Soon unilateralist and multilateralist strategies will both prove equally ineffective. The multitude will have to rise to the challenge and develop a new framework for the democratic constitution of the world.

ICONOCLASTS

When the center of the Roman Empire moved east from Rome to Byzantium more than fifteen hundred years ago, the structure of its government was also profoundly transformed.[112] *The earlier, Latin version had a government distributed among three ruling bodies: the emperor ruled together with the aristocracy balanced by the* comitia, *the popular councils. The later, Byzantine version, in contrast, consolidated power under one rule, raising up the Basileus, the Holy Roman Emperor, above aristocratic and popular control. The Byzantine emperor was a new Moses who handed down tablets of laws directly from God; he was a new Elijah who rose up to the heavens and thus was the sole mediator between the human and the divine, Christlike in his redemptive mission of government. In the Byzantine Empire power was thus sanctified and its legitimation directly divine. The emperor and the high priest,* imperium *and* sacerdotium, *tended to merge into a single figure.*

One of the weapons used in Byzantium to defend this central-

ized power against both the distributed Latin model of government and any democratic spirit or popular resistance was the ban on holy images, or iconoclasm. In the year AD 726 Leo the Isaurian, the Byzantine emperor, issued an edict forbidding his faithful subjects from worshiping icons or divine images, which they considered to be means of salvation. All icons had to be smashed. The religious justification was that worshiping images is sacrilegious, detracting from the true worship of God, an argument that explicitly recalls the Bible story of the golden calf adored by the Jews but then destroyed by Moses. "Thou shalt not make unto thee any graven image or any likeness of any thing that is in heaven above." (Exodus, 20:4). Iconoclasm was not only a religious project, but also a political one—or, rather, the religious and political projects were one and the same. At stake was the power of representation itself.

If you walked into a Byzantine basilica before the eighth century, before the iconoclastic furor broke out, you would have seen an enormous mosaic in the apse with a soaring figure of Christ Pantocrat (ruler of all) surrounded by the twelve apostles and the signs of the apocalypse. You would have already been struck by your own insignificance in the face of such an imposing representation of the divine, but this towering figure of power was not enough for the iconoclasts. The imperial subject should not even be able to enjoy the image of the Pantocrat or possess icons; the opportunity to worship the image of God and thereby attain the hope of salvation was prohibited. Iconic representation did provide, even if only in the very smallest corners of the imagination, a way to participate in the sacred and imitate the divine. The aesthetic representation, in other words, served as the vehicle for some kind of political representation. The iconoclastic monarch had to put an end to even this small opportunity of power and salvation. God must be completely separate from the multitude such that the Basileus is the only link between them, the only means of salvation.

This conception of Byzantine power played an important role in the foundation of modernity in Europe—even if at times the European imagination did not correspond very well to the reality of Byzantine history. One might say that the Byzantine figure of power resurfaced in early modern Russia when the title of caesar (czar) was accompanied by the epithet of "terrible" (groznyj). This was not really an innovation because already in the Byzantine iconoclast struggles, sovereignty had begun to adorn itself with this "terrible" quality, pretending that sovereignty could sever the relationship between who rules and who obeys. This is the conception of absolute sovereignty that solicited the indignation of Montesquieu and Voltaire; this is the figure of power against which both Edward Gibbon and Adam Smith conceived their projects of liberation; and later Herder and Niebuhr dramatically confronted Byzantium with their Romantic and excessive passion for freedom. The liberatory tradition of European modernity, in short, was built in part in opposition to the arrogance of Byzantine power.

That conception of Byzantine power, however, has also somehow found its way to our times. Today's political theories of imperial sovereignty are brimming with Byzantine cruelty. The idea of a moral ruling power legitimated in the symbiosis of the sacerdotium *and the* imperium, *in contrast to all the secular and enlightened modern conceptions of Empire, is certainly alive in our world. Already in the twentieth century the politicians of Zhadnovism and McCarthyism repeated that the priesthood of ideological dogma and the ruling power cannot be separated, and we hear this again from today's theoreticians of "just war" and "preemptive war" against indefinite, unknown enemies, as well as in the rhetoric of "security" and "zero tolerance" against the metropolitan multitudes. And, more important, we have begun to hear political leaders once again propose a notion of sovereignty that pretends to sever the relationship between the rulers and the ruled, re-creating an absolute and autonomous notion of power. These are the new iconoclasts!*

But the situation is even more complex because today's icono-clasts have also paradoxically usurped the position of the iconophiles. The new sovereign power strives to sever the relation-ship between the rulers and the ruled precisely through the use of images, through the spectacle of the media, and through the con-trol of information. The element of hope and salvation that the Byzantine multitudes found in icons now seems to have been drained from all images.

Against these new Byzantine powers we must raise a cry some-thing like that of John of Damascus, whose On Divine Images *contributed more than any other text to the defeat of iconoclasm. The Byzantine iconoclastic controversy is often understood as a debate over the relationship between the copy and the original, bringing together Platonic philosophy with patristic theology.[113] John of Damascus focuses instead on the incarnation of God and the material connection humanity has with God made flesh, which because it is material can be represented. The debate is clearly conducted in theological terms, but at stake is really a po-litical struggle over the figure of power. I cannot accept, John writes, that the Basileus usurps the priesthood in a tyrannical way.[114] The priesthood, he insists—which is to say the power of social invention and the legitimation of values and free exis-tence—belongs to the multitude. No sovereignty can be allowed to take away the icons that open the imagination to the love for free-dom. And no sovereignty can be allowed to smash the vehicle of hope and salvation that belongs to the multitude. Otherwise, if the sovereign becomes a tyrant and its power unquestionable and absolute, then sovereignty itself must be attacked and destroyed.*

3.3 DEMOCRACY OF
THE MULTITUDE

I turn now to the third and completely absolute form of
government, which we call democracy.

—BARUCH SPINOZA

Herzen once accused his friend Bakunin of invariably in
all his revolutionary enterprises taking the second month
of pregnancy for the ninth. Herzen himself was rather inclined to deny even in the ninth that pregnancy existed.

—LEON TROTSKY

The movements that express grievances against the injustices of our current
global system and the practical reform proposals, which we enumerated in
the previous section, are powerful forces of democratic transformation, but
in addition to these we need to rethink the concept of democracy in light
of the new challenges and possibilities presented by our world. That conceptual rethinking is the primary task of our book. We do not pretend
to propose a concrete action program for the multitude but instead try to
work out the conceptual bases on which a new project for democracy
can stand.

SOVEREIGNTY AND DEMOCRACY

The entire tradition of political theory seems to agree on one basic principle: only "the one" can rule, whether that one be conceived as the monarch,
the state, the nation, the people, or the party. The three traditional forms
of government that form the basis of ancient and modern European political thought—monarchy, aristocracy, and democracy—reduce, from

this perspective, to one single form. Aristocracy may be the rule of the few, but only insofar as these few are united in one single body or voice. Democracy, similarly, can be conceived as the rule of the many or all, but only insofar as they are unified as "the people" or some such single subject. It should be clear, however, that this mandate of political thought that only the one can rule undermines and negates the concept of democracy. Democracy, along with aristocracy in this respect, is merely a facade because power is de facto monarchical.

The concept of sovereignty dominates the tradition of political philosophy and serves as the foundation of all that is political precisely because it requires that one must always rule and decide. Only the one can be sovereign, the tradition tells us, and there can be no politics without sovereignty. This is espoused by theories of dictatorship and Jacobinism as well as by all the versions of liberalism as a kind of blackmail that one cannot avoid. The choice is absolute: either sovereignty or anarchy! Liberalism, we should emphasize, for all its insistence on plurality and the division of powers, always concedes in the final instance to the necessities of sovereignty. Someone must rule, someone must decide. It is constantly presented to us as a truism, reinforced even in popular sayings. Too many cooks spoil the broth. To rule, to decide, to take responsibility and control, there must be one, otherwise disaster.

In European thought, this insistence on the one is often characterized as the continuing legacy of Plato. The one is the immutable ontological foundation, both origin and telos, substance and command. This false alternative between the rule of one and chaos is indeed repeated in various permutations throughout European political and legal philosophy. In the silver age of European philosophy at the turn of the twentieth century, for instance, legal philosophers used this alternative as the basis of a notion of "natural law" that they conceived as a "pure theory of law." Rudolf Stammler, to take a representative example, poses the legal order as the material representation of that ideal, formal unity.[115] This insistence on the rule of one, however, is certainly not limited to the European tradition. The history of Chinese philosophy too, for example, is dominated by notions of immutable unity and a dictating center.

The necessity of the sovereign is the fundamental truth expressed in the traditional analogy between the social body and the human body. The illustration on the original frontispiece of Thomas Hobbes's *Leviathan* designed by Hobbes himself captures this truth wonderfully.[116] Viewed from a distance the illustration shows the body of the king towering over the earth, but closer one can see that below the king's head the body is composed of hundreds of tiny bodies of the citizens, making up his arms and torso. The body of the sovereign is literally the social body as a whole. The analogy serves not only to emphasize organic unity but also to reinforce and naturalize the division of social functions. There is only one head, and the various limbs and organs must obey its decisions and commands. Physiology and psychology thus add force to the obvious truth of the theory of sovereignty. There is in each body a single subjectivity and rational mind that must rule over the passions of the body.

We insisted earlier that the multitude is not a social body for precisely this reason: that the multitude cannot be reduced to a unity and does not submit to the rule of one. The multitude cannot be sovereign. For this same reason, the democracy that Spinoza calls absolute cannot be considered a form of government in the traditional sense because it does not reduce the plurality of everyone to the unitary figure of sovereignty. From the strictly practical, functional point of view, the tradition tells us, multiplicities cannot make decisions for society and are thus not relevant for politics proper.

Carl Schmitt is the modern philosopher who posed most clearly the centrality of sovereignty to politics, renewing the early modern European theories of absolute sovereignty articulated by authors such as Hobbes and Jean Bodin. It is particularly interesting, in fact, how Schmitt manages to bring together the various medieval and feudal theories of sovereignty of the ancien régime with the modern theories of dictatorship: from old notions of the divine charisma of the monarch to Jacobin theories of the autonomy of the political, and from theories of bureaucratic dictatorship to those of populist and fundamentalist tyrannies. Schmitt insists that in all cases the sovereign stands above society, transcendent, and thus politics is always founded on theology: power is sacred. The sovereign is defined, in other words, positively as the one above whom there is no power and who is thus free to decide and, negatively, as the one potentially excepted from every social norm and rule. Schmitt's theological-political notion of the "total state," which poses the sovereign above every other form of power as the only possible source of legitimation, develops the modern conception of sovereignty toward a form coherent with fascist ideology. Schmitt did argue bitterly in Weimar Germany against the forces of liberal, parliamentary pluralism, which he thought either naively negate the rule of the sovereign and thus inevitably lead toward anarchy or dishonestly mask the sovereign behind the play of plural powers, undermining its capacities. We should emphasize once again, however, that modern sovereignty does not require that a single individual—an emperor, a führer, or a caesar—stand alone above society and decide, but it does require that some unitary political subject—such as a party, a people, or a nation—fulfill that role.[117]

The theory of modern sovereignty in politics dovetails with capitalist theories and practices of economic management. There must be a single, unitary figure that can take responsibility and decide in the field of production not only for there to be economic order but also for there to be innovation. The capitalist is the one who brings the workers together in productive cooperation, in the factory, for instance. The capitalist is a modern Lycurgus, sovereign over the private domain of the factory, but pressed always to go beyond the steady state and innovate. Schumpeter is the economist who best describes the economic cycle of innovation and links it to the form of political command.[118] To sovereign exceptionalism corresponds economic innovation as the form of industrial government. A large number of workers are engaged in the material practices of production, but the capitalist is the one responsible for innovation. Just as only the one can decide in politics, we are told, only the one can innovate in economics.

The Two Sides of Sovereignty

The theory of sovereignty leads many to conceive the realm of the political as the terrain of the sovereign itself, focusing on the state, for instance, but this is too narrow a view of the political. Sovereignty is necessarily two sided. Sovereign power is not an autonomous substance and it is never absolute but rather consists of a relationship between rulers and ruled, between protection and obedience, between rights and obligations. Wherever tyrants have tried to make sovereignty into something unilateral, the ruled have always eventually revolted and restored the two-sided nature of the relationship. Those who obey are no less essential to the concept and the functioning of sovereignty than the one who commands. Sovereignty is thus, necessarily, a dual system of power.

The two-sided nature of sovereignty makes clear, as Machiavelli explained, the limited utility of violence and force in political rule. Military force can be useful for conquest and short-term control, but force alone cannot achieve stable rule and sovereignty. Military force is, in fact, because it is so one-sided, the weakest form of power; it is hard but brittle. Sovereignty also requires the consent of the ruled. In addition to force, the sovereign power must exert hegemony over its subjects, generating in them not only fear but also reverence, dedication, and obedience through a form of power that is soft and supple. The sovereign power must constantly be able to negotiate the relationship with the ruled.

Once we recognize sovereignty as a dynamic two-sided relationship we can begin to recognize the contradictions that continually appear within sovereignty. Consider, first of all, the modern military figure of sovereignty, that is, the power to decide over the life and death of subjects. The constant development of technologies of mass destruction throughout the modern era arriving finally at nuclear weapons has, as we saw earlier in part 1, made this prerogative of sovereignty approach something absolute. The sovereign in possession of nuclear weapons rules almost completely over death. Even this seemingly absolute power, however, is radically thrown into question by practices that refuse the control over life, such as, for example, suicidal actions, from the protest of the Buddhist monk who sets himself on fire to the terrorist suicide bomber. When life itself is negated in the struggle to challenge sovereignty, the power over life and death that the sovereign exercises becomes useless. The absolute weapons against bodies are neutralized by the voluntary and absolute negation of the body. Furthermore, the death of subjects in general undermines the power of the sovereign: without the subjects the sovereign rules not over a society but an empty wasteland. The exercise of this absolute sovereignty becomes contradictory with sovereignty itself.

The sovereign is similarly constrained to negotiate a relationship with the ruled and solicit its consent in the economic sphere. The early political economists, such as Adam Smith and David Ricardo, recognized this relationship at the heart of capitalist production. Labor, they said, is in capitalist society the source of all wealth. Capital needs labor just as much as labor needs capital. Marx recognized here a fundamental contradiction. Labor is antagonistic to capital and constantly represents a threat to production through its strikes, sabotage, and other forms of subterfuge, but capital cannot do without labor. It is forced to cohabit intimately with the enemy. Capital, in other words, must exploit the labor of workers but it cannot really oppress, repress, or exclude them. It cannot do without their productivity. The concept of exploitation itself might serve to summarize the contradiction at the heart of the capitalist relationship of rule: workers are subordinated under the command of the capitalist, and a portion of the wealth they produce is stolen from them. And yet they are not powerless victims. They are, in fact, extremely powerful, because they are the source of wealth. "The oppressed" may name a marginal and powerless mass, but "the exploited" is necessarily a central, productive, and powerful subject.

That sovereignty is two-sided means not only that it is a relationship but also that it is a constant struggle. This relationship is perpetually an obstacle for sovereign power that can block or limit, at least temporarily, the will of those in power. From the other side, this relationship is the point on which sovereignty can be challenged and overthrown. In politics as in economics, one weapon that is constantly at the disposal of the ruled, in other words, is the threat to refuse their position of servitude and subtract themselves from the relationship. This act of refusing the relationship with the sovereign is a kind of exodus, fleeing the forces of oppression, servitude, and persecution in search of freedom. It is an elemental act of liberation and a threat that every form of sovereignty constantly has to manage, contain, or displace. If sovereign power were an autonomous substance, then the refusal, subtraction, or exodus of the subordinated would only be an aid to the sovereign: they cannot cause problems who are not present. Since sovereign power is not autonomous, since sovereignty is a relationship, then such acts of refusal are indeed a real threat. Without the active participation of the subordinated, sovereignty crumbles.

In our era, however, in the age of global Empire, the struggle represented by the two-sided nature of sovereignty becomes even more dramatic and intense. One might say that the obstacle that has traditionally been posed to sovereignty by the need for consent, submission, and obedience becomes an ineluctable active adversary. An initial approach to the question can be posed in terms of what we call biopower, that is, the tendency for sovereignty to become power over life itself. One new aspect of the present global order is that, in step with the processes of globalization, it tends to blur the boundaries between political, economic, social, and cultural forms of power and production. On one hand, political power is no longer simply oriented toward legislating norms and preserving order in public affairs but must bring into play the production of social relationships in all aspects of life. We argued in part 1 that war has gone from an instrument of politics, used in the last resort, to the foundation of politics, the basis for discipline and control. This does not mean that all of politics has been reduced to a question of brute force, but rather that military power has to accommodate and address not only political questions but also the production of social life in its entirety. Sovereign power must not only rule over death but also produce social life. Economic production, on the other hand, is increasingly biopolitical, aimed not only at the production of goods, but ultimately at the production of information, communication, cooperation—in short, the production of social relationships and social order. Culture is thus directly both an element of political order and economic production. Together, in a sort of concert or convergence of the various forms of power, war, politics, economics, and culture in Empire become finally a mode of producing social life in its entirety and hence a form of biopower. Or, rather, in a different idiom, we might say that in Empire capital and sovereignty tend to overlap completely.

Once we recognize this convergence in biopower, we can see that imperial sovereignty is completely dependent on the productive social agents over which it rules. In effect, the political relationship of sovereignty becomes increasingly similar to the economic relationship between capital and labor. Just as capital constantly relies on the productivity of labor and thus, although it is antagonistic, must assure its health and survival, so too imperial sovereignty depends not only on the consent but also on the social productivity of the ruled. The circuits of social producers are the lifeblood of Empire, and if they were to refuse the relationship of power, to subtract themselves from the relationship, it would simply collapse in a lifeless heap. The film trilogy *The Matrix* interprets this dependence of power. The Matrix survives not only by sucking the energy from millions of incubated humans but also by responding to the creative attacks of Neo, Morpheus, and the partisans of Zion. The Matrix needs us to survive.

A second and more complex approach to the novelty of imperial sovereignty involves the unlimited nature of Empire. Previous forms of sovereignty and production have all depended on a limited population that could be divided in numerous ways to allow the rulers to surmount the obstacles posed by the relationship of sovereignty. If any specific group refused to consent or submit to the sovereign power, in other words, it could be excluded from the primary circuits of social life or, at the limit, exterminated. It was necessary for the sovereign power to maintain the relationship with the general population but any specific group could be made unnecessary, disposable, cast aside. In Empire, by contrast, since it is an expansive, inclusive biopolitical system, the entire global population tends to become necessary to sovereign power not only as producers but also as consumers, or, as users or participants in the interactive circuits of the network. Empire creates and rules over a truly global society that becomes ever more autonomous while Empire relies on it ever more heavily. There are, of course, boundaries and thresholds that maintain the hierarchies that divide the global population, and the sovereign rulers can subordinate specific populations even in dramatic and cruel conditions of misery, but exclusion of any population from the processes of biopolitical production tends to become a self-defeating act for Empire. No group is "disposable" because global society functions together as a complex, integrated whole. Imperial sovereignty thus cannot avoid or displace its necessary relationship with this unlimited global multitude. Those over whom Empire rules can be *exploited*—in fact, their social productivity must be exploited—and for this very reason they cannot be *excluded*. Empire must constantly confront the relationship of rule and production with the global multitude as a whole and face the threat it poses.

In the era of imperial sovereignty and biopolitical production, the balance has tipped such that the ruled now tend to be the exclusive producers of social organization. This does not mean that sovereignty immediately crumbles and the rulers lose all their power. It does mean that the rulers become ever more parasitical and that sovereignty becomes increasingly unnecessary. Correspondingly, the ruled become increasingly autonomous, capable of forming society on their own. We spoke earlier of the newly hegemonic forms of "immaterial" labor that rely on communicative and collaborative networks that we share in common and that, in turn, also produce new networks of intellectual, affective, and social relationships. Such new forms of labor, we explained, present new possibilities for economic self-management, since the mechanisms of cooperation necessary for production are contained in the labor itself. Now we can see that this potential applies not only to economic self-management but also political and social self-organization. Indeed when the products of labor are not material goods but social relationships, networks of communication, and forms of life, then it becomes clear that economic production immediately implies a kind of political production, or the production of society itself. We are thus no longer bound by the old blackmail; the choice is not between sovereignty or anarchy. The power of the multitude to create social relationships in common stands between sovereignty and anarchy, and it thus presents a new possibility for politics.

INGENIUM MULTITUDINIS

Recognizing how the balance has tipped in the relationship of sovereignty and how the ruled increasingly tend to hold a position of priority over the rulers allows us to question the truisms that support the theory of sovereignty. Suddenly, with our new perspective, it appears that not only is it not necessary for the one to rule, but in fact that the one never rules! In contrast to the transcendental model that poses a unitary sovereign subject standing above society, biopolitical social organization begins to appear absolutely immanent, where all the elements interact on the same plane. In such an immanent model, in other words, instead of an external authority imposing order on society from above, the various elements present in society are able collaboratively to organize society themselves.

Consider, for example, the realms of physiology and psychology that stood as an analogy for the functioning and organization of the social body. For years neurobiologists have argued against the traditional Cartesian model of the mind autonomous from and capable of ruling over the body. Their research shows instead that mind and body are attributes of the same substance and that they interact equally and constantly in the production of reason, imagination, desire, emotions, feelings, and affects.[119] The brain itself, moreover, does not function according to a centralized model of intelligence with a unitary agent. Thought is better understood, the scientists tell us, as a chemical event or the coordination of billions of neurons in a coherent pattern. There is no one that makes a decision in the brain, but rather a swarm, a multitude that acts in concert. From the perspective of neurobiologists, the one never decides. It seems that some scientific developments are following a path parallel to our own thinking. Perhaps we were wrong earlier in chapter 2.3 to say that the multitude betrays the traditional analogy between the human body and the social body, that the multitude is not a body—but, if so, we were wrong for the right reason. If the analogy holds, in other words, it is because the human body is itself a multitude organized on the plane of immanence.

In economics too we can see numerous instances in which unitary control is not necessary for innovation and that, on the contrary, innovation requires common resources, open access, and free interaction. This is most clearly true in the sectors that have most recently emerged as central to the global economy, such as information, knowledge, and communication. Internet practitioners and cybernetic specialists insist that the openness of the electronic commons was the primary factor that allowed for the great

innovation of the early period of the information revolution and that today innovation is increasingly thwarted by private property and government controls that limit open access and free exchange. The same is true
in the various realms of knowledge production. We recognized earlier some
of the contradictions between collectively produced traditional knowledges, from agriculturists developing improved seeds to communities producing medical knowledges, and the private ownership of these knowledges
through patents. Scientific knowledges too are produced in wide collective
networks that are hampered by private ownership and unitary control.
The productive realm of communication, finally, makes it abundantly
clear that innovation always necessarily takes place in common. Such instances of innovation in networks might be thought of as an orchestra
with no conductor—an orchestra that through constant communication
determines its own beat and would be thrown off and silenced only by the
imposition of a conductor's central authority. We have to rid ourselves of
the notion that innovation relies on the genius of an individual. We produce and innovate together only in networks. If there is an act of genius,
it is the genius of the multitude.

Now we can recognize the full importance of our earlier argument that
the various forms of labor throughout the global economy are today becoming common. Agricultural labor, industrial labor, and immaterial labor, we argued, along with the productive social activity of the poor, are
taking increasingly common characteristics. This becoming common presents the possibility of not only the equality of the various forms of labor
but also their free exchange and communication. Producing in common
presents the possibility of the production of the common, which is itself a
condition of the creation of the multitude.

What needs to be understood, and this is indeed the central point, is
how the multitude can arrive at a decision. The model of brain functioning that neurobiologists describe gives us one way to understand this. The
brain does not decide through the dictation of some center of command.
Its decision is the common disposition or configuration of the entire neural network in communication with the body as a whole and its environment. A single decision is produced by a multitude in the brain and body.

The fact of economic innovation in networks gives perhaps a clearer model for the multitude's political decision-making. Just as the multitude produces in common, just as it produces the common, it can produce political decisions. In fact, to the extent that the distinction between economic production and political rule is breaking down, the common production of the multitude itself produces the political organization of society. What the multitude produces is not just goods or services; the multitude also and most importantly produces cooperation, communication, forms of life, and social relationships. The economic production of the multitude, in other words, is not only a *model* for political decision-making but also tends itself to *become* political decision-making.

Perhaps we can understand the decision making of the multitude as a form of expression. Indeed the multitude is organized something like a language. All of the elements of a language are defined by their differences one from the other, and yet they all function together. A language is a flexible web of meanings that combine according to accepted rules in an infinite number of possible ways. A specific expression, then, is not only the combination of linguistic elements but the production of real meanings: expression gives a name to an event. Just as expression emerges from language, then, a decision emerges from the multitude in such a way as to give meaning to the whole and name an event. For linguistic expression, however, there must be a separate subject that employs the language in expression. This is the limit of our analogy because unlike language the multitude is itself an active subject—something like a language that can express itself.

We might also understand the decision-making capacity of the multitude in analogy with the collaborative development of computer software and the innovations of the open-source movement. Traditional, proprietary software makes it impossible for users to see the source code that shows how a program works. Programmers had thought of their programs, as Eric Raymond puts it, as pristine cathedrals created by individual geniuses.[120] The open-source movement takes the opposite approach. When the source code is open so that anyone can see it, more of its bugs are fixed, and better programs are produced: the more eyes that see it and the more people allowed to contribute to it, the better a program it becomes. Raymond calls this, in contrast to the cathedral style, the bazaar method of software development, since a variety of different programmers with different approaches and agendas all contribute collaboratively. As we noted earlier with respect to "swarm intelligence," we are more intelligent together than any one of us is alone. The important point here is that open-source, collaborative programming does not lead to confusion and wasted energy. It actually works. One approach to understanding the democracy of the multitude, then, is as an open-source society, that is, a society whose source code is revealed so that we all can work collaboratively to solve its bugs and create new, better social programs.

The decision-making ability of the multitude, we should note, inverts the traditional relationship of obligation. For Thomas Hobbes, for example, and in different ways in the entire tradition of sovereign politics, the obligation to obey is the basis for all civil laws and must precede the laws.[121] There is never in the multitude, however, any obligation in principle to power. On the contrary, in the multitude the right to disobedience and the right to difference are fundamental. The constitution of the multitude is based on the constant legitimate possibility of disobedience. Obligation arises for the multitude only in the process of decision making, as the result of its active political will, and the obligation lasts as long as that political will continues.

The creation of the multitude, its innovation in networks, and its decision-making ability in common makes democracy possible for the first time today. Political sovereignty and the rule of the one, which has always undermined any real notion of democracy, tends to appear not only unnecessary but absolutely impossible. Sovereignty, although it was based on the myth of the one, has always been a relationship grounded in the consent and obedience of the ruled. As the balance of this relationship has tipped to the side of the ruled, and as they have gained the capacity to produce social relations autonomously and emerge as a multitude, the unitary sovereign becomes ever more superfluous. The autonomy of the multitude and its capacities for economic, political, and social self-organization take away any role for sovereignty. Not only is sovereignty no longer the exclusive terrain of the political, the multitude banishes sovereignty from politics. When the multitude is finally able to rule itself, democracy becomes possible.

MAY THE FORCE BE WITH YOU

The new possibilities for democracy are confronted by the obstacle of war. As we saw in part 1, our contemporary world is characterized by a generalized, permanent global civil war, by the constant threat of violence that effectively suspends democracy. Not only does the permanent state of war suspend democracy indefinitely; the existence of new pressures and possibilities of democracy are answered by the sovereign powers with war. War acts as a mechanism of containment. As the balance tips in the relationship of sovereignty, every nondemocratic power tends to need war and violence as its basis. The modern relationship between politics and war has thus been inverted. War is no longer an instrument at the disposal of political powers to be used in limited instances, but rather war itself tends to define the foundation of the political system. War tends to become a form of rule. This shift is reflected, as we argued in part 1, in the mechanisms of the legitimation of violence employed by the sovereign powers. Violence tends no longer to be legitimated on the basis of legal structures or even moral principles. Rather the legitimation of violence tends only to come after the fact, based on the effect of the violence, its capacities to create and maintain order. From this perspective too we can see that the modern order of priority has been reversed: violence comes first as basis and political or moral negotiation follows on its results. The emergence of the possibilities of democracy has forced sovereignty to adopt ever purer forms of domination and violence.

The forces of democracy must counter this violence of sovereignty but not as its polar opposite in symmetrical fashion. It would be logical if one thinks purely in terms of opposites, in other words, to pose democracy, in opposition to the permanent war of sovereignty, as an absolutely peaceful force, but such conceptual oppositions seldom correspond to our real condition. The emerging forces of democracy today find themselves in a context of violence that they cannot simply ignore or wish away. Democracy today takes the form of a subtraction, a flight, an exodus from sovereignty, but, as we know well from the Bible story, the pharaoh does not let the Jews flee in peace. The ten plagues have to rain down on Egypt before he lets them leave; Aaron has to fight a rearguard battle against the pharaoh's pursuing army; and finally Moses has to part the Red Sea and crash it back on the pharaoh's forces before the exodus is successful. This ancient example shows that there is no dialectal rule (of the kind so widespread in theories of pacifism) by which the behavior of the multitude in exodus must respond to the attack of sovereign power with its symmetrical opposite, meeting the repressive violence with the absolute lack of violence. Exodus has never been and will never be irenic, that is, absolutely pacific and conciliatory. Moses and Aaron were not, and much less were the plagues brought against Egypt. Every exodus requires an active resistance, a rearguard war against the pursuing powers of sovereignty. "Flee," as Gilles Deleuze says, "but while fleeing grab a weapon."[122]

The exodus and emergence of democracy is thus a war against war. Here, however, we seem to fall into conceptual confusion. If democracy cannot adopt the opposite strategy from sovereignty and pose pure pacifism against its permanent war, then must it necessarily be no different? Is its war against war a simple nonsense? Such confusions arise when we can think only in opposites. A *democratic* use of force and violence is neither the same as nor the opposite of the war of sovereignty; it is different.[123]

In the first place, in contrast to the new arrangement of sovereignty in which war tends to take a primary role and form the basis of politics, democracy must use violence only as an instrument to pursue political goals. This subordination of the military to the political is indeed one of the principles of the Zapatistas in Chiapas. In many ways the Zapatistas have adopted the tradition of Latin American guerrilla armies with an ironic twist. They do call themselves an army and have commandantes, but they invert the traditional structure. Whereas the traditional Cuban model poses the military leader dressed in fatigues as the supreme political power, the Zapatistas insist that all military activity must remain subordinate, at the service of the political decisions of the community.[124] The subordination of violence to politics should also be brought within each of us. As André Malraux says, *"Que la victoire demeure à ceux qui auront fait la guerre sans l'aimer"*[125] ("I hope the victory goes to those who will have made war without loving it"). Subordinating violence to politics is not in itself sufficient for its use to be democratic, but it is necessary.

The second principle of the democratic use of violence, which is much more substantial but also much more complex, is that such violence is only used in defense. Once again this is captured well in the image of the fleeing Jews protecting themselves against the pharaoh's pursuing armies. The extreme modern example of the necessity of defensive violence is the revolt of the Warsaw ghetto against the occupying Nazi army. The Warsaw Jews, who had already been corralled into a walled ghetto and had seen their neighbors and families shipped off to work and death camps, finally in desperation organized a military attack. Faced with the choice between death in passive submission and death in combat, there is no doubt that it is just and necessary that they chose the latter. Their resistance could at least inspire the resistance of others. Such an extreme example, however, might give the impression that democratic, defensive violence is simply a futile gesture. We should also link the defensive use of violence to the long republican tradition of the right to resistance against tyranny. Shakespeare's Brutus expresses rhetorically the need for this republican use of violence: "Had you rather Caesar were living, and die all slaves, / Than that Caesar were dead, to live all free men?"[126] The disobedience to authority and even the use of violence against tyranny is in this sense a kind of resistance, or defensive use of violence. This republican right to resistance is the real meaning of the Second Amendment of the U.S. Constitution: "A well regulated Militia, being necessary to the security of a free State, the right of the people to keep and bear Arms, shall not be infringed." The issue of the right to bear arms has devolved in the United States into a debate about the right of individuals to own handguns, hunting rifles, and other dangerous weapons, but the legacy of English law and more generally the republican tradition from which the amendment derives conceptually rests instead on the right of the multitude, of the "people in arms," to resist against tyranny.[127] The Black Panthers certainly understood the spirit of this right when on May 2, 1967, they theatrically strolled into the California Capitol Building in Sacramento with rifles to proclaim their constitutional right to defense of the black community. They misunderstood completely and tragically that the adequate form of resistance changes historically and must be invented for each new situation—specifically, that a gun is no longer an adequate arm for defense. The Panthers' guns and military spectacles tended to distort their organization and get them and others killed. The republican right to bear arms today has nothing to do with individuals, or communities, or states owning guns. New weapons are clearly needed to defend the multitude.

An important corollary of this principle of defensive violence is that, from the perspective of democracy, violence cannot create anything but can only preserve what has already been created. Note that this is a very weak notion of violence. It has none of the capacities, for example, that Walter Benjamin attributes to either the mythical violence that is able to create the law or the divine violence that destroys the law.[128] Our defensive notion of violence is weaker than these concepts. Democratic violence can only defend society, not create it. This is equally true in revolutionary situations. Democratic violence does not initiate the revolutionary process but rather comes only at the end, when the political and social transformation has already taken place, to defend its accomplishments. In this sense, the democratic use of violence in a revolutionary context is not really different than an act of resistance.

We should note that this principle of defensive violence, although conceptually clear, is often very confused in practice. There are innumerable examples of violent aggressions and conquests that have been mystified as defensive measures. Occupying the Sudetenland in 1938, for example, the Nazis claimed to be acting in defense of the Sudeten Germans; just as the Soviet tanks rolled into Hungary in 1956, Czechoslovakia in 1968, and Afghanistan in 1979 with the claim of defending the local governments; just as the United States intervened in numerous "defense" actions in the twentieth century, such as the invasion of Granada to defend U.S. medical students. Even the Crusades claimed to be in defense of Eastern Chistendom. The most sophisticated and elegant version of this mystification is the theory of just war, which has been resurrected in recent years by scholars, journalists, and politicians.[129] We should be clear that the notion of just war does not refer to a defensive action. The defense of the Jews in exodus against the pharaoh's armies does not need any such justification. The notion of just war instead is used to justify an aggression on moral grounds. If such a just war is conceived as a defense, it is a defense of values that are being threatened, and this is how the contemporary theory of just war is in fact closely linked with the old, premodern conception that was so effective in Europe's long religious wars. A "just war" is really a military aggression thought to be justified on a moral foundation and thus has nothing to do with the defensive posture of democratic violence. The principle of the defensive use of violence can only make sense once we separate it from all these mystifications that dress the wolf in sheep's clothing.

The third principle of the democratic use of violence has to do with democratic organization itself. If according to the first principle the use of violence is always subordinated to political process and decision, and if that political process is democratic, organized in the horizontal, common formation of the multitude, then the use of violence too must be organized democratically. Wars waged by sovereign powers have always required the suspension of freedoms and democracy. The organized violence of its military requires strict, unquestioned authority. The democratic use of violence must be entirely different. There can be no separation between means and ends.

To these three principles any democratic use of violence must also add a critique of arms, that is, a reflection on what weapons today are effective and appropriate. All the old weapons and methods are still around, from passive resistance to sabotage, and they can still in certain contexts be effective, but they are not at all sufficient. Leon Trotsky learned his lesson in the Russian Revolution of 1917—"A revolution," he says, "teaches you the value of a rifle"[130]—but a rifle does not have the same value today as it did in 1917. One element that has changed is that the development of weapons of mass destruction, especially nuclear weapons, has tended to pose an all-or-nothing logic on the use of violence: either absolute destruction or tense and fearful inaction. A rifle is of little use against an atom bomb. Nuclear weapons have generally stood, after the dramatic demonstration of their destructive might in Hiroshima and Nagasaki, as a threat to create fear in the enemy. Precisely because nuclear bombs and other weapons of mass destruction pose such generalized consequences, they cannot be used in most cases, and the armies of sovereign powers have to resort to other weapons. A second element that has changed is that there is also an ever greater asymmetry of technology in weapons of limited (rather than mass) destruction. In the series of recent wars, particularly as they have been broadcast on television, the U.S. military has demonstrated the vast superiority of its guns and bombs aided by communication and intelligence networks. It makes no sense to enter on the same terrain of violence with such asymmetry.

What we really need are weapons that make no pretense to symmetry with the ruling military power but also break the tragic asymmetry of the many forms of contemporary violence that do not threaten the current order but merely replicate a strange new symmetry: the military official is infuriated at the dishonest tactics of the suicide bomber and the suicide bomber is indignant at the arrogance of the tyrant. The forces of imperial command lament the very idea of terror, claiming that the weak will react to the asymmetry of power by using new, easily transportable weapons against large innocent populations. And this will probably happen, but it will not make the world better or even change for the better the relationship of power. It will rather allow those in control to consolidate their power, claiming the need to unite under their power in the name of humanity and life itself. The fact is that a weapon adequate to the project of the multitude cannot bear either a symmetrical or an asymmetrical relation to the weapons of power. To do so is both counterproductive and suicidal.

This reflection on new weapons helps us clarify the concept of martyrdom, which in various religions traditions can be divided into two primary forms. The one form, which is exemplified by the suicide bomber, poses martyrdom as a response of destruction, including self-destruction, to an act of injustice. The other form of martyrdom, however, is completely different. In this form the martyr does not seek destruction but is rather struck down by the violence of the powerful. Martyrdom in this form is really a kind of *testimony*—testimony not so much to the injustices of power but to the possibility of a new world, an alternative not only to that specific destructive power but to every such power. The entire republican tradition from the heroes of Plutarch to Martin Luther is based on this second form of martyrdom. This martyrdom is really an act of love; a constituent act aimed at the future and against the sovereignty of the present. Our analysis of this second martyrdom, the republican martyrdom that testifies to the possibility of a new world, should not be understood as a call or invitation to action. It would be ridiculous to *seek* such martyrdom. That martyrdom is rather, when it arrives, only a by-product of real political action and the reactions of sovereignty against it. We need to look elsewhere, clearly, for the logic of political activism.

We need to invent new weapons for democracy today. There are indeed numerous creative attempts to find new weapons.[131] Consider, for example, as an experiment with new weapons, the kiss-ins conducted by Queer Nation in which men would kiss men and women women in a public place to shock people who are homophobic, which was the case in the Queer Nation action held at a Mormon convention in Utah. The various forms of carnival and mimicry that are so common today at globalization protests might be considered another form of weaponry. Simply having millions of people in the streets for a demonstration is a kind of weapon, as is also, in a rather different way, the pressure of illegal migrations. All of these efforts are useful, but they are clearly not sufficient. We need to create weapons that are not merely destructive but are themselves forms of constituent power, weapons capable of constructing democracy and defeating the armies of Empire. These biopolitical weapons will probably be more similar to those proposed by Lysistrata to overcome the Athenian men's decision to go to war than those put in circulation by ideologues and politicians today. It is not unreasonable to hope that in a biopolitical future (after the defeat of biopower) war will no longer be possible, and the intensity of the cooperation and communication among singularities (workers and/or citizens) will destroy its possibility. A one-week global biopolitical strike would block any war. In any case, we can imagine the day when the multitude will invent a weapon that will not only allow it to defend itself but will also be constructive, expansive, and constituent. It is not a matter of taking power and commanding the armies but destroying their very possibility.

THE NEW SCIENCE OF DEMOCRACY: MADISON AND LENIN

At the beginning of chapter 3.3 we recognized how sovereignty requires a relationship between two parties, the rulers and the ruled, and this division within sovereignty poses the constant potential of crisis. This point of division is where the multitude appears as a subject and declares, "Another world is possible," fleeing from the relationship with the sovereign and applying itself to create that world. In exodus, the multitude deepens the crisis of the dual figure of sovereignty. In the next section we focus on the fact that when the sovereign power cannot hold this relationship together by peaceful, political means it resorts to violence and war as its basis. The democratic project of the multitude is thus necessarily exposed to both military violence and police repression: war follows the multitude in exodus, forcing it to defend itself, imposing on the project of absolute democracy the paradox of defining itself as resistance. In this section, then, we find ourselves at the end of this line of reasoning. Not only must the multitude configure its exodus as resistance, it must also transform that resistance into a form of constituent power, creating the social relations and institutions of a new society.

Throughout the course of this book we have studied the ontological, social, and political bases of the constituent power of the multitude. Now we have to pull them together into a coherent ensemble. From the *ontological standpoint*, we have dwelled at length on the biopolitical nature of the multitude and the intense, mutually defining relationship between the production of the multitude and the production of the common. Biopolitical production is a matter of ontology in that it constantly creates a new social being, a new human nature. The conditions of the production and reproduction of the social life of the multitude, from its most general and abstract aspects to the most concrete and subtle, are developed within the continuous encounters, communications, and concatenations of bodies. Paradoxically, the common appears at both ends of biopolitical production: it is both the final product and also the preliminary condition of production. The common is both natural and artificial; it is our first, second, third, and *n*th nature. There is no singularity, then, that is not itself established in the common; there is no communication that does not have a common connection that sustains and puts it into action; and there is no production that is not cooperation based on commonality. On this biopolitical fabric, multitudes intersect with other multitudes, and from the thousand points of intersection, from the thousand rhizomes that link these multitudinous productions, from the thousand reflections born in every singularity emerge inevitably the life of the multitude. The multitude is a diffuse set of singularities that produce a common life; it is a kind of social flesh that organizes itself into a new social body. This is what defines biopolitics. The common, which is at once an artificial result and constitutive basis, is what configures the mobile and flexible substance of the multitude. The constituent power of the multitude, from an ontological standpoint, is thus the expression of this complexity and the key that moves through the biopolitical common to express it ever more widely and effectively.

From the *sociological standpoint*, the constituent power of the multitude appears in the cooperative and communicative networks of social labor. The relationship of the common to the multitude, which appeared paradoxical from the ontological standpoint, in that the common is both precondition and result of the production of the multitude, now appears perfectly unproblematic in social terms, and specifically in terms of labor. As we argued earlier, there is today a progressive becoming common of the various forms of labor throughout the economy and throughout the world. We are witnessing a decline of the previously unbreachable divisions that separated agricultural from industrial workers, the working classes from the poor, and so forth. Instead, increasingly common conditions of labor in all sectors place new importance on knowledge, information, affective relations, cooperation, and communication. Although each form of labor remains singular—agricultural labor remains tied to the soil, just as industrial labor to the machine—they all nonetheless develop common bases, which today tend to be the condition for all economic production; and, in turn, that production itself produces the common—common relationships, common knowledge, and so forth. Production based on cooperation and communication makes perfectly clear how the common is both presupposition and result: there can be no cooperation without an existing commonality, and the result of cooperative production is the creation of a new commonality; similarly, communication cannot take place without a common basis, and the result of communication is a new common expression. The production of the multitude launches the common in an expanding, virtuous spiral. This increasing production of the common does not in any way negate the singularity of the subjectivities that constitute the multitude. Rather there is a reciprocal exchange between the singularities and the multitude as a whole, affecting them both, tending to form a kind of constituent motor. This common production of the multitude implies a form of constituent power insofar as the networks of cooperative production themselves designate an institutional logic of society. Here again we can recognize the importance of the fact that in the production of the multitude the distinction between the economic and the political tends to disappear and that the production of economic goods tends also to be the production of social relationships and ultimately of society itself. The future institutional structure of this new society is embedded in the affective, cooperative, and communicative relationships of social production. The networks of social production, in other words, provide an institutional logic capable of sustaining a new society. The social labor of the multitude thus leads directly to the proposition of the multitude as constituent power.

The fact that biopolitical production is at once economic and political, that it directly creates social relationships, and that it poses the bases for a constituent power help us understand that the democracy of the multitude we are dealing with here bears little resemblance to "direct democracy" traditionally understood, in which each of us would take time out of our lives and our work to vote continually on every political decision. Remember Oscar Wilde's ironic remark that the problem with socialism is that it would take too many evenings. Biopolitical production presents the possibility that we do the political work of creating and maintaining social relationships collaboratively in the same communicative, cooperative networks of social production, not at interminable evening meetings. Producing social relationships, after all, not only has economic value but is also the work of politics. In this sense, economic production and political production would coincide, and the collaborative networks of production would suggest a framework for a new institutional structure of society. This democracy in which all of us through our biopolitical production collaboratively create and maintain society is what we call "absolute."

So far, from the ontological and sociological perspectives, we have articulated the democracy of the multitude as a theoretical possibility—a possibility that is based in the real developments of our social world. The definition of the democracy of the multitude and its constituent power also requires a *political standpoint* that is able to put together in a determinate time and place the common power of the multitude and its decision-making capacity. This does not mean that what we have recognized thus far from the ontological and sociological standpoints is merely secondary or irrelevant. One of the gravest errors of political theorists is considering constituent power a pure political act separate from existing social being, mere irrational creativity, the obscure point of some violent expression of power. Carl Schmitt, along with all the fascist and reactionary thinkers of the nineteenth and twentieth centuries, always tried to exorcise constituent power this way, with a shiver of fear. Constituent power, however, is something completely different. It is a decision that emerges out of the ontological and social process of productive labor; it is an institutional form that develops a common content; it is a deployment of force that defends the historical progression of emancipation and liberation; it is, in short, an act of love.

People today seem unable to understand love as a political concept, but a concept of love is just what we need to grasp the constituent power of the multitude. The modern concept of love is almost exclusively limited to the bourgeois couple and the claustrophobic confines of the nuclear family. Love has become a strictly private affair. We need a more generous and more unrestrained conception of love. We need to recuperate the public and political conception of love common to premodern traditions. Christianity and Judaism, for example, both conceive love as a political act that constructs the multitude. Love means precisely that our expansive encounters and continuous collaborations bring us joy. There is really nothing necessarily metaphysical about the Christian and Judaic love of God: both God's love of humanity and humanity's love of God are expressed and incarnated in the common material political project of the multitude. We need to recover today this material and political sense of love, a love as strong as death. This does not mean you cannot love your spouse, your mother, and your child. It only means that your love does not end there, that love serves as the basis for our political projects in common and the construction of a new society. Without this love, we are nothing.

This political project of the multitude, however, must find a way to confront the conditions of our contemporary reality. Its project of love might seem out of place in a world like ours in which the global order bases and legitimates its power in war, degrading and suspending all democratic mechanisms. This crisis of democracy is not specific to Euro-America or any region of the globe; the crisis of representation and the corruption of the forms of democracy is a planetary condition, immediately evident in all the nation-states, insuperable in the regional communities of contiguous states, and violently expressed at the global, imperial level. The global crisis of democracy affects every form of government in the world. The interminable state of global war is a condition that contributes to the contemporary tendency toward the formation of a single, monarchical system of domination over the world. We are not convinced, in fact we are highly skeptical, that such monarchical, unilateralist control over Empire can be successfully established, but the tendency itself, even without being realized, destabilizes all previous forms of authority, throws every political order in crisis, and pushes farther away the hope of democracy. Political, economic, and social crises accumulate one on the other and link to each other in insolvable knots. They send ripples, waves, and monsoons of crisis and rupture across the oceans: across the North Atlantic from North America to Europe, across the South Atlantic from Latin America to Africa, across the Indian Ocean from the Arab world to South Asia, across the Pacific from East Asia to the Americas. It seems to many today that the global order of our recent past, the cold war, was paradoxically the last moment of relatively peaceful global cohabitation and the bipolar arrangement of explicit violence and reciprocal, mutually legitimating regimes was perhaps the limit of a situation that quickly became extremely destructive. Now, with the cold war over and the first experiments of global order completed, we cannot help but recognize the planet as a sick body and the global crisis of democracy as a symptom of corruption and disorder.

There is, however, another side to the real conditions that confront the political project of the multitude. Despite the constant threat of violence and war, despite the sickness of the planet and its political systems, never before has the restlessness for freedom and democracy been so widespread throughout the world. As we saw earlier, there are interminable lists of grievances against the current global order, not only against poverty and starvation and not only against political and economic inequalities and injustices, but also against the corruption of life in its entirety. We also saw that in addition to the grievances there are countless proposals to reform the global system to make it more democratic. All of this global ferment and all these expressions of fury and hope demonstrate a growing and indomitable desire for a democratic world. Every sign of the corruption of power and every crisis of democratic representation, on all levels of the global hierarchy, is confronted by a democratic will to power. This world of rage and love is the real foundation on which the constituent power of the multitude rests.

The democracy of the multitude needs a "new science," that is, a new theoretical paradigm to confront this new situation. The first and primary agenda of this new science is the destruction of sovereignty in favor of democracy. Sovereignty in all its forms inevitably poses power as the rule of the one and undermines the possibility of a full and absolute democracy. The project of democracy must today challenge all existing forms of sovereignty as a precondition for establishing democracy. In the past the destruction of sovereignty was the essential core of the communist and anarchist conception of the abolition of the state. Lenin in *State and Revolution* renewed theoretically the conception of the abolition of the state, just as the soviets aimed at reinventing it in practice during the revolutionary period. The state was considered the primary locus of sovereignty, standing above society, transcendent, blocking democratic expression. The multitude today needs to abolish sovereignty at a global level. This is what the slogan "Another world is possible" means to us: that sovereignty and authority must be destroyed. What Lenin and the soviets proposed as the objective of the insurrectional activity of an elite vanguard, however, must be expressed today through the desire of the entire multitude.[132] (Perhaps precisely because the Soviet experience was organized in a hierarchical, vanguard form, its project to abolish state sovereignty ended up in the creation of another sovereign state.) The conditions are emerging today that give the multitude the capacity of democratic decision-making and that thus make sovereignty unnecessary.

This process is anything but spontaneous and improvised. The destruction of sovereignty must be organized to go hand in hand with the constitution of new democratic institutional structures based on existing conditions. The writings of James Madison in the *Federalist Papers* provide a method for such a constitutional project, organized through the pessimism of the will—creating a system of checks and balances, rights and guarantees. Madison considered the constitutional republic to be a progressive path that had to be protected from corruption and dissolution by an internal mechanism, and the constitutional techniques of public law were instruments for the gradual building of political organization. The content of Madison's constitutionalism, which has since been called democratic but was really liberal, can be described, and often has been, as a mode of maintaining an equilibrium of social classes, whereby equilibrium of social classes one assumes the command of the stronger over the weaker. That said, we should not forget that Madison's thought is completely permeated by a republican utopianism, the same utopianism that we find today in the popular revolts and insurrectionism of the global poor. Madison's project was to discover an institutional form that could realize this utopian desire to the extent that the real conditions of his day would allow.

How can we organize today the objectives of *State and Revolution*— that is, the destruction of sovereignty through the power of the common—in coordination with the institutional methods of the *Federalist* that can realize and sustain a democratic project in our global world? How can we discover in the constituent power of the multitude the project of "Another world is possible"—a world beyond sovereignty, beyond authority, beyond every tyranny—that is endowed with an institutional method of guarantees and constitutional motors? We need to build the project on the institutional mechanisms we recognized earlier, suggested by the emerging forms of biopolitical production. The institutions of democracy today must coincide with the communicative and collaborative networks that constantly produce and reproduce social life. Today, would it be possible for a revolution, aware of the violence of biopower and the structural forms of authority, to use the constitutional instruments of the republican tradition to destroy sovereignty and establish a democracy from below of free men and women? By combining Madison and Lenin we are not simply throwing together incompatible traditions of political thought and practice in a sacrilegious way. We are trying rather to insure that our dream of democracy and desire for freedom does not fall back to yet another form of sovereignty and wake up in a nightmare of tyranny. Revolutionaries have long noted that up until now all revolutions have only perfected the form of the state, not destroyed it. The revolution of the multitude can no longer suffer the curse of the Thermidor. It must organize its project in step with the times, determined by constituent mechanisms and institutional procedures that guard against dramatic reversals and suicidal errors.

This new science of the multitude based on the common, we should be careful to point out, does not imply any unification of the multitude or any subordination of differences. The multitude is composed of radical differences, singularities, that can never be synthesized in an identity. The radicality of gender difference, for example, can be included in the biopolitical organization of social life, the life renovated by the multitude, only when every discipline of labor, affect, and power that makes gender difference into an index of hierarchy is destroyed. "The whole world will have to change," as Clarice Lispector says, "for me to fit into it."[133] Only then will gender difference become a creative, singular power and only then will the multitude become possible, on the basis of such differences. Such a radical transformation of the world to allow singularities to express themselves freely, is not a far-off utopian dream; it is grounded in the developments of our concrete social reality. The U.S. revolutionaries in the eighteenth century used to say, "The rising race is all republican." Similarly today we could say, "The rising race is all multitudinous." The new movements demanding global democracy not only value the singularity of each as a fundamental organizing principle but they also pose it as a process of self-transformation, hybridization, and miscegenation. The multiplicity of the multitude is not just a matter of being different but also of becoming different. Become different than you are! These singularities, act in common and thus form a new race, that is, a politically coordinated subjectivity that the multitude produces. The primary decision made by the multitude is really the decision to create a new race or, rather, a new humanity. When love is conceived politically, then, this creation of a new humanity is the ultimate act of love.

What we need to bring the multitude into being is a form of grand politics that has traditionally been called Realpolitik, or political realism. We need a politics, in other words, based on the transformative power of reality and grounded in our current historical epoch. Political realism is most often thought to be conservative or reactionary, based strictly on force, hegemony, and necessity. From Thucydides' Melian dialogue to Winston Churchill's memoirs, the histories of political realism have always celebrated force as the decisive element, but today this perspective is inadequate. The revolutionary need be no less realist than the reactionary: Saint-Just at Valmy, in fact, was no less realist than Metternich, Lenin no less than Kornilov, and Mao no less than Chang Kai Shek. What the revolutionary imposes, however, is not so much the pure coherence of force but rather the insistent mechanism of desire. The force that the revolutionary organizes and imposes does not appear at the beginning but only at the end of the process: revolutionary realism produces and reproduces the becoming and proliferation of desire. But this immersion in the revolutionary movement always involves, like all Realpolitik, the capacity to separate oneself from the immediate situation and tirelessly construct mediations, feigning (if necessary) coherence, and playing different tactical games in the continuity of strategy. As Tito Livy and Machiavelli teach us, there is never only one "political realism" but always at least two or, really, a single standpoint that splits into two conflicting recognitions: one organizing the desire of life and the other the fear of death, biopolitics against biopower.

If we are thus obliged to enter the horizon of political realism, are we forced to repeat the old Maoist slogan, "Great is the disorder under the skies; the situation is excellent"? No, our current situation is propitious not because of the global crisis of democracy, the permanent state of exception, and the interminable global war, but rather because the constituent power of the multitude has matured to such an extent that it is becoming able, through its networks of communication and cooperation, through its production of the common, to sustain an alternative democratic society on its own. Here is where the question of time becomes essential. When does the moment of rupture come? Earlier we spoke of political decision-making in terms of networks of biopolitical determinations and an apparatus of cooperation of the singular wills, but here we have to recognize decision also as an event—not the linear accumulation of Chronos and the monotonous ticking of its clocks but the sudden expression of Kairòs. Kairòs is the moment when the arrow is shot by the bowstring, the moment when a decision of action is made. Revolutionary politics must grasp, in the movement of the multitudes and through the accumulation of common and cooperative decisions, the moment of rupture or *clinamen* that can create a new world. In the face of the destructive state of exception of biopower, then, there is also a constituent state of exception of democratic biopolitics. Grand politics always seeks this moment, creating, as Machiavelli explains in *The Prince*, a new constitutive temporality. The bowstring shoots the arrow of a new temporality, inaugurating a new future.

Timing is crucial. Shakespeare's Brutus famously insists on the importance of timing in revolutionary practice: "There is a tide in the affairs of men / Which, taken at the flood, leads on to fortune, / Omitted, all the voyage of their life / Is bound in shallows and in miseries."[134] A philosophical book like this, however, is not the place for us to evaluate whether the time of revolutionary political decision is imminent. We have no crystal ball, and we do not pretend to read the seeds of time like Macbeth's hoary witches. There is no need for eschatology or utopianism here. A book like this is not the place either to answer the question "What is to be done?" That has to be decided concretely in collective political discussions.

We can recognize, however, that there is the unbridgeable gap that separates the desire for democracy, the production of the common, and the rebellious behaviors that express them from the global system of sovereignty. After this long season of violence and contradictions, global civil war, corruption of imperial biopower, and infinite toil of the biopolitical multitudes, the extraordinary accumulations of grievances and reform proposals must at some point be transformed by a strong event, a radical insurrectional demand. We can already recognize that today time is split between a present that is already dead and a future that is already living—and the yawning abyss between them is becoming enormous. In time, an event will thrust us like an arrow into that living future. This will be the real political act of love.

NOTES

PART 1: WAR

1. Every year impressive lists of current armed conflicts in the world are published. See, for example, Dan Smith, *The Penguin Atlas of War and Peace* (New York: Penguin, 2003); and the *Atlas* published annually by *Le monde diplomatique*.

2. Giorgio Agamben notes that the expression "world civil war" appeared in the same year, 1961, in both Hannah Arendt's *On Revolution* and Carl Schmitt's *Theorie des Partisanen*. Giorgio Agamben, *Stato di eccezione* (Turin: Bollati Boringhieri, 2003), 11. At that point, however, the civil war was probably "world" but not yet "global." Really, these authors were thinking of a civil war between the capitalist world and the socialist world, which first took the form of the Soviet Union against the Western European countries (including the fascist ones), then later against the United States. This continuous struggle against the socialist bloc on the part of fascist and liberal capitalist states was later described by revisionist historians such as Ernst Nolte and François Furet.

3. Thomas Hobbes, *Leviathan* (London: Penguin, 1968), 186.

4. Johann Jakob Christoffel von Grimmelshausen, *Simplicissimus*, trans. Mike Mitchell (U.K.: Dedalus Books, 1999).

5. Huamán Poma, *Letter to a King: A Peruvian Chief's Account of Life Under the Incas and Under Spanish Rule*, ed. Christopher Dilke (New York: Dutton, 1978). See also Mary Louise Pratt, *Imperial Eyes* (London: Routledge, 1992).

6. Carl von Clausewitz, *On War*, trans. Michael Howard and Peter Paret (Princeton: Princeton University Press, 1976). On Clausewitz, see Enrico Rusconi, *Clausewitz, il prussiano: La politica della guerra nell'equilibrio europeo* (Turin: Einaudi, 1999); and Emmanuel Terray, *Clausewitz* (Paris: Fayard, 1999).

7. The English translators of Clausewitz use the term *policy* instead of *politics* to try to capture this distinction. *Policy,* however, can refer to either domestic or interstate affairs just as *politics* does.

8. Carl Schmitt, *The Concept of the Political*, trans. George Schwab (New Brunswick, NJ: Rutgers University Press, 1976).

9. On the permanent state of exception, see Giorgio Agamben, *Stato di eccezione*; Qiao Liang and Wang Xiangsui, *Unlimited Warfare* (West Palm Beach: NewsMax, 2002); Alain Joxe, *The Empire of Chaos* (New York: Semiotexte, 2002); and Carlo Galli, *La guerra globale* (Bari: Laterza, 2002).

10. See Giorgio Agamben's brief history of the state of exception, *Stato di eccezione*, 21–32. See also Carl Schmitt, *Die Diktatur* (Munich: Duncker & Humblot, 1921); and François Saint-Bonnet, *L'état d'exception* (Paris: PUF, 2001). Clinton Rossiter provides a comparative analysis of the use of similar constitutional concepts in times of crisis in ancient Rome and twentieth-century Germany, France, Britain, and the United States in *Constitutional Dictatorship* (Princeton, NJ: Princeton University Press, 1948).

11. Madeleine Albright, *Today*, NBC, interview by Matt Lauer, February 19, 1998.

12. In the context of international law, see Harold Hongju Koh, "On American Exceptionalism," *Stanford Law Review* 55, no. 5 (May 2003): 1479–1527. In foreign policy, see Siobán McEvoy-Levy, *American Exceptionalism and US Foreign Policy* (New York: Palgrave, 2001). We should also note that "American exceptionalism" is often used to refer to at least two other distinctive characteristics of the United States: its racial mixture and its class structure.

13. See Gershom Scholem, "The Idea of the Golem" in *On the Kabbalah and Its Symbolism*, trans. Ralph Manheim (New York: Schocken, 1965), 158–204. Moshe Idel complements and extends Scholem's analysis in *Golem: Jewish Magical and Mystical Traditions on the Artificial Anthropoid* (Albany: SUNY Press, 1990).

14. H. Leivick, *The Golem* in *Three Great Jewish Plays*, trans. Joseph Landis (New York: Applause Books, 1986), 115–254. The German film *The Golem: How He Came into the World* (1920), directed by Paul Wegener, follows the same

version of the legend. Gustave Meyrink's novel *Golem*, although beautiful and mysterious in its own right, does not follow any of these legends or even relate closely to Jewish tradition. On popular and artistic appropriations of the Golem myth, see Emily Bilski, ed., *Golem! Danger, Deliverance and Art* (New York: The Jewish Museum, 1988).

15. See J. Kerrigan, *Revenge Tragedy: Aeschylus to Armageddon* (Oxford: Clarendon Press, 1996).

16. On the reversal of Clausewitz's maxim, see Michel Foucault, *"Il faut défendre la société"* (Paris: Gallimard-Seuil, 1997), especially 16 and 41; and Gilles Deleuze and Félix Guattari, *A Thousand Plateaus*, trans. Brian Massumi (Minneapolis: University of Minnesota Press, 1987), 421–29, 467.

17. Michel Foucault, *"Il faut défendre la société*, 16. See also Alessandro Pandolfi, "Foucault e la guerra," *Filosofia politica* 16, no. 3 (December 2002): 391–410.

18. For a concise definition of biopower and biopolitics, see Judith Revel, *Le vocabulaire de Foucault* (Paris: Ellipses, 2002), 13–15.

19. Carl Schmitt explicitly excludes the possibility that humanity can be united in war. "Humanity as such cannot wage war because it has no enemy, at least not on this planet" (*Concept of the Political*, 54). Jacques Derrida similarly questions the notion that "humanity" can serve as the subject of the war against terrorism. "My absolute compassion for the victims of September 11 does not stop me from saying it: I do not believe in the political innocence of anyone in this crime. And if my compassion for all innocent victims is without limit, that means it does not stop with those who were killed in the United States on September 11. This is my interpretation of what has recently been called, according to the White House's slogan, 'infinite justice' (*grenzlose Gerechtigkeit*): no one should be excused for the mistakes or errors of his or her own politics, even when the most terrible price is paid, beyond any possible proportion" (*Fichus*, Paris: Galilée, 2002, 52).

20. The classic reference that marks the turning point from the medieval celebration of the concept of just war to the modern refusal of the concept is Hugo Grotius, *De jure belli ac pacis* (On the Right of War and Peace), first published in 1625. For the recent reproposition of just war theory, at the passage from modernity to postmodernity, see Michael Walzer, *Just and Unjust Wars* (New York: Basic Books, 1992); and Jean Bethke Elshtain, *Just War Against Terror* (New York: Basic Books, 2003). In contrast to these just war theories we should remember Immanuel Kant's claim that there can be no "descriminatory definition" of war and thus no valid distinction between just and unjust wars. See Immanuel Kant, *Perpetual Peace* (New York: Macmillan, 1917). Kant's

recognition is taken up from a cynical perspective in Carl Schmitt, *Die Wendung zum diskriminierenden Kriegsbegriff* (Munich: Duncker & Humblot, 1938); from a realistic perspective in Julien Freund, *L'essence du politique* (Paris: Sirey, 1965); and from an idealist perspective in Danilo Zolo, *Invoking Humanity: War, Law, and Global Order* (New York: Continuum, 2002).

21. The primary reference for most of the arguments about the West versus Islam or other configurations of civilizational conflict is Samuel Huntington, *The Clash of Civilizations and the Remaking of World Order* (New York: Simon and Schuster, 1996).

22. See Kenneth Surin, *Theology and the Problem of Evil* (Oxford: Blackwell, 1986).

23. Noam Chomsky insists in several of his books that by the definition of terrorism used by the United States government, the United States itself is the greatest author of terrorism in the world today, pointing to the legitimate regimes it has overthrown and its record of violations of human rights and the rules of war. See, for example, *9-11* (New York: Seven Stories Press, 2001).

24. See Loïc Wacquant, "De l'Etat social à l'Etat penal," *Actes de la recherche en science sociales*, no. 124 (September 1998); and A. De Giorgi, *Il governo dell'eccedenza: Postfordismo e controllo della moltitudine* (Verona, Italy: Ombre Corte, 2002).

25. See *Empire*, 276–79.

26. Hans Kelsen, *General Theory of Law and State*, trans. Anders Wedberg (Cambridge, MA: Harvard University Press, 1945), 288.

27. This "exceptional" wartime suspension of democratic exchange did, however, in some cases become de facto the normal condition of rule. For example, the twentieth-century socialist states—the Soviet Union throughout its life span, revolutionary Cuba, and, perhaps to a lesser extent, China—were all defined by war societies because they constantly faced the explicit or implicit threat of foreign war. To a certain extent this was also true in the United States during the cold war.

28. The theorists of antinuclear pacifism in the 1950s and 1960s, primarily in Germany and the United States, were dealing with the highest levels of philosophical reflection, recognizing that nuclear war posed historicity as human essence and technology as the instrument of the destruction of history. It is no coincidence that in this same period Martin Heidegger's analysis of the danger of the destruction of being through technology takes up points that the authors of antinuclear pacifism had first articulated. By pointing this out, we are not trying to make Heidegger into an anti-nuclear activist but rather to raise the thought of antinuclear activists, such as Günther Anders, to the level of

high philosophy. See Claude Eatherly, *Burning Conscience: The Case of the Hiroshima Pilot, Claude Eatherly, Told in His Letters to Günther Anders* (New York: Monthly Review, 1961); and the two volumes of Günther Anders's collected essays, *Die Antiquiertheit des Menschens* (Munich: Verlag C. H. Beck, 1980). On Anders's work, see Pier Paolo Portinaro, *Il principio disperazione: Tre studi su G. Anders* (Turin: Bollati Boringhieri, 2003).

29. The fact that war has become confused with police action also has fundamental consequences for the politics of pacifism. For a long period now, at least since the end of the Vietnam War, traditional pacifism has been in a state of confusion, perhaps because the distinction between war and peace has become so obscure. Pacifism began to lose its political effectiveness, and all the great campaigns against nuclear armaments in Central Europe, the Mediterranean, North America, and East Asia experienced a kind of paralysis when it became clear that exercising a kind of "naked resistance" in pacifism lost its traction and could no longer create a counterpower. Ward Churchill provides an interesting critique of pacifism in *Pacifism as Pathology* (Winnipeg: Arbeiter Ring Publishing, 1999), but unfortunately he conceives political action as either pacifism or traditional armed struggle with no other alternative. In any case, we will return to the politics of pacifism and liberation movements at several points below.

30. George Orwell, *Nineteen Eighty-Four* (New York: Harcourt, Brace and Company, 1949), 269.

31. See Judith Butler, "Guantanamo Limbo," *The Nation*, April 1, 2002, 20–24; and the Amnesty International memoranda to the U.S. government on the rights of people in U.S. custody in Guantánamo Bay issued on April 15, 2002, and December 13, 2002.

32. See George W. Bush, "The National Security Strategy of the United States of America," September 2002, especially 15, available at www.whitehouse.gov/nsc/nss.pdf.

33. Richard Haass, for example, the U.S. State Department director of policy planning, explains, "Sovereignty entails obligations. One is not to massacre your own people. Another is not to support terrorism in any way. If a government fails to meet these obligations, then it forfeits some of the normal advantages of sovereignty" (Hugo Young, "A New Imperialism Cooked Up over a Texas Barbecue," *The Guardian*, April 2, 2002).

34. In his courses at the Collège de France, Michel Foucault defined this passage in the conception and practice of power and war: from government to governmentality in political science and from the rules of war to regulative war. See

Foucault, "Governmentality" in Graham Burchell, Colin Gordon, and Peter Miller, eds., *The Foucault Effect* (Chicago: University of Chicago Press, 1991), 87–104; and *Il faut défendre la société.*

35. On the concept of constituent power, see Michael Hardt and Antonio Negri, *Labor of Dionysus* (Minneapolis: University of Minnesota Press, 1994); and Antonio Negri, *Insurgencies* (Minneapolis: University of Minnesota Press, 1999).

36. For a realist view of the expansion of U.S. power and the maintenance of global order, see John Mearsheimer, *The Tragedy of Great Power Politics* (New York: Norton, 2001).

37. Giorgio Agamben explains clearly the link between the state of exception and the state's monopoly of violence in *Stato di eccezione*. Drawing on a series of legal theorists and historians of law, he demonstrates that the "state of exception" or "right of exception" defines power itself as a "monopoly of violence" because it occupies the "point of equilibrium between public law and political fact" on which the state rests. As will become clearer later, we cannot accept the generality of Agamben's claim. The state of exception or the right of exception defines the actions of only those who have power, not the actions of those who seek it, want it, or want to destroy or overturn it. "Constituent power" comes only from this second category and should not be confused with the actions of those who institutionally hold the power of exception, the power to suspend laws, and the power of dictatorship.

38. See Max Weber, *Politics as a Vocation* (Minneapolis: Fortress Press, 1965); and V. I. Lenin, *State and Revolution* (New York: International Publishers, 1988).

39. Richard Falk criticizes nonproliferation regimes because they block opportunities for nuclear disarmament (of the dominant nation-states) and diminish the legitimacy of the world order (in the eyes of the subordinate nation-states). See "Illegitimacy of the Non-Proliferation Regime" in *Predatory Globalization* (Cambridge: Polity, 1999), 83–91.

40. The delegitimation from the outside, on the basis of human rights, of the monopoly of violence of nation-states corresponds to other phenomena that delegitimate its power from the inside, such as the crisis of representation, the generalization of corruption, and the destablization of the legislative and judiciary powers of the government. This intersection among these different forces of delegitimation is a new fact, and it is one element that defines the transformation of nation-states in the era of globalization.

41. On the "Annan Doctrine," see Helen Stacy, "Relational Sovereignty," *Stanford Law Review*, 55, no. 5 (May 2003): 2029–59. The political philosophy of the

United Nations has slid increasingly toward a moral foundation of political violence. See Grenville Clark and Louis Sohn, *World Peace Through World Law* (Cambridge, MA: Harvard University Press, 1958).

42. Winston Churchill, "A Disarmament Fable," October 24, 1928, in *Complete Speeches 1897–1963*, ed. Robert Rhodes James (New York: Chelsea House Publishers, 1974), 5: 4520–21.

43. Richard Falk is one of the most authoritative advocates for international law as the basis for legitimate violence. On the Israeli-Palestinian conflict, see "Ending the Death Dance," *The Nation*, April 29, 2002; and on the U.S. military response to the September 11 attacks, see "Defining a Just War," *The Nation*, October 29, 2001.

44. See Ugo Mattei, "A Theory of Imperial Law: A Study of U.S. Hegemony and the Latin Resistance," *Indiana Journal of Global Legal Studies* 10, no. 1 (Winter 2003): 383–448.

45. See Mariano-Florentino Cuéllar, "The International Criminal Court and the Political Economy of Antitreaty Discourse," *Stanford Law Review* 55, no. 5 (May 2003): 1597–1632.

46. For the justification of preemptive wars, see George W. Bush, "The National Security Strategy of the United States of America," September 2002.

47. It should not be surprising, then, if we see in the future a coalescence under the name of security of a war against abstract enemies together with a violent campaign against the power and cooperation of the new forms of labor. See Christian Marazzi, *Capitale e linguaggio: Dalla New Economy all'economia di guerra* (Rome: Derive/Approdi, 2002).

48. See Mahmood Mamdani, *When Victims Become Killers: Colonialism, Nativism, and the Genocide in Rwanda* (Princeton, NJ: Princeton University Press, 2001).

49. Michel Crozier, Samuel Huntington, and Joji Watanuki, *The Crisis of Democracy* (New York: New York University Press, 1975).

50. See Samuel Huntington, "The Clash of Civilizations?" *Foreign Affairs* (Summer 1993) and the subsequent book version, *The Clash of Civilizations and the Remaking of World Order* (New York: Simon and Schuster, 1996).

51. Huntington's claim is "not just about the future," Wang Gungwu, a sympathetic reader, recognizes, "but may actually help shape it" (Wang Gungwu, "A Machiavelli for Our Times," *The National Interest* 46 (Winter 1996). We should note that in the original essay Huntington claims that his argument is not meant "to advocate the desirability of conflicts between civilizations. It is to set forth descriptive hypotheses as to what the future may be like." Huntington goes on in the remainder of the essay, however, to make a series of

strategic prescriptions about uniting with allied civilizations, dividing enemy civilizations, and so forth. See "The Clash of Civilizations?"

52. The White House states explicitly, "The war on terrorism is not a clash of civilizations" ("The National Security Strategy of the United States of America," September 2002, 34).

53. This periodization is drawn from Subcomandante Marcos, "The Fourth World War Has Begun," *Nepantla* 2, no. 3 (Fall 2001): 559–73. (Originally in *Le monde diplomatique*, August 1997.)

54. Two useful analyses that locate the fundamental transformation of the global economy in the early 1970s are Giovanni Arrighi, *The Long Twentieth Century* (London: Verso, 1994); and Robert Brenner, *The Boom and the Bubble* (London: Verso, 2002).

55. See, for example, Omer Bartov's analysis of "industrial killing," which he maintains was first developed in World War I and perfected in the Holocaust. By industrial killing he means not only that industrial technologies are used in warfare, but also that the ideologies of progress and improvement typical of industrial development are increasingly applied in the domain of mass killing. See Omer Bartov, *Murder in Our Midst: The Holocaust, Industrial Killing, and Representation* (Oxford: Oxford University Press, 1996).

56. Laurent Murawiec, "La république conservatrice de George Bush," *Le monde*, June 11, 2001.

57. For an innovative analysis that substantially renovates the old notions of the military-industrial complex, see James Der Derian, *Virtuous War: Mapping the Military-Industrial-Media-Entertainment Network* (Boulder, CO: Westview Press, 2001).

58. There is an enormous and highly repetitive literature on the notions of a revolution in military affairs and a defense transformation. For a brief overview, tailored to the needs of the U.S. adminstration post–September 11, see Donald Rumsfeld, "Transformating the Military," *Foreign Affairs* 81, no. 3 (May–June 2002): 20–32. For more extensive discussions, see Thierry Gongora and Harold von Rickhoff, eds., *Toward a Revolution in Military Affairs?* (Westport, CT: Greenwood, 2000); Laurent Murawiec, *La guerre au XXIeme siècle* (Paris: Odile Jacob, 2000); Douglas MacGregor, *Breaking the Phalanx: A New Design for Landpower in the 21st Century* (Westport: Praeger, 1997); George and Meredith Friedman, *The Future of War: Power, Technology, and American World Dominance in the 21st Century* (New York: Crown, 1996); and Harlan Ullman and James Wade Jr., *Rapid Dominance—A Force for All Seasons* (Lon-

don: Royal United Services Institute for Defense Studies, 1998). For a more critical perspective see Alain Joxe, *Empire of Disorder*, especially 118–26; and for the link between war and global police, see Alessandro Dal Lago, *Polizia globale: Guerra e conflitti dopo l'11 settembre* (Verona: Ombre Corte, 2003). An excellent source for online links to articles about the RMA debate can be found at http://www.comw.org/rma/index.html.

59. For one example of the technologist model of new warfare, see Andrew Bacevic and Eliot Cohen, eds., *War over Kosovo* (New York: Columbia University Press, 2001).

60. See Corey Robin, "Remembrance of Empires Past: 9/11 and the End of the Cold War," in Ellen Schrecker, ed., *Cold War Triumphalism* (New York: The New Press, forthcoming).

61. See Erich Maria Remarque, *All Quiet on the Western Front*, trans. A. W. Wheen (Boston: Little, Brown, 1929); Ernst Jünger, *Storm of Steel*, trans. Basil Creighton (Garden City, NY: Doubleday, 1929); and Louis-Ferdinand Céline, *Journey to the End of the Night*, trans. John Marks (Boston: Little, Brown, 1934).

62. This close relation between industry and war is suggested, for example, by the fact that early in Roosevelt's New Deal two generals who had served on the War Industries Board during the First World War were responsible for key recovery programs, Hugh Johnson at the National Recovery Administration and George Peek at the Agricultural Adjustment Administration.

63. For an example of the technologist's dream of pilotless planes and a war fought without soldiers, see Matthew Brzezinski, "The Unmanned Army," *New York Times Magazine*, April 20, 2003, 38–41, 80–81.

64. See, for example, Michael O'Hanlon, "A Flawed Masterpiece," *Foreign Affairs* 81, no. 3 (May–June 2002): 47–63.

65. See Leslie Wayne, "America's For-Profit Secret Army," *New York Times*, October 13, 2002.

66. Jean Genet, "Four Hours in Shatila," *Journal of Palestine Studies* 22, no. 3 (Spring 1983).

67. See James Davis, *Fortune's Warriors: Private Armies and the New World Order* (Vancouver: Douglas & McIntyre, 2000).

68. See Machiavelli, *The Prince*, trans. Mark Musa (New York: St. Martin's Press, 1964). For Machiavelli's condemnation of mercenaries, see chapter 12, pp. 99–109.

69. Ernst Kantorowicz, "Pro Patria Mori in Medieval Political Thought," *American Historical Review* 56, no. 3 (April 1951): 472–92. For an excellent account of

the republican ideal of government and patriotic life, see Quentin Skinner, *L'artiste en philosophe politique: Ambrogio Lorenzetti et le Bon Gouvernment* (Paris: Raisons d'agir, 2002).

70. Niccolò Machiavelli, *The Prince*, 223. The most explicitly humanist defense of Machiavelli's democracy we know is a rarely cited text by Maurice Merleau-Ponty, "A Note on Machiavelli" in *Signs*, trans. Richard McCleary (Evanston, IL: Northwestern University Press, 1964), 211–23.

71. *Asymmetry* has become a very common term in the vocabulary of U.S. military analysts since the late 1990s. For an excellent critical analysis of the concept and its uses, see Saïda Bédar, ed., *Vers une "grande transformation" stratégique américaine?*, *Cahiers d'Etudes Stratégiques* 31, no. 4 (2001). For a perspective that justifies the use of unconventional tactics by the United States in response to the unconventional tactics used by its enemies, see Roger Barnett, *Asymmetrical Warfare: Today's Challenge to U.S. Military Power* (Washington, DC: Brassey's, 2003). For analyses of asymmetrical combat from the standpoint of the U.S. military, see Robert David Steele, "The Asymmetric Threat: Listening to the Debate," *Joint Forces Quarterly* 20 (Autumn–Winter 1998–1999): 78–84; David Grange, "Asymmetric Warfare: Old Method, New Concern," *National Strategy Forum Review* (Winter 2000); and Steven Metz and Douglas Johnson II, "Asymmetry and U.S. Military Strategy: Definition, Background, and Strategic Concepts," U.S. Army War College Strategic Institute, January 2001.

72. Apocalyptic visions of total control run throughout much of modern and postmodern critical theory. For some varied examples, see Max Horkheimer and Theodor Adorno, *The Dialectic of Enlightenment* (New York: Continuum, 1972); Guy Debord, *The Society of the Spectacle* (New York: Zone, 1994); Paul Virilio, *Desert Screen: War at the Speed of Light* (New York: Continuum, 2002).

73. See John Arquilla and David Ronfeldt, eds., *Networks and Netwars: The Future of Terror, Crime, and Militancy* (Santa Monica: Rand Corporation, 2001).

74. For an excellent history of U.S. counterinsurgency strategy, which focuses on the behaviorist paradigm at military think tanks like the Rand Corporation, see Ron Robin, *The Making of the Cold War Enemy* (Princeton, NJ: Princeton University Press, 2001). The major part of the book deals with the Korean War, but there is a fascinating chapter on the shift in counterinsurgency strategy during the Vietnam War away from attempting "constructively" to change the psychology of the enemy—winning hearts and minds—toward simply and coercively trying to change the enemy's behavior.

75. Arquilla and Ronfeldt consider swarming the primary military strategy of net-

war. See John Arquilla and David Ronfeldt, *Swarming and the Future of Conflict* (Santa Monica: Rand Corporation, 2000).

76. Much of the U.S. writing on unilateralism is tinged with the hypocritical pathos that Rudyard Kipling's notion of the "white man's burden" carried in a previous era. For laments on the solitude and reluctance of the United States in a unilaterialist role, see Samuel Huntington, "The Lonely Superpower," *Foreign Affairs* 78, no. 2 (March–April 1999): 35–49; and Richard Haass, *The Reluctant Sheriff: The United States After the Cold War* (New York: Council on Foreign Relations, 1997).

77. We should note that human rights has become fundamental—a European legal philosopher from the last century would say "dogmatic"—in the field of international law. See, for example, Richard Falk, "The Quest for Human Rights in an Era of Globalization" in Michael Schlechter, ed., *Future Multilateralism* (New York: St. Martin's Press, 1999).

78. Saskia Sassen argues that many aspects of economic decision-making are being "denationalized" and that, for example, national economic minsters and central bankers are increasingly today acting in the interest of both national and global capital. See Saskia Sassen, "The State and Globalization" in Rodney Hall and Thomas Biersteker, eds., *The Emergence of Private Authority in Global Governance* (Cambridge: Cambridge University Press, 2002), 91–112.

79. On the economic costs of the global wars, see Christian Marazzi, *Capitale e linguaggio: Dalla New Economy all'economia di guerra*. For an analysis of the extreme difficulties facing the U.S. project of unilataleralist global control, see Emanuel Todd, *Après l'Empire* (Paris: Gallimard, 2002). Todd's argument is overly polemical and exagerated in several regards (claiming, for example, that U.S. power has already steeply declined just as Soviet power did before it), but he does give a clear view of the obstacles preventing U.S. unilateralism.

80. See, for example, Boris Porchnev, *Les soulèvements populaires en France de 1623 à 1648* (Paris: S.E.V.P.E.N., 1963); and Ranajit Guha, *Elementary Aspects of Peasant Insurgency in Colonial India* (Delhi: Oxford University Press, 1983).

81. See Friedrich Engels, *Engels as Military Critic* (Manchester: Manchester University Press, 1959). In general, on the position of Marxists in the Second and Third Internationals and on armed insurrection as "the highest form of the political struggle of the proletariat," see A. Neuberg, *Armed Insurrection*, trans. Quintin Hoare (New York: St. Martin's Press, 1970). This remarkable book, originally published in German in 1928, gives a rare inside view of communist military strategy in the early twentieth century. The book was prepared on the

initiative of the Red Army in collaboration with the Agitprop office of the Third International (Komintern). The author's name, "A. Neuberg," is completely fictitious. The various chapters were written by different authors under the direction of "Hercules," the code name used by Palmiro Togliatti. The list of authors reads like a who's who of international communist agitation at the time, including Manfred Stern (who under the name "Emilio Kleber" would later lead the International Brigades in the Spanish civil war), Mikhail Tukhachevsky (marshal of the Red Army), Vasily Blücher (military adviser to the Kuomintang under the name "Galen"), and a young Ho Chi Minh.

82. Isaak Babel, *Red Cavalry*, trans. John Harland (London: Knopf, 1923), 81–84.

83. See Benjamin Young, *From Revolution to Politics: Chinese Communists on the Long March* (Boulder, CO: Westview, 1990).

84. Carl Schmitt, *Theorie des Partisanen* (Berlin: Duncker und Humblot, 1963). As we have already emphasized, the shift from the theme of the "enemy" to that of the "partisan" in Schmitt's work is a completely reactionary movement. This is even more the case in the work of Ernst Jünger, where the individualistic characteristic of rebellion is emphasized even more strongly. See *Der Waldgang* (Frankfurt: Klostermann, 1951). These are examples of the bourgeois distortion of anticapitalist rebellions, which indeed became a fashion in late modernity.

85. See Claudio Pavone's excellent study of the antifascist resistance in Italy, *Una guerra civile: saggio storico sulla moralità nella resistenza* (Turin: Bollati Boringhieri, 1991). Although the book is focused on a specific Italian case, it develops the different concepts of civil war (national, class-based, patriotic, antifascist, and so forth) and links diverse social subjects to forms of organization in a way that illuminates a much more general problematic.

86. One example of this might be the history of the southern Balkans in the twentieth century. In the 1940s the wars of antifascist resistance were mixed with civil wars between communists and "ethnic" nationalists. Those civil wars were based in divisions between town and country and between social classes. When in the 1990s nationalist wars broke out again, these same divisions and the same class basis were in play again, but often in inverted form. In many cases at this point, the poor were struggling against socialist bureaucracies.

87. On the dictatorship of the party over popular or proletarian insurrection, see again A. Neuberg, *Armed Insurrection*.

88. See Hans Magnus Enzensberger, *Der kurze Sommer der Anarchie: Buenaventura Durrutis Leben und Tod* (Frankfurt: Surkamp, 1972). For the Soviet appreciation

of Durruti, see the book by the correspondent for *Pravda* at the time, Mikhail Koltsov, *Diario de la guerra de España* (Paris: Ediciones Ruedo Ibérico, 1963).

89. This is the central argument of Régis Debray's *Revolution in the Revolution?*, trans. Bobbye Ortiz (New York: Monthly Review Press, 1967). See also Ernesto Che Guevara, *Guerrilla Warfare* (New York: Vintage, 1961).

90. For women in the Sandinista National Liberation Front in Nicaragua, see Helen Collinson, ed., *Women and Revolution in Nicaragua* (London: Zed, 1990), especially 154–55. For women in Sendero Luminoso in Peru, see Daniel Castro, "The Iron Legions," in Daniel Castro, ed., *Revolution and Revolutionaries: Guerrilla Movements in Latin America* (Wilmington, DE: Scholarly Resources, 1999), 191–99.

91. "But in retrospect it's quite clear; the moment victory became a possibility, that's when we women who had been active participants in the struggle began to be forced out, to lose power, to be marginalized. We'd been on the front lines, and then we weren't" (Gioconda Belli, "We Were the Knights of the Round Table," in Margaret Randall, *Sandino's Daughters Revisited* [New Brunswick, NJ: Rutgers University Press, 1994], 168–90).

92. See, for example, the excellent study of the Cultural Revolution in Shanghai, Elizabeth Perry and Li Xun, *Proletarian Power: Shanghai in the Cultural Revolution* (Boulder, CO: Westview, 1997).

93. For a summary of the influences of the Chinese model on Italian revolutionary organizations in the 1960s and 1970s, see Roberto Niccolai, *Quando la Cina era vicina: La rivoluzione culturale e la sinistra extraparlamentare italiana negli anni '60 e '70* (Pisa: Franco Serantini, 1998).

94. Hannah Arendt, *On Revolution* (New York: Viking, 1963).

95. For a good example of the articulation of social and political factors in a national liberation struggle, see Franz Fanon, *The Wretched of the Earth* (New York: Grove, 1963).

96. The "young Marx" elaborates a critique of transcendence that links the violence of capital to the violence of the state. See, for example, Karl Marx, "Economic and Philosophical Manuscripts of 1844," in *Early Writings*, trans. Rodney Livingstone and Gregor Benton (New York: Vintage, 1974).

97. For a brief overview of the transition to urban guerrilla movements across the world in this period, see Ian Beckett, *Modern Insurgencies and Counterinsurgencies* (London: Routledge, 2001), 151–82.

98. For English-language description and analysis of Autonomia in Italy in the

1970s, see Steve Wright, *Storming Heaven: Class Composition and Struggle in Italian Autonomist Marxism* (London: Pluto, 2002); and Sylvere Lotringer and Christian Marazzi, eds., "Italy: Autonomia," *Semiotext(e)* 3, no. 3 (1980). See also the extensive interviews with many of the protagonists contained in Guido Borio, Francesca Pozzi, and Gigi Roggero, eds., *Futuro anteriore* (Rome: Derive/Approdi, 2002).

99. See Nick Dyer-Witherford, *Cyber-Marx* (Urbana: University of Illinois Press, 1999).

100. On the first Intifada, see Robert Hunter, *The Palestinian Uprising* (London: Tauris, 1991). On the second Intifada, see Roane Carey, ed., *The New Intifada* (London: Verso, 2001).

101. See Baruch Hirson's excellent study of the Soweto Revolt, *Year of Fire, Year of Ash* (London: Zed, 1979).

102. Hirson makes clear the sometimes uneasy relationship between the revolts and the ANC in the 1970s in *Year of Fire, Year of Ash*. Dale McKinley's analysis also demonstrates this tension, but unfortunately it is clouded by his strangely antiquated Marxist-Leninist ideology and his critiques of the reformist, petit-bourgeois nature of the ANC, *The ANC and the Liberation Struggle* (London: Pluto, 1997).

103. Lynn Stephen explains how the Zapatistas mix local Tzeltal mythology with national icons such as Zapata in *Zapata Lives! Histories and Cultural Politics in Southern Mexico* (Berkeley: University of California Press, 2002), 158–75.

104. On the network nature of the Zapatista organization structure, see Roger Burbach, *Globalization and Postmodern Politics* (London: Pluto, 2001), 116–28; Fiona Jeffries, "Zapatismo and the Intergalactic Age," in Roger Burbach, *Globalization and Postmodern Politics*, 129–44; and Harry Cleaver, "The Zapatistas and the Electronic Fabric of Struggle," in John Holloway and Eloína Paláez, eds., *Zapatista!* (London: Pluto, 1998), 81–103.

105. The style of Subcomandante Marcos's writings—at once playful and militant—is the best example of how the Zapatistas make irony into a political strategy. See Subcomandante Marcos, *Our Word Is Our Weapon* (New York: Seven Stories, 2001).

106. See John Halloway, *Change the World Without Taking Power* (London: Pluto, 2002).

107. On identity politics, see Iris Marion Young, *Justice and the Politics of Difference* (Princeton, NJ: Princeton University Press, 1990), especially 156–91.

108. On the resurgence of anarchist groups, see David Graeber, "For a New Anarchism," *New Left Review*, 2nd ser., no. 13 (January–February 2002): 61–73.

109. Here we should also add the various forms of electronic resistance and hacker movements that strive to make common the enormous resources controlled in electronic networks and thwart the new, sophisticated forms of control that use cybernetic technologies. These movements too are based in a desire for freedom and a conception of the enormous wealth and the powerful new forms of collaboration and communication that networks make possible. We will return to discuss these electronic movements when we consider questions of immaterial property in chapter 2.

110. See, for example, Arquilla and Ronfeldt, *Networks and Netwar*.

111. Pierre Clastres, *Society Against the State: Essays in Political Anthropology*, trans. Robert Hurley in collaboration with Abe Stein (New York: Zone, 1987), especially chapter 11.

112. See Arquilla and Ronfeldt, *Swarming and the Future of Conflict* (Santa Monica: Rand Corporation, 2000).

113. See, for example, James Kennedy and Russell Eberhart with Yuhai Shi, *Swarm Intelligence* (San Francisco: Morgan Kaufmann Publishers, 2001).

114. Kennedy and Russell, with Shi, 103–104. For a more colorful account of insect communication, see Karl von Frisch, *The Dancing Bees*, trans. Dora Ilse (London: Methuen, 1954).

115. Emile Zola, *La debacle* (Paris: Charpentier, 1899), 210.

116. See Kristin Ross, *The Emergence of Social Space: Rimbaud and the Paris Commune* (Minneapolis: University of Minnesota Press, 1988), 105. Ross describes beautifully the central role of the swarm in Rimbaud's poetry.

PART 2: MULTITUDE

1. On the distinction between the multitude and the people, see Paolo Virno, *Grammatica della moltitudine* (Catanzaro: Rubbettino, 2001), 5–7; and Marco Bascetta, "Multitudine, popolo, massa," in *Controimpero* (Rome: Manifestolibri, 2002), 67–80.

2. For a classic formulation of liberation based on "the interdependence of mutual (nondominant) differences," see Audre Lorde, "The Master's Tools Will Never Dismantle the Master's House," in *Sister Outsider* (Trumansburg, NY: Crossing Press, 1984), 110–13.

3. The debate between Slavoj Žižek and Ernesto Laclau demonstrates the dead end of discussing class in terms of an alternative between the Marxist unitary notion and the plural liberal notion. See Judith Butler, Ernesto Laclau, and Slavoj Žižek, *Contingency, Hegemony, Universality* (London: Verso, 2000).

4. For a sample of the old debates within Marxism about the economic and the political, see (for the political side) Georg Lukács, *History and Class Consciousness*, trans. Rodney Livingstone (Cambridge, MA: MIT Press, 1971); and (for the economic side) Nikolai Bukharin, *The ABC of Communism*, trans. Eden Paul and Cedar Paul (Ann Arbor: University of Michigan Press, 1988).

5. See Antonio Negri, "Leopardi europeo," in *Lenta ginestra*, 2nd ed. (Milan: Eterotopie, 2001), 9–16. For an English version of this essay, see Antonio Negri, "The European Leopardi," trans. Timothy Murphy, *Genre* 33, no. 1 (Spring 2000): 13–26.

6. The two great superpowers of the twentieth century, the United States and the Soviet Union, pursued industrialization as the strategy for achieving economic dominance. Antonio Gramsci clearly understood early in the century the necessity of industrialization for economic dominance. See, "Americanism and Fordism," in *Selections from Prison Notebooks*, trans. Quintin Hoare and Geoffrey Smith (New York: International Publishers, 1971), 277–318.

7. We described immaterial labor and its hegemony over other forms of labor in *Empire* (Cambridge: Harvard University Press, 2000), 280–300.

8. On the linguistic nature of contemporary forms of labor, see Paolo Virno, "Virtuosity and Revolution," in Paolo Virno and Michael Hardt, eds., *Radical Thought in Italy* (Minneapolis: University of Minnesota Press, 1996), 189–210. On "cognitive labor," see Carlo Vercellone, ed., *Sommes-nous sortis du capitalisme industriel?* (Paris: La Dispute, 2003).

9. Our notion of affect derives primarily from Baruch Spinoza, *Ethics*, Part III. For slightly different but compatible discussions of affect, see Antonio Damasio, *Looking for Spinoza* (New York: Harcourt, 2003); and Brian Massumi, *Parables of the Virtual* (Durham, NC: Duke University Press, 2002).

10. On employers' rising focus on attitude and social skills, see Doug Henwood, *After the New Economy* (New York: The New Press, 2003), 76–79.

11. For a classic essay, see Georg Simmel, "The Metropolis and Mental Life," in *The Sociology of Georg Simmel*, trans. Kurt Wolff (New York: Free Press, 1950), 409–24. More generally, see Simmel's writings on money and David Frisby's useful introduction in Georg Simmel, *The Philosophy of Money* (London: Routledge, 1990), 1–49.

12. See, for example, Dorothy Smith, *The Everyday World as Problematic: A Feminist Sociology* (Boston: Northeastern University Press, 1987); and Sara Ruddick, *Maternal Thinking* (Boston: Beacon, 1989). On care as a feminist ethic, see Joan Tronto, *Moral Boundaries* (New York: Routledge, 1993); and Eva Kittay, *Love's Labor* (New York: Routledge, 1999).

13. See Danièle Kergoat, "L'infirmière coordonnée," *Futur antérieur*, no. 6 (Summer 1991): 71–85. See also Danièle Kergoat, Françoise Imbert, Hélène Le Doaré, and Danièle Senotier, *Les infirmières et leur coordination, 1988–1989* (Paris: Lamarre, 1992).

14. On "mothering paralegals," see Jennifer Pierce, *Gender Trials: Emotional Lives in Contemporary Law Firms* (Berkeley: University of California Press, 1995), 83–102. On the alienation of emotional labor, see Arlie Russell Hochschild, *The Managed Heart: Commercialization of Human Feeling* (Berkeley: University of California Press, 1983), 204–41. Hochschild gives statistics of the gender breakdown of jobs that call for emotional labor.

15. This is the primary argument of Doug Henwood, *After the New Economy*.

16. For an overview of post-Fordism and flexible specialization, see Ash Amin, ed., *Post-Fordism: A Reader* (Oxford: Blackwell, 1994).

17. See Pascal Byé and Maria Fonte, "Is the Technical Model of Agriculture Changing Radically?" in Philip McMichael, ed., *The Global Restructuring of Agro-Food Systems* (Ithaca, NY: Cornell University Press, 1994), 241–57.

18. See Michael Flitner, "Biodiversity: Of Local Commons and Global Commodities," in Michael Goldman, ed., *Privatizing Nature: Political Struggles for the Global Commons* (London: Pluto, 1998), 144–66.

19. For the U.S. Bureau of Labor projections for fastest growing jobs from 2000 to 2010, see www.bls.gov/news.release/ecopro.toc.htm.

20. See, for example, Timothy Mitchell's critique of the traditional studies that pose Egyptian peasants as eternal and immutable, "The Invention and Reinvention of the Peasant," in *Rule of Experts: Egypt, Techo-Politics, Modernity* (Berkeley: University of California Press, 2002), 123–52.

21. See the classic definitions of peasants in Eric Wolf, *Pathways to Power* (Berkeley: University of California Press, 2000), 195–96; and Theodor Shanin, "Introduction: Peasantry as a Concept," in Teodor Shanin, ed., *Peasants and Peasant Societies*, 2nd ed. (Oxford: Blackwell, 1987), 3.

22. Note that in English the terminological distinction between "peasant" and "farmer" helps separate these different economic positions. The terms in several other languages, such as "paysan" in French, "contadino" in Italian, and

"campesino" in Spanish, make it more difficult to express this conceptual distinction.

23. Mao estimated in the 1930s that poor peasants and agricultural workers together composed 70 percent of the Chinese rural population, 20 percent were middle peasants and self-sufficient, and only 5 percent were rich peasants. See Mao Tse-tung, "Analysis of the Classes in Chinese Society" (1926), in *Selected Works of Mao Tse-Tung* (London: Lawrence and Wishart, 1954), 1:13–20; "Report of an Investigation into the Peasant Movement in Hunan" (1927), in *Selected Works*, 1:21–29; "How to Analyse the Classes in the Rural Areas" (1933), in *Selected Works*, 1:138–40; and "The Chinese Revolution and the Chinese Communist Party" (1939), in *Selected Works*, 3:72–101, especially 92–93.

24. For an excellent discussion of the debates among members of the Soviet leadership, see Moishé Lewin, *Russian Peasants and Soviet Power*, trans. Irene Nove (Evanston, IL: Northwestern University Press, 1968).

25. See Lynne Viola, *Peasant Rebels under Stalin* (Oxford: Oxford University Press, 1996). Viola claims that although the peasantry lost its battle against the Soviet state, and was thus destroyed as an economic category, it survived as a cultural identity through a tradition of resistance.

26. Mao was highly critical of many aspects of Soviet agricultural policy but not of the general project to transform peasant production and collectivize agriculture—on the contrary, he thought the Soviets did not go far enough! Mao had two primary criticisms of the Soviet process. First, the Soviets overemphasized the importance of machinery and technological development as the condition for collectivization: tractors must precede cooperatives. Mao thought the emphasis belonged instead on the transformation of the relations of production: "First the production relations have to be changed, then and only then the productive forces can be broadly developed" (Mao Tsetung, *A Critique of Soviet Economics*, trans. Moss Roberts [New York: Monthly Review, 1977], 93). Second, Mao thought the Soviets did not transform ownership radically enough. The collective or communal ownership that the Soviets developed is only the first step in a process that must arrive finally at public ownership of the land and the means of production (68, 133).

27. Contemporary Chinese cinema presents several examples of nostalgia for the peasant world, but one should not confuse that nostalgia with a claim that the peasant world has actually been re-created. See, for example, Xudong Zhang's

excellent interpretation of *Red Sorghum*, the film by Zhang Yimou, as a peasant utopia, in *Chinese Modernism in the Era of Reforms* (Durham, NC: Duke University Press, 1997), 318–22.

28. California agriculture is the classic example. The construction of huge dams and irrigation systems was a powerful lever in the transformation from small family farms toward corporate production on a large scale. The concentration of property was accompanied by the implementation of technological advances and a steep rise in productivity. See Donald Pisani, *From the Family Farm to Agribusiness: The Irrigation Crusade in California and the West, 1850–1931* (Berkeley, University of California Press, 1984).

29. See Robert Brenner, "Agrarian Class Structure and Economic Development in Pre-Industrial Europe," in T. H. Aston and C. H. E. Philpin, eds., *The Brenner Debate* (Cambridge: Cambridge University Press, 1985), 10–63.

30. On the end of the peasantry in France, see Henri Mendras, *Sociétés paysannes: éléments pour une théorie de la paysannerie* (Paris: Armand Colin, 1976). For a more general view, see David Goodman and Michael Redclift, *From Peasant to Proletarian: Capitalist Development and Agrarian Transitions* (New York: St. Martin's Press, 1982).

31. See, for example, on the history of pre-peasant land tenure in Vietnam, Ngo Vinh Long, "Communal Property and Peasant Revolutionary Struggles in Vietnam," *Peasant Studies* 17, no. 2 (Winter 1990): 121–40. For similar histories of Sub-Saharan Africa, see Enwere Dike, "Changing Land Tenure Systems in Nigeria," *Peasant Studies* 17, no. 1 (Fall 1989): 43–54; and J. S. Saul and R. Woods, "African Peasantries," in Teodor Shanin, ed., *Peasants and Peasant Societies*, 2nd ed., (Oxford: Blackwell, 1987), 80–88.

32. There is considerable debate whether the term *peasantry* ever did in fact accurately describe such systems of small-holding production, especially in Africa. See Margaret Jean Hay, " 'Peasants' in Modern East African Studies," *Peasant Studies* 8, no. 1 (Winter 1979): 17–29.

33. On the history of political conflicts over land reform in Guatemala, see Greg Grandin, *The Blood of Guatemala* (Durham, NC: Duke University Press, 2000). More generally, on the continuing inequalities of land ownership and the failures of land reform in Latin America, see Ernst Feder, *The Rape of the Peasantry: Latin America's Landholding System* (New York: Anchor Books, 1971); and William Thiesenhusen, *Broken Promises: Agrarian Reform and the Latin American Campesino* (Boulder, CO: Westview, 1995).

34. For a useful description of the structure and activities of one of the major transnational agribusiness corporations, see Brewster Kneen, *Invisible Giant: Cargill and Its Transnational Strategies* (London: Pluto Press, 1995).

35. See R. E. Elson, *The End of the Peasantry in Southeast Asia* (New York: St. Martin's Press, 1997); and Anthony Pereira, *The End of the Peasants: The Rural Labor Movement in Northeast Brazil, 1961–1988* (Pittsburgh: University of Pittsburgh Press, 1997).

36. On the proletarianization of African agricultural workers, for example, see Samir Amin, ed., *L'agriculture africaine et le capitalisme* (Paris: Anthropos, 1975).

37. The cultural function of the peasant world outside of Europe is ambiguous, just as we saw above how the economic usage of the term *peasantry* outside of Europe is often problematic. When we look at non-European literature of the mid- and late twentieth century we can certainly recognize shifts that are similar to the decline of the peasant world in European literature. Many African novels, for instance, such as Chinua Achebe's *Things Fall Apart*, Hamidou Kane's *Ambiguous Adventure*, and Tayeb Salih's *Season of Migration to the North*, trace a historical passage in which the social relations and forms of authority of the traditional village structure have been destabilized, most importantly by the colonial intrusion but also by the forces of modernity and ultimately by the introduction of capital. This structure of feeling, which is found in much colonial and postcolonial literature, certainly bears resemblances to that of the loss of the peasant world in the European context: they share a common sense of disorder, disorientation, and nostalgia. When we cast the non-European crisis of village structures in terms of the decline of the European peasant world, however, we fail to grasp its specificity. It is as if we can understand non-European cultures and societies only insofar as they conform or not to Europe's past, which serves as a universal standard.

38. Raymond Williams traces beautifully in his panoramic study, *The Country and the City*, how the happy old times of rural England was a remarkably enduring motif through the various developments of modern English literature. "English attitudes to the country, and to ideas of rural life, persisted with extraordinary power, so that even after the society was predominantly urban its literature . . . was still predominantly rural" (*The Country and the City* [Oxford: Oxford University Press, 1973], 2).

39. For modernist European art, see, for example, William Rubin, ed., *"Primitivism" in 20th Century Art*, 2 vols. (New York: Museum of Modern Art, 1984). For modernist European literature, see Mariana Torgovnick, *Gone*

Primitive: Savage Intellects, Modern Lives (Chicago: University of Chicago Press, 1990); and Elazar Barkan and Ronald Bush, eds., *Prehistories of the Future: The Primitivist Project and the Culture of Modernism* (Stanford: Stanford University Press, 1995).

40. In this paragraph we follow Michael Kearney's periodization of the field of anthropology: Michael Kearney, *Reconceptualizing the Peasantry: Anthropology in Global Perspective* (Boulder, CO: Westview, 1996), 23–41. The paradigm of the peasant in anthropology arose at the beginning of the cold war, and its use by anthropologists often corresponded to clear geopolitical positions. On one side, in line with developmentalist theories, the peasant was an "undeveloped" figure that could relatively quickly reach the developed status of the Euro-American norm. On the other side, in line with the ideology of the Chinese revolution and the various national liberation struggles, the peasant was a tricontinental concept that claimed a common socio-economic-political condition in Asia, Latin America, and Africa. The peasant was, in this sense, an anticapitalist and revolutionary figure. We should keep in mind, finally, that the concept of the peasantry is conceived ambiguously in many anthropological studies. Sydel Silvermann argues, in fact, that there has never been a coherent properly cultural definition of the peasantry; the most rigorous anthropologists have instead relied on an economic definition. See "The Concept of the Peasant and the Concept of Culture," in Joan Mendur, ed., *Social Anthropology of Peasantry* (Bombay: Somaiya Publications, 1983), 7–31.

41. Some go so far as to claim that from a political perspective the peasantry does not form a class. Eric Hobsbawm, for example, defines primitive rebels, which include rebellious peasants, as "*pre-political* people who have not yet found, or only begun to find, a specific language in which to express their aspirations about the world" (*Primitive Rebels* [New York: Norton, 1959], 2).

42. "Insofar as there is merely a local interconnection among these small-holding peasants, and the identity of their interests begets no community, no national bond and no political organization among them, they do not form a class. They are consequently incapable of enforcing their class interest in their own name, whether through a parliament or through a convention. They cannot represent themselves, they must be represented" (Marx, *The Eighteenth Brumaire of Louis Bonaparte* [New York: International Publishers, 1963], 124).

43. See, for example, Karl Kautsky, *The Agrarian Question*, trans. Peter Burgess (London: Zwan, 1988). For Marx's proposal of a peasant-based political project in Russia, see his letter of March 8, 1881, to Vera Zasulich, in Karl Marx

and Friedrich Engels, *Collected Works* (New York: International Publishers, 1975), 24:346. In this letter Marx explains that *Capital* does not contain a universal theory of historical development and does not condemn us to follow determinate stages of development. The Russian peasant communes, he claims, have the capacity to proceed directly toward communism.

44. "The peasants find their natural ally and leader in the urban proletariat" (Marx, *Eighteenth Brumaire*, 128). The proletariat itself, of course, was not always in Marx's view an active political subject but became active in the course of its historical development. The French proletariat was not capable of playing a subjective role in the revolution of 1789 but could only serve the interests of and rally behind the bourgeoisie. In the June and July revolts in 1830 and 1848 the Parisian proletariat took its first steps on the political stage as an autonomous actor and was struck down quickly each time. Only with the establishment of the Paris Commune in 1871 did the proletariat emerge as a truly political subject.

45. This insight is one of the foundational tenets of postcolonial studies. See, in particular, Gayatri Spivak, *A Critique of Postcolonial Reason* (Cambridge, MA: Harvard University Press, 1999), especially 252–66.

46. Along with Mao Zedong, Ho Chi Minh must also be mentioned as a great theoretician of the peasant-based communist revolution. See Ho Chi Minh's essay "The Party's Military Work Among the Peasants," in A. Neuberg, *Armed Insurrection*, trans. Quintin Hoare (New York: St. Martin's Press, 1970), 255–71.

47. See, once again, Mao's *Critique of Soviet Economics*, especially 55 and 136. The Soviets put too much stock in new machines and the development of productive forces, Mao complains, and pay too little attention to the transformation of the peasants themselves, that is, to superstructural, political changes.

48. We do not mean to say that there is no longer any difference between the urban and the rural but rather that these differences no longer have a political significance and that the two are equal with regard to communication and cooperation. The mass diffusion of print media, radio, television, and in some areas the Internet play a role in this, as do the radical transformations of productive practices, along with the territorial transformations of urban and rural landscapes. Some China scholars call this a process of rural urbanization. See Gregory Eliyu Goldin, ed., *Farewell to Peasant China: Rural Urbanization and Social Change in the Late Twentieth Century* (Armonk, NY: Sharpe, 1997).

49. The project of the South Asian Subaltern Studies group and, in particular, that of its founder, Ranajit Guha, may from this perspective be conceived as a fun-

damentally Maoist endeavor—or, more accurately, they assume as given the *results* of the Maoist revolutionary process insofar as they insist that peasants, just like the industrial proletarians, are capable of forming an active and autonomous political subject. The equality of political capacities is what allows peasants, industrial workers, and others to share the common category of "the subaltern." The Subaltern Studies group refuses, in other words, the notion that the peasants are merely apolitical or prepolitical, arguing that the subaltern in general and the peasant specifically is the maker of its own destiny. Whereas traditional British historians conceived the great Indian peasant uprisings in the late nineteenth and early twentieth centuries against the British Raj as spontaneous and incoherent, for example, Guha maintains that such insurgency was a motivated and conscious undertaking on the part of the Indian peasantry and thus constituted political activity properly conceived. For an excellent general assessment of the work of the South Asian Subaltern Studies group in this regard, see Dipesh Chakrabarty, "*Subaltern Studies* and Postcolonial Historiography," *Nepantla* 1, no. 1 (2000): 9–32, especially 14–21.

50. See José Bove and Yves Manguy, *La confédération paysanne* (Paris: Eden Productions, 2003); Angus Wright and Wendy Wolford, *To Inherit the Earth: The Landless Movement and the Struggle for a New Brazil* (Oakland: Food First, 2003); and Sue Bradford and Jan Rocha, *Cutting the Wire: The Story of the Landless Movement in Brazil* (London: Latin American Bureau, 2002).

51. See Michael Kearney, *Reconceptualizing the Peasant*, 23–41.

52. Singularity here, in contrast to a notion of what is different from something else, refers to what is different in itself. This notion of singularity is developed by Gilles Deleuze in *Expressionism in Philosophy: Spinoza*, trans. Martin Joughin, (New York: Zone Books, 1990); and *Difference and Repetition*, trans. Paul Patton (New York: Columbia University Press, 1995). See also the entry for "singularités pré-individuelles" in François Zourabichvili, *Le vocabulaire de Deleuze* (Paris: Ellipses, 2003), 76–78.

53. Charles Piot, *Remotely Global: Village Modernity in West Africa* (Chicago: University of Chicago Press, 1999), 22–24. Piot provides an excellent example of an anthropological model that grasps local singularity and global commonality, here in the case of village life in Northern Togo. On the issue of African modernity, see Jean and John Comaroff, "Introduction" in Jean Comaroff and John Comaroff, eds., *Modernity and Its Malcontents: Ritual and Power in Postcolonial Africa* (Chicago: University of Chicago Press, 1994), xi–xxxvii.

54. Jean Comaroff and John Comaroff, "Occult Economies and the Violence of

Abstraction: Notes from the South African Postcolony," *American Ethnologist* 26, no. 2 (May 1999): 279–303, especially 294.

55. Poverty becomes a major theme in modern sociology when its economic condition collides with its political, psychological, and ideological expressions. In German sociology, for instance, especially in the school surrounding Georg Simmel in the 1920s, it becomes a central focus when the impoverishment of the middle classes takes on a political face. Sigfried Kracauer, for example, analyzes the way poor employees drift toward fascism, a theme that is also prominent in German expressionist cinema. See Kracauer, *The Salaried Masses*, trans. Quintin Hoare (London: Verso, 1998; originally published in German, 1929). Erich Fromm in psychology, Franz Neumann in political science, and Alfred Döblin in literature all develop this close connection between the economic and cultural conditions of poverty, demonstrating the dramatic anthropological regression caused by each crisis in the cycles of capitalist development.

56. For an extensive discussion of the classical and Marxist theories of the "industrial reserve army," see Yann Moulier-Boutang, *De l'esclavage au salariat* (Paris: PUF, 1998). For the original definitions of the theory, see Karl Marx, *Capital*, vol. 1, trans. Ben Fowkes (New York: Vintage, 1976), 781–94; and Rosa Luxemburg, *The Accumulation of Capital*, trans. Agnes Schwarzschild (New York: Monthly Review, 1951), 348–67.

57. Rem Koolhas, for example, tries to understand how the city of Lagos works by focusing on the extraordinary resourcefulness of the poor, such as those selling small used machines at an open-air market. What first appears as chaos in such a market turns out to be a complex organization. See *Lagos Handbook: Project on the City 4* (New York: Taschen, forthcoming).

58. See, for example, Richard Reed, *Forest Dwellers, Forest Protecters* (Boston: Allyn and Bacon, 1997); and Debra Picchi, *The Bakairi Indians of Brazil* (Prospect Heights, IL: Waveland Press, 2000). An excellent resource for information is *Indigenous Knowledge and Development Monitor*, www.nuffic.nl/ciram/ikdm/index.html.

59. On the centrality of language in contemporary economic production, see Paolo Virno, *Scienze sociali e "natura umana"* (Catanzaro: Rubbettino, 2002), especially 49–66.

60. For the history of poor people's movements in twentieth-century United States, see Francis Fox Piven and Richard Cloward, *Poor People's Movements* (New York: Random House, 1979). A contemporary example in the United

States is the Kensington Welfare Rights Union in Philadelphia, Pennsylvania. See www.kwru.org.

61. Ashwin Desai, *We Are the Poors* (New York: Monthly Review Press, 2002), 44.

62. On the proposal of guaranteed income or citizenship income, the fundamental text from the point of view of classical and monetary economics is Philippe Van Parijs, *Real Freedom for All* (Oxford: Oxford University Press, 1995). See also André Gorz, *Reclaiming Work: Beyond the Wage-Based Society*, trans. Chris Turner (Cambridge: Polity, 1999); André Gorz, *L'immatériel* (Paris: Galilée, 2003); Ulrich Beck, *The Brave New World of Work* (Cambridge: Polity, 2000); Edoardo Matarazzo Suplicy, *Renda de cidadania* (São Paulo: Cortez, 2002); and Stanley Aronowitz and Jonathan Cutler, eds., *Post-Work* (New York: Routledge, 1998).

63. On "social-movement unionism," see Kim Moody, *Workers in a Lean World: Unions in the International Economy* (London: Verso, 1997).

64. For more information on the strikes of part-time workers and "intérimaires," see the Web site of the group "Les précaires associés de Paris," http://pap.ouvaton.org.

65. Unfortunately, twentieth-century readings of Dostoyevsky's novel have been dominated and impoverished by its relation to Russian communism. When Maxim Gorky condemned the novel in 1913 and when Albert Camus approvingly adapted it for theater in 1959, both of them could only see Dostoyevsky's devils as Russian communists. Certainly one should read the novel in terms of these political values, but it should not be reduced merely to Soviet history. Dostoyevsky's novel is grounded in a much more general and profound fear of the multitude.

66. In contrast to Dostoyevsky, Victor Zelazny, the great science fiction writer, emphasizes the refusal of authoritarian control in his novel *My Name Is Legion* (New York: Ballantine, 1976). In a future world when the vital statistics of Earth's inhabitants are maintained on a central computer, Zelazny's hero manages to gain access to his files and change his identity repeatedly, thereby escaping control. Being legion functions for him as an exodus from the oppression of identity.

67. Karl Marx, *Grundrisse*, trans. Martin Nicolaus (New York: Vintage, 1973), 81–111.

68. See Antonio Negri, *Marx Beyond Marx* (New York: Autonomedia, 1989).

69. Fredric Jameson's work provides the most fully developed example of periodization. See, for example, *The Political Unconscious* (Ithaca, NY: Cornell University Press, 1981), 74–102.

70. See Michel Foucault, *Discipline and Punish*, trans. Alan Sheridan (New York: Vintage, 1979). On Foucault's earlier investigation of the isomorphisms of knowledge or epistemic regimes, see *L'archéologie du savoir* (Paris: Gallimard, 1969), especially 177–83.

71. René Descartes, "Discourse on the Method," in *Discourse on the Method and Meditations on First Philosophy*, ed. David Weissman (New Haven: Yale University Press, 1996), 8. For detailed information about the drafting and context of the text, see Étienne Gilson's exhaustive commentary in Descartes, *Discours de la méthode*, ed. Étienne Gilson (Paris: Vrin, 1930).

72. On the "power of the flesh" in the Pauline tradition, see Henry de Lubac, *Catholicisme: Les aspects sociaux du dogme* (Paris: Le Cerf, 1941). This book, relying on Patristic and Augustinian foundations, opened up the way for a historical conception of redemption, a tradition that the contemporary forms of "liberation theology" have greatly developed.

73. The concept of the political body served to reinforce theories of the absolutist state in early modern Europe, but the analogy continued throughout modernity. On the conception of the political body as a united living organism in classical German philosophy, from Kant and Fichte to Hegel and Marx, see Pheng Cheah, *Spectral Nationality* (New York: Columbia University Press, 2003).

74. We will discuss these arguments more fully at the beginning of chapter 3. For now it is sufficient to indicate the range of arguments in the global security stream by citing Samuel Huntington, *The Clash of Civilizations and the Remaking of World Order* (New York: Touchstone, 1998); and Joseph Nye, *The Paradox of American Power* (Oxford: Oxford University Press, 2002). For the "republican" line, see the various publications that refer to "global civil society," such as Mary Kaldor, *Global Civil Society: An Answer to War* (Cambridge: Polity, 2003); and the annual journal *Global Civil Society*, which began publication in 2001.

75. On the limitations of the "domestic analogy," which attempts to link political forms on the global scene with those in the national framework, see *Empire*, 3–21.

76. Joseph Schumpeter, *Capitalism, Socialism, and Democracy* (New York: Harper and Brothers, 1942), 141.

77. See Saskia Sassen, "The State and Globalization," in Rodney Hall and Thomas Biersteker, eds., *The Emergence of Private Authority in Global Governance* (Cambridge: Cambridge University Press, 2002), 91–112. See also our *Empire*.

78. For a good summary of the theories of uneven development and unequal exchange, see B. N. Ghosh, *Dependency Theory Revisited* (Aldershot: Ashgate, 2001).

79. Examples of geographers who confront the contemporary topology of exploitation include Neil Smith, *Uneven Development: Nature, Capital, and the Production of Space* (Oxford: Blackwell, 1990); David Harvey, *Spaces of Capital: Towards a Critical Geography*, 2nd ed. (New York: Routledge, 2001); and Doreen Massey, *Spatial Divisions of Labor: Social Structures and the Geography of Production* (Basingstoke: Macmillan, 1995).

80. See James Mittelman, *The Globalization Syndrome* (Princeton, NJ: Princeton University Press, 2000).

81. See T. J. Pempel, *The Politics of the Asian Economic Crisis* (Ithaca, NY: Cornell University Press, 1999).

82. The classic text is Karl Polanyi, *The Great Transformation* (Boston: Beacon Press, 1944).

83. For some of the classic texts, see Eugen Ehrlich, *Fundamental Principles of the Sociology of Law*, trans. Walter Moll (Cambridge, MA: Harvard University Press, 1936); John R. Commons, *Legal Foundations of Capitalism* (New York: Macmillan, 1924); and John Kenneth Galbraith, *The New Industrial State* (Boston: Houghton Mifflin, 1967).

84. For analyses of several emerging forms of private authority, see Hall and Biersteker, eds., *The Emergence of Private Authority in Global Governance*.

85. For a historical definition of *lex mercatoria* and its developments, see Francesco Galgano, *Lex mercatoria* (Bologna: Il Mulino, 1998). For a legal analysis of *lex mercatoria* in the processes of globalization, see Thomas Carbonneau, ed., *Lex Mercatoria and Arbitration: A Discussion of the New Law Merchant* (Dobbs Ferry, NY: Transnational Juris Publications, 1990). For a more detailed discussion of the European context, see Maria Rosaria Ferrarese, *Le istituzioni della globalizzazione* (Bologna: Il Mulino, 2000). On the functioning of law firms in international commerce, see Yves Dezalay, "Multinationales de l'expertise et "dépérissement de l'Etat," *Actes de la recherche en sciences sociales*, no. 96–97 (March 1993): 3–20; *Marchands de droit: La restructuration de l'ordre juridique international par les multinationales du droit* (Paris: Fayard, 1992); and (with Bryant Garth), *Dealing in Virtue: International Commercial Arbitration and Construction of a Transnational Legal Order* (Chicago: University of Chicago Press, 1996).

86. On the concept of "complex sovereignty," see Kanishka Jayasuriya, "Globalization, Law, and the Transformation of Sovereignty: The Emergence of Global Regulatory Governance," *Indiana Journal of Global Legal Studies* 6, no. 2 (Spring 1999): 425–55.

87. For IMF voting power figures, see http://www.imf.org/external/np/sec/memdir/members.htm.

88. For an interesting view into the culture of the IMF from a sympathetic and well-informed journalist, see Paul Blustein, *The Chastening: Inside the Crisis that Rocked the Global Financial System and Humbled the IMF* (New York: Public Affairs, 2001).

89. For Joseph Stiglitz's speeches about the Washington Consensus, see Ha-Joon Chang, ed., *Joseph Stiglitz and the World Bank: The Rebel Within* (London: Anthem, 2001); and, more generally, Stiglitz, *Globalization and Its Discontents* (New York: Norton, 2002). See also Yves Dezalay and Bryant Garth, "Le 'Washington Consensus': Contribution à une sociologie de l'hégémonie du neoliberisme," *Actes de la Recherches en Sciences Sociales,* no. 121–22 (March 1998): 3–22.

90. For a detailed history of the World Bank, see Devesh Kapur, John Lewis, and Richard Webb, *The World Bank: Its First Half Century,* vol. 1: History (Washington, DC: Brookings Institution, 1997).

91. On scarcity and immaterial property, see Christopher May, *A Global Political Economy of Intellectual Property Rights: The New Enclosures* (London: Routledge, 2000), 45.

92. See Donna Haraway, *Modest Witness @ Second Millennium* (New York: Routledge, 1997), 79–85.

93. *Diamond v. Chakrabarty,* in *United States Reports* (Washington, DC: Government Printing Office, 1982), 447:303–22. Chief Justice Burger wrote the opinion of the court.

94. James Boyle, *Shamans, Software, and Spleens: Law and the Construction of the Information Society* (Cambridge, MA: Harvard University Press, 1996), 22, 106. There are potentially numerous cases very similar to this. In particular, numerous similar cases could result from the Human Genome Diversity Project, which collects samples of hair, blood, and cheek tissue from as wide as possible a range of ethnic groups in order to preserve the archive of genetic information. These samples too can eventually be the object of research that leads to patents.

95. See Jack Kloppenburg Jr. and Daniel Kleinman, "Seeds of Controversy: National Property Versus Common Heritage," in Jack Kloppenburg Jr., ed., *Seeds and Sovereignty: The Use and Control of Plant Genetic Resources* (Durham, NC: Duke University Press, 1988), 174–302; and Jack Kloppenburg Jr., *First the Seed: The Political Economy of Plant Biotechnology, 1492–2000* (Cambridge: Cambridge University Press, 1988), 170–90.

96. In U.S. law this was established by the Plant Patent Act of 1930, which

addresses asexually reproducing plants such as hybrid roses, and the Plant Variety Protection Act of 1970, which treats sexually reproducing plant varieties and thus seeds. See Office of Technology Assessment, *Patenting Life* (New York: Marcel Dekker, 1990), 71–75; and *United States Code Annotated* 35, sec. 161, "Patents for plants" and 7, sec. 2402, "Right to plant variety protection."

97. See, for example, Andrew Kimbrell, ed., *Fatal Harvest: The Tragedy of Industrial Agriculture* (Washington, DC: Island Press, 2002).

98. See Steven Epstein, *Impure Science: AIDS, Activism, and the Politics of Knowledge* (Berkeley: University of California Press, 1996).

99. On the neem tree, see Posey and Dutfield, *Beyond Intellectual Property*, 80; and Graham Dutfield, *Intellectual Property Rights, Trade and Biodiversity* (London: Earthscan Publications, 2000), Appendix 1, 132–34.

100. On turmeric, see Graham Dutfield, *Intellectual Property Rights, Trade and Biodiversity*, 65. On the different standard for traditional and scientific knowledges, see Naomi Roht-Arriaza, "Of Seeds and Shamans: The Appropriation of the Scientific and Technical Knowledge of Indigenous and Local Communities," in Bruce Ziff and Pratima Rao, eds., *Borrowed Power: Essays on Cultural Appropriation* (New Brunswick, NJ: Rutgers University Press, 1997), 255–87.

101. It is interesting how the orientation of the World Intellectual Property Organization (WIPO) has changed in its brief history. WIPO began by focusing almost exclusively on protecting the intellectual property of the wealthiest countries, in the form of patents and copyrights, but has progressively devoted more attention to the "emerging issues" in intellectual property that are more important to the poor countries, such as the protection of traditional knowledges and genetic resources and access to affordable pharmaceutics.

102. See Lawrence Lessig, *The Future of Ideas: The Fate of the Commons in a Connected World* (New York: Vintage, 2002); Richard Stallman, *Free Software, Free Society*, ed. by Joshua Gay (Cambridge: Free Software Society, 2002); and Chris DiBona, Sam Ockman, and Mark Stone, eds., *Opensources: Voices from the Open Source Revolution* (Cambridge: O'Reilly, 1999).

103. Karl Marx, *Economic and Philosophic Manuscripts in Early Writings*, trans. Rodney Livingstone and Gregor Benton (London: Penguin, 1975), 351.

104. Baruch Spinoza, *Ethics*, book 2, proposition 13, postulate 1 in *The Collected Works of Spinoza*, ed. Edwin Curley, 1:462.

105. The attempt to describe our present age as "late modernity" rather than "postmodernity" serves, especially among German sociologists, as part of an effort

to preserve and/or recover the central social bodies and forms of modernity. See, for example, Ulrich Beck, *The Reinvention of Politics: Rethinking Modernity in the Global Social Order*, trans. Mark Ritter (Cambridge: Polity, 1997). For representative postmodern positions, see Anne Balsamo, *Technologies of the Gendered Body* (Durham, NC: Duke University Press, 1996); and Steven Shaviro, *The Cinematic Body* (Minneapolis: University of Minnesota Press, 1993).

106. Robert Putnam, *Bowling Alone: The Collapse and Revival of American Community* (New York: Simon and Schuster, 2000). Putnam's thesis is explored comparatively in several other countries in Robert Putnam, ed., *Democracy in Flux: The Evolution of Social Capital in Contemporary Society* (Oxford: Oxford University Press, 2002).

107. See, for example, Richard Sennett, *The Corrosion of Character: The Personal Consequences of Work in the New Capitalism* (New York: Norton, 1998).

108. See, for example, Richard Rorty, *Achieving Our Country* (Cambridge, Harvard University Press, 1998); and Michael Kazin, "A Patriotic Left," *Dissent* (Fall 2002): 41–44. Jean Beth Elshtain's work is a convenient reference because she argues from a Left perspective for the defense of the traditional family and celebrates patriotic fervor in the United States's "just wars."

109. Maurice Merleau-Ponty, *The Visible and the Invisible*, trans. Alphonso Lingis (Evanston: Northwestern University Press, 1968), 139.

110. Martin Heidegger, *The Question Concerning Technology*, trans. William Lovitt (New York: Harper and Row, 1977).

111. On *Dracula* as an antifamily narrative that poses a threat to heterosexual reproduction, see Nancy Armstrong, "Feminism, Fiction, and the Utopian Potential of *Dracula*" (paper delivered at the Futures of Utopia Conference, Duke University, Durham, NC, May 2003).

112. The television series *Buffy the Vampire Slayer* is the most interesting popular example. See also the Anita Blake vampire hunter novels by Laurel K. Hamilton.

113. See François Moreau, *Spinoza: L'experience et l'éternité* (Paris: PUF, 1994).

114. See Lucien Febvre, *Le problème de l'incroyance au XVIe siècle: La religion de Rabelais* (Paris: Albin Michel, 1942).

115. See Ubaldo Fadini, Antonio Negri, and Charles Wolfe, eds., *Desiderio del mostro: Dal circo al laboratorio alla politica* (Rome: Manifestolibri, 2001).

116. See Charles Peirce, "What Pragmatism Is," in *The Essential Peirce*, Nathan Hauser et al., eds. (Bloomington: Indiana University Press, 1992), 2:331–45; and William James, *Pragmatism: A New Name for Some Old Ways of Thinking*

(New York: Longmans, Green, & Co., 1907). For an overview of the prag-matists' notion of habit, see Gail Hamner, *American Pragmatism: A Religious Genealogy* (Oxford: Oxford University Press, 2003).

117. See John Dewey, *Human Nature and Conduct* (New York: Holt, 1922), 17.

118. John Dewey, *Human Nature and Conduct*, 25.

119. Alan Ryan highlights the political nature of Dewey's thought in *John Dewey and the High Tide of American Liberalism* (New York: Norton, 1995).

120. See Dewey's polemic with Walter Lippmann on the nature of the public, *The Public and Its Problems* (New York: Holt, 1927). On his critique of Roosevelt and the New Deal, see Alan Ryan, *John Dewey*, 292–95.

121. See, among many others, Judith Butler, *Bodies That Matter* (New York: Rout-ledge, 1993); Elizabeth Grosz, *Volatile Bodies* (Bloomington: University of Indiana Press, 1994); Moira Gatens, *Imaginary Bodies* (New York: Routledge, 1996); and Vicki Kirby, *Telling Flesh* (New York: Routledge, 1997).

122. See John McKenzie, *Perform or Else: From Discipline to Performance* (New York: Routledge, 2001).

123. Paolo Virno, *Quando il verbo fa carne* (Turin: Bollati Boringhieri, 2003), 73. See also, Paolo Virno, *Scienze sociali e "natura umana"* (Catanzaro, Italy: Rubbettino, 2002), 49–66.

124. See C. B. MacPherson, *The Political Theory of Possessive Individualism* (Ox-ford: Clarendon Press, 1962).

125. See Günther Teubner, "Der Umgang mit Rechtspardoxien: Derrida, Luh-mann, Wiethölter," in Christian Joerges and Gunther Teubner, eds., *Politische Rechtsteorie* (Baden-Baden, Germany: Nomos, 2003); Günther Teubner, "Ver-fassungsfragen in der fragmentierten Weltgesellschaft" (paper presented at the Globalisierungskonferenz, Berlin, Germany, April 15, 2002); and Duncan Kennedy, "Comment on Rudolf Wiethölter's "Materialization and Procedu-ralization in Modern Law" and "Proceduralization of the Category of Law," in Christian Joerges and David Trubek, eds., *Critical Legal Thought: An American-German Debate* (Baden-Baden, Germany: Nomos, 1989), 511–24.

126. Julia Kristeva emphasizes the critique of formalism conducted by Bakhtin and his group in her introduction to the French edition, *La poétique de Dostoïevskie* (Paris: Seuil, 1970), 5–21.

127. Mikhail Bakhtin, *Problems of Dostoyevsky's Poetics*, trans. Caryl Emerson (Minneapolis: University of Minnesota Press, 1984), 101.

128. On the carnevalesque nature of the protest movements, see Notes from Nowhere, eds., *We Are Everywhere* (London: Verso, 2003), 173–301.

129. See Jean Genet, *Prisoner of Love*, trans. Barbara Bray (Hanover, NH: University of New England Press, 1992).

130. See Lynn Stephen, *Zapata Lives! Histories and Cultural Politics in Southern Mexico* (Berkeley: University of California Press, 2002), 147–75.

131. See *Empire*, 49–59.

132. Peter Linebaugh and Marcus Rediker, *The Many-Headed Hydra: Sailors, Slaves, Commoners, and the Hidden History of the Revolutionary Atlantic* (Boston: Beacon, 2000).

133. We are grateful to Valery Alzaga of the Service Employees International Union, Local 105, for information on Justice for Janitors and its members.

134. We should point out that, although in our genealogy this emergence of a new cycle could appear simply as a question of the political composition of the movements reaching maturity, political composition is always linked to the technical or social composition of the population. Specifically, the economic transformations that we described earlier in this chapter in terms of a passage to the hegemony of immaterial labor should constantly be kept in mind as the condition that makes this new political development possible. And, to complicate the question even further, the distinction between political and technical composition or between the political and the economic or the social tends to blur in this passage.

135. See Colectivo Situaciones, *19 y 20: Apuntes para el nuevo protagonismo social* (Buenos Aires: De Mano en Mano, 2002); Raúl Zibechi, *Genealogía de la revuelta* (La Plata, Argentina: Letra Libre, 2003); and Maristella Svampa and Sebastián Pereyra, *Entre la ruta y el barrio: La experiencia de las organizaciones piqueteras* (Buenos Aires: Biblos, 2003). See also, in French, the collection of essays in *Multitudes* no. 14 (Fall 2003), including Collectif Situaciones, "Causes et hasards: dilemmes du nouvel antagonisme social," 135–43; and Graciela Hopstein, "Piqueteros: limites et potentialités," 155–63.

136. See, for example, Peter Bienart, "Sidelines: The Anti-globalization Protest that Must Not Occur," *The New Republic* 23, September 24, 2001, 8.

137. See Jessica Stern, "The Protean Enemy," *Foreign Affairs* 82, no. 4 (July–August 2003): 27–40.

138. See Richard Rorty, *Achieving Our Country* (Cambridge, MA: Harvard University Press, 1999); Michael Walzer, "Can There Be a Decent Left?" *Dissent* (Spring 2002): 19–23; and "Left Conservativism: A Workshop," *boundary2* 26, no. 3 (Fall 1999): 1–62.

PART 3: DEMOCRACY

1. One of the most influential examples of this social democratic position is Paul Hirst and Grahame Thompson, *Globalization in Question*, 2nd ed. (Oxford: Polity Press, 1999).
2. For an example of liberal cosmopolitanism with an economic focus, see Mike Moore's account of his tenure as director-general of the WTO, *A World Without Walls: Freedom, Development, Free Trade and Global Governance* (Cambridge: Cambridge University Press, 2003). For examples of liberal cosmopolitanism with a political focus, see Mary Kaldor, *Global Civil Society: An Answer to War* (Cambridge: Polity, 2003); David Held, *Democracy and the Global Order* (Stanford: Stanford University Press, 1995); and Ulrick Beck, *What Is Globalization?* trans. Patrick Camiller (Oxford: Blackwell, 2000).
3. See Joseph Nye, *The Paradox of American Power: Why the World's Only Superpower Can't Go It Alone* (Oxford: Oxford University Press, 2002); and Robert Harvey, *Global Disorder: America and the Threat of World Conflict* (New York: Carroll and Graf, 2003).
4. Two influential examples that link capitalist democracy and U.S. hegemony are Thomas Friedman, *The Lexus and the Olive Tree* (New York: Anchor Books, 2000); and Francis Fukuyama, *The End of History and the Last Man* (New York: Free Press, 1992).
5. See the *National Security Strategy* document released by the White House in September 2002. One of the most widely discussed arguments for unilateral U.S. power is Robert Kagan, *Of Paradise and Power: America and Europe in the New World Order* (New York: Knopf, 2003).
6. Michael Hirsh, *At War with Ourselves: Why America Is Squandering Its Chance to Build a Better World* (Oxford: Oxford University Press, 2003), 254. Niall Ferguson, in contrast, celebrates the great benefits that the British Empire brought to the world and recommends that the United States today follow the British model. See *Empire: The Rise and Demise of the British World Order and the Lessons for Global Power* (New York: Basic Books, 2002).
7. For a coherent and impassioned critique of U.S. global hegemony from a conservative European perspective, see John Gray, *False Dawn* (New York: The New Press, 1998). Emmanuel Todd also insists on the social corruption of the United States and its inability to rule over the present globl order. See *Après l'empire: Essai sur la décomposition du système américain* (Paris: Gallimard, 2002).

8. See, for example, Patrick Buchanan, *A Republic, Not an Empire* (Washington DC: Regnery Publishing, 1999); and Patrick Buchanan, *The Death of the West* (New York: St. Martin's Press, 2002). For a rather different conservative U.S. argument against unilateralist U.S. actions abroad, see Clyde Prestowitz, *Rogue Nation: Unilaterialism and the Failure of Good Intentions* (New York: Basic Books, 2003).

9. See Fareed Zacharia, *The Future of Freedom: Illiberal Democracy at Home and Abroad* (New York: Norton, 2003).

10. On the "transition to democracy," one of the founding works is Guilhermo O'-Donnell, Philippe Schmitter, and Laurence Whitehead, eds., *Transitions from Authoritarianism* (Baltimore: Johns Hopkins University Press, 1986). For an analysis of the Spanish case as a model of transition, see Kenneth Maxwell, "Spain's Transition to Democracy: A Model for Eastern Europe?" in Nils Wassel, ed., *The New Europe: Revolution in East-West Relations* (New York: Academy of Political Science, 1991). For a general proposition of this model, see Zbigniew Brzezinski, "The Great Transformation," *The National Interest*, no. 33 (Fall 1993): 3–13; and Christiane Gauaud, "Recherches sur le phénomène de transition démocratique," *Revue de droit public et de la science politique* 107, no. 1 (February 1991).

11. See Roman Schnur, *Revolution und Weltbürgerkrieg* (Berlin: Duncker & Humblot, 1983).

12. Thucydides, *The Peloponnesian War*, bk 2, sec. 37, trans. Walter Blanco (New York: Norton, 1998), 73.

13. Spinoza, *Political Treatise*, chapter XI, paragraph 1.

14. See, for example, Hannah Arendt, *The Origins of Totalitarianism* (New York: Harcourt, Brace, 1951). For the classic articulations of the forms of government and their possible corruption, see Plato, *The Republic*, bks. 8, 9, trans. G. M. A. Grube (Indianapolis: Hackett, 1992), 213–63; and Aristotle, *Politics*, bks. 3, 4, trans. T. A. Sinclair (New York: Penguin, 1981), 189–190; 263–64.

15. It is not true, as some of the eighteenth-century revolutionaries such as James Madison claim, that political representation did not exist in the ancient world, but, as Franz Rosenzweig explains, there was certainly a radical redefinition of representation and a dramatic expansion of its role in modern political thought and practice. See Franz Rosenzweig, *The Star of Redemption*, trans. William Hallo (New York: Holt, Rinehart and Winston, 1970), 55.

16. See Giovanni Sartori, *Democratic Theory* (Detroit: Wayne State University Press, 1962). On the disjunctive synthesis, see Gilles Deleuze and Félix Guattari, *Anti-Oedipus*, trans. Robert Hurley, Mark Seem, and Helen Lane (Minneapolis: University of Minnesota Press, 1983), 9–16.

17. *The Social Contract*, bks. 3, ed. Lester Crocker (New York: Washington Square Press, 1967), 73.

18. *The Social Contract*, book 3, chapter 4, 71.

19. See Robert Derathé, *Jean-Jacques Rousseau et la science politique de son temps* (Paris: PUF, 1950).

20. *The Federalist*, no. 14, Madison, ed. Clinton Rossiter (New York: Penguin, 1961), 68.

21. See, for example, Thomas Paine, "Rights of Man," in *Basic Writings of Thomas Paine* (New York: Wiley, 1942), 168–72.

22. For the anti-Federalist arguments, see Herbert Storing, ed., *The Complete Anti-Federalist* (Chicago: University of Chicago Press, 1981).

23. *The Federalist*, no. 57, 318.

24. *Social Contract*, book 3, chapter 5, 73.

25. Joseph Nye, *The Paradox of American Power*, 109.

26. See Max Weber, *Economy and Society*, eds. Guenther Roth and Claus Wittich, 3 vols. (New York: Bedminster Press, 1968), 292–97.

27. See *The Federalist*, no. 54, 304–309.

28. Hans Kelsen claimed that this instructed form in which representatives are legally bound constantly to follow the will of the represented is the only valid form of representation. "There can be no doubt that . . . none of the existing democracies called "representative" are really representative" (*General Theory of Law and State*, trans. Anders Wedberg [Cambridge, MA: Harvard University Press, 1945], 298).

29. On the participatory budget process in Porto Alegre, see Luciano Fedozzi, *Orçamento participativo: Reflexões sobre a experiência de Porto Alegre* (Porto Alegre: Fase/IPPUR, 1999). For a brief account in English, see America Vera-Zavala, "Orçamento participativo in Porto Alegre," Znet commentary, January 22, 2003. www.zmag.org.

30. *The Adams-Jefferson Letters*, 2 vols. Lester Cappon, ed. (Chapel Hill: University of North Carolina Press, 1959), 1: 168, 173.

31. *Jefferson's Letters*, ed. Willson Whitman (Eau Claire, WI: Hale and Company, nd), 83. David McCullough recounts Abigail Adams's displeasure with Thomas Jefferson over Shays' Rebellion in *John Adams* (New York: Touchstone, 2001), 368–71. For a brief, useful historial analysis of Shays' Rebellion, see Howard Zinn, *A People's History of the United States* (New York: HarperCollins, 1980), 92–93.

32. See Charles Beard, *An Economic Interpretation of the Constitution of the United States* (New York: Macmillan, 1914).

33. Karl Marx, *Civil War in France: The Paris Commune* (New York: International Publishers), 57–58.

34. Karl Marx, *Civil War in France*, 65; and Lenin, *State and Revolution* (New York: International Publishers, 1988), 37, 41.

35. On the experiences of the Russian Soviets, see Oskar Anweiler, *Die Rätebewegung in Russland, 1905–1932* (Leiden, Holland: Brill, 1958). On worker councils as a model of democracy, see the activist assessments of Anton Pannekoek, "Massenaction und Revolution," *Die Neue Zeit* 2, no. 30 (1911–1912). Rosa Luxemburg also writes about the transformation of worker councils to become the basis of democracy. We should also point out that in addition to the Soviet constitution, the experience of worker councils was adopted as a model of enlarged parlamentarianism in both the Weimar constitution and the Austrian constitution after World War I. See Hans Kelsen, *Vom Wesen und Wert der Democratie*, 2nd ed. (Tübingen, Germany: Mohr, 1929).

36. Louis Aragon, "La nuit de Moscou," in *Le roman inachevé* (Paris: Gallimard, 1956), 231.

37. The anarchists were the most insistent in their refusal of all forms of authority, even those based on universal suffrage. See, for example, Michael Bakunin, *God and the State*, ed. Paul Arich (New York: Dover, 1970). The anarchists, however, do not manage to propose a new conception of representation or democracy.

38. On the feminist developments of the early Soviet period, see *Selected Writings of Alexandra Kollantai*, ed. Alix Holt (New York: Norton, 1977). On artistic innovations, see *The Great Utopia: The Russian and Soviet Avant-Garde, 1915–1932* (New York: Guggenheim Museum, 1992); and *Art into Life: Russian Constructivism, 1914–1932* (Seattle: Henry Art Gallery, 1990). On cinema, see Dziga Vertov, *Kino-eye* (Berkeley: University of California Press, 1984).

39. Eugeny Pashukanis, *The General Theory of Law and Marxism*, trans. Barbara Einhorn (New Brunswick, NJ: Transaction, 2002).

40. Louis Aragon, "La nuit de Moscou," 233.

41. Max Weber, *The Russian Revolutions*, trans. Gordon Wells and Peter Baehr (Cambridge: Polity, 1995).

42. Benno Sarel, *La class ouvrière d'Allemagne orientale (1945–1958)* (Paris: Editions ouvrières, 1958).

43. "A New Power in the Streets," *New York Times*, February 17, 2003.

44. James Bryce, *The American Commonwealth*, 3rd ed. (New York: Macmillan, 1985), 2:258–9. For a useful intellectual biography of Bryce, see Hugh Tul-

loch, *James Bryce's American Commonwealth* (Wolfeboro, NH: Boydell Press, 1988).

45. Gustave Le Bon, *The Crowd*, 49. For a similar view of the irrational and homogeneous mass behavior of crowds, see Elias Canetti, *Crowds and Power*, trans. Carol Steward (London: Victor Gallancz, 1962).

46. On panic, see Jean-Pierre Dupuy, *La panique* (Paris: Les empêcheurs de penser en rond, 1991).

47. We should keep in mind, however, that Hegel's notion of "Burgerliche Gesellschaft" should not be translated as "civil society," as is traditional, but rather as "bourgeois society." Johannes Agnoli makes this point in *Ueberlegungen zum burgerlichen Staat* (Berlin: Klaus Wagenbach, 1975), 60–111. The term *civil society* derives from the Scottish moral philosophers who were among the founders of political economy. Hegel read their work and transcribed it into his own idiom, powerfully transforming it, the same way Habermas, for example, transcribes "public opinion" into "public sphere."

48. On Jürgen Habermas's interpretation of Hegel's concept of civil society as interaction, see "Arbeit und Interaktion: Bemerkungen zu Hegels Jenenser Philosophie des Geiste," in Habermas, *Technik und Wissenschaft als "Ideologie"* (Frankfurt: Suhrkamp, 1968). See also Jürgen Habermas, *The Structural Transformation of the Public Sphere*, trans. Thomas Burger (Cambridge: Polity, 1989); and *The Theory of Communicative Action*, trans. Thomas McCarthy, 2 vols. (Boston: Beacon, 1984, 1987). On Habermas's notion of the public sphere, see Craig Calhoun, ed., *Habermas and the Public Sphere* (Cambridge, MA: MIT Press, 1992).

49. See Niklas Luhmann, *Essays on Self-Reference* (New York: Columbia University Press, 1990); and *The Reality of Mass Media*, trans. Kathleen Cross (Cambridge, Polity, 2000).

50. George Gallup, "Polls and the Political Process—Past, Present, and Future," *Public Opinion Quarterly* (Winter 1965–1966): 549.

51. See Robert McChesney, *Rich Media, Poor Democracy* (Urbana: University of Illinois Press, 1999). On the centralization of the U.S. media sources and the distortion of information that results from it, see the annual publications of Project Censored, such as Peter Phillips, ed., *Censored 2004* (New York: Seven Stories Press, 2003).

52. See Douglas Kellner, "Media Propaganda and Spectacle in the War on Iraq" in Y. R. Kamalipour and N. Snow, eds., *War, Media, and Propaganda: A Global Perspective* (Boulder, CO: Rowman and Littlefield, forthcoming); and more

generally, Noam Chomsky and Edward Herman, *Manufacturing Consent*, 2nd ed. (New York: Pantheon, 2002).

53. On the public psychology of political opinions, beliefs, and perceptions, see the work of Murray Edelman, such as *Politics as Symbolic Action: Mass Arousal and Quiescence* (New York: Academic Press, 1971).

54. Right-wing politicians and scholars in the United States lament what they see as the liberal bias of the mainstream media and its manipulation of public opinion. See, for example, Matthew Robinson, *Mobocracy: How the Media's Obsession with Polling Twists the News, Alters Elections, and Undermines Democracy* (Roseville, CA: Forum, 2002). There are also numerous books by left-wing journalists and scholars that counter that the mainstream media is not liberal but conservative. See, for example, Eric Alterman, *What Liberal Media? The Truth about Bias and the News* (New York: Basic Books, 2003); and Edward Herman, *The Myth of the Liberal Media* (New York: Peter Lang, 1999).

55. See David Morley and Kuan-Hsing Chen, *Stuart Hall: Critical Dialogues in Cultural Studies* (New York: Routledge, 1996).

56. For a description of the "social centers" in Italy, see Naomi Klein, *Fences and Windows: Dispatches from the Front Lines of the Globalization Debate* (New York: Picador, 2002), 224–27.

57. For a useful summary of grievances across the world, see Samir Amin and François Houtart, eds., *Mondialisation des résistances: L'état des luttes* (Paris: L'Harmattan, 2002).

58. The literature on the 2000 U.S. presidential election is voluminous and growing. For an excellent analysis that focuses on the role of the media and the dangers it poses for democracy, see Douglas Kellner, *Grand Theft 2000: Media Spectacle and a Stolen Election* (Lanham, MD: Rowman and Littlefield, 2001). For legal perspectives, see Bruce Ackermann, ed., *Bush v. Gore: The Question of Legitimacy* (New Haven: Yale University Press, 2003).

59. Media corporations are a particularly significant case, since, as we saw earlier with respect to public opinion, the media assume the task of representing and giving voice to the people. Grievances of bias or lack of representation in the media are indeed omnipresent. The "girotondi" movement in Italy, for example, protests the distortion of the state media networks and the collusion between them and Prime Minister Berlusconi's own vast private media holdings, which together form a quasi-monopoly of Italian media.

60. For a brief summary of grievances against the IMF and World Bank, see Robert Weissman, "Why We Protest," *Washington Post*, September 10, 2001.

61. For a critique of human rights discourses from a feminist perspective, with particular attention to subaltern populations, see Gayatri Spivak, "Righting Wrongs" in Nicholas Owen, ed., *Human Rights, Human Wrongs* (Oxford: Oxford University Press, 2003), 164–227.

62. On the philosophical foundations of human rights, see Thomas Keenan, *Fables of Responsibility* (Stanford: Stanford University Press, 1997); and Claude Lefort, "Droits de l'homme et politique," in *L'invention démocratique* (Paris: Fayard, 1981), 45–83.

63. See Alejandro Diago, *Hebe: Memoria y Esperanza* (Buenos Aires: Ediciones Dialectica, 1988).

64. See Mariano-Florentino Cuéllar, "The International Criminal Court and the Political Economy of Antitreaty Discourse," *Stanford Law Review* 55, no. 5 (May 2003): 1597–1632.

65. Ugo Mattei, "A Theory of Imperial Law: A Study on U.S. Hegemony and the Latin Renaissance," *Indiana Journal of Global Legal Studies* 10 no. 1. (Winter 2003): 383–448. See also, Susan Marks, "Empire's Law" in the same issue of *Indiana Journal of Global Legal Studies*, 449–66.

66. On the question of imperial justice, see Nicole Loraux's beautiful historical reconstruction of the amnesty in Athens in 403 BC, the first amnesty in history, *La cité divisé* (Paris: Payot, 1997). The return of the rebels to Athens redefines the city not as an organic unity, as Plato would have it, but rather as a site of creative conflict. The tribunals, the definitions of rights, and the city institutions cannot rely on any eternal notion of human rights but must directly confront and address this conflict.

67. The World Bank, *Attacking Poverty* (Oxford: Oxford University Press, 2001), 3.

68. Ibid., 3, 23.

69. See *Breaking the Chains: The New Jubilee Debt Cutter's Handbook* (London: Jubilee 2000 Plus, 1999). See also the Jubilee Research Web site: www.jubilee2000uk.org.

70. See Yann Moulier-Boutang, *De l'esclavage au salariat* (Paris: PUF, 1998).

71. See Kavaljit Singh, *Taming Global Financial Flows* (London: Zed, 2000).

72. It is easy to see why many consider financial markets a kind of casino capitalism with high-stakes gambling—you can bet on derivatives of almost anything, but one should also recognize that many also use derivatives as an insurance policy to mitigate risk. For example, of a price fall of the commodity they will sell or a price rise of one they must buy.

73. See Christian Marazzi, *E il denaro va* (Turin, Italy: Bollati Boringhieri, 1998).

74. See Arundhati Roy's passionate diatribe, "The Greater Common Good," in *The Cost of Living* (New York: Modern Library, 1999), 1–90. On the protests against big dams througout the world, see Patrick McCully, *Silenced Rivers: The Ecology and Politics of Large Dams* (London: Zed, 1996), 281–311.

75. One proposed solution to the conflict between the need for medicine and patent laws is "compulsory licensing," which would allow governments to grant a licence to a generic domestic or foreign producer when deemed necessary. See Aditi Bagchi, "Compulsory Licensing and the Duty of Good Faith in TRIPS," *Stanford Law Review* 55, no. 5 (May 2003): 1529–55.

76. Michel Foucault, "What Is Enlightenment?" in *The Essential Works of Michel Foucault*, vol. 1, *Ethics*, ed. Paul Rabinow (New York: New Press, 1997), 303–319.

77. See Starhawk, "How We Really Shut Down the WTO" and "Making It Real: Initiation Instructions, Seattle '99," in *Webs of Power: Notes From the Global Uprising* (Gabriola Island, Canada: New Society Publishers, 2002), 16–20, 25–28.

78. On the Jamaica protests against the IMF, see the documentary film *Life and Debt* (2001), directed by Stephanie Black. For a list of protests against the IMF in the global south, see Jessica Woodroffe and Mark Ellis-Jones, "States of Unrest: Resistance to IMF Policies in Poor Countries," in the newsletter *World Development Movement Report* (London, September 2000).

79. See Jeffrey St. Clair, "Seattle Diary: It's a Gas, Gas, Gas," *New Left Review*, no. 238 (November–December 1999): 81–96.

80. See Mike Moore's personal description of the successful path of the WTO from Seattle to Doha, *A World Without Walls: Freedom, Development, Free Trade and Global Governance* (Cambridge: Cambridge University Press, 2003).

81. The articles that Naomi Klein wrote as she traveled among the various globalization protest movements give a beautiful picture of their commonality and coherence. See *Fences and Windows: Dispatches from the Front Lines of the Globalization Debate* (New York: Picador, 2002).

82. Social democrats (ever since the famous Bernstein debate) have insisted on the contradiction between reform and revolution, emphasizing the reasonableness of the former and the absurdity of the latter. Today social democratic positions of the "third way" in Britain, expressed with some original ideas by Anthony Giddens and then in impoverished form by Tony Blair supporters, believe to have moved beyond this traditional binary, since they view revolution as completely discredited in the contemporary world. Blair's enthusiasm for participation in the 2003 Iraq War demonstrates clearly the bankruptcy of the third way.

83. For an excellent summary of numerous global reform proposals, see Heikki Patomäki, Teivo Teivainen, and Mika Rönkkö, *Global Democracy Initiatives* (Helsinki: NIGD, 2002). See also Robin Broad, ed., *Global Backlash: Citizen Initiatives for a Just World Economy* (Lanham, MD: Rowman and Littlefield, 2002) and William Fisher and Thomas Ponniah, eds., *Another World Is Possible: Popular Alternatives to Globalization at the World Social Forum* (London: Zed Books, 2003).

84. See, for example, Robert Keohane and Joseph Nye, "The Club Model of Multilateral Cooperation and Problems of Democratic Legitimacy," in Keohane, *Power and Governance in a Partially Globalized World* (New York: Routledge, 2002), 219–44.

85. See Joseph Stiglitz, *Globalization and Its Discontents*, 89–132 and 229–41.

86. We are indebted to Craig Borowiak for his analyses of the concept of accountability in the contemporary globalization discussions.

87. See, for example, Kevin Danaher, *10 Reasons to Abolish the IMF & World Bank* (New York: Seven Stories Press, 2001); Kevin Danaher, ed., *50 Years Is Enough: The Case Against the World Bank and the International Monetary Fund* (Boston: South End Press, 1994); and Lori Wallach and Michelle Sforza, *Whose Trade Organization? Corporate Globalization and the Erosion of Democracy* (Washington, DC: Public Citizen, 1999).

88. See Joseph Camilleri et al., *Reimagining the Future: Towards Democratic Governance.*

89. Cite South Centre, *For a Strong and Democratic United Nations* (London: Zed Books, 1997).

90. Harry Shutt also emphasizes that in order to reform the UN system to be more democratic, the lack of real sovereignty of the vast majority of the member nations must be addressed. See Harry Shutt, *A New Democracy: Alternatives to a Bankrupt World Order* (London: Zed, 2001), 91–95, 136–39.

91. See, for example, Richard Falk and Andrew Strauss, "Bridging the Globalization Gap: Toward Global Parliament," *Foreign Affairs* 80, no. 1 (January–February, 2001): 212–20.

92. James Madison, *The Federalist Papers*, no. 56, ed. Clinton Rossiter (New York: Penguin, 1961), 318.

93. See Heikki Patomäki, Teivo Teivainen, and Mika Rönkkö, *Global Democracy Initiatives* (Helsinki: NIGD, 2002), 113–29.

94. See Ingolf Pernice, "Multilevel Constitutionalism in the European Union," *European Law Review* 27, no. 5 (October 2002): 511–529.

95. See Michael Sharf, "The Case for a Permanent International Truth Commission," *Duke Journal of Comparative and International Law* 7, no. 2 (Spring 1997): 375–410. See also, Heikki Patomäki, Teivo Teivainen, and Mika Rönkkö, *Global Democracy Initiatives*, 131–38.

96. See Margaret Stetz and Bonnie B. C. Oh, eds., *Legacies of the Comfort Women of World War II* (Armonk, NY: M. E. Sharpe, 2001).

97. Dakar Declaration, January 22–24, 2001, Recommendation #3. On the question of reparation to descendants of slaves in the United States, see Raymond Winbush, ed., *Should America Pay? Slavery and the Raging Debate over Reparations* (New York: Amistad, 2003).

98. On the erosion of civil liberties in the United States, see Michael Ratner, "Making Us Less Free: War on Terror or War on Justice?" in Stanley Aronowitz and Heather Gautney, eds., *Implicating Empire* (New York: Basic Books, 2002), 47–64; Richard Leone and Greg Anrig Jr., eds., *The War on Our Freedoms: Civil Liberties in the Age of Terrorism* (New York: Public Affairs, 2003); and Cynthia Brown, ed., *Lost Liberties: Ashcroft and the Assault on Personal Freedom* (New York: The New Press, 2003). On the growing pattern of U.S. rejection of international treaties, see Jonathan Greenberg, "Does Power Trump Law?" *Stanford Law Review* 55, no. 5, (May 2003): 1789–1820, especially pp. 1814–18.

99. The World Bank, for example, suggests combating poverty with strategies such as making state institutions more responsive to poor people and removing social barriers within national societies. See the World Bank, *Attacking Poverty*. For a critique of the World Bank reports on poverty, see Paul Cammack, "Attacking the Poor," *New Left Review*, 2nd ser., no. 13 (January–February 2002): 125–34.

100. See Joseph Stiglitz, "Dealing with Debt: How to Reform the Global Financial System," *Harvard International Review* 25, no. 1 (Spring 2003): 54–59; Kunibert Raffer, "What's Good for the United States Must Be Good for the World: Advocating an International Chapter 9 Insolvency," in *From Cancun to Vienna: International Development in a New World* (Vienna: Bruno Kreisky Forum, 1993), 64–74; and Ann Pettifor, "Resolving International Debt Crises—The Jubilee Framework for International Insolvency," http://www.jubilee2000uk.org/analysis/reports/jubilee=_framework.html.

101. Ignacio Ramonet, "Désarmer les marchés," *Le monde diplomatique* (December 1997): 1.

102. See Heikki Patomäki, Teivo Teivainen, and Mika Rönkkö, *Global Democracy Initiatives*, 161–78.

103. Lawrence Lessig makes a similar recommendation in *The Future of Ideas*, 249–61.

104. See Jessica Litman, "War Stories," *Cardozo Arts and Entertainment Law Journal* 20 (2002): 337–59.

105. See Richard Stallman, *Free Software, Free Society* (Cambridge, MA: Free Software Society, 2002).

106. "Copyleft" is a similar alternative in which the choices are fixed: works can be reproduced for noncommercial use on the condition that the author is credited. On the Creative Commons, see Lawrence Lessig, *Free Culture* (New York: Penguin, 2004). See also the organization's Web site, www.creativecommons.org.

107. For a brief description of the creation of Indymedia at the 1999 WTO protests in Seattle, see Eric Galatas, "Building Indymedia," in Peter Philips, ed., *Censored 2001*, 331–35. See also Ana Nogueira, "The Birth and Promise of the Indymedia Revolution," in Benjamin Shepard and Ronald Hayduk, eds., *From ACT UP to the WTO* (London: Verso, 2002), 290–97. On the tradition of alternative media, see Robert Hackett, "Taking Back the Media: Notes on the Potential for a Communicative Democracy Movement," *Studies in Political Economy*, no. 62 (Fall 2000): 61–86. On earlier U.S. media reform movements, such as the struggle in the 1930s against the commercialization of radio, see Robert McChesney, *Telecommunication, Mass Media, and Democracy* (Oxford: Oxford University Press, 1993), 252–70.

108. Foucault, "Cours du 7 janvier 1976," *Dits et écrits*, vol. III (Paris: Gallimard, 1994), 160–74. It is no coincidence that the neoconservative thought that drives the foreign policy of the Bush administration is based on a similarly radical project. The neoconservatives in Washington today, in fact, seem to subscribe to the revolutionary epistemology of Paris poststructuralists of the 1960s. The policy of preemptive strikes, the practice of regime change, and the project to remake the political map of the world in accordance with their vision is an affirmation of their will to power that discards any slave logics. Just as French philosophers revealed the revolutionary face of Nietzsche's thought, these neoconservatives return to its reactionary face, with their confident assertion of aristocratic virtues and master logics at a global level. On the reactionary face of Nietzsche's thought, see Domenico Losurdo, *Nietzsche: L'aristocratico ribelle* (Turin, Italy: Bollati Borringhieri, 2002).

109. See C. B Macpherson, *The Political Theory of Possessive Individualism: Hobbes to Locke* (Oxford: Clarendon, 1962).

110. One contribution to this new science is Arjun Appadurai's study of the horizontal articulation of activist movements in Mumbai, which he sees as the basis for an expansive conception of democracy, a deep democracy without borders. See "Deep Democracy: Urban Governmentality and the Horizon of Politics," *Public Culture* 14, no. 1 (Spring 2002): 21–47.

111. See *Empire*, 260–79.

112. See Silvia Ronchey, *Lo stato bizantino* (Turin, Italy: Einaudi, 2002); and Hélène Ahrweiler, *L'idéologie politique de l'Empire Byzantin* (Paris: Presses universitaires de France, 1975).

113. See, for example, Gerhart Ladner, "The Concept of the Image in the Greek Fathers and the Byzantine Iconoclastic Controversy," *Dumbarton Oaks Papers*, no. 7, (Cambridge, MA: Harvard University Press, 1953), 1–34.

114. John of Damascus, *On the Divine Images*, trans. David Anderson (New York: St. Vladimire's Seminary Press, 1980).

115. See Rudolf Stammler, *Wirtschaft und Recht nach der materialistischen Geschichtsauffassung* (Liepzig: Veit, 1896). For a proposal of natural law in the early twentieth century, see Leo Strauss, *Natural Right and History* (Chicago: Chicago University Press, 1953). Max Weber's ferocious attacks were not enough to free twentieth-century European legal philosophy from repeating these Platonic rituals. See *Economy and Society*, especially part 1.

116. On the frontispiece to Hobbes's *Leviathan*, see Carl Schmitt, *The Leviathan in the State Theory of Thomas Hobbes* (Westport, CT: Greenwood, 1996), chapter 2.

117. See Carl Schmitt, *Political Theology*, trans. George Schwab (Cambridge, MA: MIT Press, 1985). The work of Helmut Schelsky, and later that of A. Gehlen, directly criticized Schmitt's interpretation of Hobbes and his notion of political theology. But even cleaned up of its theological elements, their mechanistic philosophies of the power of action repeated much of Schmitt's thinking. See Helmut Schelsky, "Die Totalität des Staates bei Hobbes," *Archiv für Recht- und Sozialphilosophie*, xxxv (1937–38): 176–93. The U.S. neoconservatives today similarly base their claims on the exceptional power of the U.S. global monarchy and its actions in the defense of liberty. They thus expand the theory enormously with the goal of realizing *urbi et orbi*, the U.S. social constitutional model, projecting it, in other words, toward a totalitarian celebration of power. See the White House *National Security Strategy* document of September 2002. As in Hobbes and Schmitt, here too the lan-

guage of sovereign unity is legitimated by and mixed with a conception of political theology. Casting itself as realistic—but this is a realism that has nothing to do with Machiavelli but is instead mere raison d'etat—neoconservative discourse considers globalization a project of domination, citizenship and the state as indivisibly united, patriotism as the highest virtue, and the national interest as paramount, denouncing the reluctance of their liberal critics to accept their global and totalitarian projects. To the extent that Leo Strauss is an intellectual point of reference for these neoconservatives, one might have suspected such a development after having read Strauss's book on Spinoza, in which he gives a nihilistic interpretation of the ontology, a skeptical reading of ethics, and a cold reception of prophetic Judaism. It is an interpretation remarkably close to Schmitt's reading of Hobbes.

118. See Joseph Schumpeter, *Business Cycles* (New York: McGraw-Hill, 1939). For Schumpeter's theory of crisis, see also "The Analysis of Economic Change," *Review of Economic Statistics* 17, (May 1935): 2–10; and "Theoretical Problems of Economic Growth," *Journal of Economic History* 7 (November 1947): 1–9.

119. See Antonio Damasio, *Looking for Spinoza: Joy, Sorrow, and the Feeling Brain* (New York: Harcourt, 2003).

120. Eric Raymond, *The Cathedral and the Bazaar* (Sebastopol, CA: O'Reilly, 1999). For another technology-based analysis of how people are increasingly able to create collaboratively in networks, see Howard Rheingold, *Smart Mobs* (New York: Basic, 2002).

121. Thomas Hobbes, *On the Citizen*, trans. Richard Tuck and Michael Siverthorne (Cambridge: Cambridge University Press, 1998), chapter 14.

122. Gilles Deleuze and Claire Parnet, *Dialogues II*, trans. Hugh Tomlinson and Barbara Habberjam (New York: Columbia University Press, 2002), 136, translation modified.

123. Ward Churchill argues against pacifist politics but assumes that the only alternative to pacifism is armed struggle in traditional form. Our point here is that these are not the only options. See Ward Churchill, *Pacifism as Pathology* (Winnipeg: Arbeiter Ring Publishing, 1999).

124. See Subcomandante Marcos and Yvon Le Bot, *Le rêve zapatiste* (Paris: Seuil, 1997).

125. André Malraux, *Antimémoires* (Paris: Gallimard, 1967), 315.

126. William Shakespeare, *Julius Caesar*, act 2, scene 2.

127. Much of the contemporary legal scholarship in the Second Amendment moves between an individual-rights position, which protects individual gun

ownership for various purposes, and a collective or states'-rights position, which focuses on the militia aimed at protecting the autonomy of states. See Carl Bogus, ed., *The Second Amendment in Law and History* (New York: The New Press, 2000). On the source of the amendment in English law, see Joyce Lee Malcolm, *To Keep and Bear Arms* (Cambridge, MA: Harvard University Press, 1994).

128. Walter Benjamin, "Critique of Violence," in *Reflections*, ed. Peter Demetz, trans. Edmund Jephcott (New York: Schocken, 1978), 277–300.

129. See Michael Walzer, *Just and Unjust Wars* (New York: Basic Books, 1977; 2000); and Jean Bethke Elshtain, *Just War Against Terror* (New York: Basic Books, 2003), 46–70.

130. Leon Trotsky, *The History of the Russian Revolution*, trans. Max Eastman (Ann Arbor: University of Michigan Press, 1932), 184.

131. Starhawk makes a similar point, arguing that we need a "diversity of tactics." See "Many Roads to Morning: Rethinking Nonviolence," in *Webs of Power*, 206–36.

132. It is unclear in Slavoj Žižek's provocative book *Repeating Lenin* (Zabreb: Arkzin, 2001) whether he is advocating repeating, as we are, the democratic goals of Lenin's project without the vanguard leadership of the Bolshevik Party or whether he is, on the contrary, advocating just such an elitist form of political leadership.

133. Clarisse Lispector, *The Passion according to G. H.*, trans. Ronald Sousa (Minneapolis: University of Minnesota Press, 1988), 3.

134. Shakespeare, *Julius Caesar*, act 4, scene 3.

ACKNOWLEDGMENTS

It would be impossible here to thank all of those who helped us in the course of writing this book. We would like simply to acknowledge those who read the entire manuscript and gave us comments: Naomi Klein, Scott Moyers, Judith Revel, and Kathi Weeks.

INDEX

Page numbers beginning with 359 refer to notes.

Aaron (brother of Moses), 342
abortion, 202
absolute democracy, 90–91, 221, 240, 242, 311, 330, 348, 351
abstract labor, 144–45
Acção Libertadora Nacional, 81
accountability, 290–91, 308
accounting methods, 148–49
ACT-UP, 184, 191
Adams, Abigail, 247, 248, 249
affective labor, 108, 110–11, 147, 150
affirmative action, 273
Afghanistan, 23, 39, 47, 49, 52, 60, 83, 177, 179, 320, 344
AFL-CIO, 288
Africa, 72, 73, 119, 126, 213, 253, 278, 315
African Americans, 47, 81, 297
African Ministers, 297
African National Congress (ANC), 84, 372
Agamben, Giorgio, 359, 364
agriculture, 114
    capitalism and, 118–19
    collectivization of, 117–18, 120
    genetic modification in, 183–84
    Marxist analysis and, 141
    plant genetics in, 112–13, 115, 183
    production, 112, 115–16, 118, 120
    socialist modernization of, 117
    subsistence, 120
    trade policies and, 321
    workers in, 109–10, 112, 116, 120, 349, 376
air pollution, 282
Albright, Madeleine, 8–9
alienation, 111
al-Qaeda, 26, 47, 48, 89, 218
Amazon region, 132
American Commonwealth (Bryce), 259
American Revolution, 78
amnesty, 397
analytical tasks, 108
anarchists, 86, 222, 250
anarchy, 162, 208, 329, 331, 336
ANC, *see* African National Congress
animal species, 131–32
Annan Doctrine, 27
annihilation, 18–19
antagonism, 141, 150, 153, 212

anthropological transformation, 199
anthropology, 122, 125–26, 127, 379
Anti-Ballistic Missile Treaty, 38, 39
antinuclear pacifism, 362
anti-sciences, 309
anti-Semitism, 40, 104, 274
antitrust laws, 172
apartheid/Apartheid, 84, 166–67, 174, 214
appropriated representation, 245, 247
Aragon, Louis, 252
Arendt, Hannah, 78, 359
Argentina, 137, 174, 175, 216–17, 246, 274, 275, 291, 318
aristocracy, 240, 242, 244, 328–29
armed forces, see military
Armed Insurrection (Neuberg), 369–70
Arthur Andersen, 178
artificial intelligence, 91
artificial language, 147
Asia, 72, 73, 119, 165, 174, 213, 278, 291, 315, 317, 318
asymmetrical conflicts, 51, 368
Athens, 397
ATTAC, 300
Augustine of Hippo, 196
Australia, 273
Autonomia, 82
"axis of evil," 317

Baal Shem, Elijah, 10
Babel, Isaak, 70
bacteria, 182
Bakhtin, Mikhail, 208–10, 211
Balkan region, 32
bankruptcy, 299–300
Baroque, 186
Bartov, Omer, 366
Becker, Gary, 157
Beirut, 49
Benjamin, Walter, 344
Berlin revolt (1953), 255–58
big government, 176–79
Bin Laden, Osama, 26, 27, 31, 47, 49
biodiversity, 131–32
biopolitical grievances, 282–85
biopolitical labor, 109, 148
biopolitical production, xvi, 94–95, 187, 308, 334, 336, 355
  affective labor as, 110
  common and, 207

communication as central to, 263
  guerrilla warfare and, 81
  as immeasurable yet excessive, 146
  of multitude, 101, 348, 350
  new properties of value in, 148
  poor and, 130
  of subjectivity, 78
biopolitical reforms, 303–6
biopolitics, 78, 109, 356, 357
  agricultural, 116
  class and, 105
  multitude and, 349
  see also biopolitical production
biopower, 44, 135, 161, 356, 357
  concept of the common and, 206
  full-spectrum dominance, 53
  ontological limit of, 54
  population control as, 166
  security and, 18–25
  sovereignty as, 334–35
  violence of, 355
  war as regime of, 13, 39, 94
bioproperty, 181–82, 185
Birmingham School, 263
Black Panthers, 77, 81, 213, 343–44
Blair, Tony, 233, 398
Bodin, Jean, 330
body, human, 199, 330, 337
body politic, see political body
Boeing, 40
Bolivia, 119
Bolshevik revolution, 74, 345
borders, 314, 323
Borges, Jorge Luis, 269
brain, 337, 338
Brazil, 81, 125, 165, 247, 280, 292, 315, 318, 321
Brecht, Bertolt, 36, 268
Bretton Woods conference (1944), 173
bricoleur, 50
Brothers Karamazov, The (Dostoyevsky), 210
Bryce, James, 259, 262
Budyenny, Semyon, 70
Buffon, Count de, 195
Bush, George H. W., administration of, 24, 43
Bush, George W., administration of, 24, 43, 235, 304, 401
Butler, Judith, 199–200
Byzantine Empire, 324–26, 327

INDEX

Caesar, Julius, 36
cahiers de doléances, 269
California, University of, 182–83
Cambodia, 28, 57, 83
Camus, Albert, 383
Canada, 273
capital:
  big government and, 177
  definition of, 146
  finance, 151, 280–81
  global, 234, 279
  labor and, 103, 104, 147, 333, 335
  management of, 254
  Marx on, 64
  mobility of, 279
  state regulation of, 300
  see also money
Capital (Marx), 64, 141
capitalism:
  agriculture and, 118–19
  innovation and, 331
  "late," 53
  Marx on, 64, 65, 103, 104
  multitude and, 106–7
  peasant revolts in response to, 69
  poor and, 130
  production under, 144–45, 146
  property law based on labor, 186–87
  socialism as form of, 257
  transition to socialism and guerrilla
    warfare, 73
  unregulated, 167, 235–36
capitalist globalization, 101, 164, 167, 277
Caribbean region, 213
caring labor, 110
Carlisle, Thomas, 157
carnevalesque settings, 210, 211, 265, 347
Castro, Fidel, 74, 75
Céline, Louis-Ferdinand, 43
Central America, 57
Cervantes, Miguel de, 210
charity work, 279
Chicago School of economics, 155, 157
Chile, 275
China, 71, 116, 117, 123–24, 130, 253,
  272, 316, 317, 318, 376, 380
  Cultural Revolution in, 76–77, 81, 124
Chomsky, Noam, 362
Christianity, 351
Churchill, Ward, 363, 403

Churchill, Winston, 27–28
Cicero, 3
Cincinnatus, 7
civic organizations, 190
civil disobedience, 266
civilizations, 34–35, 240, 294–95,
  365–66
civil law, 340
civil liberties, 298
civil rights, 273
civil society, 260, 295, 395
civil war, 6, 238–39, 240
  concepts of, 370
  definition of, 3
  English, 5, 238, 239
  global, 7, 341
  imperial, 4, 37
  in modernity, 69–72, 89
  revolutionary, 73
  Soviet, 70
  Spanish, 74
  telluric concept of, 72
  world, 359
clash of civilizations, 34–35
class, 104–5
  conflict, 78
  dangerous classes, 15, 103–57
  economic, 104, 105
  global, xvii
  relations, 105
  social, 103
  socioeconomic, 224
  struggle, 80, 90, 104, 105, 257, 265
  see also working class
Clastres, Pierre, 90
Clausewitz, Carl von, 6, 12, 22, 47, 48, 71
climate, 304
clinamen, 357
Clinton, Bill, 24, 43, 287
cognitive labor, 108
cold war, 24, 33–34, 38, 55, 231, 232, 239,
  352
collaboration, 147, 148, 152, 159, 186, 187,
  198, 200, 201
collateral damage, 45
collectivization, 117–18, 120
Colombia, 83, 89
colonialism, 119
"comfort women," 297
commodities, 280

common, 156, 188, 206, 303, 310
  biopolitical production and, 207
  communication and, 204, 213, 349, 350
  global, 208, 212
  intensification of, 213
  international law and, 207, 208
  labor and, xv–xvi, 103–15, 148, 222, 223,
    338, 349
  law for control over, 202
  legal theory based on, 204
  mobilization of, 211–19
  multitude and, xv, 127, 135, 208, 224,
    339, 348–49
  political construction, 204
  production of, 189, 196–202, 204, 212,
    222, 308, 348–50, 358
  singularity and, 125, 128–29, 135, 198,
    204, 208, 308, 349
common interest, 206
commons, xv, 186
communication, 186, 187
  common and, 204, 213, 349, 350
  common social being and, 159
  democratic system of, 305
  ethical, 261
  global means of, 304
  of ideas, 311
  immaterial labor and, 108, 113, 114
  immaterial production and, 147, 152
  innovation and, 337, 338
  linguistic community in, 201
  Marx's view of, 123
  multitude's production of, 339
  networks and, 142
  performance and, 200
  production and, 148, 185, 197, 198, 263,
    349
  social, 198, 222
  among struggles, 214, 216
  subjectivity produced through, 189
  of swarm, 91
  of Zapatistas, 85
communism, Communists, 55, 76, 123,
    221, 232, 250–53, 281–82, 383
community, 204
community organizations, 190
computers, 115, 147, 180, 373
  software, 301–2, 339–40
  see also Internet
condottieri, 49

Conrad, Joseph, 58
conservative traditional-values arguments,
    235–36
constitution, global, 296
Constitution, U.S., 243, 295, 343
  Second Amendment of, 343
constitutionalism, 160, 161, 273
constitution of subjectivity, 141
construction work, 255
cooperation, 113, 123, 142, 147, 186, 189,
    311, 339, 349–50
copyright, 181, 301–2
corporations, 270–71
  contracts between, 175
  global, 286
  globalization and, 168–69
  lex mercatoria and, 170
  media, 264, 305, 396
  multinational, 277, 320
  pharmaceutical, 284
  resemblance to public institutions, 168
  software owned by, 301–2
  transnational, 233
corruption, 8, 48, 50, 51, 174, 178–79, 235,
    298, 352, 353, 354
Cortés, Juan Donoso, 254
cosmopolitan democracy, 234
counterinsurgency, 36–62, 72, 78, 203, 368
counterpower, 90
craft work, 190
creation myths, 10
Creative Commons project, 302
creativity, 185
Crime and Punishment (Dostoyevsky), 210
crimes against humanity, 28, 29, 275
crisis:
  of democracy, 231–37, 352, 353
  economic, 154, 156, 319
  in era of armed globalization, 231–37
  of geopolitics, 313–15
  of representation, 352, 364
Croats, 32
crowds, 100, 260
Crozier, Michel, 33
cruel and unusual punishment, 19
Crusades, 15, 344
Cuba, 74–76, 77, 81, 253, 342
Cultural Revolution, 76–77, 81, 124
cultural studies, 263
culture, 334

currency, 172, 216, 280, 281, 319
currency transaction tax, 300–301
cybernetics, *see* computers; Internet
cycle of revolts, 213–17
Czechoslovakia, 344

dams, 282–83, 377
dangerous classes, 15, 103–57
Darstellung, 64, 67
Dassault aviation, 40
data banks, 180
Davos, 167, 176
debt, 248–49, 279, 299–300, 319, 321
decapitation model, 57
decision-making, 338–40, 351, 354, 357, 369
De Cive (Hobbes), xvii
defenestration of Prague, 4
defense, 20–21
defense transformation, *see* revolution in military affairs
Deleuze, Gilles, 158, 196, 342
democracy, 68, 74, 77, 93–94, 229–358
    absolute, 90–91, 221, 240, 242, 311, 330, 348, 351
    concepts of, 232, 237, 238, 240, 241, 243, 251, 307, 329
    in context of violence, 341–45
    cosmopolitan, 234
    crisis of, 231–37, 352, 353
    desire for, 67, 88, 355, 358
    eighteenth-century, 307
    of everyone, 240, 241
    global, xi, xvi, 268–312, 356
    Huntington on, 33
    long march of, 231–67
    of multitude, 67, 312, 328–58
    new science of, 348–58
    Nye on, 245
    offered by guerrilla movements, 75–76
    as radicalization, 220
    representation and, 244–45, 393
    resistance and, 87–88
    of socialism, 249–55
    sovereignty and, 328–40
    as unfinished project of modernity, 237–47
    in U.S., 33, 235
    war and, xi, 17–18
    of workers, 257–58

democratic transitions, 179
demography, 165
denationalization, 163
deprivation, 212
derivatives, financial, 280–81, 397
Derrida, Jacques, 361
de Sade, Marquis, xiii
Desai, Ashwin, 135
Descartes, René, 143–44, 238
Devils, The (Dostoyevsky), 139
Dewey, John, 3, 18, 198–99, 200
D'Holbach, Baron, 195
dialogue, 209, 210, 211
dictatorship, 26, 329, 330
Diderot, Denis, 195, 269
differences, as enemy of the people, 243
diplomacy from above, 303
diplomacy from below, 266, 303
Discourse on Method (Descartes), 143
disjunctive synthesis, 241, 244
disobedience, 266, 340
distributed networks, 54–55, 57, 58–59, 62, 86, 88, 89, 91, 93, 113, 115, 211, 217–18, 225
dollar, 172, 319
domestic labor, 110, 112
domestic politics, 14
Dostoyevsky, Fyodor, 139–40, 208, 209–10, 383
drugs, 14, 89, 93
dumping, 285
DuPont laboratories, 181
Durruti, Buenaventura, 74

East Asia, 317, 318
Echelon, 202–3
ecology, 282, 283
economic class, 104, 105
economic grievances, 277–82
economic production, 39–40, 51, 82, 87, 88, 94, 318–19, 334, 350
economic reforms, 299–303
economic regulation, 169, 175, 176, 178, 235
economics, 157
    crisis of, 154, 156
    decision-making in, 369
    global, 39, 149, 175, 203, 233, 279, 299–303, 319, 322
    innovation in, 337

economics *(cont.)*
  Keynesian, 154–55, 173, 177
  lex mercatoria, 169–71, 175
  military and, 177
  multitude and, xv, 106–7, 223–24
  of nation-states, 300–301
  political, 156–57, 162, 163
  political order and regulation of markets, 167–68
  postmodernization, 112
  as reactionary discipline, 153–54
  World Economic Forum, 167, 168
  see also poverty, the poor
efficiency, 112
elections, 270, 293
elite, 250
El Salvador, 53, 119, 214
Empire, 324
  exploitation and, 336
  geopolitical order of, 323
  global, 7
  inevitability of war in, xiii
  multitude and, 225
  ontological constitution of, 137
  overlap of capital and sovereignty, 334
  political hierarchy of, 29
  poor as victims of, 129
  public law of, 323
  state of war within, 4
  as tendency, xii–xiii
  unilateralist control over, 352
  unlimited nature of, 335
  U.S. unilateralist version of, 320
Empire (Hardt and Negri), xii, xvii, 374
employment, 112, 114, 131, 191
Encyclopedia (Diderot and D'Alembert), 269
enemy:
  as abstract, 15, 30–31
  as evil, 16
  friend-enemy distinction, 6, 11, 34
  new form of, 54–55
Engels, Friedrich, 70, 220
England, *see* Great Britain
Enlightenment, 309
Enron scandal, 178, 298
environmentalism, 288
environment-deprivation model, 57–58
equality, 220
Estates General, 269
ethical communication, 261

ethnicity, 278
eugenics, 195
euro, 172, 319
Eurocentrism, 125, 128
Europe, 316, 317
  early period of modernity, 237, 326
  geopolitics in, 313
  Left in, 191
  notion of democracy, 240
  public opinion in, 264
  revolts of industrial workers, 213
  unified constitution, 296
European philosophy, 329
European Union, 296, 318
evil, 16
exception, 5–9, 19, 25, 67, 235, 298, 304, 360, 364
exchange relations, 260
Executive Outcomes, 49
exodus, 341–42, 344, 348
expansionism, 313, 314
exploitation, 102, 113, 154, 201
  of agriculturalists, 111
  antagonism resulting from, 150, 212
  difference between first and third world countries, 163
  Empire and, 336
  labor and, 113, 150, 333
  Marx on, 150
  revolt against, 106
  topography of, 151, 159, 164–66, 226
expression, 108, 273, 339
externalities, 147–48
EZLN, *see* Zapatista National Liberation Army

factory work, 111, 112, 190, 200, 201, 255
family, 193, 236
FAO, *see* Food and Agriculture Organization
farming, *see* agriculture
fascism, 50, 255, 315, 370, 382
fear, 239, 240
federal government, 244
Federalist Papers, The, 243
Federalists, 244, 245, 294
feminism, 199, 214, 224, 273–74
Feurbach, Ludwig, 64
Feyerabend, Paul, 157
field of conflict, 263
finalism, 195

finance, 151, 280–81, 300, 310
First World War, 37, 38, 44
fish species, 283
foco guerrilla strategy, 75, 82
food, genetically modified, 183
Food and Agriculture Organization (FAO), 113, 174
Fordism, 112, 191
foreign debt, 279, 299–300
formalism, 209
Forschung, 64, 65, 68
Foucault, Michel, 13, 142, 284–85, 308, 309, 363
Fourth World War, 37
France, 72, 118, 122, 124, 125, 137, 269, 272, 273
Frankenfoods, 183
Frankenstein (Shelley), 11–12
freedom, 68, 74, 77, 78, 87, 220, 221, 235, 353, 355
free expression, 273
free market, 167–68
free representation, 246, 247
free trade, 158
French Revolution, 78, 269, 280, 293
Friedman, Milton, 155
friend-enemy distinction, 6, 11, 34
friendly fire, 45
Front du Libération du Québec, 81
full spectrum dominance, 53, 58
functionalism, 261–62

Gàdhafi, Mu'ammar, 31
Gallup, George, 262
Garibaldi movement, 72
Geheimrat, 33–35
G-8 protests, *see* Genoa, G-8 protests in
Gemeinschaft, 160, 206
gender, 101, 199–200, 217, 224, 278, 355
genealogy, 308–9
General Electric Company, 182
general interest, concept of, 205, 206
general theory of equilibrium, 153, 154
general will, 242
Genet, Jean, 213
genetic modification, 183–84
genetics, 112–13, 115, 132, 183, 301, 386
Geneva Conventions, 299
Genoa, G-8 protests in, 191, 267, 286, 287, 315

genocide, 18–19
geopolitics, 312–24
George Jackson Brigade, 286
Gerasene demoniac, 138, 139, 223
Germany, 292
    Berlin revolt in, 255–58
    conception of *Reich,* 160
    Krupp steel works, 40
    Nazis, 274, 344
    parliamentary pluralism in, 331
    Red Army Faction, 81
    under Schröder, 233
    state of exception in, 7, 9
    Thirty Years' War, 5, 143, 238
    tradition of public law, 161
    uprisings of 1848, 70
Giap, Vo Nguyen, 74
Gibbon, Edward, 326
gigantism, 298, 304
Giuliani, Carlo, 267
global anthropology, 125
global apartheid, 166–67, 174
global "aristocracies," 318, 320–23
global capital, 234, 279
global civil society, 295
global class, xvii
global constitution, 296
global cycle of struggles, 213–18
global democracy, xi, xvi, 268–312, 356
global economy, 39, 149, 175, 203, 233, 279, 299–303, 319, 322
global governance, 171
global institutions, *see* supranational organizations and institutions; *specific institutions*
globalization, xi, xiii, 60, 67, 162–63
    capitalist, 101, 164, 167, 277
    crisis of democracy in armed era of, 231–37
    liberal cosmopolitan view of, 234
    neoliberal, 266
    political economy of, 102, 162, 168–69
    protests against, 86–87, 89, 93, 211, 215, 217–18, 222, 266–69, 277, 285–88, 322, 347
    representation and, 271
    sovereignty imposed by, 172
    United Nations and, 316
global law, 170, 171
global parliament, 293, 294–95

global production, 109
global quasi-government, 175
global reform, 289–306, 353
global warming, 304
God, 325, 327, 351
Gogol, Nikolai, 210
golem, 10–12
Golem, The (Leivick), 11
Gorky, Maxim, 383
governance, 290–91, 319
government:
  big, 176–79
  Byzantine, 324–25
  federal, 244
  quasi-global, 175
  Rousseau on, 242
  see also democracy; politics
Gramsci, Antonio, 12, 374
Granada, 344
Grapes of Wrath, The (Steinbeck), 118
"gray" strategy, 53
gray zone, 52
Great Britain, 272
  agricultural land of, 118
  civil wars of, 5, 238, 239
  Lloyds insurance of, 40
  rural life of, 378
  seventeenth-century interregnum in, 162
  U.S. supported by, 233
greenhouse gases, 304
grievances, 269–85, 301, 358
  biopolitical, 282–85
  cahiers de doléances, 269
  economic, 277–82
  against global system, 285–88, 353
  against media, 396
  of representation, 270–73
  of rights and justice, 273–77
  against war, 284
Grimmelshausen, Johann, 5
Grossraum, 313
Grotewohl, Otto, 257
Grundrisse (Marx), 140, 152
Guantánamo Bay military base, 29, 299
guaranteed income, 136, 265
Guatemala, 275
Guattari, Félix, 158
guerrilla forces, guerrilla warfare, 51–52, 59, 78

Chinese model of, 76–77, 81
Cuban model of, 74–76, 77, 81, 82, 342
de-democratization of, 76
organizational structure of, 56–57
as peasant bands, 71, 82
from people's army to, 69–79
polycentric model of, 82–83
Sandinista, 76
Soviet, 70, 76
urban, 81
women in, 76
Zapatista model, 85
Guevara, Che, 74, 75
Guha, Ranajit, 380–81
Gulf War, *see* Iraq War (2003); Persian Gulf War (1991)
guns, 343–44, 345, 346

Haass, Richard, 363
Habermas, Jürgen, 261, 395
habit, 197–98, 199, 200, 201, 212, 222
hairy-cell leukemia, 182
Haiti, 177
Hall, Stuart, 263
Hamas, 83
Harvard University, 181
Hegel, G. W. F., 64, 225, 260, 261, 395
Heidegger, Martin, 193, 362
Heine, Heinrich, 64
Hercules, 214
Herder, Johann Gottfried von, 326
Hess, Moses, 64
hierarchies, 164, 166–67, 212, 317
high-intensity police actions, 39
Hindus, 32
historical materialism, 140
historical periodization, 142
Hobbes, Thomas, xvii, 4, 21, 238, 239, 330, 340, 402–3
Hobsbawm, Eric, 379
Ho Chi Minh, 74, 380
Holocaust, 27
homosexuality, 200, 202, 214, 347
Huamán Poma de Ayala, 5
humanity, 356, 361
  crimes against, 28, 29, 275
  evil as enemy of, 16
  God and, 327, 351
  love of, 50
  united against abstract concept, 15

human rights, 15, 234
  grievances of, 273–77
  in international law, 369
  logic of, 60
  reforms of, 296–99
  violence and, 26, 27
Hungary, 344
hunger, 174, 278, 279
Huntington, Samuel, 33–35, 239–40, 294, 365
Hussein, Saddam, 31, 48, 49
Hutu people, 32

iconoclasm, 325–27
Idea of India, An (Moravia), 127
identity politics, 86, 219
idolatry, 10
IMF, see International Monetary Fund
immaterial labor, 182–84, 188, 336
  centrality of, 115
  characteristics of, 66
  definition of, 108–9
  hegemony of, 65, 108–9, 111, 113–14, 141, 145, 223, 374, 390
  as loquacious and gregarious, 201
  productive, 146, 187
immaterial production, 65, 114–15, 142, 146–49, 152, 180, 187, 201
immaterial property, 180–82, 185–88, 311
imperialism, xii, 59–60
imperial law, 171, 277
Inca civilization, 5
income, 278
India, 127–28, 165, 184, 282–83, 286, 292, 315, 318
indifference, xiv
individualized violence, 19
industrial killing, 366
industrial reserve army, 130, 131
industrial revolution, 252
industrial workers, 70–71, 77, 107–8, 109, 123, 125, 130, 220, 223, 224, 252, 349
Indymedia, 305
information, 186, 187, 262, 263, 301, 305, 327, 334, 337, 338
innovation, 185–86, 198, 201, 210, 284, 301, 331, 337–38
insects, 92, 184
instructed representation, 246, 247
instrumentalization, 11

insurrection, 13, 69, 70, 71
intellectual labor, 108
intellectual property, 185–86
"intérimaires" workers, 137
International Court of Justice, 276
International Criminal Court, 28, 29, 276, 297
International Criminal Tribunals, 28–29
international cycle of struggles, 213–18
international institutions, 169
international law:
  common and, 207
  exception from, 8
  human rights in, 369
  imperial transformation of, 207
  legitimate violence and, 26, 28, 29
  new lex mercatoria, 170
  preemptive attacks prohibited in, 20
  war and, 22
International Monetary Fund (IMF), 119, 165, 172–76, 215, 216, 245, 271–72, 280, 286, 290, 291, 303
international relations, 14
international trade, 169, 170, 175, 177, 233, 285, 286, 287, 319
International Workers of the World, 286
Internet, xv, 185, 186, 266, 301, 337, 380
interregnum, 162–63, 166, 171, 178
Intifada, 83–84, 89–90, 214
Iran, 317
Iraq, 23, 52, 60, 177, 179, 303, 320
Iraq War (2003), 43, 67, 215, 258, 262, 315, 317, 318–19, 398
isolationism, 314
isomorphisms, 142
Israel, 26, 84, 303
Italy, 72, 81, 82, 128, 264–67, 396

Jacobinism, 206, 207, 250, 329, 330
Jamaica, 286
James, William, 197
Japan, 292
Japanese Americans, 297
Jefferson, Thomas, 185, 247, 248, 249, 268, 273, 311
Jesus Christ, 138, 325
Jews, 274, 297, 341, 343, 344
  see also anti-Semitism; Judaism
Jhering, Rudolf von, 161
jobs, see employment; labor

John, King of England, 320
John of Damascus, 327
Johnson, Hugh, 367
Jubilee Movement International, 279
Judaism, 10–11, 104, 351
Jünger, Ernst, 43, 370
justice, 15, 16, 78, 273–77, 284, 296–99
Justice for Janitors movement, 214
"just" war, 15–16, 17, 23–24, 326, 344–45, 361

kabbalah, 10, 12
Kairòs, 357
Kant, Immanuel, 189, 361
Kantorowicz, Ernst, 50
Kearney, Michael, 379
Kelsen, Hans, 17, 393
Kennan, George, 24
Keynes, John Maynard, 154, 155
Keynesianism, 154–55, 173, 177
Khmer Rouge, 83
kin work, 110
Kissinger, Henry, 24, 28
kiss-ins, 347
knowledge, 148, 151, 184–87, 283–84, 301, 337, 338
Kosovo, 27, 30, 60, 275
Krupp steel works, 40
kulaks, 117
Kuwait, 30
Kyoto Accord (1997), 304

labor, 281, 308
   abstract, 144–45
   affective, 108, 110–11, 147, 150
   agricultural, 109–10, 112, 120, 141, 349
   "becoming common" of, 103–15, 222, 223, 308, 338, 349
   Berlin revolt and, 255–58
   biopolitical, 109, 148
   in blurring of work and leisure time, 66, 111–12, 145–46
   capital and, 103, 104, 147, 333, 335
   capitalist globalization and, 164
   common and, xv–xvi
   dumping of, 130, 164
   and flexibility of market, 131
   forms of, 107
   global divisions of, 164–65, 176, 177
   immaterial good from, 200–201
      industrial, 70–71, 77, 107–8, 123, 125, 130, 220, 223, 224, 252, 349
   loss of traditional forms of, 190–91
   Marx on, 64, 152
   migrant, 133–34
   within multitude, 106–7
   new topology of, 113
   peasant, 116
   political power behind negotiations with, 168
   postmodern, 159
   property law based on, 186–87
   self-management, 252, 336
   social, 44, 144, 349, 350
   socialization of categories of, 125
   as source of wealth, 144, 149–50, 188, 333
   surplus time, 150
   unions, 136–37, 214–15, 219, 256, 258, 279, 288
   value and, 144–45, 146, 148, 150, 152
   "women's work," 110
   working class, xiv–xv, 65, 106–7, 120, 130, 131, 217, 223, 224, 252, 258
   see also immaterial labor
Lakatos, Imre, 157
Landmine Ban Treaty (1997), 304
land ownership, 116–19
language, 132, 147, 197, 201, 222, 339
Laos, 28, 57
Latin America, 39, 75, 76, 119, 213, 253, 315, 318
law:
   antitrust, 172
   civil, 340
   for control over common, 202
   of Empire, 323
   global, 170, 171
   imperial, 171, 277
   natural, 329
   postsystems theory, 204
   property, 186–87, 277
   tradition of public in Germany, 161
   see also international law
Lebanon, 49, 83
Le Bon, Gustave, 259, 260
Left, political, 190, 191, 219–20
legal authority, 25
legality, 88
legal theory, 204
Leivick, H., 11

INDEX

Lenin, Vladimir, 26, 74, 250, 353, 355, 404
Leo the Isaurian, 325
leukemia, 182
Leviathan (Hobbes), xvii, 239, 330
lex mercatoria, 169–71, 175, 177, 277
liberal cosmopolitan position, 234
liberalism, 273, 329
liberation movements, 68, 72, 73, 78, 80
life-forms, 185, 187, 284, 301
linguistic communities, 132, 148, 201
linguistic expression, 108, 339
linguistic performance, 201
linguistic theories, 200
Lispector, Clarice, 355
literary criticism, 209
literature, 209–10
living labor, 146, 152
Livy (Titus Livius), 356
Lloyds insurance, 40
Locke, John, 187
Loew, Judah, 11
Long March, 74
Louis XVI, King of France, 269
love, 351–52, 356, 358
low-intensity warfare, 39, 53
Luhmann, Niklas, 261–62
lumpenproletariat, 130
Luther, Martin, 161
Luxemburg, Rosa, 394

Machiavelli, Niccolò, 33, 47–48, 49–50, 51, 332, 356, 357
McNamara, Robert, 174
Madison, James, 243, 244, 273, 294, 354, 355, 392
Madres de Plaza de Mayo, 274
Magna Carta, 320–22
Malraux, André, 342
Malthus, Thomas, 165, 166
Mao Zedong, 12, 63, 71, 74, 76, 77, 116–17, 123–24, 357, 376, 380, 381
Marcos, Subcomandante, 85, 266, 372
martyrdom, 346–47
Marx, Karl, 149, 150, 220
  abstract labor concept of, 144–45
  on capitalist production, 64, 65, 146–47
  class theory of, 103–5
  on free trade, 158
  on labor, 64, 152, 333

living labor concept of, 146, 152
  on Paris Commune, 250, 251
  on political passivity of peasantry, 122–23, 124
  on private property, 187–88
  social theory of, 140–41
Massachusetts, 247–48
masses, xiv, 100
maternal work, 110
Matrix, The, 335
media, 260, 262, 263, 286–87, 305, 327, 396
mediation, 260, 261, 262
mercenaries, 47–51
Merleau-Ponty, Maurice, 192, 193
Mexican Revolution, 71
Mexico, 85, 119, 266
Michels, Robert, 253
microorganisms, 182
Microsoft Corporation, 145, 223
Middle Ages, 15
Middle East, 316, 318
migrants, 133–34
militarism, 50
military:
  in asymmetrical conflicts, 51, 368
  economic interest and, 177
  as mercenaries, 47–51
  power of, 334
  private contractors and, 47
  revolution in, 41–48
  technology and, 40, 48, 51
  traditional structure of, 56
  unilateralist policies and, 319
  violence and, 27, 332
  see also war
military-industrial complex, 40–41
military-vital complex, 41
Milošević, Slobodan, 29, 31
mind, 337
minorities, 273, 278
missiles, 38
Mississippi, University of, Medical Center of, 184
Mittelman, James, 165
mob, 100, 259, 260
modernism, modernity, 121–22, 387–88
  civil war in, 69–72, 89
  European, 237, 326
  pragmatism and, 199

modernism, modernity *(cont.)*
  traditional social bodies and, 190
  unfinished democratic project of, 237–47
monarchy, 240, 328
monetarist policies, 173–74
monetary essentialism, 155–56
money, 151, 155–56, 281
  see also currency
monophonic literature, 209
monopoly, 172, 301, 305
Monsanto Corporation, 280
monsters, 194–96
Montesquieu, Baron de, 273, 326
morality:
  of just war, 24
  legitimate violence and, 27, 28
  war and, 15–16
Moravia, Alberto, 127
Moses, 342
Movimento Sem Terra, 280
multiculturalism, 219
multilateralism, xii–xiii, 59, 61, 234, 312, 315
multinational corporations, 277, 320
multitude, 97–227
  biopolitical production of, 101, 348, 350
  as class concept, 103, 105
  common and, xv, 127, 135, 208, 224, 339, 348–49
  concepts of, 222–27, 308
  dangerous classes and, 15, 103–57
  decision-making capacity, 338–40, 351, 354
  deconstructionist criticism of, 225
  definition of, 99–100, 105
  and demise of peasantry, 115–27
  democracy of, 67, 312, 328–58
  demonic face of, 138–40, 223
  development of, 222
  economic aspects of, xv, 106–7, 223–24, 339
  Empire and, 225
  flesh of, 100, 101, 189, 192–94, 199, 212, 285
  formation of, 189–90, 212
  geopolitics as response to challenges of, 315
  Hegelian criticism of, 225
  historical, 221
  labor and, 224

  as network, xiii–xiv, 217, 264, 311
  new science of, 353–55
  from ontological standpoint, 221, 348–49, 351
  other social subjects vs., xiv–xv, 242
  from political standpoint, xvi, 221, 351
  potentially all-inclusive nature of, 226
  project of, xi, 95, 219, 348, 352
  and reinventing of Left, 220
  singularities and, 99, 101, 105, 127, 212, 218, 224, 225, 308, 349, 350, 355
  from sociological standpoint, 349–50, 351
  sub specie aeternitatis, 221
  traces of, 189–227
Murawiec, Laurent, 40
Musil, Robert, 196
Muslims, 32, 273
My Name Is Legion (Zelazny), 383

NAFTA, *see* North American Free Trade Agreement
napalm, 58
Napster Web site, 180–81
Narmada River, 282–83
narration, 209, 210, 211
nationalism, 50
national liberation wars, 72
nation building, 23, 52, 179, 303
nation-states, 60
  economy of, 300–301
  freedom from rule of, 234
  global order and, 161, 233
  in International Court of Justice, 276
  international law and, 207
  new *lex mercatoria*, 170–71, 175
  nuclear weapons and, 38
  political conflicts between, 6
  poverty in, 278
  sovereignty of, 3, 7, 162–63, 205, 234, 239
  violence of, 25–27, 240, 364
NATO (North Atlantic Treaty Organization), 30, 275
naturalism, 210
natural law, 329
neem tree, patented products from, 184
neoconservatism, 235, 401, 402–3
neoliberalism, 167, 168, 173, 203, 205, 233, 266, 279–80, 281, 315
network(s), 142

biopolitical, 85
distributed, 54–55, 57, 58–59, 62, 86, 88, 89, 91, 93, 113, 115, 211, 217–18, 225
  forms of, 54–62, 82–83
  global economic, 319
  innovation in, 338
  legality and, 88
  multitude as, xiii–xiv, 217, 264, 311
  organization model of, 87
  power of, xii
  social, 66, 113, 187
  struggles and, 79–91
  swarm intelligence and, 91–93
  terrorist, 93
Neue Darstellung, 65
New Deal, 198, 367
new enclosures, 186
New People's Army, Philippine, 83
New York Times, 258, 264
NGOs, *see* nongovernmental organizations
Nicaragua, 53, 76, 119, 276
Niebuhr, Reinhold, 326
Nietzsche, Friedrich, 189, 401
1984 (Orwell), 19
nongovernmental organizations (NGOs), 277–78, 294, 295, 322
Noriega, Manuel, 31
North American Free Trade Agreement (NAFTA), 215, 286
North Korea, 317
nostalgia, 190, 191, 192
nuclear weapons, 18–19, 26, 38, 332, 345, 362, 364
Nuremberg Tribunal, 275
nurses, 111
Nye, Joseph, 245

Obrigkeitsstaat, 161
occult phenomena, 126
ochlocracy, 241
Office of Homeland Security, 298
oil spills, 182, 183
OncoMouse, 181, 182, 183
On Divine Images (John of Damascus), 327
open-source movement, 301, 339–40
opinion polls, 262
Opium War, 177
oppression, 249, 309, 333
Orozco, José, 71

Orwell, George, 19
overpopulation, 165

pacifism, 362–63, 403
Palestinians, 26–27, 83–84, 214
Pan, 260
Panama, 177
paradigms, 142
paralegals, 111
Paris Commune, 250–51, 380
parliament, global, 293, 294–95
party, political, 250
Pashukanis, Eugeny, 253
Pasolini, Pier Paolo, 127
patents, 182–85, 301, 302, 338, 398
patriarchal representation, 245, 247
patriotism, 51, 191, 403
Pavone, Claudio, 370
peace, 5, 6, 7, 52, 67, 284, 311, 321
  see also pacifism
peasant production and exchange, 119
peasantry, 115–27, 375–81
  definition of, 116, 118
  in European literature, 121
  as guerrilla forces, 71, 82
  middle, 117, 119
  as politically passive, 122–23
  revolts of, in response to capitalism, 69, 213
Peek, George, 367
Pentagon attack (2001), 4, 48, 176, 178, 191, 218, 361
people, as concept, xiv, 79, 99, 242–43, 329
people's army, 71, 72–74, 79, 82
performance, 199–201, 204, 213, 222
Pericles, 240
periodization, 142
peripheral Fordism, 165
Persian Gulf War (1991), 24, 30
Peru, 83
pesticides, 184
Peter the Great, Tsar of Russia, 194
pharmaceuticals, 284, 301, 398
Philip III, King of Spain, 5
Philippines, 83
philosophy, 329
physiology, 330, 337
Pinochet, Augusto, 28
Piot, Charles, 381
piracy, 181

Plant Breeders' Rights, 113
plant genetics, 112–13, 115, 132, 183
plant species, 131–32
Plato, 329
plurality, pluralism, 103, 105, 331
Poland, 72
police action, 14–15, 19, 20, 39, 266, 267, 284, 286–87, 363
police protection, 179, 181
policy, 360
political body, 100, 160–61, 164, 167, 176, 177, 179, 189, 212, 226, 384
political economy, 156–57, 161, 163, 168–69
political institutions, 169
political party, 250
political power, 334
political production, 350–51
political realism, 356–57
political revolution, 78
politics:
    autonomy of, 249
    class and, 104
    cosmopolitan, 234
    economics and, 167–68
    domestic, 14
    geopolitics and, 312–24
    identity and, 86, 219
    John Dewey's reform efforts and, 198–99
    labor and, 168
    Left, 190, 191, 219–20
    peasant passivity in, 122–23
    poor and, 130
    queer, 200
    Right, 190, 219
    social, 254
    sovereignty in, 330–31
    subordination of violence to, 342
    U.S., 235
    war and, 6, 7, 12–13, 15, 22, 341, 342
    working class, 217
polling, 262, 263
polyphonic narrative, 209, 210–11
poor, see poverty, the poor
population, xiv, 99, 165–66, 243
populism, 255
positive externalities, 147–48
possessive individualism, 203
post-Fordism, 40, 81, 82, 112, 145, 146, 191, 200, 265

postmodernism, 190, 192
postsystems theory, 204
poverty, the poor, 13, 129–38
    creativity of, 134
    elimination of, 321
    in German sociology, 382
    global, 299, 319, 320
    global topography of, 164, 165–66
    within linguistic community, 132
    Marx on, 152
    potential of, 212
    protests against, 135–36, 277–82
    struggles of, 135
    World Bank projects and, 174
power:
    Byzantine, 326
    constituent, 22, 351, 364
    global divisions of, 164–65, 176, 177
    hierarchies of, 164, 226
    lack of vacuum of, 162–63
    network, xii
    as sacred, 330
    sovereignty and, 326–27, 353
    state's monopoly of, 249
    see also biopower
pragmatism, 197, 198–99
preemptive strike, 20, 326, 401
presidential election of 2000, 270, 396
preventive attack, 20
primitivism, 121, 122, 125
Prince, The (Machiavelli), 33, 51, 357
prisoners of war, 299
privacy, 202, 203–4
private agreement, 169
private contractual subject, 207
private property, 118, 179, 180–83, 187–88, 203, 205, 236, 311, 338
privatization, 186, 203, 205, 233, 280, 283, 286, 302–3, 321
Problems of Dostoyevsky's Poetics (Bakhtin), 208
production:
    agricultural, 115–16, 118
    biopolitical, xvi, 78, 81, 94–95, 263, 308
    capitalist, 144–45, 146
    of common, 189, 196–202, 204, 212, 222, 308, 348–50, 358
    common wealth as proper object of, 149
    communication and, 148, 185, 197, 198, 263, 349

INDEX

economic, 39–40, 41, 82, 87, 88, 94, 318–19, 334, 350
global, 109
immaterial, 65, 114–15, 142, 146–49, 152, 180, 187, 201
material, 146
political, 350–51
in poor countries, 164
post-Fordist, 40, 81, 82, 112, 146
quotas on, 255–56
real abstraction and, 144
resistance and, 94
social, xv, 80, 82, 87, 88, 135, 173, 198, 295
of subjectivity, 66, 81, 151, 160, 189
of value, 150
profit, 175, 177, 179, 284
proletariat, 103, 104, 107, 123, 250, 251, 252, 380
"Pro Patria Mori" (Kantorowicz), 50
property:
bioproperty, 181–82, 185
in capitalist society, 103
immaterial, 180–82, 185–88, 311
intellectual, 185–86
law, 186–87, 277
of peasantry, 116–17
private, 118, 179, 180–83, 187–88, 203, 205, 236–37, 311, 338
protest movements, global, 86–87, 89, 93, 211, 215, 217–18, 222, 266–69, 277, 285–88, 322, 347
Proust, Marcel, 197
Psychologie des foules (Le Bon), 259
psychology, 330, 337
public, concept of, 203–4
public goods, 205, 206
public institutions, 168
public interest, 205
public opinion, 258–64
public services, 205, 206
pure theory of law, 329
Putnam, Robert, 190

Queer Nation, 191, 347
queer theories, 199–200
Quesnay, François, 148

rabble, 100
Rabelais, François, 210
race, 101, 104, 166, 217, 224, 278

radioactive fallout, 282
rational individual expression, 261
raves, 265
Raymond, Eric, 339
Reagan, Ronald, 168
real abstraction, 141, 144
Realpolitik, 313
rebellion, 71, 247–48, 370
Red Army Faction, 81
Red Brigades, 81
Reed, John, 63
reform(s), 358, 398
biopolitical, 303–6
economic, 299–303
global, 289–306, 353
of representation, 290–96
of rights and justice, 296–99
refugees, 274
regime change, 23
regulatory mechanisms, 169, 175, 176, 178, 235–36
Reich, 160
religion, 15–16
Remarque, Erich Maria, 43
Renaissance, 49, 186
representation:
in ancient world, 392
appropriated, 245, 247
in Berlin revolt, 257–58
crisis of, 352
democracy and, 241–45, 251, 261–62, 264, 393
as disjunctive synthesis, 241
free, 246, 247
grievances of, 270–73
instructed, 246–47
labor, 254
patriarchal, 245–46, 247
reforms of, 290–96
scale and, 238, 243, 308
socialist, 249–55
in United Nations, 272, 291–92
repression, 69, 78
reproducibility, 180, 311
republic, 160, 161, 242, 354
republicanism, 242
republican virtue, 8–9
resistance, 54, 63–95
and democratic use of violence, 344
economic class and, 104

resistance *(cont.)*
  and inventing network struggles, 79–91
  legality and, 88
  from people's army to guerrilla warfare,
    69–78
  primacy of, 64–69
  in Warsaw ghetto uprising, 343
responsibility, 291
restitution, 297–98
revolt, 69, 212–17, 221
revolution, 13, 221
  Arendt on, 78
  against colonial powers, 70
  for destruction of sovereignty, 355
  formation of people's army, 71
  Kant on, 189
  in modern times, 22, 241
  reform and, 289, 398
  timing in, 357
  Trotsky on, 345
revolutionary realism, 356–57
revolution in military affairs (RMA), 41–48,
  58, 59
Ricardo, David, 144, 145, 164, 333
Right, political, 190, 219
rights, *see* civil rights; human rights
rights of singularity, 202
right to bear arms, 343, 344
Rimbaud, Arthur, 92, 93
Rivera, Diego, 71
RMA, *see* revolution in military affairs
"rogue states," 317
Rome, ancient, 49, 313, 324
Roosevelt, Franklin Delano, 198, 367
Rousseau, Jean-Jacques, 242–43, 244
Ruge, Arnold, 64
ruling class, 250
Rumsfeld, Donald, 36, 43
rural areas, 123, 378, 380
Russia, 303, 316, 317, 318
  corruption of oligarchs in, 298
  of Dostoyevsky, 139–40, 210
  in Security Council, 272
  title of "czar" in, 326
  see also Soviet Union
Ruysch, Frederik, 194
Rwanda, 28, 32, 274, 275, 276

Sabra refugee camp, 49
Saddam Hussein, 31, 48, 49

Saint Petersburg, 194–95
Samuelson, Paul, 155
Sandinistas, 76
Sardar Sarovar dam, 282–83, 286
Sarel, Benno, 255
Sartre, Jean-Paul, 104
Sassen, Saskia, 163, 369
Save the Narmada Movement, 282–83
scale, 238, 243, 308
scarcity, 180, 311
Scent of India, The (Pasolini), 127
Schmitt, Carl, 6, 72, 254, 330–31, 351,
  359, 361, 370, 402
Schröder, Gerhard, 233
Schumpeter, Joseph, 162, 331
science, 151, 188, 195, 196, 309, 338
Seattle, 1999 protests in, 86, 191, 215, 217,
  266–67, 268, 285–88, 315
Second World War, 37, 38, 44, 72, 173
security, 20–21, 31, 178, 180, 203, 320,
  321, 326
seeds, 112–13, 183
Selbmann, Fritz, 257
self-management, 252, 336
Sen, Amartya, 157
Sendero Luminoso, 83
September 11, 2001, attacks, 4, 48, 176,
  178, 191, 218, 361
Serbs, 32
serfdom, 118
service work, 108, 191
sexuality, 193, 199–200, 204, 217, 224
Shatila refugee camp, 49
Shays, Daniel, 248
Shays's Rebellion, 248, 249
Shelley, Mary, 11
Sierra Leone, 49
Sièyes, Abbé, 269
Silvermann, Sydel, 379
Simmel, Georg, 382
Simplicissimus, 5, 32
Singapore, 165
singularity, 128–29, 206
  anthropology of, 127, 381
  commonality and, 125, 198, 204, 308,
    349
  and common in international law and,
    208
  and common social being, 159
  in dialogue, 211

multitude and, 99, 101, 105, 127, 212, 218, 224, 225, 349
postsystems theory and, 204
Siqueiros, David, 71
slavery, 213, 297
Smith, Adam, 144, 145, 164, 326, 333
social being, 159
social class, *see* class
Social Contract (Rousseau), 242
social democratic position, 233, 234, 235
social equilibrium, 261, 263, 354
socialism, socialists, 73, 123, 206, 207, 219, 249–55, 257, 350
social justice, 78
social labor, 44, 144, 249, 350
social life, 146, 148, 188, 193, 199
social-movement unionism, 137
social networks, 66, 113, 187
social production, xv, 80, 82, 87, 88, 135, 173, 198, 295
social reality, 140–44
social relations, 113, 334, 336, 348, 349
social revolution, 78
social theory, 140–41
social welfare, 174, 219, 233, 302–3
software, 301–2, 339–40
Somalia, 177
Sorel, Georges, 254
Soros, George, 319
South Africa, 84, 126, 135–36, 152, 214, 275, 284
South America, 57
South Asian Subaltern Studies group, 380–81
Southeast Asia, 174, 291
South Korea, 165
sovereign, 160, 161, 239, 240, 329–31
sovereignty, xvii, 243, 252, 358
    absolute, 326
    based on consent of ruled, 332, 333, 340
    as biopower, 334–35
    concept of, 329, 331
    contradictions within, 332–33
    democracy and, 328–40
    destruction of, 353–54, 355
    exodus from, 341–42
    Haass on, 363
    human rights and, 275
    imposed by globalization, 172
    as increasingly unnecessary, 336
    of nation-states, 3, 7, 162–63, 205, 234, 239
    theories of, 254, 314
    two-sided nature of, 54, 331–36, 348
    unitary authority of, 260
soviets, 251, 353
Soviet Union, 17, 72
    in Afghanistan, 52
    agricultural collectivization in, 117–18, 376
    civil war in, 70
    cold war and, 24, 38
    democratic strains in, 253
    global capitalist market and, 179
    industrialization in, 374
    nuclear deterrence treaties and, 38, 39
    representation in, 252
    soviets and worker councils in, 251, 353, 394
    see also Russia
Soweto revolt, 84
Spanish civil war, 74
Spengler, Oswald, 34
Spinoza, Baruch, 34, 190, 194, 221, 240, 285, 311, 328, 330, 403
spontaneism, 224
Stalin, Josef, 117
Stammler, Rudolf, 329
Star Trek, 45–46
State and Revolution (Lenin), 353, 354
state of exception, 7–9, 19, 25, 67, 364
states, *see* nation-states; *specific nations*
Steinbeck, John, 118
Stephen, Lynn, 372
stock markets, 281
Stoker, Bram, 193
Strauss, David Friedrich, 64
Strauss, Leo, 403
struggle, international cycle of, 213–18
style, 213
subaltern, 225
subjective rights, 202
subjectivity, 66, 73–74, 78, 81, 83, 141, 151, 160, 189, 197, 198
submission, 54
Sudetenland, 344
suicide bombings, 45, 54, 332, 346
superstition, 34
supranational organizations and institutions, 169, 172–76, 245, 280, 290–91, 299, 320

INDEX

surplus, 150, 212, 217
surveillance, 202
surveys, 263
swarm intelligence, 91–93, 340
Swift, Jonathan, 210
Swiss Guards, 49
symbolic tasks, 108

Tableau économique, 148–49
Tacitus, 179
taxation, 300–301
T cells, 182–83
technologists, 42, 43, 44–46
technology, 283
    agricultural, 112
    of economic production, 41
    golem and, 11
    military and, 40, 48, 51
teleology, 195
telluric concept, 72, 122
tendency, xii–xiii, 141–44, 151
termites, 91
terrorism, 203
    Chomsky on, 362
    definitions of, 16–17, 27, 240
    networks of, 93
    as political concept, 16
    suicide bombings of, 45, 54, 332, 346
    war on, 14, 17, 20, 202, 240, 284, 361, 366
testimony, 346–47
Thailand, 246
Thatcher, Margaret, 168
theodicy, 16
theology, 330, 402–3
Third Estate, 269
third world, 163, 253
Third World War, 37
Thirty Years' War, 4, 5, 143, 144, 238
thought, 337
Tobin, James, 300
Tobin tax, 300–301
Tocqueville, Alexis de, 245, 259
tolerance, 16
torture, 19, 20
totalitarianism, 232, 241
trade, *see* international trade; trade agreements
trade agreements, 169, 171, 175, 286, 287
trade unions, *see* unions

traditionalists, 42–43, 44
traditional-values conservative arguments, 235–36
tragedy, 210
transaction costs, 170
transnational corporations, 233
transparency, 290–91
Trotsky, Leon, 70, 74, 328, 345
truth commissions, 275, 276, 297, 298
Tupamaros, 81
Turkey, 175
turmeric powder, 184–85
Tutsi people, 32
tyranny, 241, 309, 330, 343, 355
Tzeltal mythology, 213, 372

Uganda, 49
Ukraine, 72
unemployment, 130, 131
unequal exchange, 163–64
unilateralism, xii–xiii, 59, 61, 304, 312, 315, 316–20, 322, 369
unions, 136–37, 214–15, 219, 256, 258, 279, 288
United Kingdom, *see* Great Britain
United Nations, 291–93, 315–16
    aid agencies, 173
    Annan Doctrine, 27
    economic development organizations, 172
    Food and Agriculture Organization, 113, 174
    General Assembly, 272, 292, 293
    International Court of Justice, 276
    representation in, 272, 291–92
    Security Council, 28, 29, 272, 291–92
    World Conference on Racism, 282
    World Conference on Women, 282
    World Intellectual Property Organization, 185
United States:
    agricultural production in, 118
    decline of civic and community organizations in, 190
    democracy in, 33, 235
    exceptionalism of, 8–9, 235, 298, 304, 360
    foreign policy of, 60, 61, 234, 320, 401
    global hegemony of, 234, 235, 236, 316
    global interventions of, 235

industrialization of, 374
International Criminal Court and, 276
nuclear deterrence treaties of, 38, 39
and policy shift from defense to security,
    20–21
political system of, 235
presidential election of 2000 in, 270,
    396
proclamation of "axis of evil" by, 317
protests against, 271
revolution in military affairs of, 41–48
in Security Council, 272
as sole superpower, 161
strategic competitors, 316–17
unilateralist geopolitical strategy of,
    316–20, 322
unity, 103, 105, 243, 329–30
University of California, 182–83
University of Mississippi Medical Center,
    184
urban areas, 123, 380
urban movements, 81
Uruguay, 81
USA Patriot Act, 202, 298
utopianism, 259, 262, 263, 354

value(s), 144–45, 146, 148, 149, 150, 261
vampires, 193
vanguardism, 222, 224
Veblen, Thorstein, 154
Vietnam, 39, 52, 57
Villa, Pancho, 71
violence:
    constant threat of, 341
    defensive, 343, 344, 345
    democratic, 344, 345
    global, 239, 240
    individualized, 19
    legal structures and, 28
    legitimation of, 25–32, 79, 238, 341
    limited utility of, 332
    monopoly of, 364
    morality and, 27, 28
    of protests, 286–87
    resurgence of, 126
    in service of human rights, 27
    subordinated to politics, 342
    see also war
Virno, Paolo, 201
vitalism, 193

Voltaire, François-Marie Arouet de, 16, 210,
    326
voting, 270, 293

war, 1–95
    as absolute, 18
    abstract objects of, 31
    asymmetrical, and full-spectrum
        dominance, 51–62
    as biopower, 13, 18–25, 39, 44, 53, 54,
        94
    birth of new, 37–41
    counterinsurgencies in, 36–62, 72, 78,
        368
    crimes and, 28, 275
    definition of, 3
    democracy and, xi, 17–18
    economic production and, 39–40, 367
    Empire and, xiii
    as exception, 5–6
    as general phenomenon, 3, 4–5, 7, 8
    global state of, 12–18, 231, 233–36, 238,
        284, 303, 319, 321, 322, 341, 352
    Hobbes's view of, 4, 239
    imperial, 22, 24, 32, 60
    "just," 15–16, 17, 23–24, 326, 344–45,
        361
    legitimate violence and, 25–32, 79
    metaphors for, 13–14
    network form of, 54–62
    as ontological, 19
    as permanent social relation, 12
    police action vs., 363
    as policy shift from defense to security,
        20–21
    politics and, 6, 7, 12–13, 15, 22, 341, 342
    as regulating and ordering, 21–22
    and revolution in military affairs, 41–48
    suspension of democratic exchange in,
        362
    see also civil war; guerrilla forces, guerrilla
        warfare; military; specific wars
war on drugs, 14
war on poverty, 13
war on terrorism, 14, 17, 20, 202, 240, 284,
    361, 366
Warsaw ghetto uprising, 343
Washington Consensus, 173
Watanuki, Joji, 33
water pollution, 282

water rights, 304
wealth, 153, 176, 212, 226, 322
  along class lines in U.S., 248
  inequalities of, 278
  labor as source of, 144, 149–50, 188, 333
  Marx on, 149
  of migrants, 133
  of plant and animal species, 131–32
weapons, 343–44
  limited, 346
  of mass destruction, 18–19, 20, 345
  nuclear, 18–19, 26, 38, 332, 345, 362, 364
  for today's democracy, 347
Weber, Max, 25, 26, 79, 245–47, 253, 254
welfare, *see* social welfare
White Overalls, 264–67
Wilde, Oscar, 350
women:
  "comfort," 297
  domestic labor of, 110, 112
  feminism and, 199, 214, 224, 273–74
  in guerrilla organizations, 76, 371
  immaterial labor and, 111
  poverty among, 278
  rights of, 273–74
  and theories of body, 199
  and World Conference on Women, 282
working class, xiv–xv, 65, 106–7, 120, 130, 131, 141, 217, 223, 224, 252, 258

World Bank, 119, 172–76, 215, 245, 271–72, 278, 283, 286, 290, 291, 299
world civil war, 359
World Conference on Racism, 282, 297
World Conference on Women, 282
World Economic Forum, 167, 168
World Intellectual Property Organization, 185, 387
World Social Forum (WSF), 215, 294
World Trade Center attack (2001), 4, 48, 176, 178, 191, 218, 361
World Trade Organization (WTO), 171, 172, 175, 215, 266, 268, 285–88, 305, 321
World War I, *see* First World War
World War II, *see* Second World War
W. R. Grace and Company, 184
WSF, *see* World Social Forum
WTO, *see* World Trade Organization

Young Hegelians, 64
Yugoslavia, 26, 28, 29, 72, 274, 275, 276

Zapata, Emiliano, 71, 119, 213
Zapatista National Liberation Army (EZLN), 85, 89, 93, 213, 266, 286, 342, 372
Zelazny, Victor, 383
zero-tolerance society, 17, 326
Zhu De, 74
Zola, Emile, 92

FOR THE BEST IN PAPERBACKS, LOOK FOR THE 🐧

In every corner of the world, on every subject under the sun, Penguin represents quality and variety—the very best in publishing today.

For complete information about books available from Penguin—including Penguin Classics and Puffins—and how to order them, write to us at the appropriate address below. Please note that for copyright reasons the selection of books varies from country to country.

In the United States: Please write to *Penguin Group (USA), P.O. Box 12289 Dept. B, Newark, New Jersey 07101-5289* or call 1-800-788-6262.

In the United Kingdom: Please write to *Dept. EP, Penguin Books Ltd, Bath Road, Harmondsworth, West Drayton, Middlesex UB7 0DA.*

In Canada: Please write to *Penguin Books Canada Ltd, 90 Eglinton Avenue East, Suite 700, Toronto, Ontario M4P 2Y3.*

In Australia: Please write to *Penguin Books Australia Ltd, P.O. Box 257, Ringwood, Victoria 3134.*

In New Zealand: Please write to *Penguin Books (NZ) Ltd, Private Bag 102902, North Shore Mail Centre, Auckland 10.*

In India: Please write to *Penguin Books India Pvt Ltd, 11 Panchsheel Shopping Centre, Panchsheel Park, New Delhi 110 017.*

In the Netherlands: Please write to *Penguin Books Netherlands bv, Postbus 3507, NL-1001 AH Amsterdam.*

In Germany: Please write to *Penguin Books Deutschland GmbH, Metzlerstrasse 26, 60594 Frankfurt am Main.*

In Spain: Please write to *Penguin Books S. A., Bravo Murillo 19, 1° B, 28015 Madrid.*

In Italy: Please write to *Penguin Italia s.r.l., Via Benedetto Croce 2, 20094 Corsico, Milano.*

In France: Please write to *Penguin France, Le Carré Wilson, 62 rue Benjamin Baillaud, 31500 Toulouse.*

In Japan: Please write to *Penguin Books Japan Ltd, Kaneko Building, 2-3-25 Koraku, Bunkyo-Ku, Tokyo 112.*

In South Africa: Please write to *Penguin Books South Africa (Pty) Ltd, Private Bag X14, Parkview, 2122 Johannesburg.*